COMPUTATIONAL HUMANITIES

DEBATES IN THE DIGITAL HUMANITIES
Matthew K. Gold and Lauren F. Klein, Series Editors

COMPUTATIONAL HUMANITIES

Lauren Tilton, David Mimno, and
Jessica Marie Johnson
EDITORS

DEBATES IN THE DIGITAL HUMANITIES

University of Minnesota Press
Minneapolis
London

Copyright 2024 by the Regents of the University of Minnesota

All rights reserved. No part of this publication may be reproduced, stored in a retrieval system, or transmitted, in any form or by any means, electronic, mechanical, photocopying, recording, or otherwise, without the prior written permission of the publisher.

Published by the University of Minnesota Press
111 Third Avenue South, Suite 290
Minneapolis, MN 55401–2520
http://www.upress.umn.edu

 Available as a Manifold edition at dhdebates.gc.cuny.edu

ISBN 978-1-5179-1597-1 (hc)
ISBN 978-1-5179-1598-8 (pb)

A Cataloging-in-Publication record for this book is available from the Library of Congress.

Printed in the United States of America on acid-free paper

The University of Minnesota is an equal-opportunity educator and employer.

33 32 31 30 29 28 27 26 25 24   10 9 8 7 6 5 4 3 2 1

Contents

INTRODUCTION
What Gets Counted: Computational Humanities under Revision | *Lauren Tilton, David Mimno, and Jessica Marie Johnson*   vii

PART I
Asking With

   1 Computation and Hermeneutics: Why We Still Need Interpretation to Be by (Computational) Humanists | *Hannah Ringler*   3

   2 Computing Criticism: Humanities Concepts and Digital Methods | *Mark Algee-Hewitt*   18

   3 Born Literary Natural Language Processing | *David Bamman*   45

   4 Computational Parallax as Humanistic Inquiry | *Crystal Hall*   70

   5 Manufacturing Visual Continuity: Generative Methods in the Digital Humanities | *Fabian Offert and Peter Bell*   83

   6 Maps as Data | *Katherine McDonough*   99

   7 Fugitivities and Futures: Black Studies in the Digital Era | *Crystal Nicole Eddins*   127

PART II
Asking About

   8 Double and Triple Binds: The Barriers to Computational Ethnic Studies | *Roopika Risam*   149

   9 Two Volumes: The Lessons of Time on the Cross | *Benjamin M. Schmidt*   161

   10 Why Does Digital History Need Diachronic Semantic Search? | *Barbara McGillivray, Federico Nanni, and Kaspar Beelen*   177

   11 Freedom on the Move and Ethical Challenges in the Digital History of Slavery | *Vanessa M. Holden and Joshua D. Rothman*   195

   12 Of Coding and Quality: A Tale about Computational Humanities | *Julia Damerow, Abraham Gibson, and Manfred D. Laubichler*   215

13 The Future of Digital Humanities Research: Alone You May Go Faster, but Together You'll Get Further | *Marieke van Erp, Barbara McGillivray, and Tobias Blanke*   233

14 Voices from the Server Room: Humanists in High-Performance Computing | *Quinn Dombrowski, Tassie Gniady, David Kloster, Megan Meredith-Lobay, Jeffrey Tharsen, and Lee Zickel*   247

15 A Technology of the Vernacular: Re-centering Innovation within the Humanities | *Lisa Tagliaferri*   261

ACKNOWLEDGMENTS   279

CONTRIBUTORS   281

Introduction

What Gets Counted
Computational Humanities under Revision

LAUREN TILTON, DAVID MIMNO, AND JESSICA MARIE JOHNSON

A Shifting Debate: Hope, Care, and Critical Possibilities

Questions about whether the humanities should be engaging and shaping computational methods have moved from *if* to *how*. Sites of debate and their intersections include the qualitative and quantitative, theory and numbers, empiricism and hermeneutics, credit and labor, to name just a few. Importantly, the conversation about collaboration, labor, and policy is being pushed in new directions. We are attuned to the broader community through online communication, yet we are also more aware of the importance of institutional and community *support,* which became even more important amid local and global challenges. There is, then, a need for a capacious computational humanities to remix, reimagine, and reconfigure the world of quantification and ways of knowing that can be produced.

Computational humanities (CH) is an open term, to be defined over time, in collaboration, and never fully cemented.[1] It is a process that will extend far beyond the bounds of a book but which this project shapes. In this moment, the volume revolves around a formation of CH that focuses on the use and critique of computational methods to create and analyze data that animates inquiries in the humanities. This approach pays careful attention to the infrastructure and labor that shape what is possible. Employing computational methods that are informed by an awareness and interrogation of histories that both animate and haunt computation offers a way to reveal ghosts, forge connections, and conduct beautiful experiments guided by carework.[2] The volume functions as a part of this definition and is open to expansion, agreement, critique, and debate itself.

Our entry into the debate comes from a particular angle. This volume emerged in the context of a series of debates, some ongoing, some new about what counts as CH and what does not, who is doing CH and who is not, and who is doing it right.[3] In some cases, we wanted to move beyond questions that we felt had become stale and unproductive, while in other cases we wanted to dig in further and explore what we thought were the pressing issues that could lead to better work and better working. We chose to move past debates on what *constitutes* computing in the humanities and whether it is *possible* for computing to provide useful perspectives, particularly moving beyond writ-large accusations of neoliberalism.[4] We offer no further discussion of definitions or boundaries of the digital in the humanities.[5] Our own experience, especially these last few years, has taught us that there is no clear boundary between "distant" and "close" reading; between scholarship produced by the academy and labor happening beyond classroom walls; between quantitative and qualitative data; between learning to count humans and being one in relation, in the world.[6]

Rather, computation at its most generative demands an equal degree of interpretation. The scholarship we create is generated, designed, and cocreated by and with communities at all levels of our institutions and across international boundaries, and it is rooted in our experiences, desires, and visions of the world well beyond the ivory tower. We can turn to publications such as the *Journal of Cultural Analytics* as a model for bringing together method and interpretation, attention to collaboration and credit, and prioritizing access and transparency. Authors in this volume echo these positions with a consistent call for a better understanding of hermeneutics, of stakes, and of data itself. There is a long tradition of critical essays rejecting the notion of computation as having any contribution to the humanities.[7] These are perspectives worth considering, but for this volume we start with the assumption that quantitative approaches have something to add; our sources can be seen from many perspectives, and one of those perspectives is as data.

A more recent debate, and one that we choose to consider more directly, is a product of the very interdisciplinarity that makes computational humanities thrilling. It amounts to asking: Who are we doing this work for, and who are we accountable to? Consider a researcher brought up in computer science, a researcher who builds their career on eight-page LaTeX pdfs published at competitively reviewed conferences, and a researcher brought up in a humanities discipline that prizes monographs above all else. Can they all relate? Can they recognize each other's "rigor" and value it? Perhaps more important, can they fit alternative ways of working into the institutional structures that they must navigate to maintain their careers and their entire fields? Which new structures do we need to build and for whom?

Every one of these interactions, moreover, is embedded in a context of powerful social constructs such as race and gender, prestige, and geography. Describing how intersectionality (a Black feminist framework created by Kimberle Crenshaw) and identity politics (a Black feminist framework best attributed to Beverly Smith and the Combahee River Collective) shape *what* is possible and for *whom,* and how we can collectively remove barriers, undergirds these chapters.[8] In this volume, we approach these questions in what we hope is a new way. What are the resources, in both expertise and infrastructure, that make computational humanities successful? How can different perspectives complement and strengthen each other? And how can we more intentionally open ourselves and our work to different experiences and different histories with data, computation, or the digital and allow it to reshape how we do our work?

A context that we did not anticipate but that saturated every aspect of this volume is the global pandemic. In obsessively tracking daily case counts and the horror of sickness and death, we were constantly reminded of both the inescapable necessity of quantification and also its fundamental inadequacy. The pandemic also highlighted the necessity of human infrastructure. Who was able to keep working uninterrupted, and who was not? We saw, inescapably, the value of *support*, whether it is high-performance computing or colleagues to bounce ideas off or childcare. We saw who has support, and who does not. We saw who died (Black and non-Black people of color at disproportionate rates) and who was at risk because of decades (centuries) of systemic lack of resources, dispossession, neglect, and other violence. We saw who was mourned and who was viewed as expendable. This perspective shaped the priorities of the volume: computational humanities is not just about the work but about *how* and *where* we work and *for whom*. What are the environments that allow us to apply computational methods in ways that broaden our knowledge? What do we need to make that work possible and, more important, accessible, fruitful, careful, caring, and transformative?

As we debate, we would like to consider setting at least one parameter. This involves a common rhetorical and sometimes theoretical move that we hope we might use more carefully. A trend in scholarly discourse is to place "critical" in front of a term to forge a new area of study. Yet, such a move risks becoming an appropriation, often by groups whose subjectivity and disciplinary background are quite powerful in the academy, and erasing the important work that actually undergirds the area of study. Our configuration of CH builds on the fundamental work of movements in the digital humanities (DH), such as #DHPOCO, FemTechNet, and #transformDH, and the reconfiguration of DH being forged by collectives like #USLDH, Digital Ethnic Futures, Data 4 Black Lives, Black beyond Data, and LifexCode: DH against Enclosure.[9] Their work is not only critical but specific.

They offer theories and actions through particular frames that, in aggregate, offer a critical foundation for CH. They ask us to question the sterility of "hard" numbers, the lifelessness of a form of humanistic inquiry adverse to theory, and the building of thick boundaries. Instead, they ask us to build a more expansive, inclusive, and justice-oriented praxis that knits communities together by expressing the complexity of being people in relation to one another, animated by theories that expand our ways of knowing. We have much work to do to realize the critical and emancipatory aspirations of these movements, and we hope this volume joins the call.

Organizing Debates: Asking With and Asking About

We found it hard to settle on an organization. The chapters were proposed before a global pandemic and shifted as we all processed the tremendous change to our everyday lives and immense loss underway. The chapters transformed as a result of global and local conversations about critical topics such as data, quantification, and labor. The chapters informed each other as peer review further drew out connections, and we are grateful to the authors who worked to integrate and speak directly to each other. A prominent pattern emerged in the form of the connections across disciplinary lines as authors discussed and debated within subfields such as computational literary studies and digital history. These connections are further elucidated through links in the digital open access version of this volume.

While we anticipate many readers will pick their own pathway through the volume, we do offer a broad organization: "Asking With" and "Asking About." The organization revolves around chapters that ask questions with computational methods and chapters that are asking about computational methods. Rather than using an organization based on the objects of study, we selected an order that comes from another angle and augments the links that authors draw in their chapters. The parts are infused with questions about access, labor, and power, which is shaped by the chapter's debates alongside the subjectivity and positionality of the authors.

The first part circulates around computation and interpretation. How we know what we know is shaped by method, a constant site of debate within, between, and across disciplines, areas of study, and institutional structures. Moving beyond debates about whether computational methods can animate humanistic inquiry, part 1 engages into debates over what kind of interpretation furthers the humanities. Hannah Ringler calls for a focus on the *how* of interpretation, for developing a hermeneutics that distinguishes between interpreting artifacts through tools ("asking with") and interpreting the output of tools ("asking about") toward humanistic claims. Mark Algee-Hewitt builds on this call and asks us to shift our process from applying the interpretive methods of the humanities to the results of a digital analysis to rethink how the transformation itself becomes a new kind of evidence, which now requires that we understand what these analytics methods actually do. In other words, we need a new interpretative framework for understanding the computational and humanities models of the phenomenon that we seek to study.

Building on Ringler and Algee-Hewitt, who situate their chapters within rhetoric and computational literary studies, David Bamman calls for a shift in national language processing research that trades in models that generalize analysis, regardless of the specificities of the genre, for models that are built with and for humanistic insight. These literary-centric models, he argues, necessitate collaboration with humanities scholars, a process of building with and not just for. Bamman's call could be understood as enacting Crystal Hall's call to recover the humanistic definition of parallax provided during the late Italian Renaissance in text analysis. Hall argues that this older configuration of parallax provides a method for drawing on multiple perspectives and quantitative models to expand how one analyzes text through the humanities. Finally, Fabian Offert and Peter Bell shift perspective to the study of art history and explore how humanities scholars can harness generative AI tools. They demonstrate, like Algee-Hewitt, how "wrong" results from a particular method can actually offer powerful evidence as well as call for computational humanities to embrace discriminative and generative approaches.

Turning to debates in digital history and then Black studies, the next two chapters address pressing issues about what kinds of data we should be asking our questions with. Katherine McDonough reframes maps as data by tracing the historiography of spatial history and arguing why a more interdisciplinary computational approach can further the study of space and place. The chapter expands our understanding of data into this powerful multimodal form through the lens of computer vision, bringing together image and text analysis in powerful ways that situate CH as part of a new kind of spatial turn. Crystal Eddins discusses how reading with and against the grain of the archive is critical to working with the sources that we transform into data. By focusing on archives of slavery, the chapter demonstrates how this approach is particularly crucial when working with archives and their datafied forms, as there is a risk of reifying rather than resisting violence through data. Together, these two chapters offer ways of rethinking what counts as data, with implications for all of CH.

The second part, "Asking About," turns to structural issues for CH with a focus on research practices. Roopika Risam addresses the barriers to building computational ethnic studies by drawing on her own experience forging the field. Not only does one have to contend with the institutional challenges of creating and building ethnic studies, but one must also overcome technical barriers—specifically, learning how to code. These double and triple binds offer a powerful framework for understanding the challenges faced by many areas of study, seeking to incorporate computational methods. Additionally, they offer another critical dimension to debates over coding and programming. Benjamin Schmidt presents the history of debates over computation in the disciplinary formation of history in the United States over the past fifty years as a cautionary tale. He warns that the construction of computational humanities need not (and should not) produce a humanities that becomes more scientific or primarily defined by quantification. Instead, it should make interpretive space for a more creative humanities. Barbara McGillivray, Federico Nanni, and Kaspar Beelen turn to the search process and advocate for an information retrieval architecture that is shaped by disciplinary commitments, specifically emphasizing how search affects the practice of history. These authors all demonstrate how different disciplines within the humanities contribute powerful perspectives and needs to CH—which, we argue, will benefit from a transdisciplinary framework.

Turning to collaboration and datafication, Vanessa Holden and Joshua Rothman draw on debates in digital history. Working with the archive of slavery, they argue that how evidence is created and collected is as important as the computational analysis that follows. They call for a collaborative, participatory model of engagement with the archive and data creation that facilitates thinking with, across, and against the archive, with attention to their historical legacies. While Holden and Rothman focus on the making of data, Julia Damerow, Abraham Gibson, and Manfred Laubichler turn to another key aspect of CH: coding. Because code facilitates the creation and analysis of data, the lines of structured characters become an important documentation of interpretation. The authors argue that the computational humanities have a problem: code of low quality limits our ability to interpret, reproduce, and understand its output. They offer suggestions for how to expand the field to produce clearer and higher-quality code. In aggregate, these chapters bring to the fore debates over what kinds of data we want to create, with calls to expand what counts as data and who is collaborating and with particular attention paid to how data and coding are shaped by praxis rather than just given.

Addressing the challenge of double and triple binds that Risam outlines, Marieke van Erp, Barbara McGillivray, and Tobias Blanke argue that collaboration across disciplines, particularly computer science and the humanities, will be key to the computational humanities. They identify key pressure points, including funding, publication models, and research evaluation, that will need to be grappled with. Returning to debates over collaboration and programming, Quinn Dombrowski, Tassie Gniady, David Kloster, Megan Meredith-Lobay, Jeffrey Tharsen, and Lee Zickel turn to another key aspect of computational processing: high-performance computing (HPC). They address how whoever provides support shapes which research is prioritized, and they advocate for humanities disciplinary experts as part of HPC staff to support access to these methods as we develop the computational humanities. Lisa Tagliaferri zooms out to argue that the broader "vernacular" world of startups and tech companies can both benefit from the humanities perspective and be a source for innovation relevant to humanists. These chapters speak to new and ongoing debates over the role of disciplinarity, interdisciplinarity, and transdisciplinarity and the barrier to entry to the computational humanities that, as editors, we are responsible for acknowledging, addressing, resisting, and removing. In aggregate, part 2 addresses larger debates over which ways of knowing have been erased or rendered illegitimate and which are considered prestigious, convincing, and worth investment. These chapters demonstrate how CH is less of a science and more of a situated knowledge, best when attuned to issues of field formation, history, labor, and power.

No categorization fully captures the complexity of the conversation. Like the data that we work with, there will be limits, omissions, and silences. At the same time, we hope that expected and unexpected connections and patterns will be illuminated. Listening to critiques of digital humanities from collectives such as #DHPOCO, FemTechNet, and #transformDH, we are attuned to the authors' positionality as shaped by disciplinary, geographical, institutional, and related structures of power. While we worked to create a robust and expansive conversation, there are inevitably gaps, and we are excited to see where communities bring these debates.

Future Debates: Power, Pedagogy, and Reflexive Openness

As we look to next steps, we highlight several components that we want to amplify and flag with caution. First, the growth of CH is occurring in the context of the largest shift in the balance of academic power and prestige in recent memory. We are in a moment where data and computation enjoy great prominence, both positive and, increasingly, negative. At the same time, both the institutional support for and perceived cultural impact of humanities are crashing. The incredible expansion of computer science, which struggled in the academy in the early 2000s following the dotcom crash, and the rapid ascent of data science are a testament to this moment of quantification. There are many calls in this volume and in other spaces to think across boundaries, particularly involving these two fields.

Yet, the challenges of these fields, along with the digital humanities, are well documented, ranging from a destructive "move fast and break things" ethos to long-standing cultural dynamics that reject and marginalize the contributions of all but a narrow "codebro" profile. The humanities face similar challenges of elitism and inaccessibility, compounded by isolation, glacial publication cycles, and training that is mismatched with the realities of the market. As we build out this area, it is crucial to pay attention to the structures we are creating and those we are replicating.

We are researchers, and the essays in this volume reflect that, but we are also educators. CH asks us to address our pedagogy. On the one hand, CH offers ways to think about how the humanities can expand their methodological and evidential repertoire. On the other hand, CH offers an expanded idea of why and how we pursue fields such as computer science and data science. In our own courses, we have seen significant interest in humanities-oriented computational courses from non-humanities students. When we have this kind of narrow window of opportunity, what should we teach to leave students with a long-term excitement about reaching past purely technical work?

Expanding beyond disciplinary boundaries in our classes at the secondary, undergraduate, and graduate levels will be key. Achieving balance has consistently been difficult: Can we train students in both Sanskrit and Python? What the current volume suggests is that we should not so much attempt to train generalists or unicorns as learn how to become generous collaborators. We can turn to exciting models, such as hiring scholars trained in computer science, English, and history at information science programs in the United States and interdisciplinary PhDs in Europe. But turning a pattern of work and a research agenda into a structured, measurable curriculum will take dedication.[10]

Perhaps one of the largest social and structural shifts that is underway because of CH is how digital humanities will configure itself in relation to the computational social sciences.[11] While much of the discussion in DH has involved discussing collaboration between computer science and the humanities, CH requires engagement with data science, information science, and statistics, among other disciplines. This is bringing DH in closer collaboration with the social sciences. The rapid growth of the computational social sciences in higher education, perhaps counterintuitively, is also shifting the sciences closer to the social sciences. By embracing these opportunities to create, collaborate, and debate across the humanities, social sciences, and sciences, CH makes space for the humanities to be at the center of debates over our computational world and how to computationally understand the world.

The realization of an expansive CH will require experimentation, openness, collaboration, and critical reflexivity.[12] We need to create an environment where researchers from many backgrounds can feel comfortable, productive, and valued, through a "vernacular" culture that radically expands accessibility. CH will have a sturdier foundation if we are open to listening and collaborating across boundaries, rather than trying to build a space apart. By knitting in tandem, we can create together: try new patterns, rip out, and try again.

A Final Note

When we began discussing an edited volume within the Debates in the Digital Humanities book series, compiled under the umbrella of "computational humanities," we could not have predicted how the world would change on our watch. Since the winter of 2019, when the call for papers was first issued, the world has undergone successive waves of mobilization and calamity, political and viral reverberations of an unprecedented nature, all mediated by charts and tables and graphs. We are living through history, rocked by personal grief and bathed in quantification. The larger reality risked being obscured in scale, diffusion, and complexity. Abstraction and numbers could render invisible as much as they could illuminate. We have struggled to reconcile our feelings that our subject is insignificant in the face of so much calamity, and simultaneously that the subject of this volume has never been more pressing. We are grateful to the authors, peer reviewers, series editors Matt Gold and Lauren Klein, and the team at the University of Minnesota for being a part of this critical and timely debate.

Notes

1. The term and definitions are in formation. There is the Computational Humanities Forum that "serves as an asynchronous platform to discuss all ideas and questions related to computational humanities research." Another formation is a lab, such as the

Computational Humanities Lab (2012–2014) at the University of Wisconsin–Madison and centers such as the Rhoads Computational Humanities Center at Duke University. There are also efforts to define computational humanities in relation to specific fields; see Tilton, "American Studies + Computational Humanities." Another area of development is coursework, such as Info 190: Computational Humanities at Berkeley–School of Information, taught by David Bamman, who is an author in this volume.

2. We explicitly seek to situate this version of computational humanities in Black studies and cultural theory such as described by Saidiya Hartman and Avery Gordon. We also see this volume joining the calls of other volumes in the Debates in the Digital Humanities series, such as *Bodies of Information* edited by Elizabeth Losh and Jacqueline Wernimont and *People, Practice, Power: Digital Humanities outside the Center* edited by Anna McGrail, Angel David Nieves, and Siobhan Senier.

3. For example, a group came together around 2019 to build the computational humanities research community. Primarily among scholars in Western Europe, the emerging conversation elicited critique because of initial framings that positioned CH as finally a return to more scientific engagement. This was understood as an effort to split off from the rest of DH to not have to grapple with the hard work of DH scholars to bring important questions about intersectionality and power to the field through the guise of making the field more of a science. Much of the debate ensued on X (formerly known as Twitter). For a lovely call to find an intersection between the humanities and sciences in DH, see the introduction to Miguel Escobar Varela's *Theatre as Data*. The version of the computational humanities research community that we are seeing today has taken this into account and worked to shed the problematic frames that led to a storm cloud over the initial launch of the community.

4. See, for example, Allington, Brouillette, and Golumbia, "Neoliberal Tools (and Archives): A Political History of Digital Humanities," and *Digital Humanities Now*'s "Editors' Choice: Round-up of Responses to 'The LA Neoliberal Tools (and Archives)'" at https://digitalhumanitiesnow.org/2016/05/editors-choice-round-up-of-responses-to-the-la-neoliberal-tools-and-archives/. For more about past debates on the topic in the debates series, see Greenspan, "The Scandal of Digital Humanities."

5. For more on this debate, see Terras, "Peering Inside the Big Tent: Digital Humanities and the Crisis of Inclusion"; Svensson, "Beyond the Big Tent"; and Weingart and Eichmann-Kalwara, "What's under the Big Tent?: A Study of ADHO Conference Abstracts."

6. For example, see Antoniak, Mimno, and Levy, "Narrative Paths and Negotiation of Power in Birth Stories"; Rhody, "Topic Modeling and Figurative Language"; and So, *Redlining Culture: A Data History of Racial Inequality and Postwar Fiction*.

7. For example, Nan Z. Da's "The Computational Case against Computational Literary Studies" ignited a debate about the interpretative limits of computational literary studies, including a 2019 forum in *Critical Inquiry*, which is available at https://critinq.wordpress.com/2019/03/31/computational-literary-studies-a-critical-inquiry-online-forum/ and https://critinq.wordpress.com/2019/04/12/more-responses-to-the-computational-case-against-computational-literary-studies/.

8. For more on the origins of intersectionality, see Crenshaw, "Mapping the Margins," and the Combahee River Collective, "A Black Feminist Statement." For a breakdown of intersectionality and other terms relevant to data and digital humanities work broadly, see D'Ignazio and Klein, *Data Feminism*.

9. For more about these movements, see the following websites: https://dhpoco.org/, http://digitalethnicfutures.org/, https://www.femtechnet.org/, https://www.lifexcode.org/, and https://transformdh.org/. For articles about these movements, see Gajjala, Risam, and Gairol, "What Is Postcolonial Digital Humanities (#DHpoco)?"; Johnson, "4DH + 1 Black Code/Black Femme Forms of Knowledge and Practice"; and Lothian, "From Transformative Works to #transformDH: Digital Humanities as (Critical) Fandom."

10. Recent examples of textbooks include Arnold and Tilton's *Humanities Data in R*; Walsh's *Introduction to Cultural Analytics & Python*; Jockers and Thalken's *Text Analysis with R for Students of Literature*; and Karsdorp, Kestemont, and Riddell's *Humanities Data Analysis: Case Studies with Python*.

11. We want to thank the anonymous external reviewer for bringing this important point to our attention. Along with your generous feedback and witty writing style, we are greatly appreciative of the time that you took to review the entire volume.

12. One area of emphasis in DH is building it around values. We draw on Spiro, "'This Is Why We Fight': Defining the Values of the Digital Humanities."

Bibliography

Allington, Daniel, Sarah Brouillette, and David Golumbia. "Neoliberal Tools (and Archives): A Political History of Digital Humanities." *Los Angeles Review of Books*, May 1, 2016. https://lareviewofbooks.org/article/neoliberal-tools-archives-political-history-digital-humanities.

Antoniak, Maria, David Mimno, and Karen Levy. "Narrative Paths and Negotiation of Power in Birth Stories." *Proceedings of the ACM on Human-Computer Interaction* 3, no. CSCW, art. 88 (November 2019): 1–27. https://doi.org/10.1145/3359190.

Arnold, Taylor, and Lauren Tilton. *Humanities Data in R: Exploring Networks, Geospatial Data, Images and Text*. New York: Springer, 2015.

Combahee River Collective. "A Black Feminist Statement." *Women's Studies Quarterly* 42, no. 3/4 (2014): 271–80.

"Computational Literary Studies: A Critical Inquiry Online Forum." *Critical Inquiry—In the Moment*, March 31, 2019. https://critinq.wordpress.com/2019/03/31/computational-literary-studies-a-critical-inquiry-online-forum/.

"Computational Humanities." Duke University, n.d. https://bigdata.duke.edu/computational-humanities.

Crenshaw, Kimberle. "Mapping the Margins: Intersectionality, Identity Politics, and Violence against Women of Color." *Stanford Law Review* 43, no. 6 (1991): 1241–99.

Da, Nan Z. "The Computational Case against Computational Literary Studies." *Critical Inquiry* 45, no. 3 (2019): 601–39. https://doi.org/10.1086/702594.

D'Ignazio, Catherine, and Lauren F. Klein. *Data Feminism.* Cambridge, Mass.: MIT Press, 2020.

Gajjala, Radhika, Roopika Risam, and Rahul K. Gairol. "What Is Postcolonial Digital Humanities (#DHpoco)?" *Salaam: The Newsletter of the South Asian Literary Association* 38, no. 1 (2014): 7–11.

Gordon, Avery. *Ghostly Matters: Haunting and Sociological Imagination.* Minneapolis: University of Minnesota Press, 1997.

Greenspan, Brian. "The Scandal of the Digital Humanities." In *Debates in the Digital Humanities 2019,* edited by Matthew K. Gold and Lauren F. Klein, chap. 9. Minneapolis: University of Minnesota Press, 2019.

Hartman, Saidiya. *Wayward Lives, Beautiful Experiments: Intimate Histories of Social Upheaval.* New York: W.W. Norton, 2019.

Henrickson, Leah. "Humanities Computing, Digital Humanities, and Computational Humanities: What's in a Name?" *3:AM Magazine,* October 24, 2019. https://www.3ammagazine.com/3am/humanities-computing-digital-humanities-and-computational-humanities-whats-in-a-name/.

"Info 190: Computational Humanities." Berkeley School of Information. Accessed January 13, 2024. https://www.ischool.berkeley.edu/courses/info/190/ch.

Jockers, Matthew L., and Rosamond Thalken. *Text Analysis with R for Students of Literature.* 2nd ed. New York: Springer, 2020.

"Join the Community." Computational Humanities Research, 2021. https://2021.computational-humanities-research.org/contact/.

Johnson, Jessica Marie. "4DH + 1 Black Code/Black Femme Forms of Knowledge and Practice." *American Quarterly* 70, no. 3 (2018): 665–70. https://doi.org/10.1353/aq.2018.0050.

Karsdorp, Folgert, Mike Kestemont, and Allen Riddell. *Humanities Data Analysis: Case Studies with Python.* Princeton, N.J.: Princeton University Press, 2021.

Losh, Elizabeth, and Jacqueline Wernimont, eds. *Bodies of Information: Intersectional Feminism and Digital Humanities.* Minneapolis: University of Minnesota Press, 2018. https://dhdebates.gc.cuny.edu/projects/bodies-of-information.

Lothian, Alexis. "From Transformative Works to #transformDH: Digital Humanities as (Critical) Fandom." *American Quarterly* 70, no. 3 (2018): 371–93. https://doi.org/10.1353/aq.2018.0027.

McGrail, Anne, Angel David Nieves, and Siobhan Senier, eds. *People, Practice, Power: Digital Humanities outside the Center.* Minneapolis: University of Minnesota Press, 2021. https://www.jstor.org/stable/10.5749/j.ctv2782dmw.

"More Responses to 'The Computational Case against Computational Literary Studies.'" *Critical Inquiry—In the Moment,* April 12, 2019. https://critinq.wordpress.com/2019/04/12/more-responses-to-the-computational-case-against-computational-literary-studies/.

Rhody, Lisa M. "Topic Modeling and Figurative Language." *Journal of Digital Humanities* 2, no. 1 (2012). http://journalofdigitalhumanities.org/2-1/topic-modeling-and-figurative-language-by-lisa-m-rhody/.

So, Richard Jean. *Redlining Culture: A Data History of Racial Inequality and Postwar Fiction.* New York: Columbia Press University, 2021.

Spiro, Lisa. "'This Is Why We Fight': Defining the Values of the Digital Humanities." In *Debates in Digital Humanities,* edited by Matthew K. Gold, chap. 3. Minneapolis: University of Minnesota Press, 2012.

Svensson, Patrik. "Beyond the Big Tent." In *Debates in Digital Humanities,* edited by Matthew K. Gold, chap. 4. Minneapolis: University of Minnesota Press, 2012.

Terras, Melissa. "Peering Inside the Big Tent: Digital Humanities and the Crisis of Inclusion." *Melissa Terras's Blog,* July 26, 2011. https://melissaterras.org/2011/07/26/peering-inside-the-big-tent-digital-humanities-and-the-crisis-of-inclusion/.

Tilton, Lauren. "American Studies + Computational Humanities." *American Quarterly* 70, no. 3 (2018): 633–39. https://doi.org/10.1353/aq.2018.0046.

Varela, Miguel Escobar. *Theatre as Data.* Ann Arbor: University of Michigan, 2021.

Walsh, Melanie. *Introduction to Cultural Analytics & Python.* Version 1, 2021. https://melaniewalsh.github.io/Intro-Cultural-Analytics/welcome.html.

Weingart, S. B., and N. Eichmann-Kalwara. "What's under the Big Tent?: A Study of ADHO Conference Abstracts." *Digital Studies/le Champ Numérique* 7, no. 1, art. 6 (2017). https://doi.org/10.16995/dscn.284.

PART I

ASKING WITH

PART I][Chapter 1

Computation and Hermeneutics
Why We Still Need Interpretation to Be by (Computational) Humanists

HANNAH RINGLER

In *Graphesis*, Johanna Drucker uses train timetables as an example of a visual form that produces knowledge as well as represents it. A train timetable, on the one hand, simply represents the departure times of various trains, but it also allows its reader to calculate all various itineraries for how and when to get from point A to point B. These are not itineraries that the table itself provides; rather, they are knowledge produced by the reader from interpreting the table for their own purposes (perhaps to determine if their train is late or to evaluate the timeliness of a certain route). This example separates out the *how* of interpretation, which becomes salient usually when we do not know how to do it: many of us have likely stood confused in front of a train schedule when traveling ourselves, grappling with the distinction of knowing what a train schedule is but not having the same skills as those around us to figure out the information that we need.

In this chapter, I argue for a focus on the *how* of interpretation, or for developing hermeneutics. In computational humanities work, we are frequently traversing in new tools and forms of data where the method of interpretation is not even implicit but rather yet to be developed at all. For example, if we can distinguish two corpora using a logistic regression model or stylometry analysis, how do we move from those tables of numbers to insightful humanistic claims? How do you go about interpreting a table of weighted words or "distances" between pairs of texts in order to learn about the texts themselves? While new tools may construct new reads on artifacts like texts, the data they produce does not speak for itself and tell you what those new pieces of data *mean*. To be computational *humanists*, wherein our work fits within the broader scope of the humanities, our computation needs a hermeneutics to match.

Toward developing hermeneutics for computation, my goals with this piece are twofold: First, I hope to clarify the need for and the challenge of developing theories of interpretation by distinguishing two separate phases of interpretation. In particular, I distinguish between interpreting artifacts through tools and interpreting the output of tools toward humanistic claims. Second, I want to focus in on this second step of interpretation as a next major area of growth for computational humanities work and offer a framework for the types of questions that might be asked when interpreting the output of tools. In particular, I outline how we can think about hermeneutics in computational humanities as asking questions *with* and *about* digital tools. Ultimately, developing tools in tandem with careful thinking about how to interpret them not only opens up the use of those methods by a broader humanities audience, but it is a necessary part of computational method building in order to make our processes transparent and our claims insightful to the broader humanities.

Interpretation, Knowledge Production, and Disciplinarity

Interpretation, hermeneutics, and methods of knowledge production more generally have a long and varied history that dates back at least to the ancient Greek Sophists. The history of hermeneutics even just in computational humanities work is too long and complex to treat thoroughly here (see van Zundert for an excellent review), but thinking through a few key concepts is useful for clarifying some of what developing hermeneutics for computational work might entail.

In particular, a brief example drawn from social scientists Bruno Latour and Steve Woolgar is useful for thinking theoretically about method, tools, and the various forms and complexities of interpretation. In *Laboratory Life,* their book-length study on knowledge production, Latour and Woolgar are interested in how a biology lab goes about constructing facts, by which they do not mean to construe knowledge as completely relativistic but rather to highlight that facts have a process by which they come to be. They provide a whole narrative of the lengthy process by which biologists in one particular lab went about determining the structure of a certain hormone: first by using one tool and coming to a conclusion based on those results, then learning of a problem with that method that threw its accuracy into question and invalidated their conclusion, and finally devising a new tool altogether. The biologists eventually were satisfied with the results of the new method, finding it conclusive as to the hormone's structure because it "eliminate[d] all but a few possibilities" as to the structure, while other methods only eliminated a few possibilities at a time and thus were not conclusive enough (146). At this point, the new conclusion about the hormone's structure was taken as fact in the wider scientific community.

This example, especially coming from a biology lab where method is so apparent, is helpful for distinguishing three key terms: tool, interpretation (which appears in two forms), and method. Tools are identifiable in this example as that which produces some data about the artifact (note that "data" is not a neutral term and has been used to refer to a wide variety of things, e.g., the text as data movement; in this discussion, I use "data" in its more common contemporary usage to refer to a tool's output). The use of a tool itself is one form of interpretation, though: the biologists here imposed an interpretive screen in the form of a tool that could produce some data about the hormone, thus re-imagining and interpreting the hormone as data. The use of this tool was a choice (indeed, they developed the second one specifically for investigating this hormone), shaped by their evolving beliefs about what kind of data would be helpful for answering their questions. After imposing an interpretive screen, though, the biologists move to a second step of interpretation in that they interpreted that data toward a claim. The movement from tool usage to claim might normally go unnoticed, but it is especially salient in this example because it was at first misguided by an inaccurate belief about how accurate and conclusive their method was. When the biologists decided to use a new tool to determine the structure, they did so believing that using it eliminated *enough* other possibilities as to the structure that its results could be taken as conclusive. Their conclusions were shaped by their beliefs at the given time, their trust in tools, and their weighing of possible other alternatives: "It is thus important to realise that when a deduction is said not to be logical, or when we say that a logical possibility was deflected by belief, or that other deductions later became possible, this is done with the benefit of hindsight, and this hindsight provides another context within which we pronounce on the logic or illogic of a deduction" (Latour and Woolgar, 136). The entirety of these decisions—from choosing artifacts to using tools and interpreting toward claims—and all of the socially and culturally dependent decisions around them comprise the method.

Knowledge production methods as a whole, including these two forms of interpretation, are processes guided by social norms and beliefs. The biology example demonstrates how methodological decisions were made communally by those in the discipline based on prevailing beliefs; more generally, though, the design of tools and hermeneutical decisions about how to make sense of a tool's output are shaped by social beliefs rather than neutrally objective or intuitive (Rockwell and Sinclair). Knowledge production itself is heavily informed and shaped by the social and historical rather than by disinterested and objective observation, especially in decisions around how to move from tool usage to claim or interpretation. Theoretically speaking, thinking about knowledge as socially constructed in this way became more accepted in the mid-twentieth century, post-Kant, and especially in the aftermath of World War II with key thinkers like Thomas Kuhn, Michel Foucault, Karl Popper, Tara McPherson, and others.[1]

The collective decisions about what types of tools to use, how to design them, and how to interpret their outputs to come up with claims are made by social communities known as disciplines. Focusing on the social and historical forces of knowledge production allows us to conceptualize disciplines as communities with accepted "active ways of knowing" rather than "repositories and delivery systems for relatively static content knowledge" (Carter, 387). In effect, this reconceptualization of disciplines as ways of constructing knowledge introduces not only method narrowly conceived as data gathering as part of knowledge production but also the ways we interpret data as an integral part of methods and how we define a discipline and its work. While the state of digital humanities as a discipline is often shifting, it is nonetheless a social community engaging in similar types of work that is often oriented around methods and the digital, and thus it is in a position to theorize about and make these types of decisions.

Computation and Hermeneutics

As an area of study situated within the broader digital humanities, computational humanities is a space to think carefully about what "ways of knowing," hermeneutics, or interpretive strategies might define the humanities' use of computational tools. Exciting work in computational humanities thus far has focused on the first phase of interpretation, or interpreting artifacts through tools. That is, somewhere in the messy, iterative, and sometimes playful process of computational analyses, we run some form(s) of a computational tool that produces data in the form of numbers or visualizations—perhaps we create a ranked feature list, a network visualization, a clustering of texts, or a list of topic models. Geoffrey Rockwell and Stéfan Sinclair refer to these tools as "analytical tools" and explain that they are "instantiations of interpretive methods" in that they focus our attention on certain elements of texts or other artifacts to think about them and through them in new ways (4). As an example, Jacques Savoy visualized the stylistic differences between nine 2016 presidential candidates' speeches, allowing for a view of not just different groups of candidates but a representation of their relationships and magnitudes of differences at a glance. This work imposed an interpretive screen on those texts, made possible through the tool by focusing attention on particular features to see them in a new way. As analysts, we might try on several of these tools, reading and rereading our artifacts with different tools and views until we figure out interesting questions to ask and how to answer them (Rockwell and Sinclair, 169–87).

While these tools can construct new reads on texts, they leave open what those new pieces of data mean. A study like Savoy's is useful for its new visualization of candidates' possible relations to each other, but it also introduces a whole new realm of questions that are hard to answer: Why did candidates group together in the ways they did? Does it relate to the topics they focused on? The values they believed their bases to have? And if so, how? The clustering itself can be used as a jumping off point to thinking more critically about what makes up verbal style and how it might be connected to topic, genre, beliefs about audience, values, and so forth. These questions are also interpretive questions, but of a different kind than the interpretive screen the tool provides. Answering them requires developing different hermeneutical processes to interpret the data. In addition, the use of computational tools not only changes the kinds of interpretive questions we might ask but also complicates how we answer them: Who does this kind of interpretation and how is it wrapped up in issues of power and identity (D'Ignazio and Klein), and as such, we must think critically about how interpretation happens and what it means to avoid treating it as a neutral process wherein ideas simply emerge from the tools and their output themselves (Bode).

When we use computational tools as part of methods in the humanities, then, they may help us to explore and impose new kinds of interpretive screens on our artifacts, but they ultimately stop short of interpreting the data they produce. To undertake "algorithmic criticism" wherein tools enable critical engagement (Ramsay), it is important to recognize that doing so requires careful theorizing not just about how the tool is built and used but also about how we engage interpretively with its output. As computational humanists, if we want to contribute to humanistic inquiry, computational analysis is only useful for us insofar as it is paired with a careful interpretation of data that aligns with the humanistic tradition. In other words, our computation needs a hermeneutics. To stop short of engaging with hermeneutical questions, or to only engage with interpretive questions about how tools act as interpretive screens rather than interpreting their outputs toward claims, is a different disciplinary space of tool-building rather than holistic method-building. For while methods involve the whole range of activities from artifact-gathering to claim-making (and all are filled with interpretive choices), methods in the humanities, even if digital, must move us toward humanistic claims, which requires engagement with these difficult interpretive challenges as part of our methodological engagement with tools more broadly.

A large amount of scholarship in computational humanities thus far has engaged well with the first phase of interpreting artifacts through tools. Taylor Arnold and Lauren Tilton explain how computational tools allow for exploring data in new ways, which is evident in their work on Photogrammar as well as other technical approaches like Maciej Eder's influential work thinking through the complexities of visual techniques in stylometry. While this is a necessary, and frequently theoretically challenging space, interpreting the output of those tools is a separate phase to theorize that still needs work. Ryan Heuser and Long Le-Khac, for example, narrate how challenging it is to find yourself face-to-face with a table of data to make meaning of, and Sculley and Pasanek point to the difficulties in making sense of outputs given the assumptions built into computational tools. Traditional humanities work has a long history of engaging with hermeneutics and theories of interpretation to the point that analyses may not even mention them explicitly (e.g., Clement notes that close reading often goes unquestioned as a methodological approach in textual scholarship). Given the relative newness of many computational tools though, their hermeneutics could benefit from being clearer. Computational humanities has an opportunity to develop these theories in partnership with tool-builders such that the analyses produced can speak fruitfully to humanistic inquiry.

As a step toward developing these hermeneutics more fully as a field, I offer in the next section a framework for the types of questions that might be asked when interpreting the output of tools in computational humanities work. Some initial scholarship has begun higher-level theorizing a hermeneutics for interpreting the output of tools. For example, Andrew Piper conceptualizes the movement back and forth from close to distant reading, Jo Guldi outlines a process called "critical search," and Heuser and Le-Khac explore how we can think of interpretation as hypothesis-testing. In earlier work, I talked about the process of building up evidence toward an understanding as a way of constructing arguments in the face of uncertainty (Ringler). In considering more broadly the types of interpretive questions we might encounter in analyses, I join David Bamman and Mark Algee-Hewitt in making space in this volume and the computational humanities for more critical thought about the types of hermeneutical processes we need to continue developing and the words and structure needed to define what this development might look like for future methodological work. More broadly, focusing on this second step of interpretation, of interpreting the output of tools and how that contributes to what Lincoln Mullen calls a "braided narrative" between method and interpretation, speaks to the distinction that Dennis Tenen makes between methods and tools. It also responds to concerns raised by scholars like Alan Liu and Tanya Clement about connecting method and theory. Developing tools in tandem with careful thinking about how to interpret them makes these methods more accessible to a broader humanities audience. In addition, it is also a necessary part of computational method exploration in order to make our processes transparent and our claims insightful to the broader humanities community.

A Framework for Humanistic Inquiry in Computational Humanities

As we further develop our hermeneutics for computation and focus on the second step of interpretation, what might that look like? What does interpreting the outputs of tools look like? To a large extent, this varies based on specific disciplines: the types of research questions and trajectories, methods, and orientation to the humanities broadly will affect how the results of a tool are interpreted and what counts as productive interpretation and claims for a disciplinary community (Robertson). Despite this level of variation, though, we can think generally about what interpretation of computational data in the humanities looks like based on the work being produced in computational humanities spaces now. In this section, I sketch a framework for the types of hermeneutical questions that might be asked of computational methods in the humanities. While definitions of digital humanities abound, to structure this particular framework, Kathleen Fitzpatrick's definition of digital humanities is useful for clarifying the broad types of work that digital humanities does: DH both "use[s] computing technologies to investigate the kinds of questions that are traditional to the humanities" and "ask[s] traditional kinds of humanities-oriented questions about computing technologies." This definition poses two categories of questions—asking questions *with* and *about* computing technologies—which is a productive frame for thinking about the types of interpretation we do with computation in the humanities.

Asking With

To ask questions *with* computing technologies is akin to what Rockwell and Sinclair describe when they explain hermeneutics in digital humanities as an iterative process between exploring and hypothesis testing. In this process, an analyst starts with artifacts, asks humanistic questions of them, and uses tools to help them answer those questions. Text analysis is thus the practice of "re-reading a text in different ways with the assistance of computers that make it practicable to ask formalized questions and get back artificial views" (Rockwell and Sinclair, 189). While various tools might help with broad exploration of the artifacts, as with an exploratory data analysis (EDA) framework (Tukey; Arnold and Tilton), the driving focus is the analytical humanistic question, and the tool helps answer it by pointing to specific features of interest. As we explore new tools, though, and how they interact with messy, humanistic artifacts, the key challenge for computationalists is to figure out how to interpret the tool's output to make an interpretive claim. The humanities are fundamentally about complicating, interpreting, and understanding the messy human experience (MacDonald), which means the challenge for working with computational methods is to interpret numerical models to create well-supported insights into humanities areas. This challenge is not trivial but is fundamental to using computation in humanistic spaces.

A few examples are helpful for demonstrating what it looks like to ask questions with computing technologies, and especially what it looks like to think carefully about how to interpret the results of tools toward research questions. As one useful illustration, a piece by David Kaufer and Shawn Parry-Giles uses a corpus text analysis tool called DocuScope (Kaufer and Ishizaki) to identify different identities that Hillary Clinton displays in her two memoirs, *Living History* and *Hard Choices*. They ultimately find seven distinct identities that Clinton enacts (e.g., litigator, political visionary, storyteller) and contextualize these identities within larger discussions of political memoirs as a genre and how these identities were strategic choices in her bid for the presidency and her role as a woman politician. They use these multiple identities to explain that women candidates in particular are "chronically 'double-binded' into 'personality problems' that impact voters' attachment to them" as they balance creating emotional connections with voters and staying socially "correct" and "appropriate" (Kaufer and Parry-Giles, 22). Ultimately, the authors can make claims about the rhetorical strategies that Hillary Clinton used in her memoirs and how those identities speak to her complicated position as a female politician.

DocuScope, the tool used in this analysis, is a freely available dictionary-based corpus tool.[2] It classifies words and phrases into rhetorical patterns that can be counted. Factor analysis can then reveal which rhetorical patterns statistically occur together in texts, and these factors can be interpreted as rhetorical strategies. This piece was published in the *Quarterly Journal of Speech,* which does not regularly publish heavily computational work, so the authors take some time in the piece to explain how they go about interpreting the factors and the results that their tool produces:

> The computer harvesting of latent factors (e.g., litigator versus storytelling prose) in texts identifies patterns that the human reading brain can evaluate post hoc but cannot reliably isolate and harvest systematically across hundreds and thousands of pages of text. . . . This harvesting supplies readers with a "third eye" able to discern recurrent textual patterns that remain invisible even to the most observant critic. Such systematic linkages between macrorhetorical strategies and microrhetorical patterns guards against selection bias and ensures that the passages selected for evidence are not cherry-picked but fill in defining components systematically dispersed across both memoirs. (Kaufer and Parry-Giles, 22)

In their analysis, then, the authors use the tool to identify recurring patterns that may go unnoticed by a normal serial reader. By having attention drawn to these recurring patterns, the authors are better poised to look at the text-level patterns as a whole and interpret them as "macrorhetorical strategies." These macro strategies are the ones that they ultimately name as different identities. In this example, the tool itself does some level of interpretation in its categorization of words and phrases into particular rhetorical categories and the statistical representation of those categories in factors. But we then see an explicit second step of interpretation, wherein the authors conceptualize this interpretation as a "third eye" on the text and make their own interpretations of the factors based on their readings of the texts and understandings of their contexts. The second step of interpretation is somewhat closer to a traditional/non-corpus rhetorical analysis in its close focus on context, identity, and rhetorical situation but involves a different interpretive process due to the nature of the data produced by the method. In particular, the authors return to serial reading representative pieces of the text with an intense focus on certain types of vocabulary (highlighted visually by the tool) and think critically about how the vocabulary types in one factor might collectively support a particular identity. The various identities of Clinton, then, are a result of the authors' interpretations of the tool's output, rather than something created through just the tool itself.

Another piece by Marissa Gemma, Frédéric Glorieux, and Jean-Gabriel Ganascia uses slightly more traditional computational methods on texts but also highlights this second step of interpretation. In this piece, the authors explain that literary critics have agreed that American literature emerged as a distinct style that was more colloquial in the postbellum period, but that we do not know a lot about what linguistic features make up that style. They frame their study as testing the claim about the emergence of a more colloquial style in American literature and as an investigation of features that make up that style by focusing specifically on the prevalence of repetition. In the first part of this study, they find that American fiction does increase in its rate of repetition overall, but that the results are inconclusive because British fiction measures an increase in repetition by one measure but no increase by another. The authors call these results "inconclusive" and look for tests that will provide "more interpretable historical results" (321). Based on the first results, they use different measures to find that repetition actually increases when more speech is represented in writing, and that there is a clear increase in this feature over time, though it is ambiguous whether it is unique to American fiction.

This study does not necessarily wind up confirming the hypothesis that a colloquial style is unique to American fiction, but it offers some novel insight into trends in American and possibly British fiction in the long nineteenth century. In particular, because the repetition results seemed inconclusive at first, this prompted the authors to explore with new metrics, which allowed them to discover that represented speech (and therefore repetition) increased in American and British fiction in this time period. Ultimately, the authors are able to explain what a colloquial style means in fiction by demonstrating how represented speech and dialogue increases. The claim here is ultimately one about colloquial style in American and British fiction, which was discovered through interpretation *by* the tool (i.e., counting repetition in novels over time) and interpretation *of* the tool's output (i.e., using the results of which words were repeated frequently to map this trend onto represented speech and dialogue between characters in fiction and connecting this to broader literary criticism about colloquial style in the long nineteenth century).

Both pieces (Kaufer and Parry-Giles; Gemma, Glorieux, and Ganascia) explicitly highlight the unique challenges of interpretation in computational work and the development of a new hermeneutics for making sense of these data. With DocuScope, the authors had to grapple with a question of how to interpret factors as rhetorical strategies. How do you look at a list of rhetorical patterns or types of words that cluster into a factor and decide that it suggests a "litigator" identity? Doing so requires a familiarity with how identity instantiates itself rhetorically (especially in regard to public figures and feminist theory) as well as a deep cultural knowledge of how political memoirs function to create public identities. With measuring repetition, how can the authors know how much of the repetition is made up by increased speech? And even if they can, how do we know that this is what literary critics mean when they say fiction seems more colloquial in America by the early twentieth century? Answering these questions requires not only a thorough understanding of American literary history but also of what it means for a novel to be seen as colloquial and how colloquial language takes its form in speech and literature more broadly.

These kinds of hermeneutical questions that we must grapple with when using computational methods speak deeply to our training as humanists in that they are somewhat messy and not clearly verifiable in statistical terms but rather connect to contextual understandings of the artifacts being worked with. Both of these interpretive challenges appear to have been addressed at least in part by some degree of serial reading of each corpus, with a focus on the features highlighted by the tools and a deep understanding by the authors of not only the tools but also the texts and contexts they were working with. This, then, allowed them to draw on their more traditional humanistic training in their disciplines to interpret the results toward an argumentative claim that fits within the paradigms of rhetorical and literary studies, respectively. These interpretive decisions and processes may be more or less explicit in the papers themselves, but they are the kinds of challenging methodological processes that we are well poised to think about critically in computational humanities as they draw on both the expertise of humanists (in subject matter) and data scientists (in tools) in order to figure out how to create insight from reams of data.

Asking About

While asking questions *with* computing technologies puts the analytic questions front and center, asking questions *about* computing technologies instead highlights the hermeneutic questions more explicitly. Regarding computational tools and methods specifically, this type of question prompts us to think about what particular tools or methods offer us and how they might change or add to our thinking about a concept. For example, the Six Degrees of Francis Bacon project (Warren et al.) reconstructs and visualizes a large social network in early modern Britain. This visualization allows early modernist researchers to think about relationships in entirely new ways by seeing connections between people at scale. Indeed, another social network visualization project focusing on medieval Scotland revealed a previously undiscovered role played by Duncan II, Earl of Fife (Jackson). On a more abstract level, visualizations like these ask us to question and redefine our concepts of community and what it means to be part of a social network with others in a specific context. By visualizing these connections, we have to make decisions: How do we decide someone is connected enough to warrant a link in a social network? How connected must someone be? For how long? What kind of interactions count as being connected? The tools themselves prompt a whole variety of reflective questions and ask us to make interpretive choices while also challenging our concepts of messy, humanistic concepts like *community*. In this sense, the tool and how we design it raises hermeneutic questions about how to interpret its design and output, which connect explicitly to broader questions that a discipline is already invested in and, as others have demonstrated (e.g., Cox and Tilton), can also prompt new interdisciplinary lines of argument and inquiry.

Asking questions about computational methods also opens up space for being puzzled by the outputs of tools and investigating deeply why they produce the results that they do. In the last several years, there has been growing interest in interpretable machine learning (Belinkov and Glass; Lipton). This interest points to a class of question that arises when a computational tool produces a result that seems in some way accurate or matches with our understanding of the world, but we are puzzled as to why. For example, a tool may classify texts by author gender very well (thus matching with a preexisting category we place on authors), but it may be unclear why this can be done, given the features the tool uses. Many of the more complex computational methods can be described as somewhat of a black box, making it difficult to determine why they produce the results that they do. Hugh Craig raised a version of this kind of question about stylometry methods in a paper's subtitle: "If you can tell authors apart, have you learned anything about them?" A few explorations of why particular textual features connect to authors or speakers have been taken up inside and outside the context of stylometry (McKenna and Antonia; Argamon, Dodick, and Chase; Pennebaker), but the question is still frequently a puzzling one.

These kinds of difficult questions about computational methods are interesting, though, because they point to places where we have clear humanistic insight to gain: In stylometry, for example, why is it that certain function words map onto the gender of fiction authors in particular time periods? What would we learn about function words, gender, and language more broadly by being able to answer this question? In his piece on "computing criticism" in chapter 2 in this volume, Algee-Hewitt challenges digital humanists to engage with puzzling models by seeing unexplainable models as an opportunity to reevaluate the artifacts in question rather than assuming the model is an inaccurate or useless representation. Much like the "asking with" examples used patterns to draw the analysts' attention to certain features in their reading, these kinds of puzzling results can be seen as lenses that draw our attention to certain features of texts, images, or other artifacts that warrant further investigation and thought about how they connect to other social aspects of the data. Developing the interpretive processes to answer these kinds of puzzling questions is an active new area of study, and one that requires collaboration and crossover with computer and data scientists to deeply understand the tools themselves and with humanists to deeply understand the artifacts and their contexts.

Using computational tools in the humanities opens up a wide space for thinking about how to interpret data toward humanistic inquiry. Tools themselves can be thought of as interpretive screens on artifacts, but they ultimately stop short of answering questions about what their outputs mean, which is a crucial though often implicit part of knowledge production as a theoretical process. Computational tools offer a new challenge for moving from lens to claim because of the entirely different nature of the lenses themselves. With computational tools in the humanities, then, we need to both keep learning how to apply tools as well as develop hermeneutics for different tools and artifacts.

Asking questions *with* and *about* these computational tools are two ways of thinking about the types of hermeneutical theories we might develop for different tools. Figuring out what the numbers mean, and how to go about doing that, is not a trivial process and should be interdisciplinary. While computational fields are well equipped to construct these tools and understand the assumptions and processes behind them, humanists are poised to think critically about what these tools tell us about artifacts and how interpretive practices fit within a humanistic tradition that acknowledges how feminist, intersectional, postcolonial, and other types of perspectives shape meaning-making. In this sense, computationalists and humanists have a lot to offer each other in considering a broader challenge of how to interpret and make meaning in the age of big data and machine learning. As we build computational humanities, a key component will be further thinking through the entire methodological process by considering tools as interpretation and interpretation of tools as processes that need hermeneutics. Collaboration will be key. Communally developing those hermeneutics explicitly as an integral part of method-building will help us to be more transparent in our research and able to use those tools in ways that contributes productively to the broader humanities and our computational world.

Notes

1. Considering knowledge as socially constructed rather than objectively emerging has grown out of a huge range of scholarship from different perspectives. A few notable examples include Kuhn, who revealed the social aspects of scientific knowledge developing with his theorization of paradigms; Foucault, who offered a lens on knowledge construction through language; and McPherson, who pointed to the role of social justice and civil rights movements in shaping knowledge.

2. DocuScope is developed and hosted by Carnegie Mellon University: https://www.cmu.edu/dietrich/english/research-and-publications/docuscope.html.

Bibliography

Argamon, Shlomo, Jeff Dodick, and Paul Chase. "Language Use Reflects Scientific Methodology: A Corpus-Based Study of Peer-Reviewed Journal Articles." *Scientometrics* 75, no. 2 (2008): 203–38.

Arnold, Taylor, and Lauren Tilton. "New Data? The Role of Statistics in DH." In *Debates in the Digital Humanities 2019*, edited by Matthew K. Gold and Lauren F. Klein, 293–99. Minneapolis: University of Minnesota Press, 2019.

Belinkov, Yonatan, and James Glass. "Analysis Methods in Neural Language Processing: A Survey." *Transactions of the Association for Computational Linguistics* 7 (2019): 49–72.

Bode, Katherine. "The Equivalence of 'Close' and 'Distant' Reading: or, toward a New Object for Data-Rich Literary History." *Modern Language Quarterly* 78, no. 1 (2017): 77–106.

Carter, Michael. "Ways of Knowing, Doing, and Writing in the Disciplines." *College Composition and Communication* 58, no. 3 (2007): 385–418.

Clement, Tanya E. "Where Is Methodology in Digital Humanities?" In *Debates in the Digital Humanities 2016,* edited by Matthew K. Gold and Lauren F. Klein, 153–75. Minneapolis: University of Minnesota Press, 2016.

Cox, Jordana, and Lauren Tilton. "The Digital Public Humanities: Giving New Arguments and New Ways to Argue." *Review of Communication* 19, no. 2 (2019): 127–46.

Craig, Hugh. "Authorial Attribution and Computational Stylistics: If You Can Tell Authors Apart, Have You Learned Anything about Them?" *Literary and Linguistic Computing* 14, no. 1 (1999): 103–13.

D'Ignazio, Catherine, and Lauren F. Klein. *Data Feminism.* Cambridge, Mass.: MIT Press, 2020.

Drucker, Johanna. *Graphesis: Visual Forms of Knowledge Production.* Cambridge, Mass.: Harvard University Press, 2014.

Eder, Maciej. "Visualization in Stylometry: Cluster Analysis Using Networks." *Digital Scholarship in the Humanities* 32, no. 1 (2017): 50–64.

Fitzpatrick, Kathleen. "Reporting from the Digital Humanities 2010 Conference." *ProfHacker,* July 13, 2010. http://chronicle.com/blogs/profhacker/reporting-from-the-digital-humanities-2010-conference/25473.

Foucault, Michel. *The Archaeology of Knowledge.* New York: Pantheon Books, 1972.

Foucault, Michel. *The Order of Things: An Archaeology of the Human Sciences.* New York: Pantheon Books, 1970.

Gemma, Marissa, Frédéric Glorieux, and Jean-Gabriel Ganascia. "Operationalizing the Colloquial Style: Repetition in 19th-Century American Fiction." *Digital Scholarship in the Humanities* 32, no. 2 (2017): 312–35.

Guldi, Jo. "Critical Search: A Procedure for Reading in Large-Scale Textual Corpora." *Journal of Cultural Analytics* 3, no. 1 (2018).

Heuser, Ryan, and Long Le-Khac. "Learning to Read Data: Bringing Out the Humanistic in the Digital Humanities." *Victorian Studies* 54, no. 1 (2011): 79–86.

Jackson, Cornell. "Using Social Network Analysis to Reveal Unseen Relationships in Medieval Scotland." *Digital Scholarship in the Humanities* 32, no. 2 (2017): 336–43.

Kaufer, David, and Suguru Ishizaki. "Computer-Aided Rhetorical Analysis." In *Applied Natural Language Processing and Content Analysis: Advances in Identification, Investigation, and Resolution,* edited by Philip M. McCarthy and Chutima Boonthum-Denecke, 276–96. Hershey, Pa.: IGI Global, 2012.

Kaufer, David S., and Shawn J. Parry-Giles. "Hillary Clinton's Presidential Campaign Memoirs: A Study in Contrasting Identities." *Quarterly Journal of Speech* 103, no. 1–2 (2017): 7–32.

Kuhn, Thomas S. *The Structure of Scientific Revolutions.* Chicago: University of Chicago Press, 1962.

Latour, Bruno, and Steve Woolgar. *Laboratory Life: The Construction of Scientific Facts.* Princeton, N.J.: Princeton University Press, 1986.

Lipton, Zachary C. "The Mythos of Model Interpretability." *Queue* 16, no. 3 (June 2018): 31–57.

Liu, Alan. "Where Is Cultural Criticism in the Digital Humanities?" In *Debates in the Digital Humanities,* edited by Matthew K. Gold, 490–510. Minneapolis: University of Minnesota Press, 2012.

MacDonald, Susan P. *Professional Academic Writing in the Humanities and Social Sciences.* Carbondale: Southern Illinois University Press, 2010.

McKenna, C. W. F., and Alexia Antonia. "The Statistical Analysis of Style: Reflections on Form, Meaning, and Ideology in the 'Nausicaa' Episode of Ulysses." *Literary and Linguistic Computing* 16, no. 4 (2001): 353–73.

McPherson, Tara. "U.S. Operating Systems at Mid-Century: The Intertwining of Race and Unix." In *Race after the Internet,* edited by Lisa Nakamura and Peter A. Chow-White, 21–37. New York: Routledge, 2013.

Mullen, Lincoln. "A Braided Narrative for Digital History." In *Debates in the Digital Humanities 2019,* edited by Matthew K. Gold and Lauren F. Klein, 382–88. Minneapolis: University of Minnesota Press, 2019.

Pennebaker, James W. *The Secret Life of Pronouns: What Our Words Say about Us.* New York: Bloomsbury Press, 2011.

Piper, Andrew. "Novel Devotions: Conversional Reading, Computational Modeling, and the Modern Novel." *New Literary History* 46 (2015): 63–98.

Popper, Karl R. *The Logic of Scientific Discovery.* London: Hutchinson, 1959.

Ramsay, Stephen. *Reaching Machines: Toward an Algorithmic Criticism.* Champaign: University of Illinois Press, 2011.

Ringler, Hannah. "'We Can't Read It All': Theorizing a Hermeneutics for Large-Scale Data in the Humanities with a Case Study in Stylometry." *Digital Scholarship in the Humanities* (2021).

Robertson, Stephen. "The Differences between Digital Humanities and Digital History." In *Debates in the Digital Humanities 2016,* edited by Matthew K. Gold and Lauren F. Klein. Minneapolis: University of Minnesota Press, 2016.

Rockwell, Geoffrey, and Stéfan Sinclair. *Hermeneutica: Computer-Assisted Interpretation in the Humanities.* Cambridge, Mass.: MIT Press, 2016.

Savoy, Jacques. "Analysis of the Style and the Rhetoric of the 2016 US Presidential Primaries." *Digital Scholarship in the Humanities* 33, no. 1 (2018): 143–59.

Sculley, David, and Bradley M. Pasanek. "Meaning and Mining: The Impact of Implicit Assumptions in Data Mining for the Humanities." *Literary and Linguistic Computing* 23, no. 4 (2008): 409–24.

Tenen, Dennis. "Blunt Instrumentalism: On Tools and Methods." In *Debates in the Digital Humanities 2016,* edited by Matthew K. Gold and Lauren F. Klein, 83–91. Minneapolis: University of Minnesota Press, 2016.

Tukey, John Wilder. *Exploratory Data Analysis.* Reading, Mass.: Addison-Wesley, 1977.

van Zundert, Joris J. "Screwmeneutics and Hermenumericals: The Computationality of Hermeneutics." In *A New Companion to Digital Humanities,* edited by Susan Schreibman, Ray Siemens, and John Unsworth, 331–47. New York: John Wiley, 2016.

Warren, Christopher N., Daniel Shore, Jessica Otis, Lawrence Wang, Mike Finegold, and Cosma Shalizi. "Six Degrees of Francis Bacon: A Statistical Method for Reconstructing Large Historical Social Networks." *Digital Humanities Quarterly* 10, no. 3 (2016).

PART I][Chapter 2

Computing Criticism
Humanities Concepts and Digital Methods

MARK ALGEE-HEWITT

There is a tension present when we use computational methods to explore questions that originate in the disciplines of the humanities, one felt equally by practitioners of the field as well as those who are resistant to it. This is not simply a function of the distance between the methods involved, from computation to statistics to hermeneutics and interpretation, but something more fundamental to the different epistemes of the fields in which the methods originate. Too often, when we seek to bridge the difference between computation and interpretation, we privilege one side over the other. Either computation is presented as a method that can act as a corrective to humanities practices that are unable to take a larger context into consideration, or more often, it is suggested that hermeneutics and interpretation can help us understand where our computation goes wrong. At best, we can imagine the interplay between these poles as a set of separate but mutually informative models: we use phenomena familiar to, for example, literary theory (genre, character, theme, or setting) in order to train computational models that can recognize these phenomena, and then, in turn, we use these models to explore the phenomena within a context traditionally unavailable to humanities analysis in order to help us expand the theory that we used to train the model in the first place.[1] In this feedback loop, the models (literary and computational) are mutually informative, but the distance between them is maintained. In this chapter, I argue that there are other, perhaps more productive ways of managing this tension. If we bring these fields into contact with each other in the space of our analysis, if we treat the transformations that the theoretical object must undergo to become computationally tractable not simply as a proxy for the phenomenon but instead allow it to persist as a radical reconceptualization of the object, then we open up a whole new set of possibilities for computational analysis.

Consider the following simplified schematic for how computational text analysis often takes place in humanities contexts. First, researchers assemble a digital corpus through which they will pose the questions of humanities interest that motivate their project. Next, the specifics of the question posed by the researchers are either operationalized through a computational model, which can be as simple as a word-frequency table and as complex as a deep learning encoder, or they are assessed through a supervised model (and the resulting patterns are post hoc associated with disciplinary concepts).[2] Finally, the results are collected and interpreted in light of the original question and the specific features of the texts that are being modeled. Regardless of whether we understand the modeling process as a mechanism for producing empirical results in and of themselves (Underwood, 34–67; So, Long, and Zhu), or whether we intend to create a hermeneutics in which the results of a computational analysis serve to redirect our interpretive lens toward specific parts of a text (Piper, 66–93; Froehlich), these steps often serve as a three-part framework for the process of text analysis in the humanities. At the center of this schema, the interface between the critical and digital or between the hermeneutic and the computational maintains the theoretical distance between the model and the object of its operationalization.

The effects of this distance impose artificial limits on how we can combine computation and interpretation in our research. When the results of our analysis go awry, when they provide unexpected answers that contradict aspects of the corpus that we know to be true, we seek fault at exactly this junction. We assume that either the corpus that we have created to investigate our question is insufficient (in size or in focus) to represent the textual field that we seek to investigate or, more commonly, that the methods that we have selected through which to operationalize our question are not capturing the specific phenomena that we want to explore. The iterative work of text analysis (returning to the model to adjust our parameters, reconfiguring our corpus, changing the underlying methodology of our analysis, and then running the experiment again) depends on our ability to trace the faulty model to its root in order to create a better fit between what we want to investigate and the computational methods through which we seek to represent it. If the results of an authorship attribution assign differently authored books to a single author (or if the corpus of a single author is unpredictably bifurcated into multiple authors), if a topic model is full of "junk" topics, or if a named entity recognition (NER) parse collapses or divides character mentions into unexpected configurations, then we return to the model to correct the fault and run the analysis again.[3]

Such a unidirectional approach toward operationalizing textual phenomena presumes that we know what we are looking for. In other words, it assumes that when we model author or theme or character, we understand what those objects are, such that any discrepancy between our understanding of these phenomena and our computational model lies in an error of how the model represents the real-world object. But this approach misses the fact that none of these phenomena *are* real-world objects: rather, they are the apparatus of a textual theory whose parameters are equally as approximate as the computational model to the complexities of the text itself. By assuming that our interpretive or theoretical models are better representations of the text than our computational ones, we overlook one of the most potentially productive uses of quantitative textual analysis: that by modeling one of these theoretical phenomena through computation, we can actually gain a new understanding of the textual phenomenon that we model as an author, a theme, or character. That is, rather than interpret flaws in the analysis as an underlying fault in our ability to represent real-world objects digitally, it is entirely possible to use these discrepancies to reevaluate what we think we know about the object in question.

A new strategy of this kind requires a turn in our thinking. Instead of assuming that the quantitative model represents an imperfect proxy for a real-world object (i.e., the text), it encourages us to take the quantitative results at face value and ask what they can tell us about our theories of text. This is a process that would be familiar to much early work in the digital humanities: it shares, for example, the defamiliarizing process that different textual transformations (through quantification or even just through digitization) make possible.[4] Through this chapter, I want to recover this process in order to understand what changes, both in our analyses and in our theories, when we elect to take the quantitative results that produce an authorship analysis, a named entity recognition parse, or a topic model at face value rather than as imperfect measurements. By putting quantitative textual analysis back in contact with the textual, often literary theory that destabilized and called into question these supposedly stable categories, we can return some of the revolutionary potential of early digital humanities work to our current practice.

Distributions of Authorship

The goal of stylometry is often understood to be particularly straightforward, at least when it is applied to questions of author attribution. Given a set of texts with known authors can we (a) derive a quantitative approximation of an author's style, (b) group known authors together so that individual words cluster (or classify) with their respective author, and (c) create a model robust enough that an unknown work can be correctly associated with a known author? Due to the strength of the so-called author signal within a collection of texts, stylometry operates most effectively on the most frequent words in a corpus, whose minute variation at large scales creates the distributions that can most easily differentiate between authors. Although the exact number of features is a subject of some debate in the literature, it remains an astonishing effect that relatively few function words, often no more than the 300 most frequent words (MFWs), can so effectively sort a corpus into authorial groups.[5] Take, for example, a plot of 518 works of detective fiction (written between 1881 and 2000) by twenty-five authors (Figure 2.1).[6] Here, the icons on the graph represent individual novels; their shapes, which generally group together neatly, represent the known authors of each text. The effect of this analysis is startling: across over a century of difference, authors' corpora still remained tightly bound in distinct,

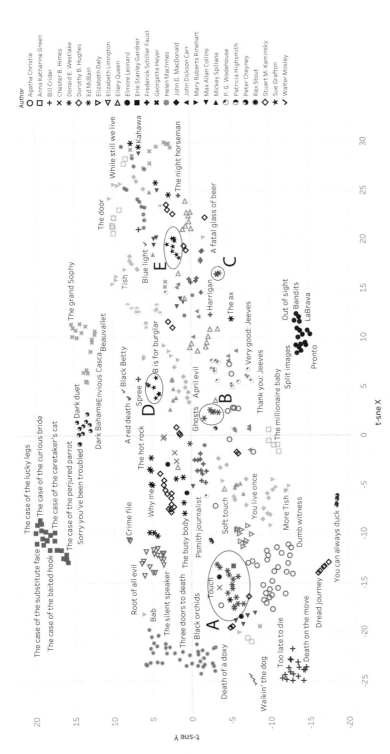

Figure 2.1. Authorship similarity between twenty-five twentieth-century authors of detective fiction based on 200 most frequent words, visualized through a t-distributed stochastic neighbor embedding (t-sne) plot, which uses a modeling algorithm to best position each text to represent its similarity to other texts in the corpus (texts closer to each other in the plot have a greater similarity).

recognizable clusters (for the most part), whether those groups are found at the center of the diagram (like the works of Ellery Queen) or in a cluster on the periphery (like the corpus of Erle Stanley Gardner).

Such an analysis might be disorienting to students or scholars without experience in the digital humanities. The notion that quantifying such a small and nominally content-free word set can capture something as meaningful, as deeply *human*, as style or authorship seems at once miraculous and terrifying. But it is worth being specific about what a plot such as this actually captures. Authorship, unlike many other literary or textual phenomena, has a real-world extension in the persons of the authors that we credit with writing the texts. When we say that an analysis such as this captures the style of Ed McBain, we are implicitly making an argument that connects the words (the high-frequency MFWs) to the embodied personhood of the author such that there seems to be something connecting the physical author to their style. Practitioners of authorship attribution have devoted a significant amount of text to explaining this phenomenon in terms of an often rather naive cognitive psychology. The variations between authors, we are told, can be resolved into differences in "background and training," where "function words are used in a largely unconscious manner" and can therefore capture "pure stylistic choices" that are "somehow affected by an unconscious personal stamp" (Baayen et al., 1; Stamatatos, 540; Eder, 103). Some even go farther and use the same statistical processes to ascertain "basic psychological processes" or even infer personality and mental health, including trauma and depression (Argamon et al.; Juola, 74). Confounding factors in the analysis are ascribed to the chosen model features or are perhaps "due to personal development of the author over time" (Diederich et al., 110). These claims have two key aspects in common: first, the authors of these studies supply little evidence linking the cognitive state of a real-world human mind to variations in the statistical patterns that their attributional findings use to associate groups of texts; second, aside from the studies that specifically try to link psychological processes to textual patterns, there is no reason to even engage cognitive or psychological theory at all.[7]

After all, when treating authorship attribution as a purely text classification problem, the actual persona or even embodiment of the author is often immaterial to the analysis. If the texts cluster together such that texts with the same author's name are associated, the link between that name and the physical human, or their mental state, is arbitrary at best.[8] In fact, relating commonalities in word frequency distributions back to a unique unconscious is frequently complicated by the slippery nature of authorship itself. Ed McBain, clustered somewhat reliably by the graph in Figure 2.1, is the name under which Evan Hunter wrote his best-selling genre fiction, and Evan Hunter is the adopted pen name of Salvatore Lombino, who also wrote under the pseudonym Hunt Collins and Richard Marsten (MacDonald). While on the surface, this seems like the ideal case for an authorial attribution study (whose goal would be to reassociate the various pen names used by Lombino under a single category), such a study would heavily weight the biographical theory of authorship while, at the same time, undercutting the ways in which Lombino's books were marketed and sold to the public. In fact, in Figure 2.1, McBain's novels are actually located in three distinctive clusters: (A) toward the left-hand side of the graph, (B) to the right, separated by the clusters of Elizabeth Daly and Frederick Schiller Faust, and (C) on the right periphery of the central cluster. In classic authorship attribution, this would be read as an error: one unique individual whose works are wrongly differentiated into three distinct authors. But given the complexities of his own authorial identity, the fractured nature of McBain/Lombino/Marsten/Collins is partially captured by the apparent "flaws" in the analysis.[9]

This complexity of authorial layering—the relationship between the author as human and the author as signatory of a body of work—is deeply familiar in a literary studies context. It is precisely the nexus of bibliographic, performative, and fictional identities that drives Michel Foucault's "What Is an Author?" (Foucault).[10] Foucault's essay remains valuable in its reconfiguration of the author into the author-function: a recognition of the purely *classificatory* work of the authorial signature. "A name can group together a number of texts and thus differentiate them from others. A name also establishes different forms of relationships among texts" (123). In this grouping function, the author becomes a convenient shorthand to describe similarities among a body of work. In discussing the Nancy Drew series as the work of Carolyn Keene or the Baby-Sitters Club as the work of Ann M. Martin, we are typically less interested in the presence of ghostwriters or an editorial house style than we are in understanding each collection of texts as belonging to a meaningful classificatory group. This is not to say that differentiating Ann M. Martin from her ghostwriters might not have value within the context of a particular authorship study; rather, understanding the group as "by" a single or multiple author-function(s) is equally valid, depending on the perspective of the analysis.

It is in Foucault's theory that we can find an unexpected power in stylometric authorship attribution if we let go of the implicit connection between author and author-function (that is, between the lived experience of an individual and the signatory on a collection of texts) that lives in the pseudo-psychological explanations for the connection between style and (un)consciousness. In its statistical model, stylometry provides an unexpectedly simple yet powerful answer to the question animating (and titling) Foucault's work: What is an author? The answer, according to the computational model, is that it is a set of word frequencies that cluster texts into recognizable groups with high probability. Such an explanation of authorship does not need the apparatus of cognitive psychology, not merely because, in the contexts of the articles that I discuss above, such connections are worse than arbitrary, but more importantly because defining authorship in this way offers a greater explanatory power for associations between texts that do not rest on the mere accident of a single individual authoring a cluster of books. The other kinds of work that the author-function performs—conceptual, theoretical, social, and classificatory—can actually be better observed if we allow authors to recede from stylometry and rest our theories specifically on the new ways in which quantitative analysis allows us to reconfigure the classification of texts. What I am suggesting here is a radicalization of *what is already central to stylometry*: the substitution of word patterns for the figure of the author as a unique consciousness. Our theories, unprepared to grapple with this reconfiguration of authorship, seek the comfort of offering a cognitive explanation for a statistical phenomenon: by preventing or resisting this, we are able to leverage stylometry to understand different kinds of author-functions.

Such an approach is particularly relevant in cases wherein a stylometric analysis either groups together authors known to be different (for example, in the presence of a strong editorial or house style) or breaks apart clusters known to be by a single signatory author. In Figure 2.1, for example, Sue Grafton, author of the "alphabet series" of detective novels, is neatly divided into two distinct clusters (D and E). With some refinement to the graph (changing the feature set, adjusting the number of authors, or moving to a different clustering method), it is difficult but possible to resolve this split and cluster Grafton's works together; however, doing so again reifies the a priori author over the potential information that the quantitative methods reveal.[11] The split in Grafton's alphabet series, as it turns out, is not random: books *A Is for Alibi* through *F Is for Fugitive* lie on the left side of the Mary Roberts Rinehart cluster (D), while books *G Is for Gumshoe* through *N Is for Noose* are on the right side (E). Such a split marks out a clear change in Grafton's writing over time: the fact that the split persists over different feature sets and models as two distinct clusters (as opposed to a drawn-out gradient) suggests that this division represents something fundamental about Grafton's writing. While it is tempting to use this division to explore the possibilities of a so-called late style, there is another, equally important historical dimension to this change.[12] In Grafton's case, *F Is for Fugitive* marked the first entry of one of her novels into the *New York Times* Best Seller list (Cowles). What the analysis naively divides, then, is the group of novels written before the prestige of a bestseller with an eye toward creating a popular readership and the group of novels belonging to a series that has already achieved bestseller status. The changes in publishing, marketing, editorial practices, and Grafton's own attention to the series that occur alongside this shift in popularity create a gulf in the novels that, although imperceptible to readerly attention, is still captured by the minute changes registered by stylometry. What this suggests is that we are right to understand the identity of "Sue Grafton," author, as bifurcated: there are two Sue Graftons that are fundamentally irreducible within a social understanding of the publishing and bookselling industry.

This is not to say that the data indicates the presence of a ghostwriter or even necessarily a heavy editorial hand: the data, I want to argue, does not indicate anything about the embodied author at all. Rather, it suggests that among the different ways that the author function can be understood, there is a detectable difference between texts written before and after they belong to a set that has come to prominence through such a mechanism of popularity as the *New York Times* Best Seller list. We can call this set either the "alphabet mystery" novels, or "the novels of Sue Grafton": the label is largely immaterial. What is material is the ways that the set can be reliably differentiated based on a very specific historical circumstance. Of course, the interpretive steps that follow rest on how we want to understand the division. If we do want to speak to the figure of the author as traditionally understood, we might seek to interpret the difference as that between an author before and after they are aware of their success. Or, if we want to analyze the series, we could examine the difference in editorial practices in a publishing house before and after they know that they have a hit. What the quantitative analysis gives us (along with the data that reveals this bifurcation) is the choice between these interpretive avenues. Neither of these interpretations were hypotheses driving the analysis at the outset or fundamental to the model: the choice between them is driven by scholarly interest rather than the parameters of the data.

This, I want to suggest, is the power of quantitative analysis: despite our desire to describe it with reference to our intuitive understanding of authors as the origin points of texts, the data itself describes similarity through the semantics alone. Splitting traditionally one-author corpora or grouping multiple authors together within a single unitary cluster adds dimensions to our understanding of similarity and difference within a corpus. By letting go of the connection between pattern similarity and authorial embodiment, we can gain a fuller understanding of the different ways that texts might be understood as similar or different based on social, political, conceptual, or even authorial pressures. If we allow a computational model of authorship to guide our exploration of the corpus, we can surface new patterns of relationship between texts that may not conform to our assumptions about "authors" but that can nevertheless powerfully alter our understanding of the texts themselves.

Character Patterns

The works of Jane Austen are central not only to understanding character but also to understanding the history of how character has been theorized and analyzed, both critically and computationally. Just as studies of character centralize Austen's creation of the first modern character-system, so too do Austen's works provide a key testing and pedagogical ground for natural language processing (NLP) methods.[13] In particular, research into the application of named entity recognition (NER) as a potentially reliable way to extract (and resolve) character coreferences has depended on Austen's corpus to a surprising extent.[14] Characters in Austen occupy a unique inflection point. No longer the parodic or archetypal figures of eighteenth-century fiction, they have still not assumed the more experimental aspects that characterize the novels of the late nineteenth or twentieth centuries. Austen's protagonists, in particular, appear to the reader as "rounded" or "deep" and well situated within a system of major and minor characters that offers a fully psychologized world familiar to her readers. It is for this reason that Austen's texts, more than any other, serve as the primary example of NER. Her ability to give the impression of an inner psychology to Elizabeth Bennet or Mr. Darcy of *Pride and Prejudice* suggests the possibility of a psychological *permanence* within the text: an inner life of a character whose various names, actions, and pronouns can be resolved into a single individual being that takes on the attributes of personhood.[15]

The question of the inner life of literary characters resides at the roots of the debates that surround them. It is clear that characters are one of the most recognizable and transportable phenomena of literature: when describing books, students leap to characters much more quickly than they do plot, theme, or even setting (Vermeule, 49). For all of their recognizability, however, they are notoriously hard to define. Even when they form the basis of a formalist theory of text, they remain slippery entities to pin down. To Vladimir Propp, the formalist critic, for example, characters are the foundational unit of the story, the medium through which action propagates. Propp is a crucial figure in this history, as his reading of character can be traced through the work of poststructuralist theory in which (much like the death of the author) characters become either psychoanalytic archetypes or reduced to mere rhetorical effects—the words on the page (Lacan, 6–50; Barthes). Recent work has refashioned the character into a nexus of the interactions between the text and the expectations, ideas, and desires that readers bring to it (Frow; Vermeule; Lynch). Yet once again, a hard look at the specifics of the closest analogue to character that computation has to offer reveals not only a key strategy for extracting and tracing the appearance of characters across a corpus of texts but also a new understanding of the material of character itself.

A computational approach to NER and, equally as important, coreference resolution is, by definition, pattern-based.[16] From early coreference resolution systems that used decision trees and complex syntactical rules, to contemporary models that use neural solutions, coreference resolution—the operation of deciding object permanence in characters—has always relied, like readers, on patterns of reference (Elango; J. Wu and W. Ma). This method, however, converges on contemporary literary theories of characters within texts. The complex assemblage of rhetorical effects (Barthes), narrative necessities (Propp), and readerly expectations (Lynch) creates a system of reference through which readers can come to understand the individual identities and roles of characters within a particular novelistic world. Austen's work serves as a particularly cogent example of this process at work: Alex Woloch's theory of major and minor characters rests of what he calls the "character-system" of *Pride and Prejudice* that weaves an inter-referentiality among the Bennet sisters according to their narrative (and economic) movements throughout the text (Woloch, 61). Where Woloch's theory and contemporary NER align is in their use of patterns of character relationships to establish the rules of a system

Table 2.1. Counts of Tokens Resolved as Coreferences to Mr. Darcy (Character 2) in *Pride and Prejudice* Using BookNLP

Character	*Token*	Count
2	darcy	374
2	he	318
2	her	10
2	him	189
2	his	299
2	mr.	273
2	she	9

through which each character can be understood as part of the whole. NER, however, takes rules of the system seriously and, in doing so, once again suggests a more radical reading of the character-system than is offered in contemporary literary theories. As with the author, the seemingly straightforward answer to what a character *is* that is supplied by NER—a referential set of terms that exists in a structured relationship to the syntactical universe of the text—opens up a new set of possibilities for understanding exactly how characterization happens within a novel. The naive reading of the NLP model, its successes, and more importantly, its failures, in tandem offer us a way to understand the actual operation of character within a text without the baggage of our own assumptions about the permanence of identity and the identifiably of individual characters.[17]

A key breakdown of NLP that gives us insight into complex modes of characterization in *Pride and Prejudice* itself occurs midway through the novel.[18] Woloch places the binary of Elizabeth Bennet and Mr. Darcy at the center of his theory, arguing that the sharpness with which this pair is defined and juxtaposed creates a dialectic through which the minor characters of the novel are resolved into the same world (Woloch, 50). The differentiation between Elizabeth and Darcy seems key to the character system of the text: the gendered nature of their relationship situates the individual identities of the characters within both an intersubjective and social system that rests on the separation of the two as individuals fulfilling the necessary roles in the romance plot. From an NLP perspective, the "he" and "she" of the romance narrative should be among the most concretely identifiable based on the patterns of the novel. A BookNLP parse of the novel, however, reveals critical moments where this binary breaks down. As Table 2.1 shows, Mr. Darcy, identified by the model as character 2, is resolved into 1,472 coreferential tokens, where 647 are a variation of "Mr. Darcy" and 806 are some variation of a male pronoun. That leaves 19 instances when Mr. Darcy is referred to as "she" or "her." If we assume that each of these instances is an error on the part of the parse, then the overall correctness is 98.7 percent, which is an acceptably high rate of precision. When we examine the individual points at which Darcy is misgendered with female pronouns, however, many of these so-called errors reveal something much more complex in the text.

At the beginning of chapter 10 of the second volume of the novel, Elizabeth, residing in Kent, has begun to encounter Mr. Darcy during her walks in a seeming coincidence that indicates, to the reader, Darcy's interest in a romantic attachment:

> **He** never said a great deal, nor did **she** give herself the trouble of talking or of listening much; but it struck **her** in the course of their third recontre that **he** was asking some odd unconnected questions—about **her** pleasure in being at Hunsford, **her** love of solitary walks, and **her** opinion of Mr. and Mrs. Collins's happiness; and that in speaking of Rosings and **her** not perfectly understanding the house, **he** seemed to expect that whenever **she** came into Kent again **she** would be staying *there* too. His words seemed to imply it. Could he have Colonel Fitzwilliam in his thoughts? **She** supposed, if he meant any thing, he must mean an allusion to what might arise in that quarter. It distressed **her** a little, and **she** was quite glad to find herself at the gate in the pales opposite the Parsonage. (Austen, emphasis mine)

Here, the highlighted pronouns indicate all of the entities resolved into character 2—everything that the model guessed was Mr. Darcy. Far from being separate, Darcy and Elizabeth are collapsed into the same entity within the first sentence ("**He** never said a great deal, nor did **she** give herself the trouble"). The reference passes back and forth between them until it is entirely resolved into Elizabeth by the end of the passage. The syntax here complicates the ability of the model to easily resolve the pronouns into a character, despite their gendered nature. The movement of the first sentence as the clauses trade between the two halves of the dialogic exchange (or lack thereof) run the two characters together as, narratively, both converge on the same interpersonal tactic: as co-participants in the social act of walking and not talking, they act effectively as one. Moreover, as the passage continues, it becomes clear that this is Austen using a form of free indirect discourse to probe Elizabeth's thoughts and suppositions about Darcy. Her lack of certainty over his goals in their interactions is relayed in a passage focalized through Elizabeth as she seeks to understand Darcy's motivations, effectively creating her own version of his character to herself: "She supposed, if he meant any thing, he must mean an allusion to what might arise in that quarter." By this point, all references to character 2 are inhabited exclusively by Elizabeth. Or, more accurately, they are inhabited by her suppositions about his character. As Elizabeth begins to cognitively *perform* Darcy, she takes over his referentiality: she effectively *becomes* Mr. Darcy from the point of view of the narrative.

What the coreference captures as it "mistakes" one character for the other is the convergence of the two in Elizabeth's mind, which becomes an act of virtual puppetry as her mental model of Darcy escapes the boundaries of the "real" Darcy and becomes a version of the character created for and by her, fully inhabited by her subjectivity. In its naivete regarding the character's gendered roles, the coreference resolution model has uncovered something profound about Austen's characterization. The interpenetration of the two characters at this point disturbs the boundary that separates them. Temporarily, their back-and-forth intersubjectivity followed by the performance of Darcy within Elizabeth's focalization blends the two characters together, dissolving the space between them and creating an amalgam of Darcy-as-Elizabeth-as-Darcy that is crucial to a pivotal moment in the romance plot (immediately following this chapter, Elizabeth discovers Darcy's agency in separating her sister from her fiancé, which again drives a wedge between the two characters). The indistinguishability of the two central characters is not a flaw in the NLP model, nor an effect of the general similarity between all characters, but rather a crucial, carefully plotted set of effects that demonstrates the interplay between the various psychological states that Austen has established for her characters. Once again, this insight is made available not through a careful close reading but rather through the transformation of character into a syntactic and semantic pattern through the NLP parse. Like an authorship attribution, reducing the characters to the language patterns that animate them on the page reveals the extent to which they occupy the same set of spaces and identities. When we, as readers, bring the assumptions of psychological interiority and individuality to our encounter with the characters, we miss the extent to which the boundaries between them are permeable in ways that are crucial to both the plot and the effect of characterization itself.

What would it mean, then, to *improve* a natural language parse to the point where this slippage disappears? An updated version of BookNLP built on the LitBank work that Bamman describes in chapter 3 of this volume requires, in Bamman's words, "a stable entity for each character [given through coreference] that such counts can apply to." Such stability, however, imposes a specific reading on the text—namely, one that requires characters to remain stable entities rather than shifting, interpenetrated, and contingent figures that always exist in a complex negotiation between writer and reader. If we do understand the misgendered Darcy as a function of Elizabeth's performance of the character in her own act of reading, then the model that Bamman proposes privileges the reader's reading performance over Elizabeth's, just as the current BookNLP model makes Elizabeth visible as a reader of Darcy. In arguing for a *born-literary* NLP—that is, an NLP model that treats literary phenomena, such as character, as a referent to be modeled rather than as an *alternate model* of the text—Bamman privileges an understanding of character as a persistent, stable entity over the textual complexities of Austen's diegesis. To be clear, such a model would not be wrong: my point is that it is not objectively *right* or that we should understand the model as *improved* by the loss of this complex nuance in the text.

Just as in the previous section, my intent is not to remove the author from consideration but rather to open up a manifold space of possibility for what an author could be (not Barthes's death but Foucalt's function). My goal here is not to return to the flatness of the poststructural character-as-rhetorical effect but rather to understand the kinds of malleability afforded to the assemblage of words, syntax, and impressions (both external and internal) that we call character. Literary characters are not persons: we as readers understand this. Yet on the page and outside of it, we imbue them with a spectrum of possibilities that exceeds mere personhood and rests on our dual understanding that these are rhetorical effects that we can treat as objects, archetypes, or categories of being. Darcy's ability to transcend the page for the reader begins with his ability to transcend the boundaries of his own characterization: in a very real sense, Elizabeth is the first reader of Darcy and the first to imbue him with a psychological interiority, setting the pattern for generations of readers to come (Vermeule, 51). Although this model of nested character interaction, in which characterization becomes a performance of a psychologized interiority, has precedence in literary scholarship, particularly that on Austen, a computational model can aid us in radicalizing our understanding of what character is, thereby deepening our understanding on how it works in the text itself.[19] Characters modeled "incorrectly" by NLP software therefore do not necessarily result from errors in the fitting of object to model: rather, they can direct our attention toward the ways in which characters themselves are hybrid and contingent proxies, less real-world objects than literary critical models of being.

Topic and Theme

In the case of authors and characters, there is a clear line between the statistical approximation and the object it seeks to represent. After all, the challenge in thinking through the relationships revealed by authorship analysis is in moving beyond the embodied author; even if characters are slightly more ephemeral, few readers would dispute that Elizabeth or Mr. Darcy are characters. When it comes to topic models, however, the object of analysis is much more opaque. Simply by calling the algorithm a "topic" model, we are already making an implicit case that what we are modeling are topics; however, this just displaces the question from the computational to the textual node. In other words, we are still left with the question of what a "topic" is in the context of a text.

Much of the critique of the use of topic modeling in humanities contexts lies in the tendency of readers to overinterpret the individual topics themselves, investing the wordlists that stand in for topics with thematic, discursive, or relational meanings that they may not carry (this is particularly the case for low-coherence topics).[20] In fact, it is still unclear as to the best way to represent a topic (which, in itself, is a distribution of posterior probabilities over a vocabulary). While scholars most often relay topics as a wordlist of top terms per topic (replicating the output of the most popular topic modeling software), it is also possible to describe topics with a series of meaningful names assigned by the analyst or as a network of semantic connections (McCallum; Lau et al.; Goldstone and Underwood). All suffer from particular weaknesses: lists of top terms may overrepresent extremely high-frequency or low-frequency terms at the expense of more meaningful words; labeling topics often overgeneralizes their specificity; and networks of topics are still based on a limited list of top terms. As such, the status of topic models in the humanities remains in flux: it is a popular method, but one with significant drawbacks in interpretability or meaningfulness.

Many early critiques of topic modeling stemmed from the disjunction between the design of the algorithm and its use by humanists: as an information-retrieval tool, the models would generate lists of co-occurring terms as a mechanism for labeling clusters of documents, not for the kind of close reading that humanities scholars try to bring to bear on them (Schmidt; Mimno et al.).[21] A key sign of the success of these critiques lies in the caution with which humanists now deploy them: scholars are encouraged to think critically about the kind of information that a topic model produces and how that might be read as meaningful (or not) within humanities contexts.[22] Even as we think through the best ways to represent topics within the work of the computational humanities, however, the problem of their referentiality remains a significant obstacle to understanding the results that they produce.

Much as in authorship attribution, where the assumed connection between the distribution of frequencies and the embodied author leads scholars to gesture toward causal cognitive explanations for the clusters, scholars working with topic models will similarly gesture toward "discourses," "aboutness," or above all, "theme."[23] The problem here is that even if topics could be resolved into themes with some rigor, the use of "theme" in literary studies is even less rigorous than that of "topic." Propp's turn to character in his classification of folktales is predicated on the impossibility of classifying texts according to a higher-order taxonomy, particularly that of theme: "If a division into categories is unsuccessful, a division into theme leads to total chaos" (Propp, 7). In Erich Auerbach's *Mimesis*, theme appears to be an important consideration, and yet theme and motif slide into each other with such regularity that both lose a degree of rigor (Auerbach, 470–71).[24] In other words, theme is no more helpful than topic for understanding what is being revealed by the unsupervised probabilistic model. Without this conceptual apparatus, relating each topic to its textual equivalent becomes doubly fraught. If we understood topics as representing themes *and* we had a rigorous definition of "theme," then we would be able to hermeneutically read topics in the ways that so many scholars of the digital humanities seek to do. When Andrew Piper describes a topic as "a heterogeneity of statements under a semantic *field*" he is, in part, speaking to the multiplicity of things that a topic can carry within its distribution (Piper, 74, emphasis in original). But it might be equally as meaningful to apply this heterogeneity to what we can mean by both topic and theme.

The problem is one of scale: a theme or motif, in Auerbach's sense, may be as sprawling and complex as romance or as limited and singular as the garden in which the lovers meet. This is why Propp found it impossible to create a taxonomy based on such differences. Likewise, a computational topic might easily be as expansive or specific, depending on the frequency of the words it contains and its probability distribution across the texts of a corpus. For a taxonomy, such heterogeneity makes comparison (and thus differentiation) impossible. In even the best topic models, we still remove a significant percentage of topics, not because they fall into one of the categories of low-quality topics described by David Mimno and colleagues, but because the phenomenon they capture is incommensurate with those captured by the rest of the topics within that model.[25] Reading two topics with this degree of difference, not just of subject, but of scale, is as much an exercise in futility as the Borgesian categorization that Propp describes in which tales about unjust persecution are differentiated from tales with three brothers (Propp, 8).[26]

Once again, the solution that I want to suggest lies in taking the methodology literally. As an information-retrieval tool, topic models excel at organizing documents into clusters of texts based on shared clusters of terms that themselves occur together with high probability. In the instructional literature on topic models, the list of terms associated with each topic (as distinct from the posterior probabilities of terms in topics) is generated as a heuristic to help analysts give labels that assist in indexing the clusters generated by the posterior probabilities in the model, not as an end of the analysis in and of itself. If a topic model is applied to a large, undifferentiated corpus of texts and generates recognizable clusters of documents in ways that answer questions about difference and similarity, then the actual topical composition that creates the clusters may be, in many cases, immaterial, given that we have much better information with which to diagnose cluster membership, once those clusters are identified. In fact, I want to put this in even stronger terms: the desire to "read" the topic can be, in many cases, detrimental to understanding the principle behind the distribution of texts generated by the model because we, as human readers, are trained to treat any set of word clusters as if they all belonged to the same hermeneutic space.

Take, for example, a topic plot of the Gale American Fiction corpus, which contains 18,040 novels.[27] To generate this plot, I applied a topic model with 150 topics in Mallet and reduced the posterior probabilities of the topics in texts to a two-dimensional plot using T-sne.[28] Each dot represents a novel whose relative position is a function of the topical similarities and differences from the texts that surround it: the posterior probabilities of topics in documents index the similarities and differences between texts. The individual points are colored according to the most distinctive topic in each text, allowing us to explore the graph both for the clusters that reveal the underlying structure of the data and the topics whose probabilities determine these patterns. What is immediately apparent is that a clear set of clusters does emerge from the analysis. Texts are predominately grouped by shared topics (particularly in the well-defined clusters at the periphery of the graph), and adjacent clusters typically share topics among their top three most distinctive topics.

But while the data reveals that there is an underlying structure to this corpus of novels, the nature of that structure is surprisingly difficult to decipher from the topics alone. The cluster of novels at the very bottom of the graph (A) predominately shares a topic (topic number 6) whose ten top terms are captain, ship, deck, men, board, vessel, crew, sea, cabin, mate. Conversely, the top of the graph features a small but significant cluster (B) whose top topic (topic number 42) contains professor, college, class, one, said, university, room, year, student, study. Together these two topics point to two key genres of nineteenth- and early-twentieth-century American literature: sea tales and college novels. Genre, therefore, seems to be a key element of the structure of the graph; and genre, from these two topics, seems largely concerned with setting: at opposite poles of the graph, we find novels set at sea and novels set at college campuses. But what, then, are we to make of the sizable cluster (C) on the top left of the graph? It appears to be as equally distinct as either the sea or college novels, but its top topic (topic number 137) contains a much different set of words: man, door, roof, house, one, found, two, night, woman, find. While topics 6 and 42 can explain the settings/genres of their respective clusters (ships and cabins versus professors and colleges), topic 137 offers very few clues as to the relationality of the texts that it groups. Most novels, after all, contain men and women, or doors and houses.

If, however, we move beyond the topic to the fact that these texts form a coherent cluster and actually look at its members, the logic behind the cluster immediately becomes clear. Among others, the cluster contains *A Tragic Mystery, The Trevor Case,* and *The Silver Blade: A True Chronicle of a Double Mystery.* What the model has revealed, then, is the mystery/detective genre. Working backward from this knowledge to the topic, we can certainly imagine the ways in which the terms night, woman, house, and above all, found and find, work within this genre; but, crucially, this reconstruction can only happen iteratively, *in retrospect.* The process of finding the cluster and identifying its commonality can only be done without any reference to the topics themselves. The same can be said for the other two clusters. Our sea tales cluster contains such novels as *Thirty Years at Sea, The Adventures of a Naval Officer,* and of course, *Moby Dick.* Likewise, with titles such as *A Princetonian, College Girls,* and *When Patty Went to College,* the connecting theme of the college cluster is also apparent from the metadata. Again, the topic model reveals crucial information about how texts cluster without reference to the composition of the topics at all; what it reveals is a set of clusters that seem to follow the same logic as Vólkov's catalog of themes that Propp believes approaches chaos. We understand sea tales and college tales primarily in terms of their setting, but mysteries are predominately plot driven.[29] Exploring the clusters further, we find religious novels (both realist novels of faith and historical novels set in the biblical past), fiction about women in the workforce, and a cluster of temperance novels. To catalog these as "themes" is to make the same mistake as trying to decipher the clusters from the lists of words that are the topics themselves.[30]

By resisting the urge to begin by reading the topics and (over)interpreting the wordlists that they contain, we can explore the large- (and small-) scale clusters through the metadata that we already have. The incommensurability of the topics (much like that of themes) resolves into a set of distinctive groupings whose identity offers a complex but interpretable set of phenomena or discourses around which this set of American novels of the nineteenth and early twentieth centuries are structured. The topics, of course, remain a crucial part of the downstream analysis, but rather than being led by the naive interpretation of the method itself as a way of revealing structure within a collection of documents, we can gain a new understanding of the variety of things that "theme" or "motif" (or even "plot" or "setting") might represent within the context of a corpus. Much in the same way that a literal approach to stylometry allows us to rethink what we mean when we talk about an author, or how coreference resolution helps us to understand where character lives in the space between the text and the reader, topic models can help us understand the heterogeneous ways in which texts can group together outside of, or beyond, a comprehensive definition of theme, field, or discourse. Topic models call our attention to the ways in which these categories themselves are technologies of information retrieval: all represent higher order ways of organizing, relating, and categorizing texts. When a topic model sorts a corpus into an unexpected arrangement, then, it can defamiliarize our understanding of its organization and surface new connections that are equally as meaningful for that corpus as any of the critical schemas that we may seek to impose on it.

Reading the Model

What unites all of the brief experiments that I have offered here is an argument in favor of complicating the standard practices of operationalization and modeling in the computational humanities by taking the results of these practices at face value. Our traditional ways of understanding both operationalizing and modeling begin with the presumption that we are using computational methods to approximate something "out there": a phenomenon that exists independently of our analysis.[31] Taking this approach, however, mischaracterizes the relationship between literary theory and the computational model that seeks to approximate it: both are, in fact, models of the text, and both approximate the complexity and multivalenced nature of the object itself. It is only because we have become so long habituated to the ways that we read and talk about text that our critical models of literature (author, character, theme) appear to be the "real" object that our computational methods simulate. We can therefore understand the analytic distance between the two, the literary and the computational (or the humanities and the computational), as an effect of this habituation. By recognizing both approximations as models (the author as a unique, singular genius solely responsible for the text and the author as a collection of word probabilities), we can finally bring both halves into contact with each other and create a mutually informative account of the object that can reveal surprising new aspects. Doing this within the space of humanities research alone involves pushing against a surprising amount of inertia: for example, our understanding of an author is freighted with a set of social, cultural, psychological, and economic concerns whose viability requires that there be a single authorial source for a text. By complicating our understanding of a phenomenon like authorship through a computational model, we give ourselves the opportunity to revise our understanding of the underlying phenomena outside the constraints of habituation and practice such that we can radically alter our understanding of the object itself.[32]

A turn such as this, however, is not without its risks. For example, Hannah Ringler argues for a strong hermeneutic approach to computational analysis, arguing that methods alone are unable to interpret the data that they produce. In the new framework that she proposes, however, the process of "asking with" returns us again to our habituated forms of humanities knowledge: "in this process, an analyst starts with artifacts that they know well, asks humanistic questions of them, and uses tools to help them answer those questions."[33] The methodological intervention that I propose in this chapter asks us to let go of the idea that we know our artifacts well. Interpretation is still a crucial part of the research process, but rather than simply bringing humanities interpretive methods to the results of a digital analysis, we allow the results to guide our analysis, taking seriously and literally the sometimes radical transformations that they enact on the artifacts that we only thought we knew. Interpretation, then, ceases to be a second-order operation on the results of the analysis and becomes a negotiation between computational and humanities models of the phenomenon that we seek to study. The second pillar of Ringler's framework, "asking about," comes much closer to what I propose here. Interrogating our methods, both computational and hermeneutic, for their underlying assumptions allows us to understand their interaction and the mutually constitutive ways through which they alter our understanding of the objects of our analysis. Taking the results of our computational analysis seriously and using them as a platform for our interpretive practices demands that we understand what these analytic methods actually do.

Herein lies the risk of the analytic transformation that I am proposing. If we give our computational results the same interpretive weight as our humanities theories, then we need to fully understand how they function. If we do not, then we risk resting our hermeneutics on a set of faulty assumptions or a contingent, nonreplicable set of results. The methods of the computational humanities often include statistical validation practices: these can aid us in differentiating between a model that has gone awry and returned arbitrary, random, or otherwise mathematically invalid results and a working model that returns an unexpected yet productive set of results that do not conform to our habituated hypotheses about the object that we are modeling. Ringler's implicit critique of tools (black boxes that obfuscate the actual computational work to facilitate ease of use) as opposed to methods can help point us toward the ways in which we can validate our models without recourse to a ground truth that, in the humanities, is frequently only another model itself. Only by fully engaging with the *methods* that inform our analysis, both those that come from the humanities and those that are computational or statistical in nature, can we take full advantage of the radical nature of the insights that computation can bring to our research.

When we seek to operationalize a literary or textual concept, or when we train a supervised model, we presume (either tacitly or explicitly) to begin at the point at which we understand the object of our analysis. These types of analyses are valuable in the field of computational humanities because they serve to help test our assumptions of how certain phenomena work at very large or small scales, or they can redirect our reading toward particularly meaningful examples within a corpus of text. But all of these approaches overlook the radical reconfigurations that the proxies for the objects of our analysis must undergo in order to be computationally tractable and, in turn, the ways in which these reconfigurations can help us understand the objects themselves as they are differently represented in the quantitative analysis. By approximating authors as distributions of word frequencies and not insisting on an explanatory connection between these frequencies and the mental state of a real, embodied author, we can expand our definition of what an author might be and reveal the multiplicity of factors that influence a text's origin. By modeling characters as patterns of referentiality, we can begin to question how they are being referred to and who is doing the referring, allowing us to reconfigure a character as a nexus of textual possibility that exists between the rhetoric of the text and the reader within the matrix of a character-system. And by forgoing the a priori close reading of topics in an attempt to model genre or theme within a corpus of texts, we can use the resulting probabilities to uncover clusters of texts that demonstrate the malleability of these terms and the ways in which classifications of certain kinds of text bring together multiple systems of referentiality simultaneously.

This approach not only gives us new purchase on the ways in which computational text analysis can be of use in the humanities, but it also restores a crucial potential of the computational humanities and the digital humanities more broadly. By being guided by the methods that we adopt, by paying attention to how we approximate textual phenomena through quantification, and by taking the results of our clusters and models as reflexively interpretable objects themselves (rather than simply as proxies for the true objects that we seek to study), we can use the methods and strategies of computation to put pressure on our received theoretical and historical objects and uncover alternative ways of thinking about the material that we study.

Notes

1. This is the premise behind, for example, Ted Underwood's study of "the life spans of genres" in *Distant Horizons* or even David Bamman's promise of a "born-literary natural language processing" in chapter 3 of this volume.

2. Ted Underwood, in *Distant Horizons,* has argued that we should focus our efforts on using supervised modeling to reveal effect sizes of variables that differentiate pre-classified groups rather than creating "arbitrary measurements" to operationalize concepts (Underwood, 181). In practice, both equally involve the fitting of measurement to theory. When adopting a modeling approach, the selection of training groups and feature sets does the work of creating a quantitative proxy for a textual phenomenon: training a model on a group of texts divided by genre whose features are word frequencies still requires an operative theory of genre.

3. The wealth of articles on "improving" results through these three methods demonstrate the centrality of this approach. See, for example, Rybicki and Eder; Hoover, "Testing"; Elango; J. Wu and W. Ma; Mimno et al. Lisa Rhody, in "Topic Modeling and Figurative Language," offers an approach more in line with what I suggest here; however, as we will see in the discussion of topic modeling below, her own discourse on topic modeling falls into a slightly different binary.

4. This deformation/defamiliarization of the text through computational means is a hallmark of Stephen Ramsay's *Reading Machines: Toward an Algorithmic Criticism* (Ramsay).

5. The precise number of terms varies between practitioners. John Burrows, in his foundational article, tests a range of most frequent words (MFWs), from 200 down through 40, settling on 150 words as the optimal number (Burrows, "'Delta,'" 274). David Hoover argues that expanding the wordlist to 800 MFW (while filtering the list for contractions and personal pronouns) leads to improvements in author classification, while others, such as Jan Rybicki and Maciej Eder, have demonstrated that while success varies with language, word sets with even the top 2,000 words removed still show some success in author classification tasks (Hoover, "Testing"; Rybicki and Eder). Because the debate over the specific feature set used in authorship attribution is not germane to my argument in this chapter, for my work here I adopt the optimizing improvements to stylometry suggested by Peter Smith and W. Aldridge, who argue that limiting the feature set to between 200 and 300 MFWs and using cosine similarity measurements (as opposed to Manhattan or Euclidean distances) greatly improve classification (Smith and Aldridge).

6. My analysis here follows Peter Smith and W. Aldridge's suggestion of comparing the normalized z-scores of the 200 MFW in a corpus of texts using cosine similarity, with very few modifications or refinements to the initial clustering. The plot was generated by a t-stochastic neighbor embedding of the z-scores of the feature set and is largely in agreement with a clustering solution using the cosine similarity between all texts (Smith and Aldridge).

7. This is true in the textual analysis settings that I describe here, although it is worth noting that there is a robust psychological literature on the meaning of function word usage, for example (Chung and Pennebaker; Simmons, Gordon, and Chambless). The gestures toward cognitive theory in the examples that I provide above, however, are typically used as a way of explaining the relationship between feature and author without recourse to an actual engagement with psychological theory.

8. In literary contexts, the most famous case of using stylometric features to detect authorial mental states is the claim that the late works of Agatha Christie feature a dramatically reduced vocabulary and syntactic complexity, indicating an onset of dementia. This is work that has been extended to the senescent work of other authors (Le et al.). These metrics, however, are not the same as the feature set used in authorship attribution and are often only meaningful, in this sense, in intra-corpus comparisons. In Figure 2.1, the works of Christie, both early and late, form one coherent cluster.

9. It is worth noting that the three clusters do not separate neatly into the three different pen names under which McBain published; however, there does seem to be a temporal distinction separating the groups, with most of the earlier works in the left-hand group. It is also notable that Walter Mosley's work also separates into three clusters with his earliest novel in the "Easy Rawlins" series and the first novels in the "Socrates Fortlow" series sharing the far-left cluster.

10. The traditional concept of the author, as a unitary, embodied individual with authority over the work, such as I describe here, is currently facing challenges from a number of directions. Postcolonial critiques have revealed the extent to which this concept of the "author" is originally a European construct, and many are working to explore alternate modalities of assigning origins to text—for example, the *In the Same Boats* project by Kaiama Glover and Alex Gil. Other researchers are putting pressure on the author as a legal fiction, particularly in the face of new technologies that complicate the concept of the author and, by extension, the equally Western idea of copyright law (Tay, Sik, and Chen).

11. While this split is echoed in a dendrogram cluster based on the cosine similarity (again following Smith and Aldridge), a linear discriminant analysis (with a reduced variable set) clusters all of Grafton's works as by the same author with high probability.

12. When the computational misclustering of authors through stylometry has been taken seriously, it has mostly happened under the rubric of the late style of authors, such as Hoover's work on Henry James or Andrew Piper's exploration of Said's theory (Hoover, "Corpus Stylistics"; Piper, 167–77).

13. It is no coincidence that Alex Woloch centralizes *Pride and Prejudice* in his seminal study of character-system, *The One vs. the Many*: works on literary character from a humanities perspective reliably reference Austen's corpus (Woloch; Frow; Lynch). In NLP research, Austen's corpus has become a "gold standard" of testable material, partly because of its availability as an out-of-copyright work but also because of its ubiquity and the various heavily annotated copies held by prominent NLP practitioners (Pereira and Paraboni; Dekker, Kuhn, and van Erp; Bird, Klein, and Loper; Manning and Schutze).

14. For example, the foundational paper on David Bamman's BookNLP, the method that I employ here, not only uses Austen as one of the sample groups but also makes frequent reference to Austen's characters as exemplars of the ways in which characters behave in texts (Bamman, Underwood, and Smith). Similarly, in his work on LitBank in this volume, Bamman again uses Austen's *Pride and Prejudice* as a starting point for explaining coreference resolution, describing the difficulty in assigning the label of "Miss Bennet" to the "correct" Bennet sister.

15. Even Burrows's early study of authorship attribution sought to resolve Austen's character in the same manner as authors, to mixed results (Burrows).

16. Named entity recognition describes the task of extracting proper nouns from a text and resolving these to the *kind* of entity that they represent (most often persons or places, but sometimes organizations, corporations, or even ideologies). Coreference resolution applies primarily to person entities and describes the task of resolving the individual mentions of a single person (or character) into a single entity. This can include both resolving variations of names ("Elizabeth," "Miss Bennet," or "Elizabeth Bennet") as well as the pronouns (she, her, hers) that refer to the character throughout the text.

17. Andrew Piper explores the lack of individuality among characters as a path toward identifying the specifically gendered social functions that they maintain in the novel, using, of course, *Pride and Prejudice* (Piper, 123–24).

18. I am indebted for this reading to my collaborators on the Literary Lab Project "The Grammar of Gender," particularly Regina Ta, who first noticed the discrepancies that led to this insight.

19. Elizabeth's doubling of Darcy's character here is very much in line with Mary Poovey's description of her "psychological economy" as this is a key moment in the novel at which "she directs her intelligence toward defending herself against emotional vulnerability" (Poovey, 198). In its narratological implications, it is also deeply resonant with Austen's use of free indirect discourse, which Daniel Gunn reads as "primarily an *imitation* of figural speech or thought, in which the narrator echoes or mimics the idiom of the character" (Gunn, 37, emphasis in original). Although here, it is Elizabeth who stands in for the narrator mimicking the idioms of Darcy, it appears that the NER is picking up on what Gunn calls "stylistic contagion" in Austen's characterization.

20. Ben Schmidt's early critique of this tendency is particularly cogent (Schmidt). David Mimno and colleagues' metric of topic coherence can be used to assess topics for their relative meaningfulness to experts in the field on which the corpus is based (Mimno et al.).

21. Much of David Blei's early work on topic models focused specifically on the relevance of topic modeling to information retrieval (Blei and Lafferty).

22. It is notable, for example, that Piper finds more meaning in a cluster of words around art and water that emerges in passages identified by an entirely different topic in his exploration of "reading topologically" in *Enumerations* (Piper, 75–83). Underwood's *Distant Horizons* only mentions topic models once, on the final pages of his chapter on the "risks of distant reading" (Underwood, 168).

23. According to Blei, a topic model "discovers a set of 'topics'—recurring themes that are discussed in the collection" (Blei). The relationship between topics and themes was also explored in the eighth pamphlet of the Stanford Literary Lab, "On Paragraphs." Here, the key finding, that paragraphs are the unit of the topical coherence in fiction, is linked to the idea that topics represent themes or motifs. Although compelling, this connection is purely interpretive and is based on the finding of the relationship between paragraphs and topics (Algee-Hewitt, Heuser, and Moretti).

24. More contemporary approaches are no more helpful in understanding themes, which remain significantly under-theorized in literary study. For example, Shlomith Rimmon-Kenan's contribution to the volume *Thematics: New Approaches* offers what seems to be a prescient version of topic modeling as she connects theme to "aboutness" and then to "topic," which is a "construct put together from discontinuous elements of the text" (Rimmon-Kenan, 14). In the end, however, she is only able to offer a partial and incomplete catalog that points to the indeterminacy of the term, as are her fellow critics in the volume.

25. The four categories are chained, intruded, random, and unbalanced (Mimno et al., 264). Of the four, the unbalanced topic (which contains a mix of general and specific words) might come closest to what I describe here, but closer still would be a model that contained a number of topics with specific words and one with general terms, or vice versa.

26. Lisa Rhody uses Latent Dirichlet Allocation topic modeling to explore the figurative language of poetry; in "Topic Modeling and Figurative Language," she focuses on topics that do not, in her words, exhibit "thematic clarity" (Rhody). Here too, however, "thematic" remains deeply undertheorized, as she contrasts a "thematic" topic such as "genetics" in a science corpus with a topic from Anne Sexton's "The Starry Night" that she says "draws from the language of elegy" with a relation to "death, loss and internal turmoil." Such as a topic, Rhody argues, is not "thematic"; however, when compared with Rimmon-Kenan's discussion of the thematics of Tolstoy's *The Death of Ivan Illych,* which she reads as "the life-giving, because insight providing, power of death," Rhody's reasoning behind differentiating topics on the basis of whether or not they mark "theme" becomes, at best, opaque, and at worst, arbitrary (Rimmon-Kenan, 16).

27. See *American Fiction, 1774–1920* (Farmington Hills, Mich.: Gale, 2020), https://www.gale.com/c/american-fiction-1774-1920. This corpus, based on the Lyle H. Wright bibliography of American fiction, is one of the largest bibliographically based corpora of American fiction. It purports to include all novels by American authors published by major publishing houses between 1774 and 1920. It is important to note, then, that this, by definition, excludes crucial categories of American novels, particularly those published by smaller, bespoke publishing houses or those circulated in magazines, newspapers, or by manuscript. Considering that these missing categories were largely peopled by women authors and authors of color, who systematically lacked access to the publishing and bookselling industry, the bibliography and therefore the corpus skews both white and male in its representation of American fiction. While there are novels by authors of color and women authors in the corpus, they are underrepresented. My demonstration here should therefore be taken to represent a slice of fiction written in America during this period, not "American fiction" writ large.

28. My choice of 150 topics in this analysis was based on a sampling of other models with different numbers of topics (75, 100, 150, 175, and 200). All demonstrated some resolution around genre, although the clusters in the 150 topic model above were more distinct.

29. This is not to say that there are not specific concerns to the sea tale or the college novel, but those concerns are a product of the setting (the ocean or a campus), which sets the stage for the specific types of actions that can take place within the genre.

30. Contemporary religious fiction, for example, groups around topic 103: church, god, Christian, faith, minister; while historical religious fiction is clustered by topic 91: god, shall, lord, great. Again, the difference here can be interpreted once we know what the clusters represent, but this interpretation rests on the metadata of the novels themselves and not from the topics that, to a naive reader, are mostly undifferentiable.

31. Although my examples here are drawn from literary criticism and computational text analysis, my conclusions are equally extensible to other humanities fields that bring computational methods to bear on supposedly "real world" objects. The use of Geographic Information Systems in the spatial humanities, for example, similarly creates models of complex relationships between society, geography, history, and space that frequently rest on ideas of a literal "ground truth" but whose "errors" and deformed geographies frequently point to critical, and often overlooked, assumptions in the model itself. Ideas of "space" and "history" are equally as abstract as "theme" or "topic."

32. Given the origin of the single genius author of the literary work as a function of white, male authorial practices in the Romantic period, a computational approach that calls this version of authorship into question can also create room for other (non-white, non-male) authorial traditions to surface.

33. See chapter 1 in this volume.

Bibliography

Algee-Hewitt, Mark, Ryan Heuser, and Franco Moretti. *On Paragraphs: Scale, Themes and Narrative Form*. Stanford, Calif.: Stanford Literary Lab, 2015.

Argamon, Shlomo, Sushant Dhawle, Moshe Koppel, and James W. Pennebaker. "Lexical Predictors of Personality Type." *Proceedings of the 2005 Joint Annual Meeting of the Interface and the Classification Society of North America*, 1–16. St. Louis: Interface, 2005.

Auerbach, Erich. *Mimesis: The Representation of Reality in Western Literature–New and Expanded Edition*. Translated by Willard R. Trask. Princeton, N.J.: Princeton University Press, 2013.

Austen, Jane. *Pride and Prejudice*. Edited by Vivian Jones. London: Penguin, 2006.

Baayen, Harald, Hans van Halteren, Anneke Neijt, and Fiona Tweedie. "An Experiment in Authorship Attribution." *6th JADT* (2002).

Bamman, David, Ted Underwood, and Noah A. Smith. "A Bayesian Mixed Effects Model of Literary Character." *Proceedings of the 52nd Annual Meeting of the Association for Computational Linguistics. Volume 1: Long Papers*, 370–79. Baltimore: Association for Computational Linguistics, 2014.

Barthes, Roland. *S/Z*. Translated by Richard Miller. Vol. 76. New York: Hill and Wang, 1974.

Bird, Steven, Ewan Klein, and Edward Loper. *Natural Language Processing with Python: Analyzing Text with the Natural Language Toolkit*. Sebastopol, Calif.: O'Reilly Media, 2009.

Blei, David M. "Topic Modeling and Digital Humanities." *Journal of Digital Humanities* 2, no. 1 (2012): 8–11.

Blei, David M., and John D. Lafferty. "Topic Models." *Text Mining: Classification, Clustering, and Applications* 10, no. 71 (2009): 34.

Burrows, John. "'Delta': A Measure of Stylistic Difference and a Guide to Likely Authorship." *Literary and Linguistic Computing* 17, no. 3 (2002): 267–87.

Burrows, John Frederick. *Computation into Criticism: A Study of Jane Austen's Novels and an Experiment in Method.* Oxford: Clarendon Press, 1987.

Chung, Cindy, and James W. Pennebaker. "The Psychological Functions of Function Words." In *Social Communication,* edited by Klaus Fiedler, 343–59. Vol. 1. Sussex, UK: Psychology Press, 2007.

Cowles, Gregory. "Before Sue Grafton Was a Star: Inside the List." *New York Times Books,* January 5, 2018.

Dekker, Niels, Tobias Kuhn, and Marieke van Erp. "Evaluating Named Entity Recognition Tools for Extracting Social Networks from Novels." *PeerJ Computer Science* 5 (2019): e189.

Diederich, Joachim, Jörg Kindermann, Edda Leopold, and Gerhard Paass. "Authorship Attribution with Support Vector Machines." *Applied Intelligence* 19, no. 1–2 (2003): 109–23.

Eder, Maciej. "Style-Markers in Authorship Attribution: A Cross-Language Study of the Authorial Fingerprint." *Studies in Polish Linguistics* 6, no. 1 (2011).

Elango, Pradheep. "Coreference Resolution: A Survey." Technical Report, University of Wisconsin, Madison, 2005.

Foucault, Michel. *Language, Counter-Memory, Practice: Selected Essays and Interviews.* Ithaca, N.Y.: Cornell University Press, 1980.

Froehlich, Heather. "Dramatic Structure and Social Status in Shakespeare's Plays." *Journal of Cultural Analytics* 5, no. 1 (2020).

Frow, John. *Character and Person.* Oxford: Oxford University Press, 2014.

Glover, Kaiama, and Alex Gil. *In the Same Boats,* accessed February 2022. www.sameboats.org.

Goldstone, Andrew, and Ted Underwood. "What Can Topic Models of PMLA Teach Us about the History of Literary Scholarship." *Journal of Digital Humanities* 2, no. 1 (2012): 39–48.

Gunn, Daniel P. "Free Indirect Discourse and Narrative Authority in 'Emma.'" *Narrative* 12, no. 1 (2004): 35–54.

Hoover, David L. "Corpus Stylistics, Stylometry, and the Styles of Henry James." *Style* 41, no. 2 (2007): 174–203.

Hoover, David L. "Testing Burrows's Delta." *Literary and Linguistic Computing* 19, no. 4 (2004): 453–75.

Juola, Patrick. *Authorship Attribution.* Vol. 3. Boston: Now Publishers, 2008.

Lacan, Jacques. *Écrits.* Translated by Bruce Fink. New York: W. W. Norton, 2006.

Lau, Jey Han, Karl Grieser, David Newman, and Timothy Baldwin. "Automatic Labelling of Topic Models." *Proceedings of the 49th Annual Meeting of the Association for Computational Linguistics: Human Language Technologies,* 1536–45. Portland, Ore.: Association for Computational Linguistics, 2011.

Le, Xuan, Ian Lancashire, Graeme Hirst, and Regina Jokel. "Longitudinal Detection of Dementia through Lexical and Syntactic Changes in Writing: A Case Study of Three British Novelists." *Literary and Linguistic Computing* 26, no. 4 (2011): 435–61.

Lynch, Deidre Shauna. *The Economy of Character: Novels, Market Culture, and the Business of Inner Meaning.* Chicago: University of Chicago Press, 1998.

MacDonald, Erin E. *Ed McBain/Evan Hunter: A Literary Companion.* Jefferson, N.C.: McFarland & Company, 2012.

Manning, Christopher, and Hinrich Schutze. *Foundations of Statistical Natural Language Processing.* Cambridge, Mass.: MIT Press, 1999.

McCallum, Andrew Kachites. *MALLET: A Machine Learning for Language Toolkit.* http://mallet.cs.umass.edu. 2002.

Mimno, David, Hanna Wallach, Edmund Talley, Miriam Leenders, and Andrew McCallum. "Optimizing Semantic Coherence in Topic Models." *Proceedings of the 2011 Conference on Empirical Methods in Natural Language Processing,* 262–72. Edinburgh, UK: Association for Computational Linguistics, 2011.

Pereira, Daniel Bastos, and Ivandré Paraboni. "A Language Modelling Tool for Statistical NLP." *Anais do V Workshop em Tecnologia da Informação e da Linguagem Humana–TIL,* 1679–88. Rio de Janeiro: Congresso da SBC, 2007.

Piper, Andrew. *Enumerations: Data and Literary Study.* Chicago: University of Chicago Press, 2018.

Poovey, Mary. *The Proper Lady and the Woman Writer: Ideology as Style in the Works of Mary Wollstonecraft, Mary Shelley, and Jane Austen.* Chicago: University of Chicago Press, 1985.

Propp, Vladimir. *Morphology of the Folktale.* Vol. 9. Austin: University of Texas Press, 2010.

Ramsay, Stephen. *Reading Machines: Toward an Algorithmic Criticism.* Champaign: University of Illinois Press, 2011.

Rhody, Lisa M. "Topic Modeling and Figurative Language." *Journal of Digital Humanities* 2, no. 1 (2012).

Rimmon-Kenan, Shlomith. "What Is Theme and How Do We Get at It?" In *Thematics: New Approaches,* edited by Claude Bremond, Joshua Landy, and Thomas Pavel, 9–20. Albany: State University of New York Press, 1995.

Rybicki, Jan, and Maciej Eder. "Deeper Delta across Genres and Languages: Do We Really Need the Most Frequent Words?" *Literary and Linguistic Computing* 26, no. 3 (2011): 315–21.

Schmidt, Benjamin M. "Words Alone: Dismantling Topic Models in the Humanities." *Journal of Digital Humanities* 2, no. 1 (2012): 49–65.

Simmons, Rachel A., Peter C. Gordon, and Dianne L. Chambless. "Pronouns in Marital Interaction: What Do 'You' and 'I' Say about Marital Health?" *Psychological Science* 16, no. 12 (2005): 932–36.

Smith, Peter W. H., and W. Aldridge. "Improving Authorship Attribution: Optimizing Burrows' Delta Method*." *Journal of Quantitative Linguistics* 18, no. 1 (2011): 63–88.

So, Richard Jean, Hoyt Long, and Yuancheng Zhu. "Race, Writing, and Computation: Racial Difference and the US Novel, 1880–2000." *Journal of Cultural Analytics* 3, no. 2 (2018).

Stamatatos, Efstathios. "A Survey of Modern Authorship Attribution Methods." *Journal of the American Society for Information Science and Technology* 60, no. 3 (2009): 538–56.

Tay, Pek San, Cheng Peng Sik, and Wai Meng Chen. "Rethinking the Concept of an 'Author' in the Face of Digital Technology Advances: A Perspective from the Copyright Law of a Commonwealth Country." *Digital Scholarship in the Humanities* 33, no. 1 (2018): 160–72.

Underwood, Ted. *Distant Horizons: Digital Evidence and Literary Change.* Chicago: University of Chicago Press, 2019.

Vermeule, Blakey. *Why Do We Care about Literary Characters?* Baltimore: Johns Hopkins University Press, 2010.

Woloch, Alex. *The One vs. the Many: Minor Characters and the Space of the Protagonist in the Novel.* Princeton, N.J.: Princeton University Press, 2009.

Wu, J., and W. Ma. "A Deep Learning Framework for Coreference Resolution Based on Convolutional Neural Network." *IEEE 11th International Conference on Semantic Computing (ICSC),* 61–64. San Diego: IEEE Computer Society Press, 2017.

PART I][Chapter 3

Born Literary Natural Language Processing

DAVID BAMMAN

In many ways, literary texts push the limits of natural language processing (NLP). The long, complex sentences in novels strain the limits of syntactic parsers, their use of figurative language challenges representations of meaning based on neo-Davidsonian semantics, and the sheer number of words in a book rules out existing solutions for problems like coreference resolution that expect short documents with a small set of candidate antecedents. This complexity of literature motivates the core argument of this article: if methods in NLP are to be used for analyses to help drive humanistic insight, we must develop resources and models in NLP that are *literary-centric*—models trained specifically on literary data that attests to the phenomena that we might want to measure, that encodes representations of the world we deem more appropriate than those encoded in other datasets designed for other purposes, and that specifically considers the needs of researchers working with fictional material—for example, by historicizing categories of gender (Mandell, "Gender and Cultural Analytics").

This stance comes from an increasing use of NLP as a measuring instrument, where the individual low-level linguistic representations of morphology, syntax, and discourse are employed in analyses that depend on them for argumentation. In these cases, the fundamental research question is not in solving an NLP problem but in treating NLP as an *algorithmic measuring device*—representing text in a way that allows a comparison of measures to be made, whether for the purpose of explicit hypothesis testing, exploratory analysis, or an iterative, grounded interpretive process (Nelson). While measurement modeling has a long research history in the social sciences (Fariss, Kenwick, and Reuning; Jacobs and Wallach), work in the computational humanities—which focuses on applying empirical and computational methods for humanistic inquiry—likewise has drawn on NLP as an algorithmic measuring device for a wide range of work. Automatic part-of-speech taggers have been used to explore poetic enjambment (Houston, "Enjambment and the Poetic Line") and characterize the patterns that distinguish the literary canon from the archive (Algee-Hewitt et al., "Canon/Archive"). Syntactic parsers have been used to attribute events to the characters who participate in them (Jockers and Kirilloff; Underwood, Bamman, and Lee) and characterize the complexity of sentences in Henry James (Reeve). Coreference resolution has been used to explore the prominence of major and minor characters as a function of their gender (Kraicer and Piper). Named entity recognizers have been used to explore the relationship between places in British fiction and cultural identity (Evans and Wilkens); geographic markers extracted from named entity recognition (NER) have been used to create visualizations of the places mentioned in texts, both for toponyms in Joyce's *Ulysses* (Derven, Teehan, and Keating) and short fiction by Edward P. Jones (Rambsy and Ossom-Williamson). Topics help organize a range of work in the humanities, from identifying the characteristics of colonial fiction in Australian newspapers (Bode) to unveiling editorial labor in nineteenth-century U.S. publications (Klein) and organizing reader responses to "classics" (Walsh and Antoniak). And moving beyond text to sound studies, work has also explored using NLP to extract prosodic features from texts (Clement et al.) and directly model audio data to investigate questions revolving around applause (Clement and McLaughlin) and poet voice (MacArthur, Zellou, and Miller). In each of these cases, NLP is used to extract some aspect of linguistic structure from text and take measurements on those aspects in order to advance an argument.

As NLP is increasingly used in this measurement capacity for inquiry within the humanities, it is important to establish its *instrument validity*—the degree to which a measuring device (whether mechanical or algorithmic) is measuring what it is supposed to. While there are, of course, many applications of computational methods to literary texts that will resist comparison to a preexisting gold standard (and that subsequently require other methods for establishing validity), consensus is often possible for the low-level linguistic phenomena on which those methods depend, such as classifying a word as a noun or a verb or identifying the mentions of people in a sentence. One source of potential trouble in this case, however, is the mismatch in domains between literary texts and the relatively small set of domains that mainstream NLP has tended to focus on. A prominent source is news, which forms the overwhelming basis for benchmark corpora. Examples include MUC (Sundheim), the Penn Treebank (Marcus, Santorini, and Marcinkiewicz), ACE (Walker et al.), the New York Times Annotated Corpus (Sandhaus), and OntoNotes (Hovy et al.). Another prominent source is Wikipedia, which provides the benchmark datasets for question answering (Rajpurkar et al.; Rajpurkar, Jia, and Liang) and named entity linking (Cucerzan). It also provides the training material for many language models in multiple languages (Mikolov et al.; Pennington, Socher, and Manning; Devlin et al.).

As methods developed within the context of NLP are increasingly used for humanistic inquiry, much work has explored adapting unsupervised models (such as topic models) to issues commonly encountered in datasets used by humanists. This includes understanding the impact of text duplication in large digital libraries

(Schofield, Thompson, and Mimno), moderating the influence of authorial voice on topic inference (Thompson and Mimno), and exploring the impact of applying such models to figurative texts (Rhody). This chapter makes an argument for extending this scrutiny to supervised models as well, charting the drop in performance that comes when training supervised models on one domain and applying them to another. I introduce LitBank, a dataset of literary texts annotated with a range of linguistic phenomena that can provide the basis for training literary-centric NLP. As we think about the ways in which researchers in the digital humanities interact with NLP (McGillivray, Poibeau, and Fabo), a focus on literary-centric NLP not only seeks to improve the state of the art for NLP in the domain of literature but also examines the specific research questions that are only afforded *within* literature. While other work in NLP touches on aspects of narrative that are common with news, such as inferring narrative event chains (Chambers), literature presents a number of unique opportunities, including modeling suspense, the passage of time, and focalization. Importantly, literary-centric NLP also entails a widening of opportunity for researchers in the computational humanities; either those with training in both computational methods and a literary theory or a part of a team that has expertise in both. While much work in NLP has been dominated by researchers in the fields of computer science, information science, and linguistics, the researchers poised to make the biggest advances in this area are those with training and collaborators in the humanities. These researchers and teams can not only leverage their expertise in the specific subject matter to define the appropriate boundaries of datasets, but they also use their own disciplinary expertise to define the literary phenomena that are worth modeling in the first place. In so doing, they are uniquely positioned to use their hermeneutic expertise to both interpret the ways in which measurements of those phenomena can be turned into knowledge (as Hannah Ringler points out in this volume) and challenge the initial theoretical objects such work often begins with (as Mark Algee-Hewitt highlights in this volume as well).

Performance across Domains

Progress in natural language processing is primarily driven by comparative performance on benchmark datasets—progress in phrase-structure syntactic parsing, for example, has been defined for thirty years by performance on the Penn Treebank (Marcus, Santorini, and Marcinkiewicz). Benchmark datasets provide an external control: given a fixed dataset, researchers can be more confident that an increase in performance by their model for the task relative to another model can be attributed to their work alone and not simply be the result of incomparable performance on different datasets. At the same time, benchmark datasets tend to myopically focus attention on the domains they represent, and the ability of models to perform well on domains *outside* the domain they have trained on (their "generalization" performance) can be quite poor. Table 3.1 represents a metareview illustrating this

Table 3.1. In-Domain and Out-of-Domain Performance for Several NLP Tasks

Includes POS tagging, phrase structure (PS) parsing, dependency (dep.) parsing, named entity recognition (NER), coreference resolution, and event trigger identification. Accuracies are reported in percentages; phrase structure parsing, NER, coreference resolution, and event identification are reported in F1 measure.

Citation	Task	In domain	Accuracy	Out of domain	Accuracy
Rayson et al. (2007)	POS	English news	97.0%	Shakespeare	81.9%
Scheible et al. (2011)	POS	German news	97.0%	Early Modern German	69.6%
Moon and Baldridge (2007)	POS	WSJ	97.3%	Middle English	56.2%
Pennacchiotti and Zanzotto (2008)	POS	Italian news	97.0%	Dante	75.0%
Derczynski, Ritter, et al. (2013)	POS	WSJ	97.3%	Twitter	73.7%
Gildea (2001)	PS parsing	WSJ	86.3 F	Brown corpus	80.6 F
Lease and Charniak (2005)	PS parsing	WSJ	89.5 F	GENIA medical texts	76.3 F
Burga et al. (2013)	Dep. parsing	WSJ	88.2%	Patent data	79.6%
Pekar et al. (2014)	Dep. parsing	WSJ	86.9%	Broadcast news	79.4%
				Magazines	77.1%
				Broadcast conversation	73.4%
Derczynski, Maynard, et al. (2013)	NER	CoNLL 2003	89.0 F	Twitter	41.0 F
Bamman, Popat, and Shen (2019)	Nested NER	News	68.8 F	English literature	45.7 F
Bamman, Lewke, and Mansoor (2020)	Coreference	News	83.2 F	English literature	72.9 F
Naik and Rose (2020)	Events	News	82.6 F	English literature	44.1 F

performance degradation across a range of training/test scenarios. A model trained on one domain may yield high performance when evaluated on data from that same domain, but it often suffers a steep drop in performance when evaluated on data from another domain. In the few cases that involve training on news and evaluating on literature, these drops in performance can amount to twenty absolute points or more, effectively rendering a tool unusable.

Perhaps more pernicious than a simple drop in performance, however, are the forms of representational bias that are present in any dataset. For literary texts, an entity recognition model trained on news (the ACE 2005 dataset) is heavily biased toward recognizing men, simply given the frequency with which men are present in that news data (Bamman, Popat, and Shen). When tested on literature, where men and women are mentioned with greater parity, the recall at recognizing women is much worse, recognizing only 38.0 percent of mentions, compared to 49.6 percent for men (a difference of −11.6 points). A model trained natively on literature, however, corrects this disparity, recognizing 69.3 percent of mentions who are women and 68.2 percent of those who are men (a difference +1.1 points). Literature naturally presents its own representational bias when considered from the viewpoint of other datasets (e.g., the depiction of gender roles in a nineteenth-century novel of manners is certainly different from that of a twenty-first-century biography), and this is part of the point: the models we use should reflect the characteristics of the data we are applying it to—the words that are being used and the worlds they are depicting.

One motivation for literary-centric NLP is to simply improve this dismal performance—if a model is able to reach an F-score of 68.8 for entity recognition in English news, then we should not have to settle for an F-score of 45.7 for English literature. But beyond that overall goal is a concern that strikes at the heart of methods in the computational humanities—if we are using empirical methods as algorithmic measuring devices, then absolute accuracy is less important than the source of any measurement error: if error is nonrandom, such that measurement accuracy is dependent on a variable that is at the core of subsequent analysis (such as gender), then we need to account for it. While methods from the social sciences that deal with survey data—like multilevel regression and poststratification (Gelman and Little)—may provide one means of correcting the disparity between a biased sample and the true population they are meant to reflect (if error rates are known and we only care about aggregate statistics), there are many situations where such methods fail.

This is not to say that generalizing from a nonliterary domain to a literary one is not possible; methods in NLP already have several strategies for narrowing this gap with domain adaptation (adapting the parameters of a model toward a domain for which it has little, or perhaps no, training data) and distributed representations of words so that a model has some information that a word like "rockaway" (a nineteenth-century four-wheeled carriage) has some lexical similarity to "car," even if it never appears in its labeled data. But if our goal is to use these methods for work in literature, then we should be centering metrics of validity on literature as a domain, including both overall accuracy and the biases that reflect those that appear in the texts under study. In the absence of any other method to optimize both of those concerns, an alternative is much simpler: we can train models natively on literary data and encode the biases present in representatives of the data we will later analyze.

LitBank

By training a model on data that resembles what it will see in the future, we can expect our performance on that future data to be similar to the performance on data we have seen during training. Several efforts have done just this for a range of linguistic phenomena, including part-of-speech tagging (Mueller) and syntactic parsing in a variety of historical and literary registers—including Portuguese (Galves and Faria), Greek and Latin (Bamman and Crane; Passarotti; Haug and Jøhndal), and English (Taylor and Kroch; Kroch, Santorini, and Delfs; Taylor et al.). By annotating data within the domain we care to analyze, we can train better methods to analyze data that looks similar to it in the future.

LitBank is one such resource: an open-source, literary-centric dataset to support a variety of contemporary work in the computational humanities working with English texts. To date, it contains 210,532 tokens drawn from 100 different English-language novels, annotated for four primary phenomena: entities, coreference, quotations, and events (each described in more detail below). By layering multiple phenomena on the same fixed set of texts, the annotations in LitBank are able to support interdependence between the layers—coreference, for example, groups mentions of entities (*Tom, the boy*) into the unique characters they refer to (TOM SAWYER), and quotation attribution assigns each act of dialogue to the unique character (i.e., coreference chain) who speaks it.

SOURCES

The texts in LitBank are all drawn from public domain texts in Project Gutenberg and include a mix of high literary style (e.g., Edith Wharton's *Age of Innocence,* James Joyce's *Ulysses*) and popular pulp fiction (e.g., H. Rider Haggard's *King Solomon's Mines,* Horatio Alger's *Ragged Dick*). All of the texts in LitBank were originally published before 1923 and, as Figure 3.1 illustrates, predominantly fall at the turn of the twentieth century.

Phenomena

ENTITIES

Entities define one of the core objects of interest in the computational humanities. Entities capture the characters that are involved in stories, the places where

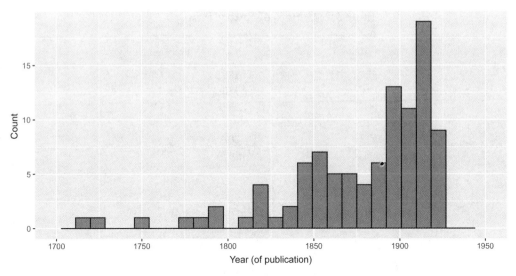

Figure 3.1. Distribution of texts in LitBank over time.

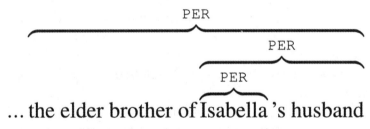

Figure 3.2. A hierarchical structure of a passage from Jane Austen's *Emma*.

they operate, and the things they interact with. Much work in the computational humanities reasons about these entities, including character (Underwood, Bamman, and Lee), places (Evans and Wilkens), and objects (Tenen), and has focused on both evaluating and improving NER for specifically the literary domain (Brooke, Hammond, and Baldwin; Dekker, Kuhn, and van Erp).

Traditional NER systems for other domains like news typically disallow hierarchical structure within names—flat structure is easier to reason about computationally where it can be treated as a single-layer sequence labeling problem and largely fits the structure of the phenomenon, where common geopolitical entities (such as Russia) and people (such as Bill Clinton) lack hierarchical structure. But literature abounds with hierarchical entities, many of which are not named at all (Figure 3.2). In this passage from Jane Austen's *Emma*, we see multiple entities expressed: *Isabella, Isabella's husband,* and *the elder brother of Isabella's husband.* Even though they are not named, all are potentially significant as mentions of characters within this story.

Table 3.2. Counts of Entity Type

Category	n	Frequency
PER	24,180	83.1%
FAC	2,330	8.0%
LOC	1,289	4.4%
GPE	948	3.3%
VEH	207	0.7%
ORG	149	0.5%

Table 3.3. Counts of Entity Category

Category	n	Frequency
PRON	15,816	54.3%
NOM	9,737	33.5%
PROP	3,550	12.2%

To capture this distinctive characteristic of literary texts, the first annotation layer of LitBank identifies all entities of six types—people (PER), facilities (FAC), geopolitical entities (GPE), locations (LOC), organizations (ORG), and vehicles (VEH), as illustrated in Table 3.2—and classifies their status as a proper name (PROP), common noun phrase (NOM), or pronoun (PRON).[1] Table 3.3 shows that the proportion of entities that traditional NER would capture (PROP) is quite small—common entities (*her sister*) are mentioned nearly three times as often as proper names (*Jane*) and both far less frequently than pronouns.

What can we do with books labeled with these entity categories? At their simplest, entities provide an organizing system for the collection, as Erin Wolfe ("Natural Language Processing in the Humanities") has demonstrated by applying models trained on LitBank to texts in the Black Books Interactive Project (https://bbip.ku.edu). This work extracts a ranked list of the most frequent people and places mentioned in a text, which provides a high-level overview of the content of a work.

At the same time, entity types abstract away common patterns that provide insight into narrative structure. As David McClure ("Distributions of Words across Narrative Time in 27,266 Novels") points out at the scale of individual words, many terms exhibit strong temporal associations with the narrative time of a book: significant plot elements like *death* show up near the end of a novel, while many terms that introduce people show up earlier. By tagging the entities that exist within a text, we can move beyond measuring individual words like "John" or "she" to capture the relative frequency of people as a whole. As Figure 3.3 illustrates, we also find different temporal dynamics when considering all people mentioned by proper name (*Sherlock, Jane Eyre*), common noun phrases (*the boy, her sister*), and pronouns

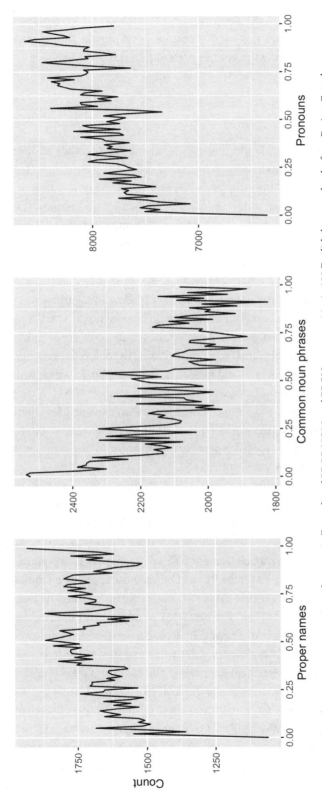

Figure 3.3. Distribution over narrative time of automatically predicted PROP, NOM, and PRON person entities in 100 English-language books from Project Gutenberg, excluding all paratextual material from Project Gutenberg (legal boilerplate) and the print original (tables of contents, advertisements, etc.).

(*he, she, they*). While proper names and pronouns increase in frequency as a book progresses from its beginning to end, common noun phrases show a marked decline in frequency. Identifying the entities present in a text gives us the ability to study behavior at these different levels of granularity.

COREFERENCE

Coreference resolution is the challenge of clustering together all mentions that refer to the same distinct entity. While some mentions have names that are determinative of their identity—for example, just about every mention of New York City in a text will refer to the unique city known by that name—there is often ambiguity in mapping mentions to entities. The same term (e.g., "she") can often refer to many different people, and the same person (e.g., Tom Sawyer) can be known by many different expressions ("Tom," "that boy," "him").

The benchmark dataset for coreference in English is OntoNotes 5 (Weischedel et al.), which includes the domains of news (broadcast, magazine, and newswire), conversation, the web, and even some literature (though restricted to include only the Bible). There are many ways, however, in which coreference in literature differs from that in factual textual sources, including the delayed revelation of identity (common in detective stories and mysteries, for example), in which two characters portrayed as separate entities are revealed to be the same person. Narratives in literary texts also tend to span longer time frames than news articles—perhaps years, decades, or even centuries—which raises difficult questions on the metaphysical nature of identity (e.g., is Shakespeare's LONDON of 1599 the same entity as Zadie Smith's LONDON in the year 2000?).

To address these issues, the second layer of annotations in LitBank covers coreference for the entities annotated above.[2] We specifically consider the ways in which literary coreference differs from coreference in news and other short, factual texts and manually assign the 29,103 mentions annotated above into 7,235 unique entities. As a result, coreference models trained on this native literary data perform much better on literary text (79.3F average F1 score) than those trained on OntoNotes (average 72.9F). This joins existing datasets for literature, including the work of Hardick Vala and colleagues ("Mr. Bennet, His Coachman, and the Archbishop Walk into a Bar but Only One of Them Gets Recognized"), which annotates character aliases in *Sherlock Holmes*, *Pride and Prejudice*, and *The Moonstone* and annotated datasets of conference in German novels (Krug et al.) and plays (Pagel and Reiter).

What does coreference make possible for cultural analysis? Coreference is critical for aggregating information about distinct entities like characters. For example, in "The Transformation of Gender in English-Language Fiction" (Underwood, Bamman, and Lee), we measured the amount of "attention" that characters receive in novels over 200 years of literary history by counting up the number of actions each character participates in. This is only possible by having a stable entity for each character that such counts can apply to, and since over half of all entity mentions are pronominal in nature, including pronouns in coreference is critical for that characterization. Limited attention has been devoted to the potential of coreference for other entity categories beyond people, but coreference for such classes as place (forests and marshes, houses and rooms, cities and countries and villages) is in many ways a precondition for the analysis of setting and its relationship to plot. In order to chart that characters in *Lord of the Rings* begin in the Shire, venture to Mount Doom, and return home in the end, we need to understand that "the Shire" and "home" refer to the same physical location. Coreference resolution would help make this kind of spatial analysis possible.

QUOTATION ATTRIBUTION

Much work in the computational humanities has explored the affordances of speaker attribution—identifying the speaker of a given piece of dialogue. Such attributed dialogue has been used in the past to create character networks by defining characters to be nodes and forming an edge between two characters who speak to one another (Elson, Dames, and McKeown). Literary-centric quotation data exists for both English and German: for English, this data encompasses Austen's *Pride and Prejudice* and *Emma* as well as Chekhov's *The Steppe* (He, Barbosa, and Kondrak; Muzny et al.), while the Columbia Quoted Speech Corpus (Elson and McKeown) includes six texts by Austen, Dickens, Flaubert, Doyle, and Chekhov. For German, 489,459 tokens were annotated for speech, thought, and writing, including direct, indirect, free indirect, and reported speech (Brunner et al.).

To provide a more diverse set of data for English, the third layer of LitBank includes dialogue attribution for the 100 texts in its collection.[3] This includes 1,765 dialogue acts across 279 characters in the 100 novels present in LitBank, which allows us to measure the accuracy of both quotation identification and attribution across a much broader range of texts than previously studied. Table 3.4 provides a summary of the characters with the most dialogue in this annotated dataset.

What can we do with such attribution data? Expanding on the use of quotations to define character interaction networks, in "Measuring Information Propagation in

Table 3.4. Characters with Most Annotated Dialogue from LitBank Database of 278 Characters across 100 Novels

Character	Text	n
Buck Mulligan	*Ulysses*	43
Convict	*Great Expectations*	33
Mrs. Bennet	*Pride and Prejudice*	29
Ragged Dick	*Ragged Dick*	28
Mr. Bennet	*Pride and Prejudice*	28

Literary Social Networks" (Sims and Bamman), we use quotations to extract atomic units of information and measure how those units propagate through the network defined by people speaking to each other. We specifically find both that information propagates through weak ties and that women are often depicted as being the linchpins of information flow.

Quotation also enables direct analysis of character idiolects, allowing us to ask what linguistic properties differentiate dialogue from narrative (Muzny, Algee-Hewitt, and Jurafsky) and the speech of characters from each other (Vishnubhotla, Hammond, and Hirst)—including the degree to which speech is predictive of other traits like personality (Flekova and Gurevych). While our work in "Measuring Information Propagation" (Sims and Bamman) exploits the notion of "listeners" of dialogue in order to track propagation, there is a range of work to be done in analyzing what differentiates the speech of a single character as they address different listeners, following the fundamental principle of audience design (Bell).

EVENTS

While entity recognition captures the important characters and objects in literature, recognizing events is important for grounding actions in plot. Event-annotated datasets in NLP have historically focused on the domain of news, including MUC (Sundheim), ACE (Walker et al., ACE 2005), and DEFT (Aguilar et al.), with some exceptions—in particular, an annotated dataset for historical texts that captures important classes of events in consultation with historians (Sprugnoli and Tonelli). But the depiction of events in literary texts tends to be very different from events in news. Literary texts include long and complex structures of narrative and multiple diagetic frames in which some events properly belong to the space of the plot, while others exist only in the commentary by the author. To address the specificity of the problem for literature, the fourth layer of annotation in LitBank focuses on *realis* events—events that are depicted as actually taking place within the narrative—which excludes hypotheticals, conditionals, and extra-diagetic events.[4] The criteria for what constitutes a realis event fall into four distinct categories (in the examples below, only realis events appear in boldface):

- **Polarity:** events must be asserted as actually occurring and not marked as having *not* taken place (John **walked** by Frank and didn't say hello).
- **Tense:** events must be in past or present tense; they must not be future events that have not yet occurred (John **walked** to the store and will buy some groceries).
- **Specificity:** events must involve specific entities and take place at a specific place and time (John **walked** to work Friday morning); they must not be unqualified statements about classes (Doctors walk to work).

- **Modality:** events must be asserted as actually occurring, as distinct from events that are the targets of other modalities, including beliefs, hypotheticals, and desires (John **walked** to the store to buy some groceries).

We annotate a total of 7,849 events in the 100 novels of LitBank. As Aakanksha Naik and Carolyn Rose ("Towards Open Domain Event Trigger Identification Using Adversarial Domain Adaptation") have shown, models trained natively on news (TimeBank) tend to perform quite poorly on LitBank (leading to a cross-domain drop in performance of 38.5 points), attesting to the benefit of annotated data within the domain we care about.

What can we do with events? In "Literary Event Detection" (Sims, Park, and Bamman), we show that examining realis events reveals a meaningful difference between popular texts and texts with high prestige, which is marked as the number of times an author's works were reviewed by elite literary journals, following Ted Underwood (*Distant Horizons*). Authors with high prestige not only present a lower intensity of realis events in their work than authors of popular texts, but they also have much more variability in their rates of eventfulness; popular texts, in contrast, have much less freedom in this respect, exhibiting a much narrower range of variation. Additionally, Maarten Sap and colleagues ("Recollection versus Imagination") build on this work by leveraging models trained on LitBank events to measure the difference between imagined and recalled events, showing that stories that are recalled contain more realis events than those that are entirely fictional. While existing work to date has focused on measurements of events on their own, there is much space for exploring the interaction between events and other narrative components—such as which characters participate in the most realis events and which works have the highest ratio of realis events per page (to capture a measure of pacing).

COVERAGE

One critique that we might level at this work is that "literature" is not a monolithic domain—and, in fact, the differences between individual texts that fall into what we call literature can be much greater than the cross-domain difference between a random novel and a news article. One of the biggest differences on this front is due to time—methods that are trained on texts published before 1923 will help us little in recognizing entities in contemporary novels like Facebook, jets, and Teslas, along with events like googling and texting.

LitBank contains texts published before 1923 in order to work exclusively with public domain texts, so that the original text can be published along with the annotations we layer. While texts published before 1923 capture a wide range of literature, this decision is restrictive, missing nearly a century of more contemporary texts, along with the more diverse voices represented in novels published today. Our current efforts are focused on expanding LitBank to include samples from 500 books published between 1924 and 2020, including 100 works written by Black authors drawn from the Black Books Interactive Project, 100 works by global Anglophone writers, 100 bestsellers, 100 prizewinning books, and 100 works of genre fiction. While these texts are in copyright, we will publish small samples of the texts along with linguistic annotations in order to enable reproducibility. We do so under the belief that such work is a transformative use of the original text that adds new value and does not affect the market for the original work and hence falls under the protections of fair use (Samberg and Hennesy).

At the same time, LitBank also is focused on works of fiction in the English language, further exacerbating what Roopika Risam notes is "the Anglophone focus of the field" of digital humanities (Risam, "Other Worlds, Other DHs"). NLP pipelines developed in many languages likewise perform quite poorly for literary texts such as NER for Spanish literary texts (Isasi), exposing the need for literary datasets across a wide range of languages. Current work is also focused on expanding the languages represented in LitBank to include Chinese and Russian, with more to follow.

Literary-Centric Questions

There is a rich research space building methods and datasets to adapt existing components of the NLP pipeline to work better on literary texts. But at the same time, an emphasis on literary-centric NLP requires attending to specifically literary questions that current NLP systems cannot directly address. As Lauren Klein notes, we should not let our questions be guided by the performance of our algorithms (Klein, "Distant Reading after Moretti"). What are these questions that are uniquely literary?

One set of questions models the relationship between readers and the texts they read, including the state of knowledge that we might surmise a reader has at a given point in the text. This is a problem that uniquely pertains to narrative text, where a reader builds up a model of the represented world over the course of reading and can make predictions about future events that might transpire within it. While some work in NLP addresses the question of the temporal order with which stories unfold (Mostafazadeh et al.), one phenomenon that appears frequently within some genres of literature is suspense—the potential anxious uncertainty about what is yet to come. Mark Algee-Hewitt ("The Machinery of Suspense") models this phenomenon by soliciting judgments of suspense from readers and building a model to predict that rating from an input passage that is 2 percent the length of a book, and David Wilmot and Frank Keller ("Modelling Suspense in Short Stories as Uncertainty Reduction over Neural Representation") model suspense in short stories by measuring the reduction in future uncertainty. While most document-level classification tasks presume simultaneous access to the entirety of a text, suspense is one phenomenon where the sequential ordering of narrative is critical for understanding—we are essentially modeling a reader's state of mind at time *t* having read the text through time *t* but not after it. Work in the computational humanities has begun to explore this phenomenon from the perspective of intratextual novelty and repetition (McGrath, Higgins, and Hintze; Long, Detwyler, and Zhu)—modeling the degree to which authors repeat information within a book—but there are many other related phenomena such as foreshadowing that remain to be explored.

A second set of questions arises from the formal nature of novels and longer literary texts. Unlike news, Wikipedia articles, and tweets, novels are long; they are roughly 100,000 words, on average. This length presents challenges for NLP that was designed for other domains—in particular, interesting questions that we might ask of the nature of objects and things more generally (Brown, "Thing Theory") are resisted by the quality of coreference resolution for common entities like cars, guns, and houses over long distances of narrative time. Tenen's "Toward a Computational Archaeology of Fictional Space" is one example of the kind of work that can be done when reasoning about the nature of objecthood—in that case, considering the density of objects mentioned. What we often want is not only a measure of how objects in the abstract behave, but how *specific* objects are depicted—such as the eponymous houses in E. M. Forster's *Howards End,* Nathaniel Hawthorne's *House of Seven Gables,* or Mark Danielewski's *House of Leaves.* Characterizing those distinct houses requires us to identify when any individual mention of the word *house* refers to the named house in question—a task challenging even for short documents but far more difficult at the moment for hundreds of mentions of such a common phrase potentially describing dozens of unique entities. Even though this is more of a computational challenge than a literary one, it is driven exclusively by the characteristics of literary texts and is unlikely to be solved by anyone not working in the computational humanities.

Finally, a third set of questions are narratological ones—how do we recognize the individual components of narrative and assemble them together into a representation of plot? A wealth of work has explored this question from different angles (Piper, So, and Bamman), including inferring sentiment arcs (Jockers; Reagan et al.), identifying "turning points" in movies (Papalampidi, Keller, and Lapata), disentangling storylines in *Infinite Jest* (Wallace, "Multiple Narrative Disentanglement"), and separating segments in *The Waste Land* (Brooke, Hammond, and Hirst). Other work has focused on identifying Proppian narrative functions in fairy tales (Finlayson), recognizing free indirect speech (Brunner et al.), modeling stream of consciousness (Long and So), and measuring the passage of time (Underwood). Much of the difficulty for modeling complex narratological phenomena is embedded in the difficulty of simply operationalizing what a concept like "plot" means as a computational form. Recent work attempts to tackle this theoretical question head on by comparing different narratological annotation schemes as a first step toward computational modeling (Reiter, Willand, and Gius). But in many ways, modeling narratological questions is uniquely positioned at the intersection of computation and the humanities—requiring not only expertise in models of linguistic structure but also a deep foundation in literary and narrative theory (Genette; Bal). The breadth of areas in this space—ranging from identifying characters and settings to inferring storylines and hierarchical narrative levels—makes modeling narratological phenomena one of the most vibrant areas poised for transformative work going forward.

Future

There is a range of work in the computational humanities that relies on linguistic structure—established phenomena like named entity recognition, uniquely literary tasks like predicting the passage of time, and a variety of opportunities on the horizon—that raises the potential to generate insight by considering the inherent structure present within text. While the field of natural language processing has focused for years on developing the core computational infrastructure to infer linguistic structure, much work remains to both adapt those methods to the domain(s) of literature and also to explore the unique affordances that literature provides for computational inquiry. For existing tasks—entity recognition, coreference resolution, event identification, quotation attribution—one straightforward solution exists: we need to create more annotated data composed of the literary texts that form the basis of our analyses, for both training (to improve the models on this domain) and evaluation (so that we know they work). LitBank provides one such resource; while this dataset is expanding to encompass a greater variety of texts, it will always hold gaps—both in its representation and in the phenomena it contains. More annotated data is always needed.

Annotated data from literary texts provides a solution to one issue in literary-centric NLP: How do we go about tackling new literary-centric questions, including those research areas outlined above? For several components of these problems, we can fall back on time-tested strategies. If we can operationalize a concept and annotate its presence in text to a reliable degree, we can annotate texts and train models to predict those human judgments for new texts we have not labeled yet. The complexity of modeling can range from straightforward sentence-level classification problems of suspense to complex hierarchical models of narrative levels.

While the design of some models will require training in NLP, the most important parts of this work are often outside the realm of computation and draw on at least three different skills: first, insight into the aspects of narrative and critical theory that can provide a strong foundation for an empirical method; second, the ability to circumscribe the boundaries of a problem in a way that both simplifies it enough for computational methods to be able to address it while also still preserving enough richness to sustain its relevance for humanistic inquiry; and third—and perhaps most important—the creativity needed to identify the questions worth asking in the first place. Like its broader field of the computational humanities, literary-centric NLP necessarily draws on expertise in both disciplines that comprise its community of practice, and this need to co-construct both the questions worth working on and the methods used to address them offers a vibrant path forward in this interdisciplinary space.

Notes

Many thanks to the reviewers for helpful comments in improving this work. The research reported in this article was supported by an Amazon Research Award and NSF CAREER grant IIS-1942591, along with resources provided by NVIDIA and Berkeley Research Computing.

1. This work is described in more detail in Bamman, Popat, and Shen, "An Annotated Dataset of Literary Entities," and Bamman, Lewke, and Mansoor, "An Annotated Dataset of Coreference in English Literature."

2. More information on the coreference layer can be found in Bamman, Lewke and Mansoor, "An Annotated Dataset of Coreference in English Literature."

3. This work is described in more detail in Sims and Bamman, "Measuring Information Propagation in Literary Social Networks."

4. This layer is described in Sims, Park, and Bamman, "Literary Event Detection."

Bibliography

Aguilar, Jacqueline, Charley Beller, Paul McNamee, Benjamin Van Durme, Stephanie Strassel, Zhiyi Song, and Joe Ellis. "A Comparison of the Events and Relations across ACE, ERE, TAC-KBP, and FrameNet Annotation Standards." In *Proceedings of the Second Workshop on Events: Definition, Detection, Coreference, and Representation*, 45–53. Baltimore: Association for Computational Linguistics, 2014. https://doi.org/10.3115/v1/W14-2907.

Algee-Hewitt, Mark. "The Machinery of Suspense," 2016. http://markalgeehewitt.org/index.php/main-page/projects/the-machinery-of-suspense/.

Algee-Hewitt, Mark, Sarah Allison, Marissa Gemma, Ryan Heuser, Franco Moretti, and Hannah Walser. "Canon/Archive: Large-Scale Dynamics in the Literary Field." *Literary Lab Pamphlet* 11 (2016).

Bal, Mieke. *Narratology: Introduction to the Theory of Narrative*. Toronto: University of Toronto Press, 2017.

Bamman, David, and Gregory Crane. "The Ancient Greek and Latin Dependency Treebanks." In *Language Technology for Cultural Heritage*, 79–98. Berlin: Springer, 2011.

Bamman, David, Olivia Lewke, and Anya Mansoor. "An Annotated Dataset of Coreference in English Literature." In *Proceedings of the 12th Language Resources and Evaluation Conference*, 44–54. Marseille: European Language Resources Association, 2020. https://www.aclweb.org/anthology/2020.lrec-1.6.

Bamman, David, Sejal Popat, and Sheng Shen. "An Annotated Dataset of Literary Entities." In *Proceedings of the 2019 Conference of the North American Chapter of the Association for Computational Linguistics: Human Language Technologies, Volume 1 (Long and Short Papers)*, 2138–44. Minneapolis: Association for Computational Linguistics, 2019. https://doi.org/10.18653/v1/N19-1220.

Bell, Allan. "Language Style as Audience Design." *Language in Society* 13, no. 2 (1984): 145–204.

Bode, Katherine. "'Man People Woman Life'/'Creek Sheep Cattle Horses': Influence, Distinction, and Literary Traditions." In *A World of Fiction: Digital Collections and the Future of Literary History*, 157–98. Ann Arbor: University of Michigan Press, 2018.

Brooke, Julian, Adam Hammond, and Timothy Baldwin. "Bootstrapped Text-Level Named Entity Recognition for Literature." In *Proceedings of the 54th Annual Meeting of the Association for Computational Linguistics. Volume 2: Short Papers*, 344–50. Berlin: Association for Computational Linguistics, 2016. https://doi.org/10.18653/v1/P16-2056.

Brooke, Julian, Adam Hammond, and Graeme Hirst. "Unsupervised Stylistic Segmentation of Poetry with Change Curves and Extrinsic Features." In *Proceedings of the NAACL-HLT 2012 Workshop on Computational Linguistics for Literature*, 26–35. Montreal: Association for Computational Linguistics, 2012. https://www.aclweb.org/anthology/W12-2504.

Brown, Bill. "Thing Theory." *Critical Inquiry* 28, no. 1 (2001): 1–22. https://www.jstor.org/stable/1344258.

Brunner, Annelen, Stefan Engelberg, Fotis Jannidis, Ngoc Duyen Tanja Tu, and Lukas Weimer. "Corpus REDEWIEDERGABE." In *Proceedings of the 12th Language Resources and Evaluation Conference*, 803–12. Marseille: European Language Resources Association, 2020. https://www.aclweb.org/anthology/2020.lrec-1.100.

Brunner, Annelen, Ngoc Duyen Tanja Tu, Lukas Weimer, and Fotis Jannidis. "Deep Learning for Free Indirect Representation." *Proceedings of the 15th Conference on Natural Language Processing: KONVENS 2019*. Erlangen, Germany: German Society for Computational Linguistics & Language Technology, 2019.

Burga, Alicia, Joan Codina, Gabriella Ferraro, Horacio Saggion, and Leo Wanner. "The Challenge of Syntactic Dependency Parsing Adaptation for the Patent Domain." In *ESSLLI-13 Workshop on Extrinsic Parse Improvement*. 2013.

Chambers, Nathanael. "Inducing Event Schemas and Their Participants from Unlabeled Text." PhD thesis, Stanford University, 2011.

Clement, Tanya, and Stephen McLaughlin. "Measured Applause: Toward a Cultural Analysis of Audio Collections." *Journal of Cultural Analytics* 1, no. 1 (2018).

Clement, Tanya, David Tcheng, Loretta Auvil, Boris Capitanu, and Megan Monroe. "Sounding for Meaning: Using Theories of Knowledge Representation to Analyze Aural Patterns in Texts." *DHQ: Digital Humanities Quarterly* 7, no. 1 (2013).

Cucerzan, Silviu. "Large-Scale Named Entity Disambiguation Based on Wikipedia Data." In *Proceedings of the 2007 Joint Conference on Empirical Methods in Natural Language*

Processing and Computational Natural Language Learning (EMNLP-CoNLL), 708–16. Prague: Association for Computational Linguistics, 2007.

Dekker, Niels, Tobias Kuhn, and Marieke van Erp. "Evaluating Named Entity Recognition Tools for Extracting Social Networks from Novels." *PeerJ Computer Science* 5 (2019).

Derczynski, Leon, Diana Maynard, Niraj Aswani, and Kalina Bontcheva. "Microblog-Genre Noise and Impact on Semantic Annotation Accuracy." In *Proceedings of the 24th ACM Conference on Hypertext and Social Media,* 21–30. New York: Association for Computing Machinery, 2013.

Derczynski, Leon, Alan Ritter, Sam Clark, and Kalina Bontcheva. "Twitter Part-of-Speech Tagging for All: Overcoming Sparse and Noisy Data." In *RANLP,* 198–206. Shoumen, Bulgaria: Incoma, 2013.

Derven, Caleb, Aja Teehan, and John Keating. "Mapping and Unmapping Joyce: Geoparsing Wandering Rocks." In *Digital Humanities 2014.* 2014.

Devlin, Jacob, Ming-Wei Chang, Kenton Lee, and Kristina Toutanova. "BERT: Pre-Training of Deep Bidirectional Transformers for Language Understanding." In *Proceedings of the 2019 Conference of the North American Chapter of the Association for Computational Linguistics: Human Language Technologies. Volume 1: Long and Short Papers,* 4171–86. Minneapolis: Association for Computational Linguistics, 2019.

Elson, David K., and Kathleen R. McKeown. "Automatic Attribution of Quoted Speech in Literary Narrative." In *Proceedings of the 24th AAAI Conference on Artificial Intelligence,* 1013–9. AAAI Press, 2010.

Elson, David K., Nicholas Dames, and Kathleen R. McKeown. "Extracting Social Networks from Literary Fiction." In *Proceedings of the 48th Annual Meeting of the Association for Computational Linguistics,* 138–47. Stroudsburg, Pa.: Association for Computational Linguistics, 2010.

Evans, Elizabeth F., and Matthew Wilkens. "Nation, Ethnicity, and the Geography of British Fiction, 1880–1940." *Journal of Cultural Analytics* 3, no. 2 (2018).

Fariss, Christopher J., Michael R. Kenwick, and Kevin Reuning. "Measurement Models." In *SAGE Handbook of Research Methods in Political Science and International Relations,* edited by Luigi Curini and Robert Franzese. London: Sage, 2020.

Finlayson, Mark A. "ProppLearner: Deeply Annotating a Corpus of Russian Folktales to Enable the Machine Learning of a Russian Formalist Theory." *Digital Scholarship in the Humanities* 32, no. 2 (2015): 284–300. https://doi.org/10.1093/llc/fqv067.

Finlayson, Mark Alan. "Inferring Propp's Functions from Semantically Annotated Text." *Journal of American Folklore* 129, no. 511 (2016): 55–77. https://www.jstor.org/stable/10.5406/jamerfolk.129.511.0055.

Flekova, Lucie, and Iryna Gurevych. "Personality Profiling of Fictional Characters Using Sense-Level Links between Lexical Resources." In *Proceedings of the 2015 Conference on Empirical Methods in Natural Language Processing,* 1805–16. Lisbon: Association for Computational Linguistics, 2015. https://aclweb.org/anthology/D15-1208.

Galves, Charlotte, and Pablo Faria. "Tycho Brahe Parsed Corpus of Historical Portuguese." 2010. www.tycho.iel.unicamp.br/~tycho/corpus/en/index.html.

Gelman, Andrew, and Thomas C. Little. "Poststratification into Many Categories Using Hierarchical Logistic Regression." *Survey Methodology* 23, no. 2 (1997): 127–35.

Genette, Gérard. *Figures of Literary Discourse*. New York: Columbia University Press, 1982.

Genette, Gérard. *Narrative Discourse: An Essay in Method*. Ithaca, N.Y.: Cornell University Press, 1983.

Gildea, Daniel. "Corpus Variation and Parser Performance." In *Proceedings of the 2001 Conference on Empirical Methods in Natural Language Processing,* 167–202. Stroudsburg, Pa.: Association for Computational Linguistics, 2001.

Haug, Dag TT, and Marius Jøhndal. "Creating a Parallel Treebank of the Old Indo-European Bible Translations." In *Proceedings of the Language Technology for Cultural Heritage Data Workshop (Latech 2008), Marrakech, Morocco, 1st June 2008,* 27–34. 2008.

He, Hua, Denilson Barbosa, and Grzegorz Kondrak. "Identification of Speakers in Novels." In *Proceedings of the 51st Annual Meeting of the Association for Computational Linguistics. Volume 1: Long Papers,* 1312–20. Sofia, Bulgaria: Association for Computational Linguistics, 2013.

Houston, Natalie. "Enjambment and the Poetic Line: Towards a Computational Poetics." In *Digital Humanities 2014.* 2014.

Hovy, Eduard, Mitchell Marcus, Martha Palmer, Lance Ramshaw, and Ralph Weischedel. "OntoNotes: The 90% Solution." In *Proceedings of the Human Language Technology Conference of the NAACL. Companion Volume: Short Papers,* 57–60. Stroudsburg, Pa.: Association for Computational Linguistics, 2006.

Isasi, Jennifer. "Posibilidades de La Minería de Datos Digital Para El Análisis Del Personaje Literario En La Novela Española: El Caso de Galdós Y Los 'Episodios Nacionales.'" PhD thesis, University of Nebraska, 2017.

Jacobs, Abigail Z., and Hanna Wallach. "Measurement and Fairness." In *Conference on Fairness, Accountability, and Transparency (FAccT '21).* 2021.

Jockers, Matthew. "Revealing Sentiment and Plot Arcs with the Syuzhet Package," February 2015. http://www.matthewjockers.net/2015/02/02/syuzhet/.

Jockers, Matthew, and Gabi Kirilloff. "Understanding Gender and Character Agency in the 19th Century Novel." *Journal of Cultural Analytics* 2, no. 2 (2017).

Klein, Lauren. "Distant Reading after Moretti." *Arcade,* January 29, 2018. https://arcade.stanford.edu/blogs/distant-reading-after-moretti.

Klein, Lauren F. "Dimensions of Scale: Invisible Labor, Editorial Work, and the Future of Quantitative Literary Studies." *PMLA* 135, no. 1 (2020): 23–39. https://doi.org/10.1632/pmla.2020.135.1.23.

Klein, Sheldon, John F. Aeschlimann, David F. Balsiger, Steven L. Converse, Claudine Court, Mark Foster, Robin Lao, John D. Oakley, and Joel Smith. "Automatic Novel Writing." University of Wisconsin-Madison, 1973.

Kraicer, Eve, and Andrew Piper. "Social Characters: The Hierarchy of Gender in Contemporary English-Language Fiction." *Journal of Cultural Analytics* 3, no. 2 (2018).

Kroch, Anthony, Beatrice Santorini, and Lauren Delfs. "Penn-Helsinki Parsed Corpus of Early Modern English." Department of Linguistics, University of Pennsylvania, 2004.

Krug, Markus, Lukas Weimer, Isabella Reger, Luisa Macharowsky, Stephan Feldhaus, Frank Puppe, and Fotis Jannidis. "Description of a Corpus of Character References in German Novels—DROC [Deutsches ROman Corpus]." DARIAH-DE Working Papers No. 27, 2017.

Lease, Matthew, and Eugene Charniak. "Parsing Biomedical Literature." In *Natural Language Processing-IJCNLP 2005,* 58–69. Berlin: Springer, 2005.

Long, Hoyt, and Richard Jean So. "Turbulent Flow: A Computational Model of World Literature." *Modern Language Quarterly* 77, no. 3 (2016): 345–67. https://doi.org/10.1215/00267929-3570656.

Long, Hoyt, Anatoly Detwyler, and Yuancheng Zhu. "Self-Repetition and East Asian Literary Modernity, 1900–1930." *Journal of Cultural Analytics* 2, no. 1 (May 2018).

MacArthur, Marit J., Georgia Zellou, and Lee M. Miller. "Beyond Poet Voice: Sampling the (Non-) Performance Styles of 100 American Poets." *Journal of Cultural Analytics* 3, no. 1 (2018).

Mandell, Laura. "Gender and Cultural Analytics: Finding or Making Stereotypes?" In *Debates in Digital Humanities 2019,* edited by Matthew K. Gold and Lauren F. Klein. Minneapolis: University of Minnesota Press, 2019.

Marcus, Mitchell P., Beatrice Santorini, and Mary Ann Marcinkiewicz. "Building a Large Annotated Corpus of English: The Penn Treebank." *Computational Linguistics* 19, no. 2 (1993): 313–30.

McClure, David. "Distributions of Words across Narrative Time in 27,266 Novels." *Stanford Literary Lab,* July 10, 2017. https://litlab.stanford.edu/distributions-of-words-27k-novels/.

McGillivray, Barbara, Thierry Poibeau, and Pablo Ruiz Fabo. "Digital Humanities and Natural Language Processing: 'Je t'aime . . . Moi non plus.'" *DHQ: Digital Humanities Quarterly* 14, no. 2 (2020).

McGrath, Laura B., Devin Higgins, and Arend Hintze. "Measuring Modernist Novelty." *Journal of Cultural Analytics* 3, no. 1 (2018).

Meehan, James R. "TALE-SPIN, an Interactive Program That Writes Stories." *IJCAI* 77 (1977): 91–98.

Mendenhall, T. C. "The Characteristic Curves of Composition." *Science* (1887).

Mikolov, Tomas, Kai Chen, Greg Corrado, and Jeffrey Dean. "Efficient Estimation of Word Representations in Vector Space." *ICLR* (2013).

Moon, Taesun, and Jason Baldridge. "Part-of-Speech Tagging for Middle English through Alignment and Projection of Parallel Diachronic Texts." In *Proceedings of the 2007 Joint Conference on Empirical Methods in Natural Language Processing and Computational Natural Language Learning (EMNLP-CoNLL),* 390–99. Prague: Association for Computational Linguistics, 2007.

Mostafazadeh, Nasrin, Nathanael Chambers, Xiaodong He, Devi Parikh, Dhruv Batra, Lucy Vanderwende, Pushmeet Kohli, and James Allen. "A Corpus and Evaluation Framework for Deeper Understanding of Commonsense Stories." *NAACL* (2016).

Mosteller, F., and D. Wallace. *Inference and Disputed Authorship: The Federalist.* Boston: Addison-Wesley, 1964.

Mueller, Martin. "WordHoard," 2015. https://wordhoard.northwestern.edu/userman/martin-data.html.

Muzny, Grace, Mark Algee-Hewitt, and Dan Jurafsky. "Dialogism in the Novel: A Computational Model of the Dialogic Nature of Narration and Quotations." *Digital Scholarship in the Humanities* 32 (July 2017).

Muzny, Grace, Michael Fang, Angel Chang, and Dan Jurafsky. "A Two-Stage Sieve Approach for Quote Attribution." In *Proceedings of the 15th Conference of the European Chapter of the Association for Computational Linguistics. Volume 1: Long Papers,* 460–70. Valencia, Spain: Association for Computational Linguistics, 2017.

Naik, Aakanksha, and Carolyn Rose. "Towards Open Domain Event Trigger Identification Using Adversarial Domain Adaptation." In *Proceedings of the 58th Annual Meeting of the Association for Computational Linguistics,* 7618–24. Online: Association for Computational Linguistics, 2020. https://www.aclweb.org/anthology/2020.acl-main.681.

Nelson, Laura K. 2020. "Computational Grounded Theory: A Methodological Framework." *Sociological Methods & Research* 49, no. 1 (2020): 3–42.

Pagel, Janis, and Nils Reiter. "GerDraCor-Coref: A Coreference Corpus for Dramatic Texts in German." In *Proceedings of the 12th Language Resources and Evaluation Conference,* 55–64. Marseille: European Language Resources Association, 2020. https://www.aclweb.org/anthology/2020.lrec-1.7.

Papalampidi, Pinelopi, Frank Keller, and Mirella Lapata. "Movie Plot Analysis via Turning Point Identification." In *Proceedings of the 2019 Conference on Empirical Methods in Natural Language Processing and the 9th International Joint Conference on Natural Language Processing (Emnlp-Ijcnlp),* 1707–17. Hong Kong: Association for Computational Linguistics, 2019. https://doi.org/10.18653/v1/D19-1180.

Passarotti, Marco. "Verso Il Lessico Tomistico Biculturale. La Treebank Dell'Index Thomisticus." In *Il Filo Del Discorso. Intrecci Testuali, Articolazioni Linguistiche, Composizioni Logiche. Atti Del Xiii Congresso Nazionale Della Società Di Filosofia Del Linguaggio, Viterbo, Settembre 2006,* edited by Petrilli Raffaella and Femia Diego, 187–205. Rome: Aracne Editrice, Pubblicazioni della Società di Filosofia del Linguaggio, 2007.

Pekar, Viktor, Juntao Yu, Mohab El-karef, and Bernd Bohnet. "Exploring Options for Fast Domain Adaptation of Dependency Parsers." *First Joint Workshop on Statistical Parsing of Morphologically Rich Languages and Syntactic Analysis of Non-Canonical Languages (SPMRL-SANCL 2014),* 54–65. 2014.

Pennacchiotti, Marco, and Fabio Massimo Zanzotto. "Natural Language Processing across Time: An Empirical Investigation on Italian." In *Advances in Natural Language Processing,* 371–82. Springer, 2008.

Pennington, Jeffrey, Richard Socher, and Christopher Manning. "Glove: Global Vectors for Word Representation." In *Proceedings of the 2014 Conference on Empirical Methods in Natural Language Processing (EMNLP),* 1532–43. 2014.

Piper, Andrew, Richard Jean So, and David Bamman. "Narrative Theory for Computational Narrative Understanding." In *Proceedings of the 2021 Conference on Empirical Methods in Natural Language Processing (EMNLP).* 2021.

Rajpurkar, Pranav, Robin Jia, and Percy Liang. "Know What You Don't Know: Unanswerable Questions for SQuAD." In *Proceedings of the 56th Annual Meeting of the Association for Computational Linguistics (Volume 2: Short Papers),* 784–89. Melbourne: Association for Computational Linguistics, 2018.

Rajpurkar, Pranav, Jian Zhang, Konstantin Lopyrev, and Percy Liang. "SQuAD: 100,000+ Questions for Machine Comprehension of Text." In *Proceedings of the 2016 Conference on Empirical Methods in Natural Language Processing,* 2383–92. Austin, Tex.: Association for Computational Linguistics, 2016.

Rambsy, Kenton, and Peace Ossom-Williamson. *Lost in the City: An Exploration of Edward P. Jones's Short Fiction*. Urbana, Ill.: Publishing Without Walls, 2019. https://iopn.library.illinois.edu/scalar/lost-in-the-city-a-exploration-of-edward-p-joness-short-fiction-/index.

Rayson, Paul, Dawn Archer, Alistair Baron, Jonathan Culpeper, and Nicholas Smith. "Tagging the Bard: Evaluating the Accuracy of a Modern POS Tagger on Early Modern English Corpora." In *Proceedings of Corpus Linguistics (Cl2007).* 2007.

Reagan, Andrew J., Lewis Mitchell, Dilan Kiley, Christopher M. Danforth, and Peter Sheridan Dodds. "The Emotional Arcs of Stories Are Dominated by Six Basic Shapes." *EPJ Data Science* 5, no. 1 (2016): 31.

Reeve, Jonathan. "The Henry James Sentence: New Quantitative Approaches," June 7, 2017. https://jonreeve.com/2017/06/henry-james-sentence/.

Reiter, Nils, Marcus Willand, and Evelyn Gius. "A Shared Task for the Digital Humanities Chapter 1: Introduction to Annotation, Narrative Levels and Shared Tasks." *Journal of Cultural Analytics* 4, no. 3 (December 2019).

Rhody, Lisa M. 2012. "Topic Modeling and Figurative Language." *CUNY Academic Works,* 2012. https://academicworks.cuny.edu/cgi/viewcontent.cgi?article=1557&context=gc_pubs.

Risam, Roopika. "Other Worlds, Other DHs: Notes towards a DH Accent." *Digital Scholarship in the Humanities* 32, no. 2 (2016): 377–84. https://doi.org/10.1093/llc/fqv063.

Samberg, Rachael G., and Cody Hennesy. "Law and Literacy in Non-Consumptive Text Mining: Guiding Researchers through the Landscape of Computational Text Analysis." In *Copyright Conversations: Rights Literacy in a Digital World.* 2019. https://escholarship.org/uc/item/55j0h74g.

Sandhaus, Evan. "The New York Times Annotated Corpus." LDC. 2008.

Sap, Maarten, Eric Horvitz, Yejin Choi, Noah A. Smith, and James Pennebaker. "Recollection versus Imagination: Exploring Human Memory and Cognition via Neural Language Models." In *Proceedings of the 58th Annual Meeting of the Association for*

Computational Linguistics, 1970–8. Online: Association for Computational Linguistics, 2020. https://www.aclweb.org/anthology/2020.acl-main.178.

Scheible, Silke, Richard J. Whitt, Martin Durrell, and Paul Bennett. "Evaluating an 'Off-the-Shelf' POS-Tagger on Early Modern German Text." In *Proceedings of the 5th ACL-HLT Workshop on Language Technology for Cultural Heritage, Social Sciences, and Humanities,* 19–23. Portland, Ore.: Association for Computational Linguistics, 2011.

Schofield, Alexandra, Laure Thompson, and David Mimno. "Quantifying the Effects of Text Duplication on Semantic Models." *Proceedings of the 15th Conference of the European Chapter of the Association for Computational Linguistics: Volume 2, Short Papers.* 2017.

Sims, Matthew, and David Bamman. "Measuring Information Propagation in Literary Social Networks." In *Proceedings of the 2020 Conference on Empirical Methods in Natural Language Processing (EMNLP),* 642–52. Association for Computational Linguistics, 2020.

Sims, Matthew, Jong Ho Park, and David Bamman. "Literary Event Detection." In *Proceedings of the 57th Annual Meeting of the Association for Computational Linguistics,* 3623–34. Florence, Italy: Association for Computational Linguistics, 2019. https://doi.org/10.18653/v1/P19-1353.

Sprugnoli, R., and S. Tonelli. "One, No One and One Hundred Thousand Events: Defining and Processing Events in an Inter-Disciplinary Perspective." *Natural Language Engineering* 23, no. 4 (2017): 485–506. https://doi.org/10.1017/S1351324916000292.

Sundheim, Beth M. "Overview of the Third Message Understanding Conference." In *Processing of the Third Message Understanding Conference.* 1991.

Taylor, Ann, and Anthony S. Kroch. "The Penn-Helsinki Parsed Corpus of Middle English." University of Pennsylvania, 2000.

Taylor, Ann, Arja Nurmi, Anthony Warner, Susan Pintzuk, and Terttu Nevalainen. "Parsed Corpus of Early English Correspondence." Oxford Text Archive, 2006.

Tenen, Dennis Yi. "Toward a Computational Archaeology of Fictional Space." *New Literary History* (2018).

Thompson, Laure, and David Mimno. "Authorless Topic Models: Biasing Models Away from Known Structure." In *Proceedings of the 27th International Conference on Computational Linguistics.* 2018.

Underwood, Ted. "Why Literary Time Is Measured in Minutes." University of Illinois, 2016.

Underwood, Ted. *Distant Horizons: Digital Evidence and Literary Change.* University of Chicago Press, 2019.

Underwood, Ted, David Bamman, and Sabrina Lee. "The Transformation of Gender in English-Language Fiction." *Journal of Cultural Analytics* 3, no. 2 (2018).

Vala, Hardik, David Jurgens, Andrew Piper, and Derek Ruths. "Mr. Bennet, His Coachman, and the Archbishop Walk into a Bar but Only One of Them Gets Recognized: On the Difficulty of Detecting Characters in Literary Texts." In *Proceedings of the 2015 Conference on Empirical Methods in Natural Language Processing,* 769–74. Lisbon: Association for Computational Linguistics, 2015.

Vishnubhotla, Krishnapriya, Adam Hammond, and Graeme Hirst. "Are Fictional Voices Distinguishable? Classifying Character Voices in Modern Drama." In *Proceedings of the 3rd Joint SIGHUM Workshop on Computational Linguistics for Cultural Heritage, Social Sciences, Humanities and Literature,* 29–34. Minneapolis: Association for Computational Linguistics, 2019. https://doi.org/10.18653/v1/W19-2504.

Walker, Christopher, Stephanie Strassel, Julie Medero, and Kazuaki Maeda. "ACE 2005 Multilingual Training Corpus." LDC. 2006.

Wallace, Byron. "Multiple Narrative Disentanglement: Unraveling Infinite Jest." In *Proceedings of the 2012 Conference of the North American Chapter of the Association for Computational Linguistics: Human Language Technologies,* 1–10. Montreal: Association for Computational Linguistics, 2012. https://www.aclweb.org/anthology/N12-1001.

Walsh, Melanie, and Maria Antoniak. "The Goodreads 'Classics': A Computational Study of Readers, Amazon, and Crowdsourced Amateur Criticism." *Journal of Cultural Analytics* 6, no. 2 (2021).

Weischedel, Ralph, Sameer Pradhan, Lance Ramshaw, Jeff Kaufman, Michelle Franchini, Mohammed El-Bachouti, Nianwen Xue, et al. "OntoNotes Release 5.0." 2012.

Wilmot, David, and Frank Keller. "Modelling Suspense in Short Stories as Uncertainty Reduction over Neural Representation." In *Proceedings of the 58th Annual Meeting of the Association for Computational Linguistics,* 1763–88. Online: Association for Computational Linguistics, 2020. https://www.aclweb.org/anthology/2020.acl-main.161.

Wolfe, Erin. "Natural Language Processing in the Humanities: A Case Study in Automated Metadata Enhancement." *Code4lib* 46 (2019).

PART I][Chapter 4

Computational Parallax as Humanistic Inquiry

CRYSTAL HALL

Humanistic Parallax

European astronomers in the seventeenth century faced a situation familiar to computational humanists: their instruments and methods were embroiled in controversies over disciplinary territory and status at the university, definitions of their objects of study, and reliability of techniques for reconciling mathematical observations with received historical and theoretical understandings of these objects (Westman, 230–34). In particular, the astronomers debated parallax, a theorized effect that would allow for modeling the cosmos using the calculation of the distance between celestial objects based on measurements related to observer positions on earth. To make effective use of parallax, the fractious natural philosophers would have needed to agree on the overall dimensions of their objects of study, establish an accurate underlying model of their relationships in time, and adhere to stable taxonomies of those objects. For textual scholars, these astronomical disagreements might echo current literary and historical questions about the ideal collection of texts or corpus to study, which features determine a meaningful relationship between texts, and the consistency or even validity of genre categories. This chapter does not propose a solution to these long-standing debates but rather a method for expanding humanistic interpretation of text using computation, in spite of the unsettled nature of the textual environment in which we operate.

This method takes its inspiration from the fusion of astronomy and literary studies that was frequently practiced in seventeenth-century Europe. The provisional solution to the astronomers' apparent impasse was not mathematical but humanistic, in the European Renaissance sense of the term: the examination of particulars of textual variants in search of common contexts and stability of relationships across documents (Mueller, 83).[1] Rather than wait for agreement on dimensions, models, and categories of objects (which would only arrive centuries later), the unsigned, jocose "Dialogue of Cecco di Ronchitti" (1604), often attributed to Galileo Galilei, shifts the goal of parallax away from measurement toward aggregating relative attributes of the objects of study using these early humanistic methods. In the dialogue, two mathematically inclined farmers *experience* difference instead of *calculating* it by viewing trees in a forest from different perspectives. Their geometric, not measured, experiments lead to the declaration: "Parallax just means a difference of viewpoint [*deferientia de guardamento*]" (Galileo, 48). To be more precise, parallax is the accumulation of attributes of an object when seen in multiple contexts generated by an observer's changed position. Importantly, it means keeping our (computational) eye trained on one object while we change the ways in which we observe it or the backdrops against which it is compared.

Computational humanities research frequently makes reference to parallax, but with inconsistent definitions that often foreclose a study of ambiguity, polyphony, and critical imagination that are bedrock elements of much current humanistic study. Adapting the metaphor from the farmer-astronomers in 1604, calculating the forest often obscures our ability to experience a tree. I argue for framing computational experiments that rely on parallax for interpretation with the recovered late-Italian Renaissance articulation of the roles of the observer, the objects of study, and contexts. I am intentional about referring to this as computational rather than digital parallax. Admittedly, parallax can be created digitally through graphical display tools. This can be through a background that scrolls more slowly than a foreground in digital storytelling, or through interfaces that overlay or juxtapose partial views of an object's colocation in a collection (Whitelaw, 36–37). For my purposes, computation refers to repeated, complex calculations of relationships between humanistic objects of study. Those calculations, made for multiple models that reflect changes in corpora, parameters, or scale, artificially create a sense of space in which the objects exist. The analyst, then, experiences and interprets that space.

Adopting the visual, geometric framework of parallax that emphasizes the analyst's change in perspectives unites existing threads of discourse in digital humanities (DH). As such, computational humanistic parallax responds to Johanna Drucker's related suggestion that "parallax and difference" in computational methodologies could emphasize variability, irregularity, and complexity as opposed to representations of humanistic data that otherwise risk a "self-evident or self-identical presentation of knowledge" in diagrammatic or numeric results ("Humanistic Theory," 91). Computational humanistic parallax offers a valuable heuristic for interpreting expression by units of analysis that exist within and across collections of texts: varying backdrops (different corpora), multiple perspectives (parameters of observation), and attention to scale (levels of addressability). I will describe each of these features after offering an overview of the appearance of parallax in other digital humanities research.

Importantly, my synthesis comes from a white, multilingual settler perspective that is privileged and not all-encompassing. Right to left (RTL) and multilingual DH are actively resisting the limitations of previous computational humanistic approaches and building alternative designs that include rather than exclude perspectives for analysis.[2] Moreover, the scholarship that I present reflects the languages that I can navigate, and given the information architectures that create filters in the name of expediency, it is quite likely that even the examples here are but a limited portion of what exists in those critical traditions. This limitation invites expansion from colleagues within and outside the Anglophone and Romance language traditions of text analysis. Does my argument nonetheless move away from a universalizing, normalizing approach to data? Yes, I think so. Does it give agency to more voices in the documents? Here, too, I am optimistic that it creates possibilities to explore connections foreclosed by post hoc categories imposed by majority-organized archives and information practices.

Survey of the Field

In DH, the concept of parallax has been deployed already as a way to add perspectives and layers to computational humanistic analysis, with a particular emphasis on change over time and the use of extratextual data for adding depth to resulting models. Johanna Drucker, using graphics credited to Xárene Eskandar, initially presented graphical design interventions for representing parallax of witnesses and participants in narrative events ("Humanities Approaches," 36). Stephen Nichols later proposed parallax as layering and juxtaposition of a digitized library of manuscript variants, which is quite aligned with the method for using parallax adopted by Galileo's farmers. Mark Sample has presented parallax as a hermeneutic for scalable reading by placing one text in the contexts of different corpora in order to ask questions about the multiple meanings that a work offers to readers over time, here too maintaining the object of study while changing parameters for analysis and interpretation. Ted Underwood most recently explores parallax as perspectival modeling of genre labels over time through the use of machine learning (*Distant Horizons* and "Machine Learning"). Nonetheless, most of these publications include a section of defense that this computational work is humanistic, writing in anticipation of a presumed fractious audience.

By recovering the Renaissance humanistic definition of parallax adopted by Galileo's farmers, current humanists need not agree on the definitive model of the largest dataset; we can instead direct our computational energy toward the ways in which an individual object participates (or not) in larger patterns. Such a framework also overcomes a frequent challenge of quantitative approaches to interpreting remixed and remixable ecosystems of expression: a struggle to expand beyond sociological or historical conclusions. The recovered definition reasserts the scholar's role in creating the contextual conditions for observing relationships and the multiple, simultaneous ways that text carries or expresses meaning. This multiplicity has been identified using different descriptors across the humanities: from "massively addressable" text (Witmore) to polyrhythmic performances (Andrews) to images and spaces designed to be viewed and experienced from multiple perspectives (Ruecker and Roberts-Smith). Rather than computation aiming for contextualization or definition within the largest dataset possible, computational humanistic parallax aims for the largest possible variation of contexts and features to analyze. The definition that I propose emphasizes the scholar's active role in collating these perspectives on their objects of study through multiple observations. The scholar is also participant, experiencing the results of the change as a way to interpret the object, in line with, but not limited to, Sample's changing corpora. This approach expands Drucker and Eskandar's initial conceptualization of parallax beyond the content of the humanistic object to the process of its analysis.

Computational parallax as a process thus declares its conditionality and constructedness at the outset in ways that align with traditional humanistic inquiry. As Drucker reminds us: "The parallax views that arise in the interstices of fragmentary evidence are what give humanistic thought its purchase on the real, even with full acknowledgment that knowing is always a process of codependencies" ("Humanistic Theory," 92). From the perspectives offered by computational humanistic parallax, we have learned something that can add to our understanding of our text(s). For example, a sentiment analysis model might assign a numeric score to a passage to represent positive or negative valence, based on the sum of the scores of the words it contains. Changing passage sizes and textual environments, we can interpret the passage based on a multiplicity of results revealed by computation, without affixing a measurement to a passage as though it could only have one way of making meaning. This is one way a computational tool can work in service of humanistic concerns.

This focus on the relationship of one document to the rest of the corpus sets computational humanistic parallax apart from the related practices of exploratory data analysis (EDA). Both are iterative and rely on an attitude of experimentation rather than the application of a theory to produce multiple visualizations and analyses of a dataset. Yet, EDA's goal is to summarize the data as a whole through multiple methods of summarizing, aggregating, and visualizing variables, their categories, or their relationships before determining which statistical model(s) will best describe the objects of study. On the other hand, computational humanistic parallax makes no presumption about the possibility of creating such a model and instead draws attention to the relationship of the part to the whole as it is defined at the time, without claims to definitiveness of the corpus of texts.

Since the status of an optimized model is debatable, much like the astronomical theories that provoke Galileo's farmers, computational humanistic parallax offers a mechanism for interpreting the individual pieces of that system. It is a mechanism that both assists in reproducibility and makes evident when computational results cannot be compared because all the conditions of the original observations cannot be re-created. This separates model creation from interpretation, following Drucker's advocacy away from output that risks being mistaken as a representation instead of an analytical result that requires explanation. Our interpretations might still vary, depending on the other knowledge that we bring to these patterns and representations. This framing also moves us away from reductive criticisms that computation of humanistic study can only show aboutness and its quantities, influence and its strengths, and the stability or change of categorical labels over time (Da, 605). For example, if I change the corpus but keep the parameters and scale the same, then I can interrogate why the results might be different rather than argue that a model is wrong. Elsewhere in this volume, Mark Algee-Hewitt advocates for a similar use of unexpected quantitative results to inform textual theory (see chapter 2). Building on these examples, I want to advance the argument that the priorities of humanistic interpretation can drive computational methods through a closer examination of computational humanistic parallax at work in corpus design, parameter variation, and scales of address.

Backgrounds and Corpus Construction

Unlike Galileo's farmer-astronomers, who had an established forest for their experiential experiments, current humanists recognize how incomplete their inventory of objects might be. Computational humanistic parallax calls for designing multiple corpora in order to account for both the outsized role of certain texts that obscure our vision and the systemic forces that exclude other texts from analysis. As Lauren Klein has demonstrated, documenting absence requires disrupting the (digital) archive that is often complicit in the process of silencing some voices. Disruption requires interpretation, not declaration: a computational practice whose aim is not classification or testing conformity to a category but a process that creates analytical space.

Instead of assembling the largest environment for analysis, computational parallax invites assembling multiple possible scenarios for that environment. No matter how large the corpus, how big the big data, or how small the passage, many computational approaches such as clustering will only show the best fit based on a strongest signal determined by the features of the other texts being analyzed. To avoid this outcome, for his parallax reading, Mark Sample places one of Theodore Roethke's poems in biographical, chronological, and spoken contexts alongside keyword searching in Google Ngram Viewer and the Corpus of Historical American English. For my project, rather than optimizing one model to document Galileo's overall position among texts in the sixteenth and seventeenth centuries, I have compared his texts against the backdrops of pre-Reformation fiction, prose by Florentine authors, Italian dialogues, and Aristotelian mathematical treatises. Consider two visual examples of the overall similarity between one of Galileo's texts to seventy-three other documents circulating during his lifetime (Figure 4.1a) and to only those twenty-eight documents published in the seventeenth century (Figure 4.1b). The focus here is on the contingent nature of that similarity when the same analysis is performed on both corpora; a more detailed analysis follows in the next sections.

Many attributes have been collapsed into two dimensions in these visualizations (more on this in the next section). Thinking geometrically, like the astronomer-farmers, I want to draw our attention to the change in relative location (the relative similarity) of Galileo's text (bold) when the corpus changes. Removing the seventeenth-century documents allows us to see similarities with the earlier texts that would have escaped our attention otherwise. This immediately draws my attention to what meaning might exist in Galileo's text that originates in the expressions of the century prior in the apparently similar treatise on painting (the point labeled "Della Pittura"). We also cannot help but notice how distant and different the translation of an Arabic treatise on geometry is in Figure 4.1b (the point labeled "Superficie"). These examples are drawn from text analysis, but humanists interpret meaning through recontextualization of a variety of objects of study. As Hannah Ringler argues in chapter 1 in this volume, by seeing the computational tool as a "third eye" in our methodology, we can ask humanistic questions rather than answer quantitative ones with computation.

Perspectives and Parameters

Against these backdrops, the critic can then select from a number of instruments or settings on those instruments to accumulate different perspectives (collapsed into just two opaque dimensions of the x- and y-axes in Figure 4.1). In the example above, each perspective could address a different kind of abstraction of the texts: frequencies, bags of words without order, parts of speech, punctuated interruptions, and metadata. The perspectives show what is present or absent, how much is present in what proportions, along with what other attributes, which layers of significations and in what rhythms, and from what creators or in what containers. Andrew Piper's work in *enumerations* embodies much of this parallax spirit by creating different kinds of models to explore questions about the English, German, and French texts under consideration. The computational question is not simply if there are similarities, but under what conditions are similarities observed? For instance, his analysis of plot combines vector space models built from words in context, type-token ratios of quantities of unique and total terms, and network representations of characters named in close context with one another (42–66). In his introduction, Piper is direct about modeling being "contingent world-making that recognizes the situatedness of the critic, aka the model creator, without it being entirely subjective" (12). Some of the tools embed iteration and multiplicity of model building into their design, like topic modeling, which outputs a result optimized for statistical likelihood. Yet, often the inner workings of such output are opaque, such that the attributes that contribute to it are lost to the scholar seeking information about meaning-making.

Here we return to the question of the axes in Figure 4.1. That graph represents the reduction into two-dimensional space of 100 dimensions of information about

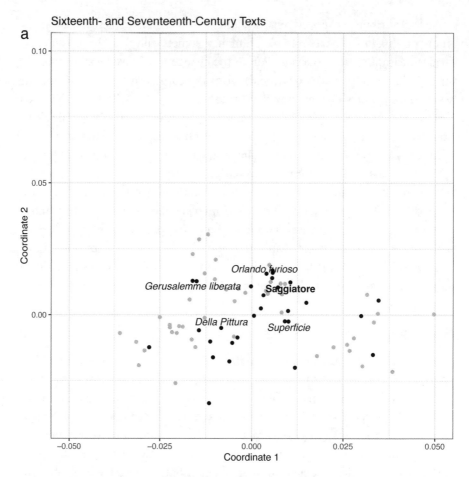

Figure 4.1. These plots use multidimensional scaling to represent the overall similarity of relative frequency of the 100 most frequent words (a common measure in stylometric analysis) in a corpus of seventy-five Italian texts published from 1532 to 1643. Labeled texts in both emphasize Galileo's letter-treatise on comets (bold), two poems shown in more detail in Figure 4.2 (*Orlando furioso* and *Gerusalemme liberata*), and two notable texts in Figure 4.1b (opposite): Lodovico Dolce's dialogue *Della Pittura*, for its greater proximity to Galileo, and the distance of the translation of Abu Bakr Muhammad Ibn 'Abd al-Bāqī al-Baghdadi's treatise on divisions of figures, *Superficie* (italics). Lines in Figure 4.1b indicate the change in position of the sixteenth-century texts in the two analyses.

most frequent words calculated as distance measurements for seventy-five texts. The graph is declarative, but without spaces for asking how it came to be and what that means for the texts it represents. Figure 4.2 provides a simplified example of how parallax can offer such transparency. The ideal output need not be visual, but it does make analysis more experiential, much like the astronomer-farmers walking through their forest. The x and y axes in Figure 4.2 could represent any perspective for analysis: types and tokens, distance from the object of interest in stylometric tests, likelihood of the presence of a topic, frequency of a character's name or

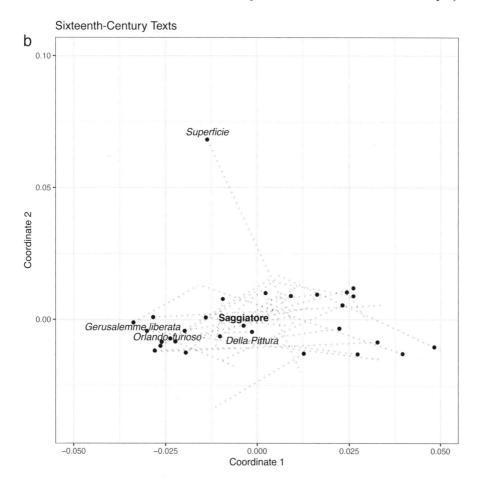

a character pair, or even the reduction to two dimensions of a matrix of quantitative attributes accumulated over iterations of analysis. Here, to keep things within the limits of this chapter, they represent the frequency of "e" (and) and "che" (that/which), two of the most frequent words in Italian texts during Galileo's period (also two of the reduced dimensions in Figure 4.1). Points are shaped by author: Galileo (triangles) and his favorite poet from a century prior (circles) along with a contemporary poet he loved to hate (squares). To anticipate the question of scale in the last section, the full text measurement is represented by a large shape surrounded by small shapes that represent each section of the respective texts.

It is even easier to see how the sections of Galileo's work participate differently in the overall relationships in the corpus when the relationships are animated instead of static.[3] As the attributes change, we experience the resonance (or not) of the texts with one another across analytical perspectives. The proximity or the spaces made evident by the visualization invite exploration. Similarly, Lisa Rhody's

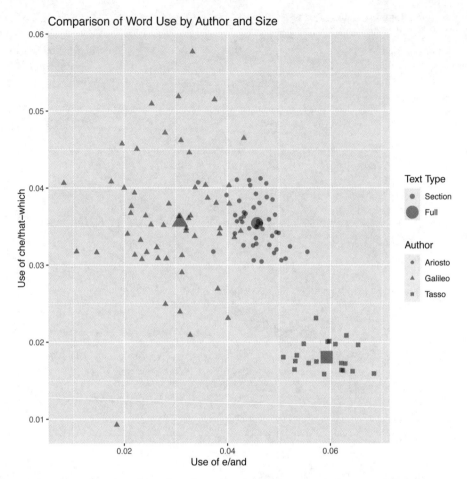

Figure 4.2. Representation of the relative frequency of use of the two most frequent words in the corpus used for Figure 4.1: *e/and* and *che/that-which*. Sections of Galileo's treatise on comets are shown as triangles, with a large triangle indicating the measure for the full text; two poems and their sections are also indicated: one that Galileo admired (overall closer to him in style, circles) and one that he critiqued (nearly consistently in the lower right corner of all plots, squares).

work on topic modeling figurative language highlights the effectiveness of exploring this interpretative space between the details of a text and the contextual understanding offered by a model. Importantly, I seek ways to identify the place of parts of expression within the whole; Rhody investigates how poetic language resists the model; and Algee-Hewitt pushes us to consider the moments "when the results of our analysis go awry," which Piper calls the "vulnerability" of texts (159–62). Fragments, resistance, and vulnerability could be extended easily to other forms of expression beyond the texts. Currently, the computational "third eye" can see these relationships, but it only reports an abstraction back to us.

Scale and Addressability

The massive addressability of humanist objects of study immediately challenges the stability implied by describing a genre or period from a collection of feature frequencies that represent only one scale of address. This final aspect of parallax asks us to consider what pieces of the text will be studied: the work in its entirety or segments? Declaring the ability of the object to simultaneously participate in different patterns connects parallax to polyrhythmic performance and analysis. These methods emphasize that aspects of the same expression can expand through time differently. Comparing those permutations through time to others (rather than the object's persistence through time) allows us to explore what Drucker called "interstices" ("Humanistic Theory," 92) and Rhody described as "rich deposits of hermeneutic possibility" in the space between what we study and its contexts.

For example, because the richness of literary analysis rests in an acceptance and exploration of the multiple simultaneous associations between texts of varying sizes, the literary scholar can take advantage of the computational ability to create conditions to observe these relationships. I find that using computational parallax for stylometric examination of most frequent words in a corpus of textual sections (the smaller points in Figure 4.2) creates space for a more nuanced interpretation than just which passages are most similar to Galileo's style. For shorter chapters in his treatise (approximately 500 words), the process reveals rhythmic similarities with other textual segments that have the same rhetorical goals (lengthy description). Yet, similar longer passages (approximately 1,000 words) share narrative devices with its cluster of documents (such as the episodic zigzag from Galileo's favorite epic poet). Full-text comparisons align the entire work with century-old prose more often than with his contemporaries. We are drawn to these similarities by what John Burrows called "tiny strokes" (268), not explicit sampling or marked, specialist vocabulary that keyword search or topic modeling would identify. Here, they point toward conventions of description, digression, and debate, not traditional genres.

Creating a workflow based on generating parallax and expressing results of varying analytical perspectives thus reduces the possibility of reconfirming interpretations shaped more by the conditions of scholarship than by the expressions of the texts. At the conclusion of her critique of text mining and gender, Laura Mandell gestures toward the value of parallax particularly regarding how some digital humanities research is structured, which risks reification and reconfirmation of categories and definitions that arise post hoc from critics rather than organically from the texts in their multiple contexts and conversations. Mandell, drawing on Donna Haraway, underlines the inordinate power of an observer for defining reality with one statistical result when computation should afford us opportunities for immersion in complexity (Mandell, 17). In chapter 6 in this volume, Katherine McDonough directs us to one solution for breaking out of the imposed or engrained categories of map attributes by using machine learning to look beyond geolocated points to patterns that change how a map can be analyzed, both saving time and possibly stepping away from some of the embedded violence and injustice that a map often represents.

Implications

Using a spatial framework like parallax for computation necessarily relies on understanding text as multidimensional and multicontextual. Interpretations rest not on reduction to a single quantification but aggregation of simultaneous measurements for comparison, contextualization, and evaluation. Expanded research will assess the extent to which this approach holds value for the study of image, sound, and the body. Next steps in computation for this definition of parallax would develop an interface to make more of the objects' dimensions available for experience and subsequent interpretation. The ARTFL project has anticipated some of these needs with the experimental reading environment for *The Intertextual Hub,* which allows for toggling between results of different reading tools for documents and corpora as a way to navigate their collection of texts. This need not be supported by a consortium like ARTFL, since the code exists in a shareable Jupyter notebook currently, but it will require collaboration across the spectra of programming and humanistic specialties to move to a more user-friendly phase with the ease and functionality of something like a Voyant Tools widget. Much like Galileo's farmers walking through an orchard rather than measuring it, the work to be done involves prioritizing experience over calculation. By using the recovered humanistic definition of parallax to guide computation, computation itself is no longer the goal, replaced by identifying as many possible perspectives on the forest as we care to explore in order to better understand the trees within them.

Notes

1. See chapter 15 in this volume.

2. RTL scholars have offered workshops at the Digital Humanities Summer Institutes in Victoria since 2018 and had been using #Right2Left, #RTL20, #RTL21, etc., to connect RTL speakers and DH researchers. The list multilingual-dh@lists.stanford.edu and the Github repository for Multilingual Digital Humanities (https://github.com/multilingual-dh) offer ways to connect with that community.

3. See animated graphic at https://www.bowdoin.edu/~chall/ParallaxAnimated.mov (also available as a gif).

Bibliography

Andrews, Richard. *Polyrhythmicity in Language, Music and Society: Complex Time Relations in the Arts, Humanities and Social Sciences.* Singapore: Springer, 2021.

ARTFL. "The Intertextual Hub. Search and Navigation across Digital Collections." Accessed July 30, 2021. https://intertextual-hub.org/.

Burrows, John. "'Delta': A Measure of Stylistic Difference and a Guide to Likely Authorship." *Literary and Linguistic Computing* 17, no. 3 (2002): 267–87.

Da, Nan Z. "The Computational Case against Computational Literary Studies." *Critical Inquiry* 45 (Spring 2019): 601–39.

Drucker, Johanna. "Humanities Approaches to Graphical Display." *DHQ: Digital Humanities Quarterly* 5, no. 1 (2011). http://www.digitalhumanities.org/dhq/vol/5/1/000091/000091.html.

Drucker, Johanna. "Humanistic Theory and Digital Scholarship." In *Debates in the Digital Humanities*, edited by Matthew K. Gold, 85–95. Minneapolis: University of Minnesota Press, 2012. https://dhdebates.gc.cuny.edu/read/untitled-88c11800-9446-469b-a3be-3fdb36bfbd1e/section/0b495250-97af-4046-91ff-98b6ea9f83c0#ch06.

Galilei, Galileo. "The Dialogue of Cecco di Ronchitti." In *Galileo against the Philosophers*, edited and translated by Stillman Drake, 33–53. Los Angeles: Zeitlin and Ver Brugge, 1976.

Klein, Lauren. *An Archive of Taste: Race and Eating in the Early United States.* Minneapolis: University of Minnesota Press, 2020.

Mandell, Laura. "Gender and Cultural Analytics: Finding or Making Stereotypes?" In *Debates in the Digital Humanities 2019,* edited by Matthew K. Gold and Lauren F. Klein, 3–26. Minneapolis: University of Minnesota Press, 2019. https://dhdebates.gc.cuny.edu/read/untitled-f2acf72c-a469-49d8-be35-67f9ac1e3a60/section/5d9c1b63-7b60-42dd-8cda-bde837f638f4#node-a34ec8b32594cb722950f75611f4038a278e7464.

Mueller, Paul R. "Textual Criticism and Early Modern Natural Philosophy: The Case of Marin Mersenne (1588–1648)." In *The Word and the World. Biblical Exegesis and Early Modern Science,* edited by Kevin Killeen and Peter J. Forshaw, 78–90. New York: Palgrave Macmillan, 2007.

Nichols, Stephen G. "The Anxiety of Irrelevance: Digital Humanities and Contemporary Critical Theory." *Poetica* 45, no. 1/2 (2013): 1–17.

Piper, Andrew. *enumerations.* Chicago: University of Chicago Press, 2018.

Rhody, Lisa. "Topic Modeling and Figurative Language." *Journal of Digital Humanities* 2, no. 1 (2012). http://journalofdigitalhumanities.org/2-1/topic-modeling-and-figurative-language-by-lisa-m-rhody/.

Ruecker, Stan, and Jennifer Roberts-Smith. "Experience Design for the Humanities: Activating Multiple Interpretations." In *Making Things and Drawing Boundaries,* edited by Jentery Sayers, 259–70. Minneapolis: University of Minnesota Press, 2017. https://doi.org/10.5749/j.ctt1pwt6wq.34.

Sample, Mark. "A Parallax Reading of Roethke's 'My Papa's Waltz.'" *samplereality.org,* May 31, 2017. https://www.samplereality.com/author/admin/page/2/.

Underwood, Ted. *Distant Horizons: Digital Evidence and Literary Change.* Chicago: University of Chicago Press, 2019.

Underwood, Ted. "Machine Learning and Human Perspective." *PMLA* 135, no. 1 (2020): 92–109.

Westman, Robert. *The Copernican Question.* Berkeley: University of California Press, 2011.

Whitelaw, Mitchell. "Generous Interfaces for Digital Cultural Collections." *DHQ: Digital Humanities Quarterly* 9, no. 1 (2015). http://www.digitalhumanities.org/dhq/vol/9/1/000205/000205.html.

Witmore, Michael. "Text: A Massively Addressable Object." In *Debates in the Digital Humanities,* edited by Matthew K. Gold. Minneapolis: University of Minnesota Press, 2012. https://dhdebates.gc.cuny.edu/read/untitled-88c11800-9446-469b-a3be-3fdb36bfbd1e/section/402e7e9a-359b-4b11-8386-a1b48e40425a.

PART I][Chapter 5

Manufacturing Visual Continuity
Generative Methods in the Digital Humanities

FABIAN OFFERT AND PETER BELL

The great promise of the computational humanities is a humanities scholarship on par with computer science, a deep exploration of state-of-the-art computational methods and their application to humanities questions. In this chapter, we argue that this technical focus requires a critical complement that becomes particularly obvious at the intersection of computer vision and machine learning in digital art history and digital visual studies—sometimes also referred to as the visual digital humanities (Münster and Terras). We suggest understanding "critical complement," in the original sense of critical theory (Horkheimer, "Traditionelle und Kritische Theorie"), as the necessity to fix a historical disjunction between theory and practice: while the computational humanities have caught up to the technical state of the art in computer science practically, the methodological reflection provided by the concepts of computer science has not been adopted in a productive manner. Hence, we propose to review the fundamental computational paradigms that currently define technical experimentation in digital art history and digital visual studies. In that way, our approach takes seriously, and specifies with regard to digital art history, Taylor Arnold and Lauren Tilton's call for collaboration with statistics in *Debates in the Digital Humanities 2019*; "the digital humanities should welcome statistics to the table, and this begins by better acknowledging the critical role of statistics in the field" (Arnold and Tilton, "New Data?"). Echoing Hannah Ringler in chapter 1 in this volume, we argue that not only do we need to consider "tools as interpretation and interpretation of tools as processes that need hermeneutics," but we should also reconsider both the theoretical and practical contributions of all disciplines involved.

Specifically, we propose that the statistical distinction between generative and discriminative approaches can not only inform the methodological discourse in digital art history and digital visual studies but also provide a starting point for the exploration of previously disregarded generative machine learning techniques. While computational literary studies and related subdisciplines of the digital humanities have already implicitly embraced generative methods, the visual digital humanities lack equivalent tools. Here, we propose to investigate generative adversarial networks (GANs) as a machine learning architecture of interest. Further, we suggest that the *manufactured continuity* that GANs provide through advanced techniques like latent space projection can guide our interpretation of an image corpus.

Studying Images with Machine Learning

Depending on the disciplinary perspective, the (digital) study of (digital) images, with the help of machine learning, is either a rather recent development or can be traced back to the very beginnings of computing: (connectionist) machine learning, after all, started as computer vision (e.g., Papert, "The Summer Vision Project"). At the same time, it is only recently that high-level machine learning–based tools and toolkits for digital art history, like the Distant Viewing Toolkit (Arnold and Tilton), PixPlot (Duhaime), imagegraph.cc (Impett), or imgs.ai (Offert and Bell) have started to emerge, due to the increasing availability of computational resources, software libraries, technical competence, and code availability in the digital humanities. Within the relatively new field of machine learning–based digital art history and digital visual studies, two major and interconnected technical directions can be identified: the use of machine learning for image retrieval and the use of machine learning for image classification. There, the focus lies on the identification of objects (Crowley and Zisserman, "The State of the Art"), poses (Bell and Impett, "The Choreography of the Annunciation through a Computational Eye"), styles, and artists (Elgammal et al., "The Shape of Art History in the Eyes of the Machine"). A similar development can be seen in the study of moving images in digital film studies and the digital humanities (DH) for A/V.[1]

As Lev Manovich observes in *Cultural Analytics*, fields like digital art history and digital visual studies examine cultural data "at scale": entire oeuvres, periods, or collections become objects of investigation. Image retrieval and image classification techniques serve to answer two different sets of questions that result from this increased scale. Image retrieval deals with questions of search: How can singular images be found within large-scale datasets without additional identifying information (i.e., metadata)? Machine learning–based solutions to retrieval problems usually involve image embeddings in combination with clustering and dimensionality reduction algorithms. Image classification, on the other hand, implies the automated labeling of images—for instance, with regard to traditional art-historical categories like provenance. Machine learning–based solutions to image classification problems often use state-of-the-art deep convolutional neural networks and high-quality training and test corpora. Importantly, both image retrieval and classification could be described as "forward" problems: an image serves as the input to a machine learning pipeline that outputs some high-level descriptor. The conceptual opposite here is a generative process, the production of images from high-level descriptors. However, while generative methods have seen a surge of popularity in artistic (Offert, "The Past, Present, and Future of AI Art") and scientific (Offert, "Latent Deep Space") contexts, they seem to be more or less absent from computational humanities work.

It is important to keep in mind, however, that these distinctions are purely application-based. On a theoretical level, the rules of statistics, even if they are applied to web-scale corpora of complex, high-dimensional data, stand as unifying principles behind all machine learning approaches. While this is obvious to computer science practitioners, it is often disregarded when machine learning is discussed in the humanities context, mirroring an often-diagnosed epistemological split between computer scientists and engineers and digital humanities scholars (Mercuriali, "Digital Art History and the Computational Imagination"). We argue that, somewhat counterintuitively, statistical notions offer an alternative critical perspective on machine learning in the humanities context. We suggest that the foundational statistical distinction between discriminative and generative approaches (Ng and Jordan) can be used to guide the further development of the computational humanities.

Discriminative versus Generative Approaches

The digital humanities have often been broadly criticized for the mere use of quantitative methods, as eloquently summarized in Ted Underwood's blog post, "It Looks like You're Writing an Argument against Data in Literary Study . . ." While some of these critiques from the early days of the field still resonate, and general critiques of quantitative methods occasionally reappear with force, as in Claire Bishop's critique of digital art history, generally, a consensus has grown that a blanket rejection has no grounding in the reality of digital humanities work. Instead, the focus of critique has shifted to the epistemological implications of exploratory data analysis.

One of the most powerful critiques that follows this trajectory is Nan Z. Da's article, "The Computational Case against Computational Literary Studies." Da writes that "all the things that appear in [computational literary studies]—network analysis, digital mapping, linear and nonlinear regressions, topic modeling, topology, entropy—are just fancier ways of talking about word frequency changes" (607). Based on a formal distinction between discriminative and generative methods, however, we can see that some of these methods are not the same.

To distinguish between two kinds of objects—say, apples and oranges—based on a dataset of labeled images of both, we can imagine two possible strategies of classification. We can design a model that learns the *most salient difference between apples and oranges* from the dataset. A good candidate for a distinctive visual feature would be color: apples are usually red; oranges are usually orange. The model then uses these most salient features to classify new, unseen samples. This is the discriminative approach. The generative approach, however, learns the *complete distribution of visual features for both apples and oranges.* Apples come in different shades of red, yellow, and green; oranges come in different shades of orange. The model then classifies new, unseen samples by comparing their visual feature distribution to the visual feature distribution for apples and the visual feature distribution for oranges. The discriminative approach attempts to model a decision boundary *between classes* (it literally learns "where to draw the line" between apples and oranges), while the generative approach attempts to model the actual distribution *of each class.* The generative approach essentially asks: What is the most likely *source* of the *signal* we are seeing, while the discriminative approach simply looks for a way to distinguish one signal from the other and does not take the source into account.

In fact, linear regression and topic modeling fall on opposite ends of the spectrum between discriminative and generative approaches, and the prevalence of latent Dirichlet allocation (LDA), also known as (one variation of) topic modeling, in computational literary studies and in the digital humanities in general, points to an even stronger claim: the digital humanities "intuitively" choose generative over discriminative approaches because they are more aligned to humanities data.

Why do the digital humanities gravitate toward generative approaches? Because generative approaches mitigate, at least in part, the alienation and the general inadequacy of quantitative methods vis-à-vis cultural artifacts. Quantitative methods, obviously, can never fully represent cultural artifacts. Precisely, both the sampling of cultural artifacts into data and the modeling of this data are reductive. In the domain of modeling, however, generative approaches stay as close to the material as possible, while discriminative approaches essentially "ignore" the material for the sake of classification. In other words, generative approaches, while not being able to mitigate the problems introduced by sampling, can mitigate the problems introduced by modeling within the realm of what can be modeled. Generative approaches will always allow for multiple interpretations to coexist, while discriminative approaches provide one, and only one, interpretation in the form of a classification decision.

Regardless, many of the problems discussed in Da's article stand with or without generative machine learning. Shoddy hypothesis building or the lack thereof, intentional or unintentional over- or misinterpretation of the empirical evidence quantitative methods can offer, or too-broad applications of narrow technical concepts are problematic irrespective of the kind of model involved. Hence, a focus on generative approaches does not "solve" or even explicitly address these issues. Generative approaches do not magically produce a "self-reflexive account of what the model has sought to measure and the limitations of its ability to produce such a measurement," as Richard Jean So writes ("All Models Are Wrong"). On the contrary, generative methods tend to actually and implicitly encourage the problematic "exploratory" approach.[2] This became a central argument in the discussion following Da's article (Underwood, "Critical Response II"; Da, "Critical Response III").

Moreover, famously, the existence of "raw data" is an illusion (Gitelman, *Raw Data Is an Oxymoron*; Latour, *Science in Action*; Dobson, *Critical Digital Humanities*), and the existence of "neutral algorithms" even more so (Benjamin, *Race after Technology*; Buolamwini and Gebru, "Gender Shades"). Thus, if we propose that generative methods "stay as close to the material as possible," we do not imply the absence of subjective guidance through the design or selection of algorithms and datasets. Indeed, it is not only dataset bias that shapes machine learning models, but inductive biases induced by pragmatic architectural decisions often further entangle subjective and machinic perspectives. In computer vision in particular, specific models will "see" things in their own idiosyncratic ways (Offert and Bell, "Perceptual Bias"; Geirhos et al., "Shortcut Learning in Deep Neural Networks").

What a critical distinction between generative and discriminative approaches offers, regardless, is a prospective path through current and future experimental work in computer science, where the digital humanities, we argue, need to critically consider the distinction between generative and discriminative methods in the evaluation of new, experimental tools and methods—all while keeping in mind that the maximum benefit of all machine learning models is a "useful-wrong" model in the sense of that George Box uses the term ("Robustness in the Strategy of Scientific Model Building")—that is, a model that stays "reasonably" close to the material.

Generative Adversarial Networks

As Leonardo Impett has pointed out in "Open Problems in Computer Vision," the computer vision problems that art history is concerned with are almost exclusively search-related—that is, they are classification problems. What if digital art history would start focusing on generative methods instead? Would a closer relation to the material also establish itself in the domain of images?

Generative methods are already implicitly employed in the neural network–based clustering of images, which has become increasingly more popular in digital art history (Wevers and Smits, "The Visual Digital Turn"). When embeddings are used, a learned subsystem of a classifier is repurposed exactly for its generative properties, which is also why recent research (Graving and Couzing, "VAE-SNE") suggests building explicitly generative systems for the specific purpose of clustering. Even more recently, better contrastive learning techniques like CLIP (Radford et al., "Learning Transferable Visual Models from Natural Language Supervision") have produced embeddings of almost universal applicability, as training corpora are continuously extended and now include large parts of the internet.[3] We argue that beyond these *implicitly* useful applications, *explicitly* generative methods can become for the visual domain what LDA became for the text domain: a universal instrument for the guided, unsupervised exploration of large-scale corpora.

Generative adversarial networks, first introduced by Ian Goodfellow and colleagues ("Generative Adversarial Nets"), leverage game theory to model the probability distribution of a corpus by means of a minimax game between two deep convolutional neural networks. Effectively, generative adversarial networks define a noise distribution p_z that is mapped to data space via $G(z; \theta g)$, where G is a "generator," an "inverted" convolutional neural network with parameters θg that "expands" an input variable into an image, rather than "compressing" an image into a classification probability. G is trained in conjunction with a "discriminator," which is a second deep convolutional neural network $D(z; \theta d)$ that outputs a single scalar. $D(x)$ represents the probability that x came from the data rather than G. Note that the whole system, not just the "generator," realizes the generative approach, as the whole system is needed to model $p(x|y = 0)$. Also note that the system effectively learns a compression: a high-dimensional data space with dimensions $> z$ is compressed to be reproducible from a data space with dimensions z. This means that details will always be lost, a detail that we should keep in mind.

The original article by Goodfellow demonstrates the potential of generative adversarial networks to synthesize images in particular by synthesizing new handwritten digits from the MNIST dataset. The MNIST dataset, however, has a resolution of 28 × 28 pixels (i.e., several orders of magnitude below standard photo resolutions). Scaling up the approach proved difficult, and while a lot of effort was made to go beyond marginal resolutions, progress was slow (for machine learning) until very recently, when StyleGAN (Karras, Laine, and Aila, "A Style-Based Generator Architecture"), a generative adversarial network that implemented several significant optimization tricks to mitigate some of the limitations of generative adversarial networks, was introduced. Current-generation models like StyleGAN2 (Karras et al., "Analyzing and Improving the Image Quality of StyleGAN"), which present another improvement over the original StyleGAN, are able to produce extremely realistic samples from large image corpora. Finally, in 2021, projects like OpenAI's DALL-E (Ramesh et al., "Zero-Shot Text-to-Image Generation") have shown the promise of architectures like deep variational autoencoders to potentially surpass GANs in the generation of realistic images.

Regardless of the concrete architecture, however, generative samples, to the humanist, feel uncanny. GANs obviously learn something (maybe everything?) about a corpus, and GAN samples "tick all the boxes" at the first glance. At the same time, GANs seem almost useless. What knowledge is there to gain from a model that essentially learns to re-create approximations to what exists and nothing *about* what exists? This questionable utility is amplified by necessary imperfections, on the one hand—after all, GANs learn a compression of an image corpus—and by a fundamental artificial, nonhuman quality, on the other. At least since the ancient Greeks, when Aristippus, on seeing geometric drawings in the sand, famously exclaimed, "Let us be of good cheer, for I see the traces of man," image-making has been understood as an exclusively human faculty—homo pictor as the synthesis of homo sapiens and homo faber (Jonas, "Homo Pictor").

Interestingly, for a long time and despite impressive early results, the utility of generative adversarial networks was not entirely clear in the computer science community either. And while today there are obvious applications in digital image processing (inpainting, superresolution, image-to-image translation, style transfer) and manipulation (deep fakes), the epistemological qualities of GANs—that is, their role in scientific (and, we argue, humanist) processes of discovery—are still not fully explored. And, in fact, such an exploration would need to start not from questions of optimization or architecture search but from the image artifacts themselves; we would need a way to properly study, analyze, and interpret images produced by generative methods. In the following, we sketch what we see as the inherent potential and limitations of such an approach.

Latent Spaces as Continuous Image Spaces

We commonly assume that works of art relate to specific sociohistorical contexts. Their aesthetic autonomy is an effect of neither fully taking in, nor completely rejecting, this sociohistorical context. According to Theodor W. Adorno (*Ästhetik*), works of art act as a "social antithesis to society" (19), and "art's double character as both autonomous and fait social is incessantly reproduced on the level of its autonomy" (16). Different approaches to interpretation propose different ways of navigating this dialectic relationship. What, then, is the sociohistorical context of a latent space image, of an image that has never existed in the real world?

Importantly, any latent space image is entirely determined by the corpus of images used to train the GAN that produced the latent space. In a sense, the sociohistorical context of a latent space image is thus the combined sociohistorical context of the training corpus. But while this understanding can be potentially productive for a very limited number of cases—those in which the training corpus is extremely homogeneous—it will usually not take us very far, particularly in the case of iconographic corpora that intentionally span multiple sociohistorical contexts.

Nevertheless, GAN latent spaces are imaginary spaces. They are reconstructions of the defining features of a corpus, and exploring such spaces is not the same thing as exploring the corpus itself. This imaginary quality, however, which is deeply problematic in any other application of generative methods (Offert, "Latent Deep Space"), can precisely be of use in the digital humanities context. Here, GAN samples are not mistaken for valid information generated from nothing, as in so many recent examples in the sciences, but can be understood as an additional means to ask questions about the information we do have about the corpus at hand. GAN latent spaces are, for better or worse, "filled to the brink" with images. This also means that for each given sample, there exist millions of other samples that look almost identical to this sample, except for tiny details. It also means that, between each two samples, we can find theoretically infinite "intermediate" samples—hybrid images that combine aspects of both of the samples between which they are positioned.

Digital humanities corpora, on the other hand, visual or otherwise, always exist as discrete collections of samples (and often as fragmented collections of samples as well, because many historical artifacts are lost). We argue that GAN images can reintroduce a certain *manufactured continuity* to such a discrete corpus, which allows study of the discreteness of the corpus itself. By reintroducing continuity to a corpus of discrete images, we are forced to precisely quantify the semantic thresholds that support its discreteness. Discrete concepts are transformed into continuous variables. What, exactly, defines a certain iconography? How far in any direction (in the literal sense of latent space hyper-directions) can we veer off until an image that is clearly recognizable as belonging to a certain iconographic tradition stops being recognizable as such? A synthetic grammar of art emerges that is not historical like Alois Riegl's *Historical Grammar of the Visual Arts,* but rather is diachronic and multimodal. In a sense, if generative approaches automatically stay close to the material, using GANs would mean staying closer to the material *than is actually possible* by amending it.

Latent Space Projection

What this approach would require, however, is finding and operationalizing meaningful relations between real and latent space images. If we want to use latent space images as intermediate images, we need to reconnect them to the space of real images, or vice versa. And if we understand the sociohistorical context of an image as the set of those circumstances that determine, to a certain degree, both its existence and its interpretation, then the space of real images, the training corpus, becomes that sociohistorical context for these GAN images.

We propose to operationalize this "reconnection" as latent space projection. Latent space projection is an optimization technique that uses gradient ascent, similar to the way it is used in feature visualization, to optimize an input with respect to certain criteria. In the case of GANs, a latent code is optimized with respect to the perceptual similarity (Zhang et al., "The Unreasonable Effectiveness of Deep Features as a Perceptual Metric") between the generated GAN image and the image that is being projected into the latent space. With latent space projection, thus, we can identify the latent *double* of a real image: the point in latent space, and its associated image, that comes closest to, but will never exactly match, a real image (Figure 5.1).

If we evaluate this idea by close-reading concrete interpolations of projected images, we immediately see how it can indeed produce insights about the corpus at large. We demonstrate this by exploring a latent space generated by a StyleGAN2-ADA network (Karras et al., "Training Generative Adversarial Networks with Limited Data") trained for 2,000 "kimg" (thousands of real images shown to the discriminator) on approximately 1,200 derivatives and reproductions of four antique statues scraped from multiple art-historical image archives: *Laocoon Group, Boy with Thorn, Farnese Hercules,* and *Apollo Belvedere.* Starting from two projected images and their respective latent space points (using the projection algorithm supplied with the StyleGAN2-ada PyTorch reference implementation), we generate

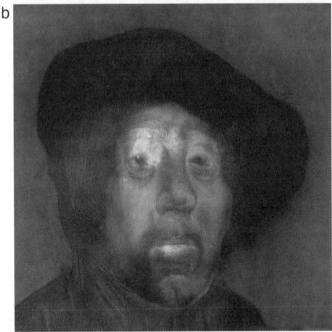

Figure 5.1. Central section of Rembrandt's *Self Portrait* (1660) and a latent space double after 5000 projection iterations (dataset: https://github.com/NVlabs/metfaces-dataset; model: https://nvlabs-fi-cdn.nvidia.com/stylegan2-ada-pytorch/pretrained/metfaces.pkl.) The self-portrait by Rembrandt (5.1a), as well as historically adjacent portraits, are likely part of the Met Faces model, but because of the compression learned by the GAN, the latent space double can only ever be an approximation. Importantly, in the GAN latent space, an approximation (5.1b) still produces a legible image, as its solution space is a "dense" solution space that always provides *a* result (Offert, "Latent Deep Space"). Public domain/CC-BY-SA.

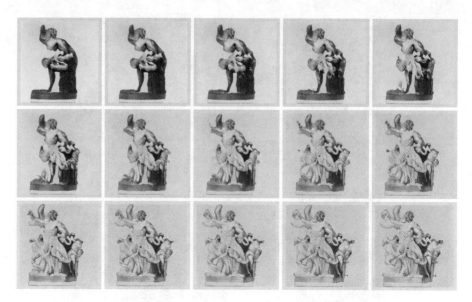

Figure 5.2. Interpolation between the latent space double of a *Boy with Thorn* derivative and a *Laocoon Group* derivative. Public domain/CC-BY-SA.

interpolations by sampling intermediate points at regular intervals with a custom-built tool.[4] Figure 5.2 shows such an interpolation, between a projection of the *Boy with Thorn* and a projection of the *Laocoon Group*. Semantically relevant in this example is what could be described as the repurposing of body parts. The boy's *hat*, in the first image, becomes Laocoon's *head* in the last image. Likewise, the boy's head in the first image becomes Laocoon's upper body in the last image. In Figure 5.3, which interpolates between the latent double of a *Laocoon Group* drawing and the latent space equivalent of an *Apollo Belvedere* black-and-white photograph, we see a similar repurposing of body parts. On the syntactic level, we see that, in Figure 5.2, the gold color of the statue's head becomes the yellowed paper in the Laocoon drawing. (The gold color can be seen in the ebook and Manifold editions of this chapter.) Likewise, in Figure 5.3, we see an increased "shading" in the drawing evolve into a three-dimensional representation in the latent space photograph.

The GAN, as apparent from these examples, has picked up on two significant aspects of the corpus. First, it has internalized the distribution of color in the corpus, which has a significant bias toward grayscale (due to the oversized presence of drawings and etchings) and yellow/gold (due to its presence on many derivatives of the *Boy with Thorn* and the paper color of many drawings and etchings). We can validate this by plotting the real images in the corpus using a semantic clustering tool developed by the authors.[5] Initially, clustering was done according to pretrained CLIP (contrastive language-image pretraining) embeddings, then according to raw color data (Figures 5.4 and 5.5, available in the ebook and Manifold editions of this chapter). Second, it has learned the importance of a central human

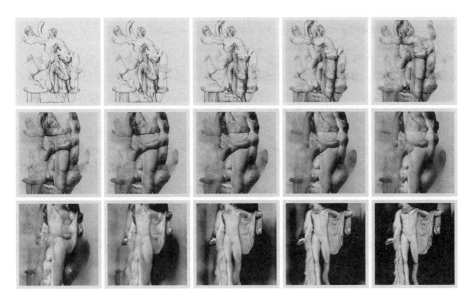

Figure 5.3. *Laocoon Group* derivative and *Apollo Belvedere* derivative interpolation. Public domain/CC-BY-SA.

figure, which explains the repurposing of body parts. Both of these conclusions, obviously, can be derived from the corpus itself or from more "traditional" clustering methods. The GAN latent space, however, gives us the unique opportunity of seeing these important traits of the corpus "in action": as actual image properties, with clear visual implications. A morphology of techniques and materials emerges. The delicate and unstable Laocoon drawing is literally set into stone. Visualizing its artificial transition, then, allows us to grasp, and visualize for ourselves, the material relations between objects in the corpus.

It is important to note that, much like the technical method we are studying here, the conclusions drawn are speculative in nature: future research and further collaboration with computer scientists will have to show if GANs and similar methods can indeed be viable tools of digital art history and digital visual studies, given the unavoidable heterogeneity of cultural image corpora, which cannot be neatly aligned like the celebrity faces we see so often in GAN papers, neither visually nor historically. Despite these obvious limitations, however, generative methods could provide us with more hands-on approaches to explore image corpora, allowing us to arrange and rearrange an image corpus beyond the permutations allowed by its original elements. Mirroring Bruno Latour's call to examine science "in action" to better understand the historical formation of scientific discoveries, the manufacturing of visual continuity would force visual relations to emerge that are usually hidden in the unbridgeable gaps between historically separate images. The speculative nature of generative methods would thus, paradoxically, provide a glimpse into a more empirical future of digital art history and digital visual studies.

Postscript: Visual Continuity in the Age of Multimodal Models

The last major revision of this chapter was submitted at the end of 2021. It is our conviction that its main argument—generative models can teach us something about the discreteness of both image corpora and image objects—still stands three years later. And yet, everything has changed. The generative models of today are not the generative models of this text: GANs, to the most part, have been succeeded by so-called multimodal models that enable the user to generate images from descriptive prompts. Multimodal models move away from the game-theoretic structure of GANs and take inspiration from natural language processing by adapting the so-called transformer architecture (Vaswani et al., "Attention Is All You Need") to the visual domain.

The transition from one to the other, historically, began in late 2021 and early 2022, when Katherine Crowson published a series of CoLab notebooks exploring ways to use CLIP (Radford et al., "Learning Transferable Visual Models") to guide GAN-based image generation.[6] CLIP learns from pairs of images and descriptive captions. In practice, this means that CLIP's internal representational logic is informed by both visual and linguistic relations: related visual properties exist in the CLIP latent space, and vice versa, for each "word."[7] This approach was almost immediately taken up and refined by OpenAI, eventually leading to the publication of the DALL-E 2 model in April 2022 (Ramesh et al., "Hierarchical Text-Conditional Image Generation with CLIP Latents").

Compared to GANs, multimodal models—like DALL-E 2 or Stable Diffusion (Rombach et al., "High-Resolution Image Synthesis with Latent Diffusion Models")—afford an entirely different approach to latent space navigation. In GANs, navigation is necessarily geometric. There exists no interface that would facilitate the discovery of images other than latent space itself. To move from one image to the next, one has to literally traverse latent space on one or multiple axes. In multimodal models, on the other hand, navigation is guided by a discrete symbolic system—natural language.

This also implies that the strategic exploration of latent space becomes more and less intuitive at the same time. More intuitive because specific visual ideas are easier to "get to." As Hannes Bajohr has argued, prompts could be understood as a kind of "operative ekphrasis." A whole terminology of "visual words," including references to existing visual properties ("in the style of") enables the user of a multimodal model to navigate latent space without knowing anything about its topology. But also it is less intuitive because, once a visual idea is realized, its immediate neighbors are difficult to address. Other than in the geometric navigation afforded by GANs, where we can easily move "a tiny bit to the right," the minimum latent space "step size" in multimodal models is that of discrete tokens. What we describe as a potential benefit of GAN latent space exploration above—to explore the in-between spaces of discrete corpora made continuous—thus seems out of reach for multimodal models.

At the same time, some new experimental methods promise to restore the kind of fine-grained control inherent in geometric approaches to latent space navigation. An architecture called ControlNet (Zhang and Agrawala, "Adding Conditional Control to Text-to-Image Diffusion Models"), for instance, reintroduces "classic" computer vision techniques as guiding principles for multimodal generative models. Techniques like edge detection, pose detection, and image segmentation allow the user to reach those parts of latent space that lie between tokens, where the generated image is just different enough to be considered "a different image" but not different enough to warrant a change in any high-level description. Even in the age of multimodal models, in other words, visual continuity continues to be a concept of interest—and thus should continue to be a field of experimentation in the computational humanities as well.

Notes

1. See, for instance, the two special issues of *DHQ: Digital Humanities Quarterly* on "Film and Video Analysis in the Digital Humanities" (ed. Manuel Burghardt et al.) and "AudioVisual Data in DH" (ed. Taylor Arnold et al.).

2. One could argue that this is an effect of the reduced interpretability of generative methods.

3. Approaches like CLIP and, to a lesser degree (at least for the moment), vision transformers, also indicate an increasing entanglement of language and vision in machine learning that promise to have a significant impact on the use of machine learning in the digital humanities.

4. Available at https://github.com/zentralwerkstatt/lit-ada.

5. Available at https://github.com/zentralwerkstatt/just-the-clusters.

6. For a more extensive overview of the transition from GANs to multimodal models, see Offert, "KI-Kunst als Skulptur."

7. In practice, the transformer architecture operates on "tokens," which can be words but also "subwords" (i.e., suffixes, prefixes, or other partials).

Bibliography

Adorno, Theodor W. *Ästhetik*. Edited by Eberhard Ortland. Vol. IV-3. Nachgelassene Schriften. Frankfurt am Main: Suhrkamp, 2009.

Arnold, Taylor, and Lauren Tilton. "Distant Viewing: Analyzing Large Visual Corpora." *Digital Scholarship in the Humanities* 34, supp. 1 (2019): i3–i16.

Arnold, Taylor, and Lauren Tilton. "New Data? The Role of Statistics in DH." *Debates in the Digital Humanities 2019,* edited by Matthew K. Gold and Lauren F. Klein. Minneapolis: University of Minnesota Press, 2019.

Bajohr, Hannes. "Operative Ekphrasis: Multimodal AI and the Text-Image Distinction." Lecture given at University of California, Berkeley, January 23, 2023.

Bell, Peter, and Leonardo Impett. "The Choreography of the Annunciation through a Computational Eye." *Revue Histoire de l'art. Les humanités numériques: de nouveaux récits en histoire de l'art?* 87 (2021): 61–76.

Benjamin, Ruha. *Race after Technology: Abolitionist Tools for the New Jim Code*. New York: John Wiley, 2019.

Bishop, Claire. "Against Digital Art History." *International Journal for Digital Art History* 3 (2018).

Box, George E. P. "Robustness in the Strategy of Scientific Model Building." *In Robustness in Statistics*, edited by Robert L. Launer and Graham N. Wilkinson, 201–36. New York: Academic Press, 1979.

Buolamwini, Joy, and Timnit Gebru. "Gender Shades: Intersectional Accuracy Disparities in Commercial Gender Classification." *Proceedings of Machine Learning Research* 81, no. 1–15 (2018): 77–91.

Crowley, E. J., and Andrew Zisserman. "The State of the Art: Object Retrieval in Paintings Using Discriminative Regions," 1–12. British Machine Vision Association, 2014.

Da, Nan Z. "The Computational Case against Computational Literary Studies." *Critical Inquiry* 45, no. 3 (2019): 601–39.

Da, Nan Z. "Critical Response III. On EDA, Complexity, and Redundancy: A Response to Underwood and Weatherby." *Critical Inquiry* 46, no. 4 (2020): 913–24.

Dobson, James E. *Critical Digital Humanities: The Search for a Methodology*. Champaign: University of Illinois Press, 2019.

Elgammal, Ahmed, Bingchen Liu, Diana Kim, Mohamed Elhoseiny, and Marian Mazzone. "The Shape of Art History in the Eyes of the Machine." *Proceedings of the AAAI Conference on Artificial Intelligence* 32, no. 1 (2018).

Geirhos, Robert, Jörn-Henrik Jacobsen, Claudio Michaelis, Richard Zemel, Wieland Brendel, Matthias Bethge, and Felix A. Wichmann. "Shortcut Learning in Deep Neural Networks." *ArXiv:2004.07780 [Cs, q-Bio]* (May 2020). https://arxiv.org/abs/2004.07780.

Gitelman, Lisa. *Raw Data Is an Oxymoron*. Cambridge, Mass.: MIT Press, 2013.

Goodfellow, Ian, Jean Pouget-Abadie, Mehdi Mirza, Bing Xu, David Warde-Farley, Sherjil Ozair, Aaron Courville, and Yoshua Bengio. "Generative Adversarial Nets." In *Advances in Neural Information Processing Systems*, 2672–80. 2014.

Graving, Jacob M., and Iain D. Couzing. "VAE-SNE: A Deep Generative Model for Simultaneous Dimensionality Reduction and Clustering." *BioRxiv Preprint* (2020).

Horkheimer, Max. "Traditionelle und Kritische Theorie." *Zeitschrift für Sozialforschung* 6, no. 2 (1937): 245–94.

Impett, Leonardo. "Open Problems in Computer Vision." Friedrich Alexander University Erlangen-Nuremberg. YouTube Video, 24:54, March 2020. https://www.youtube.com/watch?v=zsQKFxqqTto.

Jonas, Hans. "Homo Pictor. Von der Freiheit des Bildens." In *Organismus und Freiheit. Ansätze zu einer philosophischen Biologie*, 226–57. Göttingen: Vandenhoeck & Ruprecht, 1973.

Karras, Tero, Miika Aittala, Janne Hellsten, Samuli Laine, Jaakko Lehtinen, and Timo Aila. "Training Generative Adversarial Networks with Limited Data." *ArXiv:2006.06676* (2020).

Karras, Tero, Samuli Laine, and Timo Aila. "A Style-Based Generator Architecture for Generative Adversarial Networks." *ArXiv:1812.04948* (2018).

Karras, Tero, Samuli Laine, Miika Aittala, Janne Hellsten, Jaakko Lehtinen, and Timo Aila. "Analyzing and Improving the Image Quality of StyleGAN." *ArXiv:1912.04958* (2019).

Latour, Bruno. "Circulating Reference: Sampling the Soil in the Amazon Forest." In *Pandora's Hope: Essays on the Reality of Science Studies,* 24–79. Cambridge, Mass.: Harvard University Press, 1999.

Latour, Bruno. *Science in Action: How to Follow Scientists and Engineers through Society.* Cambridge, Mass.: Harvard University Press, 1987.

Manovich, Lev. *Cultural Analytics.* Cambridge, Mass.: MIT Press, 2020.

Mercuriali, Giacomo. "Digital Art History and the Computational Imagination." *International Journal for Digital Art History* 3 (2018): 141.

Münster, Sander, and Melissa Terras. "The Visual Side of Digital Humanities: A Survey on Topics, Researchers, and Epistemic Cultures." *Digital Scholarship in the Humanities* 35, no. 2 (2020): 366–89.

Ng, Andrew, and Michael Jordan. "On Discriminative vs. Generative Classifiers: A Comparison of Logistic Regression and Naive Bayes." *Advances in Neural Information Processing Systems* 14 (2001).

Offert, Fabian. "KI-Kunst als Skulptur." In *KI-Realitäten. Modelle, Praktiken und Topologien des Maschinellen Lernens,* edited by Richard Groß and Rita Jordan. Transcript, 2023.

Offert, Fabian. "Latent Deep Space: GANs in the Sciences." *Media + Environment* (2021).

Offert, Fabian. "The Past, Present, and Future of AI Art." *The Gradient* (June 2019). https://thegradient.pub/the-past-present-and-future-of-ai-art/.

Offert, Fabian, and Peter Bell. "Perceptual Bias and Technical Metapictures: Critical Machine Vision as a Humanities Challenge." *AI & Society* (2020). https://link.springer.com/article/10.1007/s00146-020-01058-z.

Papert, Seymour. "The Summer Vision Project." MIT, 1966. https://dspace.mit.edu/handle/1721.1/6125.

Radford, Alec, Jong Wook Kim, Chris Hallacy, Aditya Ramesh, Gabriel Goh, Sandhini Agarwal, Girish Sastry, et al. "Learning Transferable Visual Models from Natural Language Supervision." *Image* 2 (2021): T2.

Ramesh, Aditya, Prafulla Dhariwal, Alex Nichol, Casey Chu, and Mark Chen. "Hierarchical Text-Conditional Image Generation with CLIP Latents." *ArXiv:2204.06125* (2022).

Ramesh, Aditya, Mikhail Pavlov, Gabriel Goh, Scott Gray, Chelsea Voss, Alec Radford, Mark Chen, and Ilya Sutskever. "Zero-Shot Text-to-Image Generation." *ArXiv:2102.12092* (2021).

Riegl, Alois. *Historical Grammar of the Visual Arts.* New York: Zone Books, 2004.

Rombach, Robin, Andreas Blattmann, Dominik Lorenz, Patrick Esser, and Björn Ommer. "High-Resolution Image Synthesis with Latent Diffusion Models." In *Conference on Computer Vision and Pattern Recognition (CVPR)*, 10674–85. 2022.

So, Richard Jean. "All Models Are Wrong." *PMLA* 132, no. 3 (2017): 668–73.

Underwood, Ted. "Critical Response II: The Theoretical Divide Driving Debates about Computation." *Critical Inquiry* 46, no. 4 (2020): 900–912.

Underwood, Ted. "It Looks like You're Writing an Argument against Data in Literary Study . . ." *The Stone and the Shell* (blog), September 21, 2017. https://tedunderwood.com/2017/09/21/it-looks-like-youre-writing-an-argument-against-data-in-literary-study/.

Vaswani, Ashish, Noam Shazeer, Niki Parmar, Jakob Uszkoreit, Llion Jones, Aidan N. Gomez, Łukasz Kaiser, and Illia Polosukhin. "Attention Is All You Need." *Advances in Neural Information Processing Systems* 30 (2017).

Wevers, Melvin, and Thomas Smits. "The Visual Digital Turn: Using Neural Networks to Study Historical Images." *Digital Scholarship in the Humanities* 35, no. 1 (2020): 194–207.

Zhang, Lvmin, and Maneesh Agrawala. "Adding Conditional Control to Text-to-Image Diffusion Models." *ArXiv:2112.10752* (2023).

Zhang, Richard, Phillip Isola, Alexei A. Efros, Eli Shechtman, and Oliver Wang. "The Unreasonable Effectiveness of Deep Features as a Perceptual Metric." In *Proceedings of the IEEE Conference on Computer Vision and Pattern Recognition*, 586–95. 2018.

PART I][Chapter 6

Maps as Data

KATHERINE MCDONOUGH

What if historians could change the way we interact with maps? Though it became common to mechanically reproduce maps in the late eighteenth century, it has remained uncommon to examine them in large numbers. As with a large set of books, it is rare to work with thousands of maps since it can be difficult to examine them simultaneously. In fact, maps are particularly challenging because they can be so large. It is hard to fit more than a dozen small maps on the largest tables in map libraries. Beyond table size, other material- and preservation-related constraints come into play. Like books, maps bound in a volume can only be consulted page by page, and very delicate maps sometimes cannot be requested at all. Using maps in small numbers therefore became standard practice in the last 200 years. This is relevant here because the way we access historical documents is related to the kinds of questions we ask and the ways we answer them.

Because of those constraints, historians and other humanists tend to ask questions that require treating maps as if they were books: sequentially, rather than in sets. Many historians continue to think of maps as individual illustrations of past landscapes or, at best, as "texts" to be "read" one by one or in manageably sized sets (Edney, *Cartography*). Historians of maps and mapping practices, who often conduct studies of hundreds of maps, tend to be dedicated to understanding maps as cultural objects (for example, Withers, "On Trial").[1] Such narratives, which string maps together to show how mapping practices and products changed over time, have contributed to arguments about empire, urban development, mobility, the consolidation of state power, and scientific research.[2] Yet these claims are based on examining maps one by one, mimicking both the way we encounter them in the reading room and the way we read other texts. So, if maps have had relatively limited roles in humanistic research as large groups of primary sources because of this path dependency, we could ask ourselves how our questions and claims might change if we could access them differently.

Maps are not akin to written documents: they consist primarily of visual features—with text, numbers, or other symbols added for their explanatory power. Interpreting their rhetorical messages requires accounting for new kinds of agents involved in their creation and reproduction. More fundamentally, it can be hard to interact with maps because it can be difficult to find ones that are relevant to a given investigation. They often are not cataloged in as much detail as books, pamphlets, or archival documents. Scanning maps, or digitizing at the document level, gained momentum in libraries and archives in the 1990s and continues. This was an opportunity for researchers like me to rethink the status quo.[3] Digitization encouraged people to develop new strategies for looking at maps: moving from the reading-room table to a set of screens opened a creative space for imagining new ways of interacting with multiple maps at once, for example, as superimposed layers in geographic information systems (GIS) or visualized in other ways.

Nevertheless, even with digitized collections—celebrated by curators for improving access to rare items and by researchers for reducing the costs of research trips—the habit of thinking with one map at a time has held fast. Humanities projects that engage with scanned maps using GIS still do so in small batches. But there are other possibilities. My own research, for example, was transformed by being able to review files scanned by libraries thousands of miles away from those institutions and quickly change the size of an image. I used a high-definition screen at the David Rumsey Map Center to visualize much larger versions of small paper maps from eighteenth-century France. These maps documenting road construction took on new meaning as I deciphered faint pencil marks reappearing across the set. Digitization gave me access to high-quality images from multiple collections in France that would otherwise have been impossible to see simultaneously. Piecing together these maps on the screen brought me closer to the way that civil engineers saw them as they organized forced-labor service in rural Brittany. But more importantly, it opened up possibilities beyond simply scanning and viewing the images in finer detail and sharper focus. Next, I digitized the content of the maps by developing a dataset of the names and locations of the villages and roads drawn on the maps. More than simply an Old Regime engineers' tool for managing construction labor, the maps reflected how provincial leaders were beginning to organize rural places for political purposes. I examine, for example, which communities were not indicated on the maps and why.

My set of maps was small enough to work with manually, but now there are hundreds of thousands of maps scanned around the world. Imagine what looking closely at a much larger set might offer! But it is impossible for one pair of eyes to see so many maps with an analytical eye. How can we move beyond simply digitizing images and uniting disparate collections to asking questions about the content of very large corpora of maps? What do we need to do to turn digital images of historical maps into interpretable data for humanities research?

Soon, *looking* at maps on screens shifted to *extracting* data from maps. Map content became fodder for creating digital data. This second wave of digitization—creating discrete, structured data from maps rather than treating a sheet as one digital object—raised a new set of obstacles and opportunities. Data from maps needs to be critically created and curated; it can be linked to other data. At this point, the question became whether to spend time on manual data creation (for a historian, this often boiled down to whether to do spatial history at all).

Now, propelled into the third wave of digitization by machine learning–enabled computational image analysis and its application in the visual digital humanities (DH) since the late 2010s, we have arrived at the point where it is possible to digitize the content of maps automatically rather than manually. Given this shift, two key questions are open for debate. The first question explores the tipping point between manual and automatic methods while the other seeks to bring a humanistic eye to automated methods. In other words, what are the merits of digitizing data from maps manually versus automatically? And if we embrace automatic data creation at scale, how do we approach historical maps critically as we investigate them?

Answering these questions is fundamental to the future of research with scanned map collections. And they are timely because the number of digital map collections around the world is growing quickly. It has taken a long time for the demand to work differently with maps to surface because of the kind of deep-rooted scholarly traditions that come almost naturally to historians. More than just single images, map content is one of the next frontiers in working computationally with collections as data.[4] Because of digitization, historians—and other researchers—are now able to reimagine what we ask of maps.[5] In this chapter, I trace these three "waves" of digitization, foregrounding their chronology. The first three sections each address one wave: scanning, early uses of GIS by historians based on manual data creation, and automatic data creation from very large map collections.

The last wave introduces MapReader, a computer vision machine learning pipeline that I have developed with colleagues on Living with Machines.[6] Specifically, I use an experiment in which we develop a new dataset for capturing the footprint of railway infrastructure ("railspace") in nineteenth-century Britain as shown on early Ordnance Survey (OS) maps scanned by the National Library of Scotland. As an example of the third wave of digitization, MapReader is a method informed by deep attention to source criticism, but one that nonetheless challenges historians to work with data predicted by a machine. Like a visual census (Hosseini et al.), OS maps provide national coverage of the landscape at a very granular level but on far too many sheets for even our large team to manually digitize. MapReader combines the efficiency of speed with the flexibility of an iterative workflow designed to encourage historians to think outside the box when it comes to labeling parts of a map.

Of course, such a neat distinction between "waves," or phases, is an oversimplification: in practice, they have been and will continue to be interwoven. Nevertheless, the narrative of digitization shines a light on the emergence over time of different opportunities for studying maps. In addition to this three-part narrative, this chapter also grapples with just what "digitization" means. In the humanities, to say that a map has been digitized usually means that it has been scanned and can be accessed as an image file. In geographic information science (GIScience), "digitizing a map" means turning its content into machine-readable data. This substantial difference in disciplinary expectations of digitization highlights that scanning maps is really only the first of many potential steps. An entire set of practices for working with maps has grown in the space between these two definitions: I return to this in the final section of this chapter. Automatic methods will never replace the manual work of digitizing map content because each approach suits different research questions and sources. Will historians learn to ask new questions and develop interpretations of very large sets of maps when these are dependent on machine-generated data? In other words, can we trust data predicted by machines?

Digitization Wave 1: Historical Maps as Digital Objects

Maps as digitized (scanned) sources were hard to come by twenty years ago. But today, big (well, at least medium) map data could be a reality. Thanks to government and institutional commitments to digitization of cultural heritage materials beginning in the 1990s, today hundreds of thousands of maps have been scanned.[7] For a cross-institution overview, OldMapsOnline enables searching by location across major digitized collections: it has about 500,000 maps as of 2022.[8] With so many maps being digitized, the next crucial step is making them openly available. Because public funds underpin this work, the results are usually, but not always, freely accessible for noncommercial purposes.[9] Libraries and archives often share individual images from their digitized collections online using their own catalogs. For instance, the Library of Congress exposes each sheet of its newly scanned Sanborn Fire Insurance Maps collection this way. Other times, institutions make material available through APIs (OldMapsOnline, for example), or simply through data repositories or "lab" sites such as the National Library of Scotland's Data Foundry.[10] The British Library (BL) is, in this vein, releasing thousands of nineteenth-century Ordnance Survey maps funded by the Living with Machines project through BL Labs.[11] Prioritizing access in these ways reflects the principles of "collections as data." It demonstrates that institutions are seriously engaging with the call to build their digital collections with computational uses in mind (Padilla et al., "Santa Barbara Statement").

Creating collections as data, however, requires ongoing effort to lower barriers of access to now very large sets of digital maps held around the world. Scanning and sharing maps online are only the most basic elements in a digitization project that make it possible to use these materials as historical data. Enriching maps with sheet-level metadata (e.g., cataloging them) and georeferencing the scanned images are two key tasks that make maps discoverable and allow them to be used with computational methods. However, many maps—especially the largest serial map collections—have not been cataloged, and institutions rarely have the resources to commit to this particular task. Similarly, georeferencing has been a postprocessing task that many libraries are not equipped to complete because they often lack the resources to train or hire staff and then commit significant allocation to this intensive work. Crowdsourcing has filled this gap for some institutions that can at least oversee georeferencing done by the public. The David Rumsey Map Center, the British Library, and the National Library of Scotland have used the *Georeferencer* platform (Fleet, Kowal, and Přidal).[12] In other contexts, libraries have experimented with designing ways to georeference maps in batches; Ordnance Survey maps at the National Library of Scotland (Fleet, "Creating") are an example. More recently, the *AllMaps* project is making it easy to georeference maps shared via IIIF (International Image Interoperability Framework).[13] The power of these tasks cannot be understated: metadata about print dates, for example, is what allows us to analyze maps in time, while georeferencing is what plots them in space. Together, these two elements transform scanned maps from single images unrelated to each other into a group of items that have a chronological and spatial relationship. Authoring item-level metadata and georeferencing maps are two steps that allow us to work with maps as data.

Before the collections as data and related open data movements emerged in the mid-2010s, historians had no expectation that they might find digital maps online. Exceptions to this rule—such as the online catalogs at the David Rumsey Map Collection and the French National Library's Digital Library (Gallica)—were so stunning that it took a few years to realize that just looking at maps on these websites was not the pile of gold at the end of the rainbow. In the next section, I walk through the early experiences of using maps as sources from which data could be generated using GIS. Often done one map at a time, this was nonetheless an exciting time when researchers began to realize the opportunities and limitations of GIS.

Digitization Wave 2: Make Your Own Data from Maps

Historians and archaeologists (among others) have learned to work with GIS as a way of managing historical and prehistorical information with a spatial context.[14] Before there were large collections of scanned maps online, we might scan a map or two with the help of map librarians. Those scanned maps could be used as raster data to provide a historical base map in GIS. Many introductions to GIS begin with learning to georeference a scanned map and trace that map's features "by hand" (e.g., using a mouse or trackpad to draw features so that they appear superimposed on the scanned image). In their irreplaceable guide to using GIS in historical research, Ian Gregory and Paul Ell walk readers through scanning a map, the basics of digitizing vector data, and georeferencing (*Historical GIS,* 43–51). The latter two steps transform map content into points, lines, and polygons that are located in the real world and that can be stored in a geospatial database.[15] It is then possible to layer information from different sources and to examine those layers at different geographical scales. But as Gregory and Ell warn, GIS has a "tendency to exclude data that cannot be represented as points, lines, polygons, or pixels" (*Historical GIS,* 40). There are therefore two issues with the method of digitizing map content using GIS that are worth unpacking here in the context of this exploration of how we might work with maps differently as historians. First, there is a practical problem. Using GIS to create data manually can require immense resources. Second is an epistemological issue. GIS data has a very specific form that lends itself to specific representations of the built and natural environments.

TIME AND MONEY

This kind of digitization—making vector data from maps—has been a foundational task in spatial history and historical geography, despite warnings about the expense of creating such datasets. Gregory and Ell suggest to their readers that they "should be asking 'what are the geographical aspects of my research question' rather than 'what can I do with my dataset using this software?'" (*Historical GIS,* 1; see also Anne Kelly Knowles, "Introduction," 462). The extensive labor involved in transforming maps and other analogue documents into data has played a significant role in shaping spatial history.[16] Manually digitizing map content is a useful part of the research process, like note-taking or linguistic annotation. But the time (or, put another way, money) required to perform this labor can be a barrier for scholars who need to create their own data. Colleagues working in underresourced settings lack funding that supports data creation, whether that is for personal research or for assistants. In a growing number of large, funded projects supporting spatial history research, the manual methods of digitizing map content continue to play an important role: the large-scale, Europe-based *Time Machine* supports groups who scan, transcribe, and organize maps along with other records in openly available geohistorical databases.[17]

Tracing line or polygon data (like roads or building footprints) is a classic, time-consuming digitization task that is well suited to robust GIS software packages. But many projects increasingly want a lighter-weight solution, especially for annotating point-based or simple polygon data (like place names and the symbols depicting the location of the place on a map). For work like this, the open-source platform Recogito is a popular tool for annotating features on maps and linking them to other datasets (Vitale, "Pelagios"). But in order to annotate a place name to assign it a location (on a map that has not been georeferenced), the user needs access to a knowledge base that indexes place names with metadata about those places. These knowledge bases are known as gazetteers. They serve many purposes, including disambiguating between place names and providing location data. They therefore allow linking across datasets. However, nonscholarly gazetteers (e.g., Geonames) cause more problems than they solve for many historical places. Before the surge of community interest in gazetteer development, large parts of the world as well as premodern periods simply had no reliable digital resources to point to for linking place names to locations (McDonough, Moncla, and van de Camp, "Named Entity Recognition").[18] Working with small datasets, locating places by hand is possible: the expert researcher identifies the coordinates of each location one by one. The World Historical Gazetteer is an important contribution for helping researchers identify gazetteers built by others, reconcile records in one resource against another (such as born-digital knowledge bases like Wikidata), and download data to reuse in platforms like Recogito. Access to carefully curated, linked gazetteers that are formatted using open data is a timesaver and best practice that promotes open, reproducible research in the humanities.

Even with advances and semiautomatic tools like Recogito, building a GIS database by hand requires a large investment of personal time and institutional resources. One justification for this work is now the promise of open, reusable data. Early historical GIS projects rarely made their complete databases publicly accessible, perhaps because they reflected so much labor over the years. Even today, in the age of data papers, institutional and national research repositories, and digital object identifiers (DOIs) for nontraditional outputs, it can feel like data creation work gets short shrift. It is likely one of the reasons that many people using GIS would prefer to embark on projects small enough to complete alone or with only a couple of collaborators in order to get past the data creation stage as quickly as possible. Historians using GIS want to prioritize making claims based on their spatial evidence rather than eking out an existence tracing railway tracks across the screen. But like the constraint imposed by the size of reading-room tables, time is a barrier to working with maps at scale, even when using tools like GIS.

So the challenge is to cultivate a humanistic approach to working with maps as data that allows individuals or small groups to use large map collections as input and yet still have valuable time to explore, analyze, interpret, and write about the results. Moving away from the resource-heavy requirements of GIS data preparation can allow researchers to ask specific questions, whose concepts can be represented creatively by data structures, and to craft an argument based on that evidence.

GIS DATA MODELS

When used to translate map content into data, GIS software has made it very easy to strip maps of their richness and encourage digitization of information that lends itself to representation as points and other geometries. For example, much effort has gone into drawing boundary lines for parishes, cities, nations, and other jurisdictions. But everything we know about pre-nineteenth-century boundaries suggests that it is not appropriate to draw such well-defined lines across the digital landscape (Scholz, "Deceptive Contiguity"). Continuous information on a map becomes discrete vector data isolated from its context when it is digitized. Once you work with the vector data alone, you literally lose sight of that context in which map information was presented and begin to treat information digitized from maps as verified, real objects on the ground. Time and again, we have learned that maps can be misleading, fanciful, or even just unintentionally error-prone: reifying this information in vector data is not only time-consuming for the person doing the digitization, but it is also potentially hazardous in terms of presenting data that could be reused without an understanding of its limits.[19]

In contrast, humanities researchers might want to work in a computational environment where they can flexibly and contextually interrogate map scans. Prolonging the time spent with the map as a source of contested information and enabling change of direction after initial exploration are valuable actions that currently have no formal place in GIS approaches to working with scanned maps. Miriam Posner warned us about the dilemmas of talking about "humanities data." Researchers in the humanities struggle with thinking about our sources, maps among them, as something that can be turned into discrete pieces of information that continue to have the same value independent of their context. "You're not extracting features in order to analyze them," she writes, "you're trying to dive into it, like a pool, and understand it from within" ("Humanities Data"). This call for working with maps as data is founded on the imperative of retaining contextual meaning. We need a way to "go swimming" in a large corpus of maps as well as to be able to analyze the outputs of spatial analysis during data exploration and analysis.

Working with maps as data should allow researchers to use them as primary sources that are constituted through map-making and map-reading practices. A humanistic approach to working with maps at scale can recalibrate the danger of reading maps as truth statements. How can humanities scholars contribute to computational map processing to embrace another view of the world (shown on maps)? These questions point to places where humanists can join the conversation, changing the future of scientific *and* humanistic uses of maps. Humanistic inquiry around spatial data has already provided a number of important critiques of a decontextualized, scientific approach. The work of getting from map to data requires "knowing what is lost" and how this "is critical to understanding what can and cannot be learned from the extracted and chosen data" (Nicole Coleman, "Everything Is Data"). As we explore the potential of working with automatic methods, at scale, using different data formats, we must not lose sight of the politics of making data from maps.

GIS tools created to organize, explore, and analyze contemporary spatial information are not always well suited to understanding change over time, race, and inequality. In the last ten years, there have been challenges to the status quo that historical data should have the same shape as twenty-first-century data. If GIS has helped scholars uncover hidden histories in data, it was still designed to manage people and communities (in addition to more nefarious military applications) (Schuurman, *GIS: A Short Introduction*; Kurgan, *Close Up at a Distance*). Kim Gallon, in

"Making a Case for the Black Digital Humanities," reminds us that "computational processes might reinforce the notion of a humanity developed out of racializing systems," which brings to mind long-standing debates about the power of maps and the emergence of critical GIS studies. As we move toward working at scale with digitized maps, this is yet another reason to develop alternative modes of creating spatial data (Jefferson, "Predictable Policing").

Finally, why are we constrained by the rules set by GIS data models? Miriam Posner ("What's Next") has asked: "What would maps and data visualizations look like if they were built to show us categories like race as they have been experienced, not as they have been captured and advanced by businesses and governments?" Rather than depending on practices engrained in GIS software features, we can, as Posner suggests, "build something entirely different and weirder and more ambitious." Giving the example of David Kim's work on Edward S. Curtis's photographs of Native Americans, she calls for looking at other ways of engaging with maps, ways that offer scholars a chance to reframe what we are looking for in maps and how we translate that into machine-readable content.

Coleman, Gallon, and Posner ask us to reconsider existing ways of making and processing humanities data. I believe there is a timely intervention that begins at the level of language and carries over into method development and research workflows. Across the disciplines now using computational methods to analyze media, a rhetoric of exploitation has been used when talking about getting data from maps, texts, and other sources—they are documents to be "mined." For maps in particular, this language reverberates with the knowledge that GIS is used to document natural resource extraction around the world. Maps, like the earth itself, can be tunneled into, and data, like minerals, can be removed. Is this the way we want to interact with the past? Nuance, complexity, uncertainty, these are the historian's constant companions, and they are usually out of place in the fairly inflexible world of GIS data. So, if we are not going to mine maps, what are we doing? In my work, I am testing out alternative language: instead of drilling down, what if we generate, create, or classify? The language we use to talk about how we work with maps as data has power.

Digitizing map content using GIS has made it possible to incorporate maps into new spatial historical scholarship, but still on a small scale. DH projects dependent on manual data creation are at a crossroads. If they have the resources, and if the nature of the research lends itself to representing space with vector data, then what follows might be of little interest. But I imagine that many people will have two questions about using automatic methods dependent on machine learning: Will the results be trustworthy? And how can I think differently about representations of space? For instance, will spatial analysis reproduce historical inequalities? Will it divorce my analysis from the visual context of my objects of inquiry?

The current opportunity to ask questions of very large numbers of maps is an unprecedented chance to think both about maps as repositories of information and, with careful planning, how mapped landscapes can be read to understand social, cultural, or environmental history. Sometimes, because of the nature of the question, there is no replacement for manual data creation. When the not unreasonable error rate of 10 to 20 percent in an algorithm's predictions introduces too much doubt in a dataset, human effort is the solution. But it is likely that the way forward will embrace a hybrid approach with methods that save time by automating what machines do well and allowing experts to validate or complement machines where necessary.

Wave 3 Catalysts

I now turn to two developments that helped us move toward this third wave: automatic creation of vector data from scanned maps. Natural language processing, "text as data," machine learning, and computer vision and visual DH all contribute to emerging work analyzing map content at scale.

TEXT AS DATA

In the last five years, using text as data introduced historians to the advantages and disadvantages of working at scale. Like the growth of distant reading in literature departments, text as data is shaping research in political science economics (see Grimmer and Stewart; Gentzkow, Kelly, and Taddy). In history, take-up has been slower than in, for example, English, but this is now beginning to change with work that brings together historians, information theorists, computational linguists, and others (see Barron et al., "Individuals"; Hitchcock and Turkel, "The Old Bailey Proceedings"). Linking text analysis and spatial analysis was the next step. Using methods from natural language processing, tasks like named entity recognition (NER), where a named entity is a unique reference to a thing, such as a person or place, and more broadly, the suite of practices now known as geographic information retrieval (GIR), it is possible to explore the spatial dynamics of texts and generate datasets from them. This has been a core activity of researchers in the spatial humanities, a community that crosses multiple disciplines and is united by a shared concern with working computationally with usually historical primary sources that can be analyzed spatially. It is also a concern among geographers, computer scientists, and linguists: GIScientist May Yuan wrote a key chapter on "Mapping Text" in the 2010 volume *The Spatial Humanities: GIS and the Future of Humanities Scholarship*. At the same time, the linguistics team behind the Edinburgh Geoparser was publishing their first papers on software, which many humanities researchers still encounter as an introduction to semiautomatic identification (with NER) and geo-resolution of place names in text (Grover et al., "Use of the Edinburgh Geoparser"). Finally, a series of projects led by Ian Gregory, including *Mapping Lake District Literature* and *Spatial Humanities,* contributed to the emergence of historical, spatial text analysis at scale.[20] This work taught humanities researchers how to bridge the gap between qualitative and quantitative ways of thinking about space and place, how to assess bias in a corpus, and how to grapple with statistical measures as part of the evidentiary basis for an argument. This opened the door to translating such skills from texts to visual documents like maps.

VISUAL DH

Historians, art historians, archaeologists, curators, and others have begun to work in creative ways with computer vision and visual sources, launching a visual turn that already shows promise for combining state-of-the-art methods in machine learning, statistics, computer vision, and the humanities. This visual turn hinges on developing methods and theories for working computationally with visual and audiovisual sources. Lauren Tilton, Taylor Arnold, Thomas Smits, and Melvin Wevers have advocated for "distant viewing," and they have expanded to visual collections the computational methods already embraced by the DH community working with texts. Tilton and Arnold offer the term "distant viewing" as a framework for "making explicit the interpretive nature of extracting semantic metadata from images" (Arnold and Tilton, "Distant Viewing," i3–i4).[21] As they suggest, creating semantic metadata, or information about the content of images, in a critical and well-documented manner is at the core of a humanistic computer vision research agenda. The visual turn proposed by these authors highlights machine learning–driven computer vision using convolutional neural networks (CNNs) as a method for searching. Computer vision with CNNs—which is one type of deep learning algorithm—learns relationships between pixels and then uses those features to predict further patterns in unseen data. The visual turn in DH is simultaneously a shift in medium and a call for working at scale by embracing machine learning (the predictive part) and statistics (the quantitative part).

For example, Smits and Wevers argue in their analysis of images in newspapers that applications of computer vision are within reach of humanities scholars or at least interdisciplinary teams (Wevers and Smits, "The Visual Digital Turn").[22] The projects that I worked on at the Alan Turing Institute (Living with Machines and Machines Reading Maps) brought together expertise in multiple domains to make new contributions to computational image analysis with historical documents. But one of the goals of Living with Machines was to lower the cost of entry to this method. And we are not alone. Tools already exist that make visual DH accessible to individuals with no previous experience in this kind of research. PixPlot from the Yale DH Lab allows users to explore visual patterns in large, static image collections as a data exploration tool.[23]

The opportunity to think about maps as data in new and exciting ways is one way that the visual turn in DH is forging exciting opportunities for the computational humanities. Like the photographs, newspapers, TV programs, paintings, and born-digital images that are now being studied, maps require careful attention to transform their visual, qualitative features into quantitative data. In applying insights from the visual DH turn to maps, of particular interest is the opportunity to replace now standard GIS "codes" (e.g., interpreting a building on a map as a polygon) with a new set of codes that are appropriate to humanities research questions. New codes, in machine learning jargon, are labels or metadata about an image or a region of an image. Just like GIS data structures, these codes play a role in determining what kinds of interpretative outcomes are possible. However, we lack methods for large-scale analysis that enable this rethinking of how to capture spatial phenomena as shown on maps. In the following section on the latest digitization wave, I introduce MapReader, a computer vision pipeline that specifically focuses on what kind of task and labels are suited for working with historical maps. MapReader prompts users to ask questions of maps that might challenge existing paradigms of spatial data while offering the chance to work at the unprecedented scale of tens of thousands of maps.

Digitization Wave 3: Automatic Data

In this section, I discuss the MapReader pipeline.[24] This computer vision pipeline offers practical answers to the questions driving this chapter: how to work critically with digital maps and how and why to automate data creation and curation. MapReader is a key output from Living with Machines, a digital history project colocated at the Alan Turing Institute and the British Library in London.[25] Two key features of this project were at the heart of MapReader's creation: first, a desire to work in new ways as historians with colleagues from many disciplines in order to ask and answer historical questions of large, digitized collections; and second, a critical awareness that automating data creation requires new theories and practices for accommodating machine-generated error. I want to contextualize MapReader in relation to the new field of historical map processing that has largely developed within computer science.

The high costs of historical geospatial data creation paired with the massive explosion in online map collections has created a body of scholarship in GIScience called historical map processing (also referred to as the automatic extraction and geolocation of map content, or raster-to-vector conversion).[26] In Figure 6.1, we see what this research aspires to encompass. It includes a number of methods used frequently in the spatial humanities (georeferencing, querying gazetteers) but positions map processing as an end-to-end workflow that produces carefully created "analysis-ready historical geospatial data" mimicking the manual vectorization process.

If automatic map processing was an afterthought in 2007 (Gregory and Ell, *Historical GIS*, 45), in 2020 it is a well-funded challenge for many teams around the world. Even Google Research joined the fray (Tavakkol et al., "Kartta Labs"). Scientists and businesses see immense value in historical maps—to create fine-grained, longitudinal datasets about, for example, housing stock, forest cover, or mining resources.

Maps as Data [111

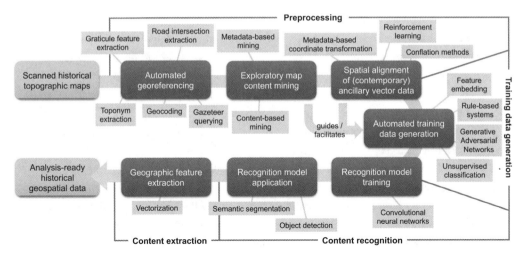

Figure 6.1. Example of a historical map processing workflow, including methodological approaches for each step (in gray boxes). Source: Uhl and Duan, "Automating Information Extraction from Large Historical Topographic Map Archives," 511.

This exciting new work will benefit from greater communication and collaboration with humanities researchers and curators, who can refine these methods and attend to the implications of turning qualitative features in maps into quantitative, precisely located data stored in a database and visually abstracted from their context. One risk of this drive to vectorize, and to do so quickly, is that it may reinforce the (very) outdated view of maps as a container of objective information. Layering different datasets has the potential to reveal dissonance between mapping cultures, but too often layers calcify around each other and turn abstracted features into factual statements about what is or was on the ground.

MAPREADER

MapReader makes it possible to ask historical questions of large collections of maps (Hosseini et al., "Maps of a Nation?").[27] When it comes to working with scanned maps at scale, we need to simplify massive collections so that visual patterns across space and time, like streets of terrace housing or industrial areas, are actually findable. Making vector data from specific features on maps is an important way to explore spatial information over time and space, but it is not the only way. Raster data assumes that the graphic primitive, or basic form, is the pixel. With MapReader, we propose a flexible, modifiable area created by systematically dividing a map sheet into equally sized squares—patches—as the unit of analysis (Hosseini et al., "MapReader").

For Living with Machines, the goal was not just to speed up the process of making vector data but rather to reframe how historians can engage with maps. We have created a method for iteratively asking questions and creating simple outputs that can then be analyzed as geolocated, structured data. The inputs to our computer vision pipeline, MapReader, are scanned maps (downloaded as web map tiles from the National Library of Scotland servers). The outputs are predictions of a researcher-defined label that correspond to a certain area of the map. These areas are "patches" of the map (see Figure 6.2), the size of which is determined by the researcher as a preprocessing step after the map tiles have been acquired and linked to collection metadata. This metadata contains bounding-box coordinates that allow us to reconstruct the limits of the physical map sheets among the downloaded tile layers.[28] Each patch represents a section of the map, which one can then ask questions of by assigning labels.

Labeling data during annotation exercises to collect gold standard or training data becomes an active process of considering what a map is and what you can ask of it, given the "skills" as well as the limitations of state-of-the-art computer vision models. Once we have enough training data, we fine-tune and then use a CNN model to predict those same labels for millions of patches across thousands of maps. Because each patch prediction is geolocated (when input maps are georeferenced), we can perform further spatial analysis on the patches and link them to other patches with different labels or external datasets. The patches are effectively raster (image) data: the label is an attribute of the patch segment of the map, but we can work with the patch as simple point data (based on the centroid of the patch) or as a square representing the bounding box of the patch (with or without the image data included).

Moving back and forth between the visual representation of patch predictions and csv files of those predictions allows us to remain in touch with the original source. This "patchwork" method used in MapReader is adaptable to any question that seeks to find patterns and distributions of visual information on a large number of maps. It is well suited to questions that are investigating phenomena that may be visual but for which having very precise locational data is not necessary. Once the patches for all labels have been predicted, we can perform standard spatial analysis to understand the results. For example, for label X, we could analyze the "density" of X in particular areas: How many X patches are surrounded entirely by other X patches? Where are they located? We can inspect the results visually (qualitatively), overlaid on the maps being investigated, and quantitatively, using software libraries like geopandas. The patch is a useful category of analysis to think about because it represents an action of dividing up the map for closer examination, rather than removing a unique feature to analyze in isolation from the rest of the map content.

One research objective of Living with Machines is to explore the impact of the arrival of rail in British communities. Therefore, understanding where railway infrastructure takes up space on British land was a key objective. Given access to the collection of scanned, georeferenced Ordnance Survey map sheets from the National Library of Scotland, we wanted to identify areas where there was a presence of any kind of rail development in the nineteenth century.[29] Existing data about British railways (tracks and stations) has a few limitations. First, they are incomplete, missing either stations or tracks (especially single-track lines). Second, they have no metadata for pinning down in time the track or station lines and points, only documenting what was present in three independent "snapshots" from 1851, 1861, and 1881 (for example, Henneberg et al., "1881"). We could not depend on these earlier open-access datasets because of their coverage gaps and the lack of metadata. But above all, we knew that we had other questions to ask of maps—not about rail. Given this, we wanted a method that could work for our rail questions but equally well for other topics in the project (and eventually for issues outside Living with Machines). Finally, while digitized images of maps sometimes have restrictions on sharing/reuse, the csv files can usually be shared as derived data with simple permissions. The patchwork method supports these goals: it is adaptable to researcher-defined labels (e.g., rail, building, coast, road), captures information on maps about the built or natural environment that might be missing other primary sources, can be easily checked by the researcher (e.g., is it a real thing or a cartographical mirage) against other sources, and can be re-released as open data about the historical landscape.

Our first experiments predict what we define as railspace (any visible rail development in a patch, including stations, depots, warehouses, sidings, and tunnels) and buildings (any size building, anywhere in a patch) using Ordnance Survey (OS) maps for England, Wales, and Scotland from the latter half of the nineteenth century and early years of the twentieth century (e.g., the six-inch-to-one-mile second edition sheets in the National Library of Scotland collections). We ask questions about railspace instead of railways to move away from the idea that we are capturing only the network of tracks. Railspace intentionally captures more than just the immediate pixels for tracks and warehouses, for example. As a concept applied to a patch, its expansiveness acknowledges the way that rail infrastructure affected the land surrounding it. From direct impacts like increased noise or air pollution to indirect ones, such as higher or lower land values (depending on the type of infrastructure), rail often imposed a buffer between it and adjacent development. Railspace brings this buffer zone into the field of vision and reminds researchers of the broader impact of the arrival of rail across the nation. Railspace is not a carefully verified version of the network of freight or passenger rail. It should not be used to calculate transport costs without further data curation and would require transforming the raster patch data into polylines.

In addition to this conceptual stance, what we are really labeling is the way that mapmakers show railspace as it sits among other elements in the landscape. We understand the map as not just a simplification of the environment at a moment in time; it also reflects a set of mapping practices (Kitchin and Dodge, "Rethinking Maps"). In deciding whether and how to label a visual feature on a map, the researcher must ask how the cartographer approached this information at the time and whether or not it is a good candidate for annotation using MapReader. So, as with any method, not everything lends itself to this approach. Often, this is because the label selected by a researcher does not coincide with the content: in dense urban areas on OS maps, for example, it is impossible to distinguish between residential, industrial, and commercial buildings. In this sense, if the researcher is interested in identifying housing, these are simply not the best sources. Thus, "residential" is not a useful label. Labels do not need to perfectly match a single visual signal (railway tracks, for example, as opposed to railspace), but the patch content needs to be visually specific enough to not overlap with other labels you wish to predict. The visual signal for a label might fill the patch entirely or be found in only part of it. The intentional coarseness of the patch (as opposed to a pixel) is part of our general goal of not reifying map features in the digital world as abstracted truth statements. Embracing patches as an alternative data format creates some critical distance between the historical map and the historical concept a researcher is interested in.

MapReader operates in a series of Jupyter notebooks, including ones for training data annotation and review. One experiment includes the steps of creating a corpus of georeferenced maps and their metadata records, labeling a subset of this corpus, testing and fine-tuning the available models, visualizing the initial results on a map to see if there are systematic biases, adding more annotations as necessary, rerunning the inference, and finally, exporting the output as a csv file. There are multiple stages at which the user can return to annotation, either to add a new label, remove a label, or completely start from scratch with new guidelines for labeling. The great peril of GIS digitization of map features is that once you begin digitizing a feature, it is difficult to change course partway through: in contrast, MapReader is fast and flexible and in fact encourages using the annotation part of the workflow as an active way of refining research questions in light of spending time looking at patches in their context. The manual labor of labeling training data for MapReader dwarfs the labor that would be needed to create vector data for the entire set of about 15,000 maps.

In seeking a humanistic approach to historical map processing, we strive to acknowledge conventional GIS approaches while also shifting our focus, quite literally, to an alternative way of looking. The railspace and building experiments are two examples of labels that a historian could use after reflecting on the relationship between what is visually documented on the map and what is of interest historically. During the training data annotation step, looking at the map through its patches focuses the eye on 100-square-meter areas. In the practice of extracting vector data, the researcher often only really looks at the tiny parts of the map where the feature of interest appears. In this sense, during the actions to select and digitize those specific features, the researcher stops looking at the whole and stops thinking about broader context and uncommon spatial relationships between features, instead homing in on the presence or absence of one thing. The patchwork method lends itself to research where the measurement of that presence or absence of, for example, the reconstruction of an actual rail network is less central. For an economic historian measuring the cost of freight travel, such a network is crucial.

Maps as Data [115

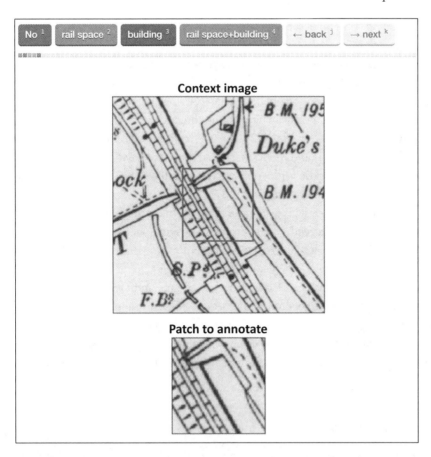

Figure 6.2. Detail of the Jupyter notebook for annotating patches in MapReader. Source: Hosseini et al., "MapReader."

For the social historian who seeks to investigate the role that the arrival (and non-arrival) of rail had on the towns and villages it passes through, the connectedness and perfection of the network is secondary to a rougher representation of that information. Patches are the friend of the researcher who seeks out context, while vector data supports the analysis of discrete entities. Both are valuable, but each serves different research communities.

For the railspace experiment, MapReader generated 30.5 million patches from the maps of England, Wales, and Scotland and predicted the label for each patch. That prediction is measured by a confidence score of how well a patch conforms to the algorithm's idea of the label: for example, a 99 percent confidence score for the rail label is very high, while a lower confidence score of 60 percent means it is less likely that this patch is actually railspace. Among these millions of patches with predicted labels, there will be errors. Riverbeds may be misclassified as railways and rocky outcroppings mistaken for terrace houses: one of the consequences of automatically creating this data is living with this error. In our future work, we will focus on describing why historians can trust the claims we make using this data and might even consider reusing it to make their own arguments.

MapReader exemplifies the potential for humanistic computer vision using maps as data. It brings the energies of text as data and visual DH to bear on collections that are now becoming openly available. Using patches as a way to simplify the data creation process, it shines a light on the choices historians make when deciding what on the map can be analyzed. Patches are flexible in size and therefore adaptable to many kinds of maps and questions: rather than representing an arbitrary shape, their regularity across the gridded map sheet puts the focus instead on how a label reflects a meaningful historical concept.

Of course, MapReader is just one of many methods that will emerge in the coming years. There are already other projects engaging with maps computationally. The Unlocking the Colonial Archive project is applying machine learning methods to analyze texts and maps in Spanish imperial collections.[30] And Machines Reading Maps, a project that I co-led with Yao-Yi Chiang and Deborah Holmes-Wong, improved methods for generating datasets of the text found on historical maps.[31] All of these projects share common objectives of reproducibility, ethical engagement with historical materials, and the ultimate goal of extending successes on large collections of European and North American maps to the rich cartographic cultures in other parts of the world.

Cautions and Next Steps

As we move toward the large-scale analysis of maps through computational methods, keeping at the fore the limits of both maps and computational methods will be key. Outside the humanities, researchers in other disciplines are beginning to use growing collections of maps to generate data about human and environmental activity in the past. They are using scanned map collections to "mine" information from them—road networks, city footprints, orchards, and more (Uhl et al., "Towards the Automated Large-Scale Reconstruction of Past Road Networks"; Uhl et al., "Combining Remote-Sensing-Derived Data and Historical Maps"; National Trust). This is an attractive proposition because it opens up map collections as sources of information about the physical environment of the past. It adds data points for measures, such as the location of certain landscape types, or proxies for others like population, which only began to be collected according to scientific methods in the late nineteenth century (Higgs, *Making Sense of the Census Revisited*).

Mimicking approaches used to process and analyze aerial and remote sensing imagery, it is tempting to think of maps as just another, older snapshot of the ground. Using extracted features from maps in quantitative spatial analysis enables research in an array of fields, such as migration studies or climate change. But so far, such approaches tend to engage with maps themselves as if they were remote sensing imagery. Knowledge of historical mapping practices and digitization challenges is rarely embedded in the design of these methods (for an exception, see the approaches developed in Uhl et al., "Map Archive Mining"). Remote sensing data can be verified on the ground by humans, who visit locations to check what might be distorted or missing from imagery because of cloud cover, recent natural disasters, or war, for instance. But you cannot ground truth or verify the contents of historical maps. You can get close through painstaking archival research, but only partially, and there is no replacement for walking the land at the time the map was surveyed. In creating a dataset of historical railroads in the United States, the economic historian Jeremy Atack concluded that many miles of track were a "figment of the cartographer's imagination" ("On the Use of Geographic Information Systems," 319). The surveyor projected rail into the landscape, and unpicking those lines on the map took significant historical research. Maps, we have learned, require careful assessment. They model the surface of the earth according to the preferences of a network of humans and their mapping practices.

So, how do we treat map data as capta, recognizing that "knowledge is constructed, taken, not simply given as a natural representation of pre-existing fact" (Drucker, "Humanities Approaches to Graphical Display")?[32] When the object of inquiry is not primarily the source itself—we are not studying map content to understand *maps*—we are adding another layer of interpretation. Even seen through the prism of the surveyor's motivations, data on maps can point to how people lived in the past. In this way, data from maps is abstracted three times: first, the map itself is a simplification of the landscape; second, it is a landscape of the past; third, digitizing its content means representing qualitative information as quantitative. Using map data as capta acknowledges these three features of the content we create from digital maps.

In practice, this means thinking about alternate methods of data creation and structures. Rather than simply using maps to gather data using predetermined categories of knowledge, we have a chance to go back to the drawing board. Analyzing regions of images (as we do with patches in MapReader), for example, is an old trick in the computer vision playbook and draws on an older tradition of embedding attributes about landscapes within the pixels of GIS raster layers. But applying it to predict the content of historical maps at scale reflects the inherent uncertainty of translating a map into a precisely located landscape feature.

Using MapReader as an example of the latest wave of digitization, this chapter shows that automatic data creation is an alternative and a complement to manual GIS work. It is a methodological offering that represents the fruits of what we have learned from working with complex historical text data and from engaging with computer scientists working on historical map processing. In the specific context of Living with Machines, automatic data creation is also the product of an ethos of showing our work from end to end and making it possible for others to recreate and repurpose our code and data. Humanistic computer vision using maps as data is all the more important because the treatment of maps as accurate representations of the built and natural environments might unintentionally reproduce the inequalities and violences embedded in these sources. If humanities scholars have been slow to take up large-scale analysis of digitized maps, the scientific and commercial community has not.

This is necessary because objectifying map content can have consequences (Crampton, *Mapping*). In her examination of the relationship between archives, data, and the past and present of commodifying black bodies, Jessica Marie Johnson articulates just what is at stake: "The brutality of black codes, the rise of Atlantic slaving, and everyday violence in the lives of the enslaved created a devastating archive. Left unattended, these devastations reproduce themselves in digital architecture, even when and where digital humanists believe they advocate for social justice" ("Markup Bodies," 58).

How one creates, organizes, and locates data about the past has social and political implications. By attempting to work with maps as "insecure" documents (Kitchin), humanities researchers can challenge existing paradigms that vacuum up map content according to the standards set by GIS decades ago. Furthermore, pinning down map content as vector data and sharing that in a database that is fixed for all time disincentivizes others from working iteratively with map content and encourages reuse of vector data. Most of the time, data reuse is great; but it has the potential to reify knowledge and stifle other views of map content. MapReader aims to allow researchers to create their own datasets based on their own questions: it does not assume that there are a finite number of features to extract and that these are known by us, the tool's creators. Yes, we will release our railspace data openly: we hope it might be reused, and we hope that it reflects the reproducibility of our method. But ultimately, the real treasure is not in the datasets: it will be in showing others how to use MapReader for their own purposes.

John Corrigan points to the humanities scholar's pursuit of complex or "dynamic" data as "data that is characterized by interaction between its various parts" ("Qualitative GIS," 80). In the first decade of the twenty-first century, GIS appeared dynamic enough. It allowed historians to toggle back and forth between different views of scanned georeferenced maps, government datasets, or painstakingly curated data from archival sources, like railway freight tables. But in 2024 there are new opportunities for introducing flexibility in how we work with historical sources. When it comes to maps, computer vision and machine learning allow us to work with maps not as resources to be mined but rather queried.

Moving away from the language of mining and toward the language of questioning celebrates the potential for iteration and reinterpretation that is valued in the humanities. It is more in tune with the ongoing connection that a historian or other humanities researcher has with a source. It evokes the idea of a conversation and acknowledges that sources are containers of multidimensional facts. Like distant viewing of photographs or film, querying scanned maps using computer vision allows scholars to interact with the data curation process, change their minds about what features are interesting, or test different ways of naming and organizing information. This malleability is not possible in a GIS workflow. Rethinking the place of maps in history and neighboring fields is a chance to democratize spatial analysis—in terms of removing both the high costs of preparing data for a GIS and the constraints around data structures and workflows that discourage iterative research.

Now is the time for DH to embrace historical maps as searchable data. Visual features and text on maps can be quickly transformed into machine-readable data. This can be used to answer historical or other research questions, to improve discoverability of maps in libraries and archives, and for other creative or scientific purposes. Data creation depends on methods that are quick and reproducible so that historians can test, for example, different approaches to labeling and then use these results to refine their research questions. Working at a national, continental, or global level with historical maps opens opportunities for research at these scales where it can be time-consuming to identify appropriate sources or difficult-to-find continuous coverage over large areas using other primary sources.

We are used to selecting case studies based on lucky archival survivals. Using tools like MapReader offers a new way to scope patterns in the built or natural environment. Indeed, it allows historians to reconsider the shapes constituting that very environment and thus understand how common or unique a place might be based on its cartographic representation. Computational approaches to digitized maps open the door to working iteratively across multiple scales of historical experience. Side by side with archival research, we can begin to make new claims about historical places and ultimately about the lives of the people in those places.

Notes

1. The History of Cartography project (https://geography.wisc.edu/histcart/) is a major contribution to the field and exemplifies the best of writing about maps and mapping since 1987. The most recent is Matthew Edney and Mary Pedley, eds., *Cartography in the European Enlightenment* (Chicago: University of Chicago Press, 2019).

2. E.g., Akerman, *Decolonizing the Map*; Guldi, "The Tangible Shape of the Nation"; Wigen, *A Malleable Map*; Heffernan, "A Paper City"; Verdier, "Plans et Cartes."

3. It also raised the thorny question of how people find maps through library catalogs or archival finding aids. Cataloging (e.g., creating metadata for collections) has been a challenge for maps. Many map collections globally are not cataloged at item level.

4. See the "Always Already Computational: Collections as Data" website at https://collectionsasdata.github.io/.

5. This chapter was written for a broad community of humanities researchers, understood to include historians but also historical geographers and archaeologists. Many times I refer to historians alone, but this is more for brevity than as a statement about disciplinary uniqueness.

6. Living with Machines (https://livingwithmachines.ac.uk/), funded by the UK Research and Innovation (UKRI) Strategic Priority Fund, is a multidisciplinary collaboration delivered by the Arts and Humanities Research Council (AHRC), with the Alan Turing Institute, the British Library, and the Universities of Cambridge, East Anglia, Exeter, and Queen Mary University of London.

7. For example, the *American Memory* initiative of the U.S. Library of Congress was an early digitization project that first provided digital images on CD-ROMs and videodiscs. Later, materials were made available online. See http://memory.loc.gov/ammem/about/techIn.html.

8. OldMapsOnline (https://www.oldmapsonline.org/).

9. Unfortunately, access to digital reproductions is not guaranteed. Whether because of copyright restrictions (which vary from country to country), licensing agreements with third-party partners, or institutional decisions to withhold access because of materials' commercial value, physical collections in the public domain cannot reliably be accessed openly as digital objects.

10. Sanborn Maps (https://www.loc.gov/collections/sanborn-maps/), National Library of Scotland Data Foundry (https://data.nls.uk/).

11. https://livingwithmachines.ac.uk/georeferencing-ordnance-survey-maps/.

12. https://www.georeferencer.com/.

13. https://allmaps.org/, https://iiif.io/.

14. This section is not meant to be a complete review of spatial humanities work. Please see the excellent overviews by Todd Presner and David Shepard, "Mapping the Geospatial Turn"; Jo Guldi, "What Is the Spatial Turn?"; and Gregory and Ell's "GIS in Historical Research" in *Historical GIS*, 15–18.

15. The role that GIS plays in allowing users simply to view overlapping, semitransparent layers of maps covering the same space has been emphasized by David Rumsey. Such a method mimics and enhances the techniques historians use in reading rooms to compare maps, but it stops short of any quantitative representation of that comparison (Rumsey and Williams, *Historical Maps in GIS*, 8–11). For tutorials that progress through these steps, see https://spatial.scholarslab.org/stepbystep/; for the first lesson in a set of early *Programming Historian* lessons, see https://programminghistorian.org/en/lessons/googlemaps-googleearth.

16. Building historical datasets—data capture—has led to new fields of inquiry in gazetteer creation, qualitative spatial relationships, and the representation of time and movement. These rich areas link spatial history to library, archive, and information science in important ways, making historical spatial data a shared interest across these fields. See, for example, Giordano and Cole, "Places of the Holocaust."

17. See, for example, the Amsterdam Time Machine's description of its geographical infrastructure (https://amsterdamtimemachine.nl/hisgis-clariah/) and the University of Antwerp Time Machine's GIStorical project (https://www.uantwerpen.be/en/projects/antwerp-time-machine/about-the-project/rapid-developments/).

18. Interest in gazetteers, in large part, was spurred by the Pelagios Commons project: see the Pelagios Network (https://pelagios.org/).

19. Furthermore, for the great majority of maps published before the nineteenth century, it is extremely difficult to create vector data that is not significantly warped because of the effects of georeferencing the scanned sheet on which that content lives.

20. Among the many outputs of these projects, see Murrieta-Flores et al., "Automatically Analyzing Large Texts in a GIS Environment," and Taylor, Gregory, and Donaldson, "Combining Close and Distant Reading."

21. Even before considering research applications, exploratory searches across digitized and born-digital image collections is a big challenge. This is why there is a growing body of literature focused on using machine learning methods to automatically generate metadata from visual collections. See, for example, Arnold et al., "Uncovering Latent Metadata," and Hu et al., "Enriching the Metadata of Map Images."

22. See also the DH2018 Computer Vision workshop at https://dh2018.adho.org/computer-vision-in-dh/.

23. PixPlot project at Yale DH Lab (https://dhlab.yale.edu/projects/pixplot/).

24. For an overview of the MapReader pipeline, see https://living-with-machines.github.io/MapReader/; see also Kasra Hosseini et al., "MapReader: A Computer Vision Pipeline for the Semantic Exploration of Maps at Scale."

25. AHRC award AH/S01179X/1, https://gtr.ukri.org/projects?ref=AH%2FS01179X%2F1.

26. For important examples of this work, see Chiang, *Using Historical Maps*; Uhl et al., "Map Archive Mining"; and Uhl and Duan, "Automatic Extraction."

27. https://github.com/Living-with-machines/MapReader.

28. See the National Library of Scotland for the historic maps API layers (https://maps.nls.uk/projects/api/).

29. See the National Library of Scotland at https://maps.nls.uk/os/.

30. Unlocking the Colonial Archive project (https://unlockingarchives.com/).

31. Machine Reading Maps project (https://www.turing.ac.uk/research/research-projects/machines-reading-maps).

32. I use the word "data" when describing what is created when we make a machine-readable version of map content (Arnold and Tilton, "New Data?"), and I find Christoph Schöch's definition of humanities data useful: "a digital, selectively constructed, machine-actionable abstraction representing some aspects of a given object of humanistic inquiry" ("Big? Smart? Clean? Messy?").

Bibliography

Akerman, James R., ed. *Decolonizing the Map: Cartography from Colony to Nation*. Kenneth Nebenzahl, Jr., Lectures in the History of Cartography. Chicago: University of Chicago Press, 2017.

Arnold, Taylor, Stacey Maples, Lauren Tilton, and Laura Wexler. "Uncovering Latent Metadata in the FSA-OWI Photographic Archive." *Digital Humanities Quarterly* 011, no. 2 (March 2017).

Arnold, Taylor, and Lauren Tilton. "Distant Viewing: Analyzing Large Visual Corpora." *Digital Scholarship in the Humanities* 34, supp. 1 (December 2019): 3–16. https://doi.org/10.1093/llc/fqz013.

Arnold, Taylor, and Lauren Tilton. "New Data? The Role of Statistics in DH." In *Debates in the Digital Humanities 2019,* edited by Matthew K. Gold and Lauren F. Klein. Minneapolis: University of Minnesota Press, 2019. https://dhdebates.gc.cuny.edu/read/untitled-f2acf72c-a469-49d8-be35-67f9ac1e3a60/section/a2a6a192-f04a-4082-afaa-97c76a75b21c#ch24.

Atack, Jeremy. "On the Use of Geographic Information Systems in Economic History: The American Transportation Revolution Revisited." *Journal of Economic History* 73, no. 2 (2013): 313–38.

Barron, Alexander T. J., Jenny Huang, Rebecca L. Spang, and Simon DeDeo. "Individuals, Institutions, and Innovation in the Debates of the French Revolution." *Proceedings of the National Academy of Sciences* 115, no. 18 (May 2018): 4607–12. https://doi.org/10.1073/pnas.1717729115.

Blevins, Cameron. "Digital History's Perpetual Future Tense." In *Debates in the Digital Humanities 2016,* edited by Matthew K. Gold and Lauren F. Klein. Minneapolis: University of Minnesota Press, 2016. https://dhdebates.gc.cuny.edu/read/untitled/section/4555da10-0561-42c1-9e34-112f0695f523.

Bodenhamer, David J., John Corrigan, and Trevor M Harris. *The Spatial Humanities: GIS and the Future of Humanities Scholarship.* Bloomington, Ind.: University of Indiana Press, 2010.

Brown, Vincent. "Mapping a Slave Revolt: Visualizing Spatial History through the Archives of Slavery." *Social Text* 33, no 4 (125) (December 2015): 134–41. https://doi.org/10.1215/01642472-3315826.

Chiang, Yao-Yi, Weiwei Duan, Stefan Leyk, Johannes H. Uhl, and Craig A. Knoblock. *Using Historical Maps in Scientific Studies: Applications, Challenges, and Best Practices.* SpringerBriefs in Geography. Cham: Springer International, 2020. https://doi.org/10.1007/978-3-319-66908-3_3.

Coleman, Catherine Nicole. "Everything Is Data, except When It Isn't." *Stanford Libraries Blog,* May 20, 2021. https://web.archive.org/web/20230705124529/https://library.stanford.edu/blogs/stanford-libraries-blog/2021/05/everything-data-except-when-it-isnt.

Corrigan, John. "Qualitative GIS and Emergent Semantics." In *The Spatial Humanities: GIS and the Future of Humanities Scholarship,* 76–88. Bloomington: University of Indiana Press, 2010.

Crampton, Jeremy W. *Mapping: A Critical Introduction to Cartography and GIS.* New York: John Wiley, 2011.

Drucker, Johanna. "Humanities Approaches to Graphical Display." *DHQ: Digital Humanities Quarterly* 5, no. 1 (March 2011).

Edney, Matthew. *Cartography: The Ideal and Its History.* Chicago: University of Chicago Press, 2019.

Fleet, Christopher. "Creating, Managing, and Maximising the Potential of Large Online Georeferenced Map Layers." *E-Perimetron* 14, no. 3 (2019): 140–49.

Fleet, Christopher, Kimberly C. Kowal, and Petr Přidal. "Georeferencer: Crowdsourced Georeferencing for Map Library Collections." *D-Lib Magazine* 18, no. 11/12 (November 2012). https://doi.org/10.1045/november2012-fleet.

Gallon, Kim. "Making a Case for the Black Digital Humanities." In *Debates in the Digital Humanities 2016,* edited by Matthew K. Gold and Lauren F. Klein. Minneapolis: University of Minnesota Press, 2016. https://dhdebates.gc.cuny.edu/read/untitled/section/fa10e2e1-0c3d-4519-a958-d823aac989eb.

Gentzkow, Matthew, Bryan Kelly, and Matt Taddy. "Text as Data." *Journal of Economic Literature* 57, no. 3 (September 2019): 535–74. https://doi.org/10.1257/jel.20181020.

Giordano, Alberto, and Tim Cole. "Places of the Holocaust: Towards a Model of GIS of Place." *Transactions in GIS*. Accessed January 14, 2020. https://doi.org/10.1111/tgis.12583.

Gregory, Ian N., and Paul S. Ell. *Historical GIS: Technologies, Methodologies and Scholarship.* Cambridge: Cambridge University Press, 2007.

Grimmer, Justin, and Brandon M. Stewart. "Text as Data: The Promise and Pitfalls of Automatic Content Analysis Methods for Political Texts." *Political Analysis* 21, no. 3 (2013): 267–97. https://doi.org/10.1093/pan/mps028.

Grover, Claire, Richard Tobin, Kate Byrne, Matthew Woollard, James Reid, Stuart Dunn, and Julian Ball. "Use of the Edinburgh Geoparser for Georeferencing Digitized Historical Collections." *Philosophical Transactions of the Royal Society of London A: Mathematical, Physical and Engineering Sciences* 368, no. 1925 (August 2010): 3875–89. https://doi.org/10.1098/rsta.2010.0149.

Guldi, Jo. "The Tangible Shape of the Nation: The State, the Cheap Printed Map, and the Manufacture of British Identity, 1784–1855." In *The Objects and Textures of Everyday Life in Imperial Britain,* edited by Janet C. Myers and Deirdre H. McMahon. London: Routledge, 2016. https://doi.org/10.4324/9781315562964-2.

Guldi, Jo. "What Is the Spatial Turn?" *Spatial Humanities*. Accessed January 14, 2020. https://spatial.scholarslab.org/spatial-turn/.

Heffernan, Michael. "A Paper City: On History, Maps, and Map Collections in 18th and 19th Century Paris." *Imago Mundi* 66, supp. 1 (September 2014): 5–20. https://doi.org/10.1080/03085694.2014.947847.

Henneberg, J., M. Satchell, X. You, L. Shaw-Taylor, and E. A. Wrigley. *1881 England, Wales and Scotland Rail Lines.* [Data Collection]. Colchester, Essex: UK Data Archive, 2017. 10.5255/UKDA-SN-852993.

Higgs, Edward. *Making Sense of the Census Revisited: Census Records for England and Wales 1801–1901: A Handbook for Historical Researchers.* London: Institute of Historical Research, 2005.

Hitchcock, Tim, and William J. Turkel. "*The Old Bailey Proceedings, 1674–1913*: Text Mining for Evidence of Court Behavior." *Law and History Review* 34, no. 04 (November 2016): 929–55. https://doi.org/10.1017/S0738248016000304.

Hosseini, Kasra, Katherine McDonough, Daniel van Strien, Olivia Vane, and Daniel C. S. Wilson. "Maps of a Nation? The Digitized Ordnance Survey for New Historical Research." *Journal of Victorian Culture* 26, no. 2 (April 2021): 284–99. https://doi.org/10.1093/jvcult/vcab009.

Hosseini, Kasra, Daniel C. S. Wilson, Kaspar Beelen, and Katherine McDonough. "MapReader: A Computer Vision Pipeline for the Semantic Exploration of Maps at Scale." *ArXiv:2111.15592 [Cs]* (November 2021). http://arxiv.org/abs/2111.15592.

Hu, Yingjie, Zhipeng Gui, Jimin Wang, and Muxian Li. "Enriching the Metadata of Map Images: A Deep Learning Approach with GIS-Based Data Augmentation." *International Journal of Geographical Information Science* 36, no. 4 (April 2022): 799–821. https://doi.org/10.1080/13658816.2021.1968407.

Jefferson, Brian Jordan. "Predictable Policing: Predictive Crime Mapping and Geographies of Policing and Race," *Annals of the American Association of Geographers* 108, no. 1 (2018): 1–16. https://doi.org/10.1080/24694452.2017.1293500.

Johnson, Jessica Marie. "Markup Bodies: Black [Life] Studies and Slavery [Death] Studies at the Digital Crossroads." *Social Text* 36, no. 4 (137) (December 2018): 57–79. https://doi.org/10.1215/01642472-7145658.

Kitchin, Rob, and Martin Dodge. "Rethinking Maps." *Progress in Human Geography* 31, no. 3 (June 2007): 331–44. https://doi.org/10.1177/0309132507077082.

Knowles, Anne Kelly. "Historical Geographic Information Systems and Social Science History." *Social Science History* 40, no. 4 (2016): 741–50. https://doi.org/10.1017/ssh.2016.29.

Knowles, Anne Kelly. "Introduction." *Social Science History* 24, no. 3 (August 2000): 451–70.

Kurgan, Laura. *Close Up at a Distance: Mapping, Technology, and Politics*. Cambridge, Mass.: MIT Press, 2013.

McDonough, Katherine, Ludovic Moncla, and Matje van de Camp. "Named Entity Recognition Goes to Old Regime France: Geographic Text Analysis for Early Modern French Corpora." *International Journal of Geographical Information Science* vol. 33, no. 12 (2019): 2498–522.

Murrieta-Flores, Patricia, Alistair Baron, Ian Gregory, Andrew Hardie, and Paul Rayson. "Automatically Analyzing Large Texts in a GIS Environment: The Registrar General's Reports and Cholera in the 19th Century." *Transactions in GIS* 19, no. 2 (2015): 296–320. https://doi.org/10.1111/tgis.12106.

Murrieta-Flores, Patricia, and Bruno Martins. "The Geospatial Humanities: Past, Present and Future." *International Journal of Geographical Information Science* 33, no. 12 (December 2019): 2424–29. https://doi.org/10.1080/13658816.2019.1645336.

National Trust. "National Trust Vows to 'Bring Back the Blossom' as New Research Reveals Massive Drop in Orchards since 1900s." Accessed March 28, 2022. https://www.nationaltrust.org.uk/press-release/national-trust-vows-to-bring-back-the-blossom-as-new-research-reveals-massive-drop-in-orchards-since-1900s.

Padilla, Thomas, Laurie Allen, Stewart Varner, Sarah Potvin, Elizabeth Russey Roke, and Hannah Frost, "Santa Barbara Statement on Collections as Data." *Always Already*

Computational: Collections as Data. 2018. Accessed March 28, 2022, https://collections asdata.github.io/statement/.

Posner, Miriam. "Humanities Data: A Necessary Contradiction." June 25, 2015. https://miriamposner.com/blog/humanities-data-a-necessary-contradiction/.

Posner, Miriam. "What's Next: The Radical, Unrealized Potential of Digital Humanities." In *Debates in the Digital Humanities 2016,* edited by Matthew K. Gold and Lauren F. Klein. Minneapolis: University of Minnesota Press, 2016. https://dhdebates.gc.cuny.edu/read/untitled/section/a22aca14-0eb0-4cc6-a622-6fee9428a357.

Presner, Todd, and David Shepard. "Mapping the Geospatial Turn." In *A New Companion to Digital Humanities,* edited by Susan Schreibman, Ray Siemens, and John Unsworth, 199–212. Malden, Mass.: Wiley-Blackwell, 2015. https://doi.org/10.1002/9781118680605.ch14.

Robertson, Stephen, and Lincoln Mullen. "Arguing with Digital History: Patterns of Historical Interpretation." *Journal of Social History* 54, no. 4 (July 2021): 1005–22. https://doi.org/10.1093/jsh/shab015.

Rumsey, David, and Meredith Williams. "Historical Maps in GIS." In *Past Time, Past Place: GIS for History,* edited by Anne Kelly Knowles, 1–18. Redlands, Calif.: ESRI Press, 2002.

Ryan, Lyndall, Jennifer Debenham, Mark Brown, and William Pascoe. "Introduction: Colonial Frontier Massacres in Eastern Australia 1788–1872." *Centre for 21st Century Humanities.* 2017. https://c21ch.newcastle.edu.au/colonialmassacres/introduction.php.

Schöch, Christof. "Big? Smart? Clean? Messy? Data in the Humanities." *Journal of Digital Humanities* 2, no. 3 (Summer 2013). http://journalofdigitalhumanities.org/2-3/big-smart-clean-messy-data-in-the-humanities/.

Scholz, Luca. "Deceptive Contiguity: The Polygon in Spatial History." *Cartographica: The International Journal for Geographic Information and Geovisualization* 54, no. 3 (Fall 2019): 206–16. https://doi.org/10.3138/cart.54.3.2018-0018.

Schuurman, Nadine. *GIS: A Short Introduction.* Malden, Mass.: Blackwell, 2004.

Tavakkol, Sasan, Yao-Yi Chiang, Tim Waters, Feng Han, Kisalaya Prasad, and Raimondas Kiveris. "Kartta Labs: Unrendering Historical Maps." In *Proceedings of the 3rd ACM SIGSPATIAL International Workshop on AI for Geographic Knowledge Discovery (GeoAI 2019),* 48–51. Chicago: Association for Computing Machinery, 2019. https://doi.org/10.1145/3356471.3365236.

Taylor, Joanna E., Ian N. Gregory, and Christopher Donaldson. "Combining Close and Distant Reading: A Multiscalar Analysis of the English Lake District's Historical Soundscape." *International Journal of Humanities and Arts Computing* 12, no. 2 (October 2018): 163–82. https://doi.org/10.3366/ijhac.2018.0220.

Uhl, Johannes H., and Weiwei Duan. "Automating Information Extraction from Large Historical Topographic Map Archives: New Opportunities and Challenges." *Handbook of Big Geospatial Data,* edited by Martin Werner and Yao-Yi Chiang, 509–22. Cham: Springer International, 2021. https://doi.org/10.1007/978-3-030-55462-0_20.

Uhl, Johannes, Stefan Leyk, Yao-Yi Chiang, Weiwei Duan, and Craig Knoblock. "Map Archive Mining: Visual-Analytical Approaches to Explore Large Historical Map Collections." *ISPRS International Journal of Geo-Information* 7, no. 4 (2018): 148.

Uhl, Johannes H., Stefan Leyk, Yao-Yi Chiang, and Craig A. Knoblock. "Towards the Automated Large-Scale Reconstruction of Past Road Networks from Historical Maps." *Computers, Environment and Urban Systems* 94 (June 2022): 101794. https://doi.org/10.1016/j.compenvurbsys.2022.101794.

Uhl, Johannes H., Stefan Leyk, Zekun Li, Weiwei Duan, Basel Shbita, Yao-Yi Chiang, and Craig A. Knoblock. "Combining Remote-Sensing-Derived Data and Historical Maps for Long-Term Back-Casting of Urban Extents." *Remote Sensing* 13, no. 18 (January 2021): 3672. https://doi.org/10.3390/rs13183672.

Verdier, Nicolas. "Plans et Cartes (France, XVIIIe Siècle)." In *Les Projets: Une Histoire Politique (XVIe-XXIe Siècles), edited by* Frédéric Graber and Martin Giraudeau, 149–61. Paris: Presses des Mines, 2018.

Vitale, Valeria, Pau de Soto, Rainer Simon, Elton Barker, Leif Isaksen, and Rebecca Kahn. "Pelagios—Connecting Histories of Place. Part I: Methods and Tools." *International Journal of Humanities and Arts Computing* 15, no. 1–2 (2021): 5–32.

Wevers, Melvin, and Thomas Smits. "The Visual Digital Turn: Using Neural Networks to Study Historical Images." *Digital Scholarship in the Humanities* 35, no. 1 (1 April 2020): 194–207. https://doi.org/10.1093/llc/fqy085.

Wigen, Kären. *A Malleable Map: Geographies of Restoration in Central Japan, 1600–1912.* Berkeley: University of California Press, 2010. https://public.eblib.com/EBLPublic/PublicView.do?ptiID=566761.

Withers, Charles W. J. "On Trial—Social Relations of Map Production in Mid-Nineteenth-Century Britain." *Imago Mundi* 71, no. 2 (July 2019): 173–95. https://doi.org/10.1080/03085694.2019.1607044.

Yuan, May. "Mapping Text." In *The Spatial Humanities: GIS and the Future of Humanities Scholarship,* edited by David J. Bodenhamer, et al. Indiana University Press, 2010. ProQuest Ebook Central, https://ebookcentral.proquest.com/lib/lancaster/detail.action?docID=1402899.

PART I][Chapter 7

Fugitivities and Futures
Black Studies in the Digital Era

CRYSTAL NICOLE EDDINS

The Black freedom struggle has not only transformed the social, economic, and political fabric of the modern world, it can also inform approaches within the realm of digital technologies. The Black studies academic field challenges the digital humanities and computational studies to advance the Black freedom struggle, rather than uphold and reify biases that are rooted in histories of racism, slavery, and surveillance. Archival records that remain from the era of racial slavery in the Americas document the dehumanizing processes that commodified, enslaved, oppressed, and exploited Black people. Such records foreshadow twenty-first-century patterns of racial discrimination and dispossession, which increasingly rely on digital tools and data yet are also challenged and upended by Black activists' usage of digital technologies. Technological developments such as the Black press, the invention of the television, and the proliferation of the internet have helped facilitate such Black mobilizations to expose the true nature of racial oppression.[1] #BlackLivesMatter and #SayHerName originated as Twitter hashtags that provided online spaces for proverbially "hacking white supremacy" and evolved into the global Black Lives Matter protest movement against the persistent patterns of racially motivated police violence, incarceration, and anti-Black discrimination in places historically linked to slavery and settler colonialism like the United States, Canada, Brazil, France, the United Kingdom, Australia, and Cuba.[2] In late spring and early summer 2020, an unprecedented number of Black Lives Matter protesters, rioters, and allies flooded U.S. cities decrying systemic racism and the killings of George Floyd, Breonna Taylor, and Ahmaud Arbery. These developments indicate how Black radical traditions and Black digital humanities cast the computational humanities, digital tools, data, and data analysis not as apolitical, ahistorical, or objective phenomena but as human constructions informed by the legacies of slavery, racial capitalism, colonialism, and surveillance in ways that counter the episteme of marronnage.

This chapter encourages those in the digital humanities and computational studies, as well as database users, to be sensitive to the ways slavery and the historical usage of runaway advertisements operated as apparatuses of surveillance, a repressive tactic that continues to undermine Black liberation efforts. Black Lives Matter, as well as global economic, health, political, and racial crises, generated public discourses about the persistence of anti-Black racism in various facets of life in postindustrial America: the racial wealth gap, mass incarceration and excessive policing of Black communities, housing segregation, educational inequalities and the school-to-prison pipeline, environmental racism and health disparities, racial terrorism and the symbolic violence of Confederate monuments and flags in public spaces are all unquestionable remnants of slavery's afterlives.[3] But, without considerations of the ways that histories of slavery and racial hierarchies also influence the digital world, the digital humanities and computational studies fields can tend to embed racial biases into the logics of online databases, algorithms, coding practices, and surveillance technologies.[4] Black studies perspectives emphasize reading digitized slavery-related historical documents "against the grain" of their original intentions, highlighting the variety of ways that enslaved people re-humanized themselves, including escaping slavery. This chapter outlines the ways in which archives of slavery and enslaved people's escapes from bondage can urge digital humanities scholarship to elevate perspectives of resistance to systems of domination connected to capitalism and legacies of racial slavery.

The heightened collective consciousness about the legacies of racial slavery has renewed public and academic interest in past, present, and future Black freedom struggles and reinvigorated the concept of marronnage—escape from enslavement—stretching it beyond its historical meanings. In nearly every society in the Americas where racial slavery existed, there was contestation to it in the form of marronnage and other resistance tactics. Rebellion against the violent dehumanization of the European slave trade and the rise of Atlantic world plantation economies was almost instantaneous—beginning as early as 1503 with the first runaway maroons of Haiti—meaning chattel slavery and slave resistance were co-constituted opposing forces that developed over time in dialectical relationship to each other.[5] Many advertisements for enslaved runaways have been digitally archived in several online databases for scholars, researchers, and students to explore and analyze. However, it is important to remember that enslavers used these advertisements as tools to commodify, track, and surveil those who attempted to free themselves from bondage and to re-enslave those self-liberators. Therefore, the advertisements were mechanisms of slavery that are invariably imbued with enslavers' racist intentions, which at times can be unintentionally upheld when the advertisements are digitally archived without critical reflection. The implications of this for the computational humanities are crucial, because they challenge scholars to refuse to see data or data collection as an objective exercise. Black digital humanities challenges computational humanists to investigate surveillance as a tool to recapture—either digitally through big data or in real-life scenarios such as policing—Black freedom-seeking people.

As Vanessa Holden and Joshua Rothman state in "Freedom on the Move and Ethical Challenges in the Digital History of Slavery," both the front- and back-end work of digitally archiving, studying, coding, and interpreting these records requires those who contribute to the database, and its users, to develop a fine understanding of the histories of slavery as well as the socially constructed nature of race and racism. Holden and Rothman argue that without the intervention of trained historians, scholars, and archivists, participants who code and process demographic information about maroons from runaway advertisements may "recreate the inspections and quantifications of Black people and their worth, which, as scholars such as Walter Johnson and Daina Ramey Berry have demonstrated, made their capital, reproductive, and labor values assessable under slavery."[6] For example, one way that database participants may inadvertently affirm the logics of slavery is to uncritically codify the racialized language that enslavers used to describe enslaved people. Holden and Rothman call for contributors and researchers to carefully consider the power dynamics embedded in the advertisements and to reflect on ways their digital practices can oppose that power. Such insights are particularly important given the rapidly changing mechanisms of invasive surveillance technologies that have been disproportionately weaponized against Black people, from eighteenth- and nineteenth-century print media runaway slave advertisements to twenty-first-century facial recognition software.[7]

Without careful consideration of these archives and the digital technologies that house them, it is possible or even likely for the computational humanities to reinforce the violent, oppressive forces that historical subjects—like enslaved rebels—attempted to circumvent. Historical records related to slavery—like advertisements for enslaved runaways—can help deepen understanding of marronnage as a state of being, a sociopolitical critique, and a resistance strategy that is foundational to the Black Radical Tradition of rebellions, revolutions, social movements, and collective actions that contest manifestations of racialized capitalism.[8] However, it is important to recognize that there are inherent contradictions that emerge from studying past, present, and future resistance traditions using the very surveillance tools and other digital technologies that power structures deploy to repress liberation efforts. As Safiya Umoja Noble and others have argued, the digital humanities field offers more than new platforms for big data projects; it also reinscribes existing structures of racial inequality through the exploitation of resources and labor from the Global South, "continuing the (neo)colonial projects of the past."[9]

The raw materials, data sources, and capitalist logics that reduce human beings to numerical values, private capital, and exploited labor pools that undergird digital technology platforms cannot be separated from racialized political economies from whence they arise.[10] Kim Gallon suggests a Black digital humanities perspective would embrace humanistic interpretations of data, such as that derived from surveillance technologies, rather than reinforce the oppressive modes of analysis for which that data was intended.[11] If slavery and colonialism have discriminatory and dispossessing afterlives that remain discernible during the age of postindustrial neoliberalism and digital technologies, then it stands to reason that there are contemporary remnants of marronnage. Given that the purpose of marronnage was, in part, to evade structural power of plantation personnel and police forces, we might assume that strategic avoidance of surveillance is an important facet of today's Black protest tradition. Therefore, this chapter encourages present and future scholars, activists, and digital humanists (including computational humanists) and archivists to employ Black studies approaches to interrogate digital archives of marronnage in ways that subvert racial and economic power relations and amplify patterns of Black resistance.

Black studies has unique perspectives and approaches that can inform broader understandings of the potential dangers of digital technologies, as well as the connections between historical and contemporary forms of oppression and insurgents' strategies to resist the reach of surveillance apparatuses. As H. L. T. Quan suggests, from the fifteenth through nineteenth centuries, marronnage foreshadowed the fact that "the propensity to run toward freedom and community building away from conditions of bondage has barely diminished within the context of persistent labor exploitation, hyper-surveillance and unending incarceration" in the twenty-first century.[12] Though our analyses cannot literally or metaphorically liberate enslaved runaways and other rebels from the technological apparatuses that facilitated their subjugation, we can commit to standing in solidarity with their efforts and work to transform material conditions until mechanisms of oppression no longer exist. The histories of oppression and resistance, paired with the concept of marronnage, offer an episteme of fugitivity that should inform the computational humanities of the future.

Maroon Episteme

Eighteenth- and nineteenth-century runaway advertisements hold potential for the study of marronnage and Black resistance, but they can be equally as disturbing as other archival sources in that they were written by plantation owners and were published widely with the specific purpose of tracking and re-enslaving runaways. To reclaim their fugitive "property," enslavers gave accounts of maroons—oftentimes using derogatory language—to describe their sex and gender, physical characteristics, personality disposition, clothing, and other pieces of information such as financial bounties to incentivize the public to identify, capture, and return suspected fugitives. Brutality is evident when runaway advertisements offer brandings, missing limbs and labor-related injuries, or whipping scars as a customary part of slaves' corporeal landscape. Enslaved women's bodies especially carried the mark of physical and sexual violence in their own scars and in the very existence of the children (sometimes biological offspring of white enslavers) they sought to protect and nurture through marronnage.[13] Rather than use archival sources and the emerging digital technologies that house them in ways that reify biased narratives or reduce the lived experiences of enslaved people to sterilized statistical data points, scholars of subaltern and oppressed communities and digital humanists are urged to read beyond the immediate texts and contexts of the sources by employing analytical perspectives that can envision the imaginary consciousness of those silenced by history without violating the boundaries of historical archives.[14] This approach aligns with historian Vincent Brown's idea of "going against the grain" of quantitative analysis in slavery studies during the current database age. As Brown points out, quantitative analysis can support the sociocultural interpretive tradition of Black studies and explain things the primary sources intended to conceal. Black radical intellectual and activist traditions thus can inform how scholars should engage slavery archives about marronnage, and the digital sphere more broadly, in meaningful ways.[15]

Advertisements for enslaved runaways contain information that provides a focused, albeit fleeting and speculative, look inside the minds of fugitives. We can look at the advertisements and discern ways maroons routinely violated the legal codes and social mores that heavily regulated and constrained enslaved people's behavior. With access to digitized archival sources, we can foreground the experiences and lives of individual runaways and begin to give needed attention to aspects of their humanity, including their motivations for escape, their social networks, labor skills, or intended geographic destinations. For example, the *Marronnage in the Atlantic World* (*Marronnage dans la monde atlantique*), an online database and open-source resource covered by an Attribution-NonCommercial license, houses runaway advertisements published in colonial Haiti and other former French colonies.[16] In the database, we find individuals like a valet and wigmaker named Julien who was born in Haiti (then called Saint-Domingue) near the port city Cap-Français (now Cap-Haitien) and escaped his owner, Msr. Larralde, on February 11, 1776. The newspaper advertisement placed to surveil and recapture Julien also made mention of his mother, a free woman named Francoise-Jeanneton Taunier, who lived at Jacquezy, as well as his sister Marie-Jeanne, who also was a free woman living at Morne-au-Diable.[17] While enslavers sought to exploit their knowledge of Julien's labor skills and familial relationships as pertinent information to aid in locating and re-enslaving him, we can also interpret this information to understand how maroons may have leveraged their human and social capital to find safe haven. Maroons created solidarity and retained their social networks by escaping in dyads, triads, or even in groups of over a dozen; locating family members and other loved ones on different plantations or neighboring towns; joining established maroon settlements in geographical isolated areas; and at times seeking harbor with free people of color. Carrying arms or appropriating money, food, and clothing were actions that demonstrated absconders intended to successfully escape and survive the dangerous journeys beyond plantations. Some maroons claimed to be free by forging written passes or by disguising themselves in the garb of free people of color or as a person of the opposite sex. A person caught perpetrating such actions could face life-threatening punishments. The boldness and craftiness that was required to take such actions exemplifies attitudes of fearlessness and deliberate opposition to slave-holding society's dominating conventions that restricted bondspeople.

I identified these behaviors associated with marronnage from content analysis of over 10,000 runaway slave advertisements that were published in colonial Haiti's eighteenth-century newspaper *Les Affiches américaines* and are now digitally archived in the *Marronnage in the Atlantic World* (*Marronnage dans la monde atlantique*). With the liberty to share and adapt the materials housed in the site, web-scraping data collection techniques facilitated acquisition of the advertisement data. The intention was to use the data for research that could "liberate" marronnage studies from traditional methods that simply quantify runaways by population, gender, and ethnic demographics and, instead, opt for a methodology that merges qualitative and quantitative analyses to highlight how enslaved Africans and African descendants developed their own understandings of self and the world, social relationships, hopes for freedom, and tools of liberation. I considered each individual enslaved runaway as a participant in a microlevel protest and created variables for analysis by coding aspects of maroons' behaviors described in the advertisements. Though there are shortcomings with the data, such as an underrepresentation of women and other missing information, the volume of runaways described in the advertisements allowed for quantitative analysis of maroons' gender and racial or ethnic identities, their social networks, their geographic locations of origin, their suspected destinations, and their oppositional behaviors such as expropriating resources, bearing arms, or passing for free. I also coded the amount of time a runaway had been missing as a continuous scale variable measured in weeks.

With the data coded, I analyzed these categories with statistical tests of frequency distribution, association, and comparison using STATA computational software to examine marronnage patterns over time. For example, chi-square tests of association showed that Africa-born enslaved runaways were more likely to escape in groups than were "creoles" born in colonial Haiti, who were more likely to have had an existing kinship tie, a labor or linguistic skill, or other form of social or human capital to facilitate their escape, as in the case of the maroon Julien described above. Similarly, women were more likely than men to have been described as seeking haven with a family member, free people of color, or other enslaved people, underscoring the importance of social networks to women and children's survival in a deadly slave society such as colonial Haiti. Lastly, chi-square tests also revealed a slow but steady increase in maroons' attempts to remain at large for longer than six months in the years leading to the Haitian Revolution, suggesting the presence of a collective liberation consciousness that fed into the 1791 uprising.[18]

Maroons are generally regarded as people who either isolated "themselves from a surrounding society in order to create a fully autonomous community" or refashioned themselves and geographic spaces dedicated to slavery and oppression for their own purposes.[19] Maroons are symbols of national heroism in places like Haiti, Cuba, Brazil, Jamaica, and Suriname, where armed communities like the Windward and Leeward Maroons and the Palmares Kingdom mounted military resistance to colonial forces and forged zones of liberation amid expanding plantation societies. Traditions of these long-term maroon struggles and cultural heritages have been shared through oral histories, music, dance and martial art forms, poetry, fictional literature, archaeological findings, as well as claims to reparations for slavery, land rights, and self-governance.[20] These legacies point to marronnage as not only a resistance tactic but a form of antislavery, anticolonial social thought and political theory. For Neil Roberts, the Haitian Revolution serves as an ideal type of "sovereign" marronnage—the country's revolutionary act of flight from the late eighteenth- and early nineteenth-century Atlantic world slave economy toward independence and sovereignty. At the microlevel, Roberts conceptualizes "sociogenic" marronnage as a community formation of shared social and political conditions as well as collective consciousness, rituals, and forms of communalism.[21] Similarly, H. L. T. Quan imagines maroon communities' collective "refusals to be governed as confirmation of democratic sensibility" as a model of resistance and a vision for living in possible futures: "the act of running away, or building independent communities . . . provides a way of knowing about life outside the state and other dominions."[22] These insights help to contextualize Black studies as a mode of inquiry that is grounded in the sociohistorical realities of resistance to racial slavery and informs further study of the Black experience in ways that emphasize Black freedom.

Black Studies as Fugitivity and the Digital Turn

Black studies was born of a tradition of fugitivity. Late-nineteenth and early-twentieth-century thinkers, as well as 1960s student protesters and think tanks like the Institute of the Black World, individually and collectively eschewed the dominance of European-centered modes of scientific and humanistic thought, fostering distinctive intellectual spaces to produce new knowledge, research, and scholarship about the global Black experience. Both marginalized from the academy and taking part in acts of epistemological flight, the charter generation of Black studies scholars abandoned the boundaries of traditional disciplines, simultaneously drawing on tools from history, sociology, journalism, philosophy, anthropology, political science, and the cultural arts. They also rejected claims to objectivity, instead pronouncing their ideological and political commitment to and solidarity with the formerly enslaved and colonized Black peoples of the world. Their sense of obligation to dismantle racist institutions, end colonialism and racial terrorism, and contest the rise of scientific racism through research, writings, and activism made people like W. E. B. Du Bois, C. L. R. James, Anna Julia Cooper, Edward Blyden, Ida B. Wells-Barnett, and Maria Stewart intellectuals of radical thought and action. These scholars' works illuminated and theorized about the many facets of the Black Radical Tradition. The proliferation of the Black studies digital humanities arena, and the resulting online distribution of university resources in an era of increasing academic neoliberalism, might further represent what Stefano Harney and Fred Moten describe as the "maroon community of the university"—networks of subversive intellectuals using their privileged status to produce academic work and activism that disrupts the status quo.[23]

The digital turn portends new interpretations of "public scholarship" that dissolves boundaries between the wider world and the academy, where walls of elitism block public access to university libraries and specialized archives, academic journals, professional organizations and their annual or biannual conferences, and even coding skills and software programs. The Black studies tradition has infused a sociocultural tradition within the digital humanities field, which is often characterized by computation void of humanistic elements.[24] Web-based visual projects, digitized archives, live-streamed conferences, academic blogs, and other endeavors engage wider audiences in new modes of knowledge production while linking scholars across disciplines, colleges and universities, and nation-state boundaries to engage in critical intellectual work. Individuals and collectives of scholars use hashtags like #Blktwitterstorians, #CiteBlackWomen, and #SlaveryArchive to speak to the nuanced experiences, contributions, and labor of Black scholars, particularly women, doing archival work on slavery and other subjects. Course syllabi such as the #LemonadeSyllabus, the #FergusonSyllabus, and the #CharlestonSyllabus provide academic peers and the public with resources to help contextualize and comprehend major cultural, social, or political events as they unfold in real time. Scholars converse about their archival findings and reflections on social media, organize working groups, and curate bibliographic blogs such as *African Diaspora, PhD* and *Black Perspectives,* the blog of the African American Intellectual History Society, providing meta-archives of the most recent advances in research and knowledge production.

These peer-sharing efforts have also been met with an increased availability of digitized primary sources related to the enslavement of Africans and African descendants in early colonial societies. Collaborations between historians and programmers have transformed and translated archival documents into large datasets, such as Gwendolyn Midlo Hall's database *Afro-Louisiana History and Genealogy, 1719–1820* and the *Slave Societies Digital Archive* directed by Jane Landers. The *Trans-Atlantic Slave Trade Database* is a comprehensive archive of nearly all known voyages of the European slave trade between the sixteenth and nineteenth centuries and has been an extensively used resource for scholars studying a range of topics related to precolonial Africa, slavery, and the Atlantic world.

Records from the U.S. Reconstruction era are housed in the *Freedom Bureau Project,* a digital portal that allows users to browse materials in search of antebellum-era ancestors.[25] Most recently, the MATRIX Center for Digital Humanities and Social Sciences at Michigan State University (MSU) initiated *Enslaved: Peoples of the Historical Slave Trade,* an online data hub to link collections from multiple universities, allowing users to search through millions of pieces of data about enslaved Africans and their descendants from a single source.[26] These materials have helped scholars understand the qualitative and quantitative nature of enslaved people's patterns of forced migration to the Americas, the composition of their African origins, their kinship and network formations, and modes of survival in "New World" colonial plantation societies. Access to these types of materials is not only helpful for scholars and citizen historians, students, and educators to gain better understanding of slavery and colonialism, but actual descendants of enslaved people can use these resources for genealogical research that can potentially support individual and collective claims to reparations.[27]

The convergence of Black protest and intellectual traditions, combined with developments in the digital humanities and turns toward public history, has created space for new and creative approaches to analyzing resistance to slavery using digitized archival materials. Online resources can highlight enslaved people's rebellions in novel ways, like Vincent Brown's interactive map *Slave Revolt in Jamaica, 1760–1761: A Cartographic Narrative,* depicting the spatial unfolding of Tacky's Revolt using materials such as primary source newspapers, maps, and journals.[28] Runaway slave advertisements that were published in colonial-era newspapers are increasingly a subject of digitization as several databases have emerged in recent years. The *North Carolina Runaway Slave Advertisements, 1750–1840,* developed at University of North Carolina Greensboro, the University of Virginia's *Geography of Slavery in Virginia,* and the Twitter-based *Adverts 250 Project* house runaway advertisements that give educators, students, and researchers alike the capability to browse, analyze, and code historical documents related to enslaved African descendants' individual and collective resistance efforts—possibilities previously only available to seasoned academics and archivists.[29]

Additionally, these resources can allow the study of microlevel action during periods of macrolevel social change and transformation. In my undergraduate course Slavery, Racism, Colonialism in the African Diaspora at the University of North Carolina at Charlotte, I highlighted an advertisement published in January 1778 in New Bern, North Carolina, for a woman named Carolina, who was "supposed to be harboured [sic] by the negroes of Col. John Patten in Beaufort County" to accompany students' reading of Julius Scott's *The Common Wind* and to help them connect microhistories to broader patterns of maroon resistance during the Age of Revolutions.[30] Cornell University's *Freedom on the Move* crowdsources volunteer transcribers and coders to bolster the site's searchability and provides resources for K–12 educators to incorporate the runaway advertisement materials into classroom settings while reflecting on how the historical archives reproduce power and violence. These databases, as well as the *Fugitive Slave Database* by scholars at the University of Bristol, primarily focus on advertisements for enslaved runaways in the Cotton Belt region of the U.S. South. Other projects expand the geographical scope of fugitivity to include areas that are often excluded in conversations about enslavement, such as the *Texas Runaway Slave Project, Runaway Connecticut,* and the *Documenting Runaway Slaves Project,* which seeks to highlight the southern United States as well as the Caribbean and Brazil. Other projects based outside the United States include the previously mentioned *Marronnage in the Atlantic World* (*Marronnage dans la monde atlantique*) database from the French Atlantic History Group, which compiles advertisements from French Caribbean and North American colonies, and *Runaway Slaves in Britain,* which gives insight to the thousands of people of African, Asian, and Indigenous American descent enslaved in eighteenth-century Britain.

Historians Vincent Brown and Jessica Marie Johnson advise that researchers be cautiously attentive to the ways in which digitized archival sources and their respective technological apparatuses can take for granted, concretize, and reinforce white enslavers' biases and acts of violence.[31] Most of the available primary sources related to enslavement in the Atlantic world come from colonial planters who owned and exploited enslaved people, slavery apologists, traffickers of captives, and brokers who inscribed their racist interpretations of Africans into the very documents—maps, plantation inventories, slave trading records, shipping logs, personal journals and notes, and runaway slave advertisements—that researchers currently use to reconstruct narratives of enslaved people's lives. Bondspeople were not regarded as human beings but as chattel property who were described in records with the same level of status as an animal or a piece of furniture. Enslavement prescribed a "social death" of alienation from kith and kin, cultural heritage, social and political rights and liberties, or economic freedoms.[32] Without social, economic, or political protections from dehumanization, white enslavers' and plantation overseers' violence and brutality toward enslaved people was quotidian. Saidiya Hartman reminds us that "scandal and excess inundate the archive" with horrifying accounts of Black deaths, rapes, and illnesses.[33] Indifference to Black humanity and the violent denial of it "determines, regulates and organizes the kinds of statements that can be made about slavery" and "creates subjects and objects of power."[34] The runaway slave advertisement archive, however, is an opportunity for scholars to deviate from witnessing the violence embedded in slavery records, an intellectual marronnage if you will, and to assume the perspective of those who rejected their reality of violent slavery by risking their lives to escape. Histories of marronnage can lend to our understanding of contemporary and future resistance tactics; however, the insights from Hartman, Johnson, and Brown remind us that the print and digital technologies that allow us to study marronnage are the very apparatuses of capital accumulation, surveillance, and capture that rebels are trying to escape.

Maroon Futures

This chapter presents a framework connecting marronnage to broader forms of collective action that demonstrates how insights about the use of digitized advertisements, which were intended to preserve slavery by surveilling and tracking runaways, can be used to interpret Black agency and meaningful human processes that challenge enslavers' original intentions. Maroon agency, grounded in the experience of enslaved Africans and their wide-ranging forms of resistance to bondage, might serve as pillars for contemporary and future collective actions that reject the racial oppression and economic exploitation embedded in global capitalism.[35] Public engagement with runaways, their self-articulations of humanity, and their pursuits for freedom—precarious as it may have been—portend inspiration for social justice activists and others attempting to carve out social, geographic, economic, political, and digital spaces that will allow them to flourish in their being and challenge institutions of anti-Blackness.[36] What does marronnage look like in the age of information and big data; the age of digital turns; the age of hypercapitalism, unprecedented wealth disparities, and widespread precarity; the age of climate change; the age of surveillance and mass incarceration—and what type of revolutionary potentiality does it hold? Based on historical study of the characteristics and principles of marronnage that I described above, I have developed a framework for identifying and understanding Black resistance both in and through computational spaces that may transcend the historical connotation of flight.

These tenets include, but may not be limited to

- reclamation of the Black self as a commodified source of capital, and redirection of time, energy, and effort toward individual, familial, or collective needs and interests;
- creation of solidarity networks of people who share social position and liberatory goals;
- networks characterized by movement or transience, having network nodes that are linked by women;
- appropriation and subversion of material goods and technologies that are typically used as apparatuses of racial capitalism;
- experiencing geographic, social, economic, and political marginalization, disempowerment, and disenfranchisement from centers of power and capital yet creating spaces organized around communal principles;
- coded forms of communication and systems of protection to enhance solidarity and to avoid surveillance or betrayal by those whose

socioeconomic mobility hinges on figurative or literal forms of re-enslavement;
- drawing on intimate knowledge of land, space, and local ecologies for survival;
- development of rituals to orient collective consciousness, to affirm collective identity, and to build solidarity;
- reimagining, rejecting, and traversing hegemonic identities, gender norms, and sociopolitical borders;
- developing self-defense or direct-action fighting techniques and tactics, such as martial arts, bearing arms, or adopting militaristic strategies to contest repression;
- disruption of capital accumulation processes that extract resources from Black spaces.

To briefly highlight solidarity networks and traversing hegemonic identities, for example, U.S. and Canadian Black women and transgendered prison abolitionists liken their work to the tactics of maroons, such as rejecting the language of state-sanctioned emancipation, opting for prison abolition, and building "black-brown" coalitions with Native American activists—not unlike historical maroons of African and Indigenous origin in places like Haiti, Florida, and Cuba. These anti-prison activists were motivated by survival imperatives and analogies between plantation slavery and the carceral state, while rejecting heteronormative gender identity and relying on spiritual sensibilities that supported their identities and ideologies.[37] Such activities also harken to figures like Magdeleine, an enslaved woman in colonial Haiti who fled her owner disguised as a man to join her lover Hyacinthe, a ritualist and rebel leader who led thousands during the Haitian Revolution.[38]

For historical maroons, freedom was precarious at best, and they were almost always vulnerable to either violent repression or re-enslavement. Evidence of this continued subjugation is found in the direct linkages between antebellum-era fugitive slave police, post-emancipation sharecropping labor, Jim Crow laws and convict leasing, and the present-day carceral state.[39] But rather than rely solely on brute force repression against insurgents, contemporary government and nongovernment entities also include covert, technology-based forms of repression such as misinformation, infiltration, and surveillance and sabotage, which seem to have been effective tactics to undermine Black mobilizations. Infiltration happens when online forums that are designated as "safe" spaces are trolled or "Zoombombed," not only by those with white supremacist leanings but by anonymous posters using "digital blackface" to delegitimize, dominate, and redirect conversations dedicated to antiracist dialogue, teaching, and organizing.[40] The Federal Bureau of Investigation (FBI) honed its counterintelligence programming by systematically undermining Marcus Garvey's Universal Negro Improvement Association, the same program that was later weaponized against members of the Civil Rights Movement, the Black

Panther Party, and the Republic of New Africa.[41] FBI surveillance of Black protesters, including monitoring their online activity, erroneously labels them as domestic terrorists—dubbed "Black Identity Extremists" whose anger over the 2014 killing of Michael Brown and other acts of state-sanctioned violence allegedly "spurred an increase in premeditated, retaliatory lethal violence against law enforcement."[42] Further, the National Security Agency has collected an assortment of raw and metadata from an untold number of our phone calls, emails, and Facebook posts for unknown purposes.[43] Combined with recent challenges to the Fourth Amendment by the U.S. Supreme Court, there is a high likelihood of increased racially driven police contacts based on questionably obtained information such as cellular phone records.[44]

The historically grounded and metaphorical state of liminality in marronnage can translate to twenty-first-century conceptions of fugitivity and has real-life implications for subversive collective actions, given ongoing transformations and adaptations of anti-Black institutions, economic modalities, and methods of re-enslaving Black people. The need for transformative subversion of state invasiveness using digital technology likely will come from mobilizers at the microlevel who, like maroons, use a range of resistance tactics to challenge and expose the contradictions of oppression and exploitation. Black people have "subverted or remixed dominant technologies using local (cultural) practices" to produce artifacts of tangible and intangible culture such as hair braiding patterns, musical forms, and artistic pieces created with discarded materials.[45] More specifically, Simone Browne offers "dark sousveillance" as a "site of critique, as it speaks to black epistemologies of contending with antiblack surveillance" and reverses the watchful anti-Black gaze from activists to state apparatuses.[46] Black Lives Matter protesters' use of "cop watching" and video activism using camera phones has been an effective countersurveillance tool in revealing police misconduct and advancing broader conversations about social movements against racial inequality.[47] Cellular phone cameras, street cameras, and police "badge cams" bore witness to the deaths of Philando Castile, Tamir Rice, Eric Garner, and Keith Lamont Scott in ways that were previously inaccessible. Similarly, the Water Protectors at the Standing Rock Sioux Reservation used drones or "aerial sousveillance" to document human rights violations and to provide counternarratives to police accounts of their actions.[48] Dark sousveillance has appeared in several other forms, such as hacking and leaking confidential documents that reveal racially motivated targeting of organizers, opposing repressive legislation, and fighting carceral expansion.[49] Other social movement activists employ tactics of secrecy, such as encrypting emails or changing cellular phone SIM cards to avoid surveillance—methods that are reminiscent of the ways fugitive slaves protected maroons communities with code words and alternative means of communication.[50]

Still, surveillance technologies, when in the control of the state and privately owned militarized entities, place limits on the effectiveness of less sophisticated video evidence from activists and have the potential power to thwart Black radical activism and societal civil liberties by magnifying "existing social control functions . . .

[and] capital accumulation imperatives" in unprecedented ways.[51] These seemingly bleak realities portend important questions for the future of fugitivity and for the role of scholars—especially digital humanists—in analyzing past, present, and future archives related to Black life. A Black digital humanities approach inherently involves fugitivity as a critique of structural inequalities and the technological platforms on which they rely, and as a mode of data analysis that seeks to free those bound by historical, present, and future archives. Marronnage was based on aspirations and struggles for freedom from hegemonic conceptions of Blackness and economically exploitative and oppressive practices that result in anti-Black outcomes, pointing toward an Afrofuture that "is explicitly antifacist insofar as it provides an imaginary domain for radical democratic politics and life-forms outside of white supremacy, racial capitalism, and hetero-patriarchy."[52] The digital humanities can stand in solidarity with social justice efforts by employing notions of Black fugitivity as a uniquely Black studies approach to recognize collective consciousness and Black agency embedded in data sources and technological platforms otherwise marked by slavery, racial oppression, and death.

Notes

1. Everett, "The Revolution Will Be Digitized"; Fleming and Morris, "Theorizing Ethnic and Racial Movements."

2. Greene-Hayes and James, "Cracking the Codes," 68; "Black Lives Matter Everywhere," *World Policy Journal*.

3. Hartman, *Lose Your Mother*.

4. Browne, *Dark Matters*; Benjamin, *Race after Technology*; Noble, *Algorithms of Oppression*.

5. For comparative overviews on marronnage in the Atlantic world, see Heuman, *Out of the House of Bondage*; Price, *Maroon Societies*; Diouf, *Fighting the Slave Trade*; Thompson, *Flight to Freedom*.

6. See chapter 11 in this volume by Holden and Rothman.

7. Browne, *Dark Matters*.

8. Robinson, *Black Marxism*.

9. Noble, "Toward a Critical Black Digital Humanities."

10. Cottom, "Where Platform Capitalism and Racial Capitalism Meet"; Hammer and Park, "Ghost in the Algorithm"; Morgan, *Reckoning with Slavery*.

11. Gallon, "Making a Case."

12. Quan, "'It's Hard to Stop Rebels,'" 184.

13. Miki, "Fleeing into Slavery"; Fuentes, *Dispossessed Lives*; Eddins, "'Rejoice!'"

14. Hartman, "Venus in Two Acts"; Brown, "Mapping a Slave Revolt"; Fuentes, *Dispossessed Lives*; Johnson, "Black [Life] Studies."

15. Brown, "Mapping a Slave Revolt"; Brown, "Designing Histories of Slavery"; Johnson, "Black [Life] Studies."

16. *Marronnage dans la monde atlantique* (Marronnage in the Atlantic World) can be accessed at http://marronnage.info/fr/index.html.

17. *Les Affiches américaines,* February 24, 1776, accessed February 24, 2021, http://www.marronnage.info/fr/document.php?id=255.

18. Eddins, "Runaways, Repertoires, and Repression"; Eddins, "'Rejoice!'"

19. Roberts, *Freedom as Marronnage,* 4; Miki, "Fleeing into Slavery."

20. Césaire, "Le verbe marronner"; Price, *Alabi's World*; Bilby, *True-Born Maroons*; White, "Maroon Archaeology"; Planas, "Brazil's 'Quilombo' Movement."

21. Roberts, *Freedom as Marronnage,* ch. 3–4.

22. Quan, "'It's Hard to Stop Rebels,'" 182.

23. Robinson, *Black Marxism*; Harney and Moten, *The Undercommons,* 26.

24. Gallon, "Making a Case."

25. Gwendolyn Midlo Hall's *Afro-Louisiana History and Genealogy, 1719–1820,* can be accessed at http://www.ibiblio.org/laslave/; Jane Landers' *Slave Societies Digital Archive* can be accessed at https://slavesocieties.org/; the *Trans-Atlantic Slave Trade Database* can be accessed at https://www.slavevoyages.org/.

26. "MSU Uses $1.5M Mellon Foundation Grant," *MSU Today.*

27. Darity, "Forty Acres and a Mule."

28. Vincent Brown's "Slave Revolt in Jamaica, 1760–1761: A Cartographic Narrative," can be accessed at http://revolt.axismaps.com/project.html.

29. Several other runaway advertisement databases are enumerated in Eddins, "On the Lives of Fugitives."

30. *North Carolina Gazette,* January 16, 1778, accessed January 11, 2024, https://dlas.uncg.edu/notices/notice/1716/.

31. Brown, "Mapping a Slave Revolt"; Johnson, "Black [Life] Studies."

32. Patterson, *Slavery and Social Death.*

33. Hartman, "Venus in Two Acts," 5.

34. Hartman, 10.

35. Robinson, *Black Marxism,* ch. 6–7.

36. Saucier and Woods, "What is the *danger.*"

37. Sudbury, "Maroon Abolitionists."

38. *Les Affiches américaines,* November 11, 1790, accessed March 11, 2021, http://www.marronnage.info/fr/document.php?id=10791; Fick, *The Making of Haiti,* 139.

39. Blackmon, *Slavery by Another Name*; Alexander, *The New Jim Crow*; Spruill, "Slave Patrols."

40. Jackson, "Memes and Misogynoir"; Lorenz and Alba, "'Zoombombing.'"

41. Davenport, *How Social Movements Die.*

42. FBI, "Black Identity Extremists," 2; Speri, "The FBI Spends a Lot of Time."

43. "FAQ: What You Need to Know about the NSA's Surveillance Programs," *ProPublica.*

44. Sorkin, "In Carpenter Case."

45. Gaskins, "Techno-Vernacular Creativity," 252.

46. Browne, *Dark Matters*, 21.
47. Canella, "Racialized Surveillance."
48. Schnepf, "Unsettling Aerial Surveillance."
49. Berger, "Mapping Resistance to Surveillance."
50. Leistert, "Resistance against Cyber-Surveillance."
51. Monahan, "Counter-surveillance as Political Intervention?" 516.
52. Quan, "'It's Hard to Stop Rebels,'" 191.

Bibliography

Alexander, Michelle. *The New Jim Crow: Mass Incarceration in the Age of Colorblindness.* New York: New Press, 2010.

Benjamin, Ruha. *Race after Technology: Abolitionist Tools for the New Jim Code.* Cambridge: Polity Press, 2019.

Berger, Dan. "Mapping Resistance to Surveillance." *Black Perspectives,* March 29, 2019. https://www.aaihs.org/mapping-resistance-to-surveillance.

Bilby, Kenneth M. *True-Born Maroons.* Gainesville: University Press of Florida, 2008.

"Black Lives Matter Everywhere." Special issue, *World Policy Journal* 33, no. 1 (2016).

Blackmon, Douglas A. *Slavery by Another Name: The Re-Enslavement of Black Americans from the Civil War to World War II.* New York: Doubleday, 2008.

Brown, Vincent. "Designing Histories of Slavery for the Database Age." *MIT Comparative Media Studies,* February 27, 2016. http://cmsw.mit.edu/podcast-vincent-brown-designing-histories-of-slavery-for-the-database-age.

Brown, Vincent. "Mapping a Slave Revolt: Visualizing Spatial History through the Archives of Slavery." *Social Text* 33, no. 4 (2015): 134–41.

Browne, Simone. *Dark Matters: On the Surveillance of Blackness.* Durham, N.C.: Duke University Press, 2015.

Canella, Gino. "Racialized Surveillance: Activist Media and the Policing of Black Bodies." *Communication Culture & Critique* 11 (2018) 378–98.

Césaire, Aimé. "Le verbe marronner/The Verb 'Marronner.'" In *The Collected Poetry,* translated by Clayton Eshleman and Annette Smith, 368–71. Berkeley: University of California Press, 1983.

Cottom, Tressie McMillan. "Where Platform Capitalism and Racial Capitalism Meet: The Sociology of Race and Racism in the Digital Society." *Sociology of Race and Ethnicity* 6 no. 4 (2020): 441–49.

Darity, William, Jr. "Forty Acres and a Mule in the 21st Century." *Social Science Quarterly* 89, no. 3 (2008): 656–64.

Davenport, Christian. *How Social Movements Die: Repression and Demobilization of the Republic of New Africa.* New York: Cambridge University Press, 2014.

Diouf, Sylvaine, ed. *Fighting the Slave Trade: West African Strategies.* Athens: Ohio University Press, 2003.

Eddins, Crystal. "On the Lives of Fugitives: Runaway Slave Advertisement Databases." *HASTAC,* March 30, 2017. https://publishing-archives.hastac.hcommons.org/2017/03/30/on-the-lives-of-fugitives-runaway-slave-advertisement-databases/.

Eddins, Crystal. "'Rejoice! Your Wombs Will Not Beget Slaves!' Marronnage as Reproductive Justice in Colonial Haiti." *Gender & History* 32, no. 3 (2020): 562–80.

Eddins, Crystal. "Runaways, Repertoires, and Repression: Marronnage and the Haitian Revolution, 1766–1791." *Journal of Haitian Studies* 25, no. 1 (2019): 4–38.

Everett, Anna. "The Revolution Will Be Digitized: Afrocentricity and the Digital Public Sphere." *Social Text* 20, no. 2 (2002): 125–46.

"FAQ: What You Need to Know about the NSA's Surveillance Programs." *ProPublica,* August 5, 2013. https://www.propublica.org/article/nsa-data-collection-faq.

Federal Bureau of Investigations. "Black Identity Extremists Likely Motivated to Target Law Enforcement Officers." Intelligence Assessment, Counterterrorism Division, August 3, 2017. https://privacysos.org/wp-content/uploads/2017/10/FBI-BlackIdentityExtremists.pdf.

Fick, Carolyn. *The Making of Haiti: The Saint Domingue Revolution from Below.* Knoxville: University of Tennessee Press, 1990.

Fleming, Crystal M., and Aldon Morris. "Theorizing Ethnic and Racial Movements in the Global Age: Lessons from the Civil Rights Movement." *Sociology of Race and Ethnicity* 1, no. 1 (2015): 105–26.

Fuentes, Marisa J. *Dispossessed Lives: Enslaved Women, Violence, and the Archive.* Philadelphia: University of Pennsylvania Press, 2016.

Gallon, Kim. "Making a Case for the Black Digital Humanities." In *Debates in the Digital Humanities,* edited by Matthew K. Gold and Lauren F. Klein. Minneapolis: University of Minnesota Press, 2016. https://dhdebates.gc.cuny.edu/read/untitled/section/fa10e2e1-0c3d-4519-a958-d823aac989eb#ch04.

Gaskins, Nettrice R. "Techno-Vernacular Creativity and Innovation across the African Diaspora and Global South." In *Captivating Technology: Race, Carceral Technoscience, and Liberatory Imagination in Everyday Life,* edited by Ruha Benjamin, 252-74. Durham, N.C.: Duke University Press, 2019.

Greene-Hayes, Ahmad, and Joy James. "Cracking the Codes of Black Power Struggles: Hacking, Hacked, and Black Lives Matter." *The Black Scholar* 47, no. 3 (2017): 68–78.

Hammer, Ricarda, and Tina M. Park. "The Ghost in the Algorithm: Racial Colonial Capitalism and the Digital Age." *Political Power and Social Theory* 38: 221–49.

Harney, Stefano, and Fred Moten. *The Undercommons: Fugitive Planning and Black Study.* Wivenhoe: Minor Compositions, 2013.

Hartman, Saidiya. *Lose Your Mother: A Journey along the Atlantic Slave Route.* New York: Farrar, Straus and Giroux, 2007.

Hartman, Saidiya. "Venus in Two Acts." *Small Axe* 12, no. 2 (2008): 1–14.

Heuman, Gad, ed. *Out of the House of Bondage: Runaways, Resistance and Marronnage in Africa and the New World.* London: Frank Cass, 1986.

Jackson, Laura M. "Memes and Misogynoir." *The Awl,* August 28, 2014. https://www.theawl.com/2014/08/memes-and-misogynoir/.

Johnson, Jessica Marie. "Black [Life] Studies and Slavery [Death] Studies at the Digital Crossroads." *Social Text* 36, no. 4 (2018): 57–79.

Leistert, Oliver. "Resistance against Cyber-Surveillance within Social Movements and How Surveillance Adapts." *Surveillance & Society* 9, no. 4 (2012): 441–56.

Lorenz, Taylor, and Davey Alba. "'Zoombombing' Becomes a Dangerous Organized Effort." *New York Times,* April 3, 2020. https://www.nytimes.com/2020/04/03/technology/zoom-harassment-abuse-racism-fbi-warning.html.

Miki, Yuko. "Fleeing into Slavery: The Insurgent Geographies of Brazilian Quilombolas (Maroons), 1880–1881." *The Americas* 68, no. 4 (2012): 495–528.

Monahan, Torin. "Counter-surveillance as Political Intervention?" *Social Semiotics* 16, no. 4 (2006): 515–534.

Morgan, Jennifer L. *Reckoning with Slavery: Gender, Kinship, and Capitalism in the Early Black Atlantic.* Durham, N.C.: Duke University Press, 2021.

"MSU Uses $1.5M Mellon Foundation Grant to Build Massive Slave Trade Database," *MSU Today,* January 9, 2018. http://msutoday.msu.edu/news/2018/msu-uses-15m-mellon-foundation-grant-to-build-massive-slave-trade-database.

Noble, Safiya Umoja. *Algorithms of Oppression: How Search Engines Reinforce Racism.* New York: New York University Press, 2018.

Noble, Safiya Umoja. "Toward a Critical Black Digital Humanities." In *Debates in the Digital Humanities,* edited by Matthew K. Gold and Lauren F. Klein. Minneapolis: University of Minnesota Press, 2019. https://dhdebates.gc.cuny.edu/read/untitled-f2acf72c-a469-49d8-be35-67f9ac1e3a60/section/5aafe7fe-db7e-4ec1-935f-09d8028a2687#ch02.

Patterson, Orlando. *Slavery and Social Death: A Comparative Study.* Cambridge: Harvard University Press, 1982.

Planas, Roque. "Brazil's 'Quilombo' Movement May Be the World's Largest Slavery Reparations Program." *The Huffington Post,* July 10, 2014. https://www.huffpost.com/entry/brazil-quilombos_n_5572236.

Price, Richard. *Alabi's World.* Baltimore: Johns Hopkins University Press, 1990.

Price, Richard, ed. *Maroon Societies: Rebel Slave Communities in the Americas.* 3rd ed. Baltimore: Johns Hopkins University Press, 1996.

Quan, H. L. T. "'It's Hard to Stop Rebels That Time Travel': Democratic Living and the Radical Reimagining of Old Worlds." *Futures of Black Radicalism,* edited by Gaye Theresa Johnson and Alex Lubin, 173–193. London: Verso, 2017.

Roberts, Neil. *Freedom as Marronnage.* Chicago: University of Chicago Press, 2015.

Robinson, Cedric J. *Black Marxism: The Making of the Black Radical Tradition.* Chapel Hill: University of North Carolina Press, 1983.

Saucier, P. Khalil, and Tryon P. Woods. "What Is the *Danger* in Black Studies and Can We Look at It Again (and Again)?" In *On Marronage: Ethical Confrontations with Antiblackness,* edited by Khalil Saucier and Tryon P. Woods, 1–32. Trenton, N.J.: Africa World Press, 2015.

Schnepf, J. D. "Unsettling Aerial Surveillance: Surveillance Studies after Standing Rock." *Surveillance & Society* 17, no. 5 (2019): 747–51.

Scott, Julius S. *The Common Wind: Afro-American Currents in the Age of the Haitian Revolution.* London: Verso Books, 2018. First published 1986.

Sorkin, Amy Davidson. "In Carpenter Case, Justice Sotomayor Tries to Picture the Smartphone Future." *The New Yorker,* November 30, 2017. https://www.newyorker.com/news/our-columnists/carpenter-justice-sotomayor-tries-to-picture-smartphone-future.

Speri, Alice. "The FBI Spends a Lot of Time Spying on Black Americans." *The Intercept,* October 29, 2019. https://theintercept.com/2019/10/29/fbi-surveillance-black-activists.

Spruill, Larry H. "Slave Patrols, 'Packs of Negro Dogs' and Policing Black Communities." *Phylon* 53, no. 1 (2016): 42–66.

Sudbury, Julia. "Maroon Abolitionists: Black Gender-Oppressed Activists in the Anti-Prison Movement in the U.S. and Canada." *Meridians: Feminism: Race, Transnationalism* 9, no. 1 (2008): 1–29.

Thompson, Alvin O. *Flight to Freedom: African Runaways and Maroons in the Americas.* Kingston: University of the West Indies Press, 2006.

White, Cheryl. "Maroon Archaeology Is Public Archaeology." *Archaeologies* 6, no. 3 (2010): 485–501.

PART II

ASKING ABOUT

PART II][Chapter 8

Double and Triple Binds
The Barriers to Computational Ethnic Studies

ROOPIKA RISAM

In the context of the tech industry, the barriers for women of color and people of color more broadly are well documented. An October 2019 *Wired* survey found that Black, Latinx, and Indigenous people make up just 5 percent of Silicon Valley tech employees. The U.S. Equal Opportunity Commission found that they make up 15 percent of tech workers more broadly, with Asians accounting for an additional 14 percent. Black, Latinx, and Indigenous women only constitute 2 percent of Silicon Valley tech workers. Women of color indicate that even when free training programs are available, the costs of housing, food, and childcare are the biggest deterrents to learning how to code.[1] These barriers are compounded by the fact that Black and Latinx students are structurally denied access to basic high school coursework and advanced STEM (science, technology, engineering, and mathematics) courses. In 2018, 25 percent of U.S. high schools with the highest percentage of Black and Latinx students did not offer prerequisites such as Algebra II (Jones). These barriers, in turn, discourage people of color and Indigenous people from pursuing college-level work in STEM and socialize them *away* from careers in tech.[2]

While these obstacles are real, are they the only barriers to computational ethnic studies? In this chapter, I reframe the barriers to learning to code for those of us who work in digital humanities within higher education. As I propose, structural inequities and the time and commitment required to overcome technical barriers are compounded by the challenges of undertaking both digital humanities *and* ethnic studies research and doing so in institutional environments that implicitly and explicitly expect that we assume heavy burdens of diversity work. Further, I offer advice for practitioners of computational humanities on how we might collectively work to move past the double and triple binds of computational ethnic studies.

[149

A Former Codephobe's Story

When I first read Miriam Posner's "Some Things to Think About Before You Exhort Everyone to Code," I thought, "THAT'S IT! As a woman of color, I have been socialized not to be able to code." I reassured myself that I could put aside the debate of whether one must be able to code to be a digital humanist, content myself with Omeka projects, and move on with my life. For years, I maintained that stance unapologetically: No, I can't code. I can't code because I am a woman of color, not a white man, and I was not encouraged to do so. In the great debate between "hack" (building) and "yack" (talking) in digital humanities (Nowviskie, 66), I was Team Yack. Out-of-the-box tools like Omeka, Scalar, and Voyant were all I needed to accomplish my goal of using digital humanities to address what I had identified as the gaps and omissions in the cultural record that are being rapidly reproduced and amplified as digital humanists build the digital cultural record (Risam, *New Digital Worlds*, 4–6).

Fast-forward to summer 2018. The administration of Donald Trump announced a new immigration policy, instructing Customs and Border Protection (CBP) and Immigration and Customs Enforcement (ICE) to separate families arriving at the Mexico–U.S. border in search of asylum. Transforming our collective despair into action, several friends and I created a team of librarians, faculty, and graduate students, wondering if our digital humanities skills might help. The result was *Torn Apart/Separados*, volume 1, a series of data visualizations demonstrating the landscape of immigrant detention in the United States, created in the span of a week. As we worked, my inability to code was not an issue. My solid research skills led to our team's clear working knowledge of the processes the government used to manage children in custody, and I took the lead on the data, curating a dataset of the locations where children were being housed by the U.S. government. My knowledge of data ethics and data visualization also figured prominently, as I repeatedly raised concerns about the children's safety as we prototyped the project. Alex Gil built the Jekyll wrapper to house the project. Several years before, Gil had patiently spent a morning teaching me to work in the command line environment and use Jekyll, so I was able to make my contributions to *Torn Apart/Separados* with ease. Coder extraordinaire Moacir P. de Sá Pereira handled the bulk of the coding in Leaflet.js, a JavaScript library for mapping, and in JavaScript to create the visualizations. The experience was, in many regards, the microcosm of a perfect digital humanities collaboration: each participant brought their knowledge to the table, everyone's expertise was respected and valued, and we successfully executed a project that was well received.[3] And never once did I think, "Oh no! I can't code."

That quickly changed when we started work on volume 2. At the Digital Humanities 2018 conference in Mexico City, we launched *Torn Apart/Separados*, volume 1, and Gil and I held a design sprint and hackathon sponsored by the Humanities, Arts, Sciences, and Technology Advanced Collaboratory (HASTAC) to share our data and explore new ways of using digital humanities to address the issue of immigrant detention. Among the promising ideas was "following the money"—understanding the fiscal landscape of immigrant detention. A week after the conference, on July 4, 2018, I was poking around government websites and discovered that we could scrape all the government contracts that ICE had given out across multiple years and explore who was reaping financial gain from immigrants' pain. Unlike the weeklong sprint to create volume 1, we took volume 2 slowly, though the process was similar. We began by scraping the data, examining it closely, and brainstorming ideas for the kinds of stories we might be able to tell. We were joined by new team members, including one with substantial coding experience. I led these conversations as we drew out complicated plans to use D3.js, a JavaScript library for data visualization. Half the time, I had no idea what our coding experts were talking about, and I did not understand the fundamentals of computation well enough to even know whether what they were proposing was feasible. But that was okay—after all, I was a woman of color, so I could not code!—until one of the coders decided they no longer had time for the project, after adding significant complexity to our design. We were faced with a choice: either we could scale back our expectations, or it was all hands on deck and, gulp, I would need to learn to code.

The answer was obvious: we should have focused on less ambitious plans. But, no, Roopika Risam, an ardent defender of the right to do digital humanities without programming knowledge, was going to learn how to code. And the team members (particularly Gil, de Sá Pereira, and Rachel Hendry) were going to have to suffer through it.

I purchased roughly every book on Amazon with the words "JavaScript," "D3," "Beginners," and "Dummies" in the title. Elijah Meeks, author of *D3.js in Action* and founder of the Data Visualization Society, sent me a copy of his book in appreciation of our work on *Torn Apart/Separados*. I read the books. I asked teammates de Sá Pereira, Hendry, Gil, and my friend Scott Weingart erudite questions like, "How do I get the code into a thingy"? (Translation: Where do I execute the code?) They didn't laugh—at least, not to my face. I printed "Hello, world." I made rectangles with lines of code. I wondered why I was making rectangles with lines of code. I realized that my knowledge of HTML and CSS meant I was not completely starting at square one. I sat through lessons where de Sá Pereira gamely taught me how to convert CSV into JSON. I learned about the Document Object Model (DOM). I called the DOM. I yelled at the DOM. I figured out how to bind data to elements in the DOM. I created force-directed graphs. I realized I should have paid more attention in physics class. Hendry pointed out countless times that my code would not run because I had missed a semicolon. And, in the end, I created a "murderboard"-style data visualization, intentionally designing a bad data visualization to emphasize the messy connections between companies and goods and services they offered ICE.

That experience, as chaotic as it was in retrospect, was a turning point for me. No, the issue wasn't that I had not been socialized to learn how to code—it was that I had not had a compelling enough reason to sit down and learn. Like many digital humanists, I had once attempted to "learn Python" for no reason beyond thinking, "I'm a digital humanist and thus should learn Python." When it didn't stick, I attributed that to race and gender, not to the fact that I did not have a strong sense of *why* I should learn it and what it could offer as a research tool. That all changed from my work on *Torn Apart/Separados,* volume 2. I realized that coding offered more control over what I could do with data than the myriad out-of-the-box tools I had been using.

The following summer, I was ready to explore the possibilities of code even further and embarked on a project called "The Global Du Bois," a series of data visualizations intended to refute the idea that W. E. B. Du Bois's investment in anticolonialism happened later in his life. This had been the topic of my dissertation, but I did not think it would have the impact I would like as a book. As a data visualization project, on the other hand, it could open up data-driven inquiry into the issue and serve as a resource for researchers. Knowing I *could* do this from my experience with *Torn Apart/Separados,* I spent the summer immersing myself in JavaScript and D3 from the ground up. I eagerly studied the fundamentals of computation. I realized that no, programmers do not have a head full of code just waiting to spill out—they build on their foundational knowledge, they use trial and error, and they talk with each other, one-to-one or through Stack Overflow. I built the backend of a web app using Node.js, Babel, and Webpack. I began designing the front end for the project. I prototyped some data visualizations. And once I knew I *could* do this, I spent the time since working on my datasets, with the goal of a 2022 launch. I bought a hoodie. I watched every Marvel movie (yes, including *Thor: The Dark World*). I had become a codebro. And, perhaps more critically, I became convinced that it is critical that more digital humanists of color learn to code—if it suits the methodological interventions they wish to make—because it can open a new world of possibilities in computational humanities: new directions for humanities research, new questions to ask about data, and new ways of engaging audiences.

Double (and Triple) Binds of Computational Ethnic Studies

While Jula Damerow, Abraham Gibson, and Manfred Laubichler describe the debate over whether computational humanists need to know how to code (settled with a firm "yes" in "Of Coding and Quality," in this volume), they fail to take into account that there are a number of barriers to entry. From interventions like Posner's blog post to the lived realities of racial disparities in STEM pipelines and the emergence of targeted interventions like Black Girls Code and the Hidden Genius Project, it may appear, at first glance, that the primary barrier to entry in computational humanities for people of color working in areas like African diaspora,

Indigenous, Latinx, Asian American, postcolonial, and ethnic studies is primarily a technical one.[4] However, the true barriers to the development of computational approaches within these areas lie in the broader challenges that people of color and Indigenous people in these fields have experienced within higher education. Thus, the primary issue lies in the double bind of undertaking ethnic studies and digital humanities research together *and* the triple bind of undertaking ethnic studies and digital humanities as people of color and Indigenous people in the academy.[5]

Far from simply being a matter of technical barriers to entry, the double and triple binds of computational ethnic studies lie in the structural challenges of the academy. The first is in biases within scholarly knowledge production. Computational humanities methods favor datasets and tools designed with white dominant cultures of the Global North in mind. This bias is compounded by the many factors that have shaped humanities knowledge production: the dominance of the English language, the concentration of academic capital in the Global North, and grant funding schemes that favor canonical topics with self-evident value. As Safiya Noble and Ruha Benjamin have noted, these technologies are built on embedded biases that marginalize communities of color and Indigenous communities. Because digitization schemes have focused on canonical histories and voices, reflecting long-standing biases within digital knowledge production (Risam, *New Digital Worlds*; Singh, "Visualizing the Uplift"), access to corpora or metadata needed for computational humanities poses a challenge for ethnic studies. Therefore, what Kim Gallon describes as the "technology of recovery" (42) is a precursor to computational humanities. Furthermore, the methodologies and workflows behind digitization efforts often fail to account for the particularities of ethnic studies materials, which in turn limits the use of computational humanities methods. In the case of HathiTrust, Nicole Brown and colleagues encountered multiple challenges identifying experiences of Black women in the 800,000 texts in the database ("Mechanized Margin to Digitized Center," 110–3). Despite these issues, which stem from the embedded biases in computational analysis, they propose that computational approaches have promise as a technology of recovery that can expand the scope of digital humanities (Brown et al., 124–5). Undertaking this work, however, can rely on a significant amount of research and intellectual labor to create datasets as a precursor to computational analysis. In the case of "The Global Du Bois," for example, I began work on my datasets, which required archival and secondary source research, then paused for three months to prototype with the data I had curated to ensure the data was appropriately structured for my research questions and that the project was feasible. I have since spent a year continuing to curate data. Similarly, in a related project visualizing key figures in Pan-Africanism undertaken with undergraduate students, we spent six months on archival and secondary source research to identify participants in Pan-Africanist gatherings between 1900 and 1959 just to be in the position to be able to begin data visualization.

Computational humanities, moreover, is poorly understood in the context of tenure and promotion decisions (Nyhan and Flinn), exacerbating the challenges that ethnic studies scholars already experience (Matthew). The phenomenon of working "double" is not unfamiliar to digital humanists, particularly those in faculty roles who are obligated to publish in traditional scholarly venues in addition to their digital scholarship. Those who work in computational humanities in any field understand the implicit expectation to do twice the work—write the books and articles and do the digital projects—for tenure and promotion (Wernimont and Losh). Black, brown, and Indigenous scholars, too, are frequently expected to work at least twice as hard to gain recognition within the white academy, particularly those in ethnic studies fields whose work is not viewed as comparatively rigorous (Ruiz and Machado-Casas; Onwuachi-Willig; Hernández). High-profile tenure denials like those of Dr. Lorgia García Peña at Harvard University and Paul Harris and Tolu Odumosu at the University of Virginia demonstrate that universities have proved to be anywhere between ambivalent to downright hostile to ethnic studies in general and ethnic studies of color and Indigenous scholars in particular (Chetty, Gonzales Seligmann, and Gil; Flaherty).

Those undertaking computational ethnic studies bear the burden of both demonstrating the value of ethnic studies *and* proving the scholarly value of computational methodologies. This is, of course, compounded harm for Black, brown, and Indigenous scholars who are additionally expected to undertake invisible diversity work, such as advising and mentoring colleagues and students of color (Risam, "Diversity Work"). Thus, the growth of computational ethnic studies is beset by the greater risk that scholars face when undertaking scholarship with experimental and poorly understood outputs because the interdisciplinary nature of their scholarship is already regarded with suspicion and ignorance (Ervin). However, this inequitable labor is magnified for those in ethnic studies and even further intensified for those of us who are scholars of color or Indigenous scholars as well. There is, thus, a triple bind for computational ethnic studies, where the additional workload (research, data curation) simply to be in the position to undertake computational analysis is accompanied by the broader challenges of evaluating and valuing digital scholarship as a form of scholarly communication *and* the devaluation of ethnic studies research.

A further issue is that resources for digital scholarship remain concentrated in predominantly white, research 1 institutions, limiting access to funding and training. Digital humanities and data science centers are most typically found at elite institutions and focus on topics of greatest interest to dominant white university cultures. As Quinn Dombrowski, Tassie Gniady, David Kloster, Megan Meredith-Lobay, Jeffrey Tharsen, and Lee Zickel note ("Voices from the Server Room," in this volume), local support is crucial to facilitating computational research by humanities scholars. They note that the people providing such support must understand the nuances of translating humanities research into digital research as well as the local infrastructure needs. In the context of computational ethnic studies, effective support also requires working knowledge of the particularities of ethnic studies. With rare exceptions like the African American Digital Humanities Initiative at the Maryland Institute for Technology in the Humanities (MITH), initially led by Catherine Knight Steele and now led by Marisa Parham; the new Center for Digital Black Research led by P. Gabrielle Foreman, Shirley Moody-Turner, and Jim Casey at Penn State; and U.S. Latinx Digital Humanities led by Gabriela Baeza Ventura and Carolina Villarroel at the University of Houston, few centers emphasize the importance of supporting computational ethnic studies. Thus, training opportunities remain limited for both early career researchers and senior scholars interested in undertaking this work. In the broader landscape of humanities graduate education, there is limited guidance for computational analysis, and institutes like the Digital Humanities Summer Institute (DHSI), Humanities Intensive Learning and Teaching (HILT) institute, the Institute for Liberal Arts Digital Scholarship (ILiADS), and DREAMLab have been providing an important service in response to this gap. Despite the work of these institutes to provide bursaries and support to make their resources accessible, being able to take advantage of such opportunities relies both on additional institutional resources and favorable personal circumstances that are not universally available. This is particularly the case for ethnic studies scholars who already contend with institutional inequities in resource allocation (Prashad; Khanmalek) and those who are Black, brown, or Indigenous and thus are more likely to have caregiving responsibilities (Griffin; Szelényi and Denson).

A final challenge to the growth of computational ethnic studies is a lack of opportunities for mentorship. Many of us who undertake this work do so at universities without doctoral programs; in libraries; or in archives, galleries, and museums. We are therefore not in positions to mentor doctoral students. When we were beginning our research, we typically did not have access to advisers or committee members who worked specifically in computational ethnic studies. Rather, we had to construct our own networks of mentors and peers with the range of expertise necessary to support our work and hope for the best. The newest generation is being forced to do the same, and this is perhaps the most significant barrier to computational ethnic studies. These circumstances can be attributed to multiple factors: the casualization of academic labor and decline in tenure-track jobs; the challenges that scholars who undertake interdisciplinary work face in the academic labor market; and the skepticism that both computational humanities and ethnic studies work can engender in departmental contexts. Consequently, scholars of computational ethnic studies cannot rely on the academic genealogies that have served those in other fields. Rather, we must construct our own scholarly ecologies and lateral and nonhierarchical networks to support our work. These networks have sustained us and held us up, but the fact that we have to rely on them, rather than on academic genealogies, means that we are in danger of being shut out from the power that those genealogies accord.

Our Collective Ways Forward

Given how deeply the challenges to computational ethnic studies are embedded in the power dynamics that shape the contemporary academy, imagining how we might address them is, at times, confounding. First, if you see value in computational humanities for your research, particularly if you are a scholar of color or an Indigenous scholar, know that you *can* do this work (hoodie optional but strongly encouraged). Yes, you may have been socialized not to, but that doesn't mean you can't.

There are a number of resources that you can use to teach yourself to code. I found the free apps for Codeacademy and SoloLearn useful for ensuring I understood the fundamentals of computation. I also used the free apps for Programming Hub and Khan Academy to find coding problems for practice. Once I began wrapping my mind around those concepts, I worked through Moacir P. de Sá Pereira's excellent free resource, *The JavaScripting English Major*. I chose to learn JavaScript because my interest in coding primarily involves data visualization. But with knowledge of the fundamentals of computation, as well as the emphasis on computational thinking in de Sá Pereira's book, I have been able to translate my knowledge to work with other languages, such as Python, when necessary. Other colleagues have found the University of Toronto's "Learn to Program: The Fundamentals" and the University of Michigan's "Python for Everybody" free courses useful.[6] I have also found the volumes published by O'Reilly (including *Becoming a Better Programmer* by Pete Goodliffe and Tom Stuart's *Understanding Computation*) incredibly helpful after exhausting freely available resources. (If you are specifically interested in data visualization, Elijah Meeks's *D3.js in Action* is indispensable.)

If you prefer learning with others and are working or studying at a university, connect with the research or teaching and learning centers on your campus to see what they offer—and express your interest in this type of programming if they are not supporting it. Talk to colleagues in computer science, information science, and data science about resources their departments offer or the possibility of auditing a course. In the realm of external resources, digital humanists have also resourcefully created their own courses, though they require access to funds for tuition and, in some cases, travel: the Programming4Humanists course has regularly run online through Texas A&M University for a number of years now and focuses on Python; Digital Mitford Coding School, which typically meets in-person, has a solid record of teaching students to work with TEI, XPath, and regular expressions (regex); and DHSI and DREAMLab are highly regarded on-site institutes.[7]

But the responsibility for creating the conditions to overcome the double and triple binds of computational ethnic studies cannot be borne by Black, brown, and Indigenous scholars alone. Rather, it requires collaborative efforts by all digital humanists across institutions, particularly those in positions of privilege, such as tenured jobs or access to institutional resources. For those at institutions undertaking digitization projects, consider what you are digitizing and how it reflects the influence of dominant white scholarly knowledge production; the more material that is made available through digitization in fields like African diaspora, Indigenous, Latinx, Asian, and postcolonial studies, as appropriate to cultural protocols on digitization and access to knowledge, the more content we have to work with for computational ethnic studies.

Consider *how* you are developing metadata schemas and the effects your practices have on inclusion, exclusion, and discovery for materials that are underrepresented in the digital cultural record. Consider the ontologies and controlled vocabularies, the metadata in digitized collections, and the metadata in library catalogs, and work toward changing subject headings. If you are developing tools, examine the biases or presumptions embedded in the tools you build and how your design practices can shift to address them. Consult with scholars and community members who have the expertise to assist with development of better metadata schema and tools—and compensate them.

If you work in a digital humanities or data science center, hold yourself and your colleagues accountable for how they are supporting computational ethnic studies. Ask how you can redistribute resources to assist scholars who do not have access to them. When you pursue grants, consider how to build in funding to support the growth of computational ethnic studies and the capacity of computational ethnic studies scholars at your campus and at other campuses. Resist models for grant funding that anoint individual scholars or projects in favor of ones that bring others in.

If you are active in your scholarly organizations, work with them to ensure that their guidelines for evaluating digital scholarship include attention to systemic racism and colonization and that they are actively working to resist these forces. In the case of publicly engaged scholarship (digital or otherwise), for example, I have been collaborating with the Modern Language Association to ensure that the practices we build into evaluation are explicitly antiracist and anticolonial. Putting these practices at the heart of guidelines and evaluation are essential to seeing them realized.

If you are working in digital humanities and committed to improving the conditions of knowledge production for your colleagues in computational ethnic studies, support the work of journals like *Reviews in Digital Humanities* and *archipelagos,* which are working to provide evaluations of digital scholarship with a strong emphasis on fields related to ethnic studies. If you are a faculty member, advocate for hiring and for the value of scholarship in computational ethnic studies. Put aside your presumptions about what scholarship—digital or otherwise—*should* look like, and encourage your colleagues to do the same.

The road ahead to undo the double and triple binds of computational ethnic studies is long. But at this moment, when institutions are committing to fighting systemic racism, let us hold them accountable to it and do our part to ensure that this battle extends to our own scholarly practices. The future of computational ethnic studies depends on it.

Notes

1. See Sara Harrison, "Five Years of Tech Diversity Reports—and Little Progress," *Wired,* October 1, 2019, https://www.wired.com/story/five-years-tech-diversity-reports-little-progress/; Galen Gruman, "The State of Ethnic Minorities in U.S. Tech: 2020," *ComputerWorld,* September 21, 2020, https://www.computerworld.com/article/3574917/the-state-of-ethnic-minorities-in-us-tech-2020.html; Chandra Steele, "Women of Color Face Extra Barriers to Entering Tech Fields," *PCMag,* July 8, 2020, https://www.pcmag.com/news/women-of-color-face-extra-barriers-to-entering-tech-fields.

2. See Allison Scott and Alexis Martin, "Perceived Barriers to Higher Education in Science, Technology, Engineering, and Mathematics," *Journal of Women and Minorities in Science and Engineering* 20, no. 3 (2014): 235–56; Kimberly McGee, "The Influence of Gender and Race/Ethnicity on Advancement in Information Technology (IT)," *Information and Organization* 28, no. 1 (2018): 1–36; J. A. Muñoz and I. Villanueva, "Latino STEM Scholars, Barriers, and Mental Health: A Review of the Literature," *Journal of Hispanic Higher Education* (2019), https://doi.org/10.1177/1538192719892148; Maya Corneille, "Developing Culturally and Structurally Responsive Approaches to STEM Education to Advance Education Equity," *Journal of Negro Education* 89, no. 1 (2020): 48–57; Maria N. Miriti, "The Elephant in the Room: Race and STEM Diversity," *BioScience* 70, no. 3 (March 2020): 237–42, https://doi.org/10.1093/biosci/biz167; Sandy Marie Bonny, "Effective STEM Outreach for Indigenous Community Contexts: Getting It Right One Community at a Time," *International Journal of Innovation in Science and Mathematics Education* 26, no. 2 (2018), https://openjournals.library.sydney.edu.au/index.php/CAL/article/view/12656; Fikile Nxumalo and Wanja Gitari, "Introduction to the Special Theme on Responding to Anti-Blackness in Science, Mathematics, Technology, and STEM Education," *Canadian Journal of Science, Mathematics and Technology Education* 21 (2021): 226–31.

3. The *Torn Apart/Separados* team consisted of untenured faculty, librarians, contingent faculty, and graduate students. At the time, I was an untenured assistant professor, which meant that while I was negotiating the research demands of tenure, I also had the privilege of stable, gainful employment where research was part of my job duties, which was not the case for the whole team.

4. For further resources on this topic, see Black Girls Code, https://lnk.bio/blackgirlscode, accessed September 15, 2021; The Hidden Genius Project, https://www.hiddengeniusproject.org/, accessed September 15, 2021; All Star Code, https://www.allstarcode.org/, accessed September 15, 2021; Black Tech Unplugged, https://blacktechunplugged.com/, accessed September 15, 2021; digitalundivided, https://www.digitalundivided.com/, accessed September 15, 2021; People of Color in Tech, https://peopleofcolorintech.com/, accessed September 15, 2021.

5. Implicitly underlying these barriers is the fraught state of labor in higher education, where 75 percent of the labor force is contingent.

6. See *The Javascripting English Major* (https://the-javascripting-english-major.org/v1/contents); University of Toronto's "Learn to Program: The Fundamentals" (https://www.coursera.org/learn/learn-to-program); and the University of Michigan's "Python for Everybody" (https://www.coursera.org/specializations/python).

7. See the Programming4Humanists course (https://programming4humanists.tamu.edu/); Digital Mitford Coding School (https://digitalmitford.wordpress.com/); DHSI (https://dhsi.org/); and DREAMLab (https://web.sas.upenn.edu/dream-lab/).

Bibliography

Benjamin, Ruha. *Race after Technology: The New Jim Code.* Cambridge: Polity, 2019.

Brown, Nicole M., Ruby Mendenhall, Michael L. Black, Mark Van Moer, Assata Zerai, and Karen Flynn. "Mechanized Margin to Digitized Center: Black Feminism's Contributions to Combatting Erasure within the Digital Humanities." *International Journal of Humanities and Arts Computing* 10, no. 1 (2016): 110–25.

Chetty, Raj, Katerina Gonzalez Seligmann, and Alex Gil. "Ethnic Studies Rise," 2019. https://ethnicrise.github.io/.

Ervin, Kelly. "The Experiences of an Academic 'Misfit.'" In *Presumed Incompetent: The Intersections of Race and Class for Women in Academia,* edited by Gabriella Gutiérrez y Muhs, Yolanda Flores Niemann, Carmen González, and Angela P. Harris, 439–45. Denver: University Press of Colorado, 2012.

Flaherty, Collen. "'Botched.'" *Inside Higher Education,* June 22, 2020. https://www.insidehighered.com/news/2020/06/22/two-black-scholars-say-uva-denied-them-tenure-after-belittling-their-work.

Gallon, Kim. "Making the Case for Black Digital Humanities." *Debates in the Digital Humanities 2016,* edited by Matthew K. Gold and Lauren F. Klein, 42–49. Minneapolis: University of Minnesota Press, 2016.

Griffin, Kimberly A. "Institutional Barriers, Strategies, and Benefits to Increasing the Representation of Women and Men of Color in the Professoriate: Looking beyond the Pipeline." In *Higher Education: Handbook of Theory and Research,* edited by Laura W. Perna, 1–73. Vol. 35. Cham: Springer, 2020.

Hernández, Francisco. "Ethnic Studies Fifty Years Later: Activism, Struggles, and Lessons." *Ethnic Studies Review* 42, no. 2 (2019): 56–61.

Jones, Carolyn. "Latino, African Americans Have Less Access to Math, Science Classes, New Data Show." *EdSource,* May 22, 2018. https://edsource.org/2018/latino-african-americans-have-less-access-to-math-science-classes-new-data-show/598083.

Khanmalek, Tala. "Looking Back (and Inward), Moving Forward: A Roundtable on Ethnic Studies." *Ethnic Studies Review* 42, no. 2 (2019): 99–114.

Matthew, Patricia, ed. *Written/Unwritten: Diversity and the Hidden Truths of Tenure.* Chapel Hill: University of North Carolina Press, 2016.

Noble, Safiya. *Algorithms of Oppression.* New York: NYU Press, 2018.

Nowviskie, Bethany. "On the Origin of 'Hack' and 'Yack.'" In *Debates in the Digital Humanities 2016,* edited by Matthew K. Gold and Lauren F. Klein, 66–70. Minneapolis: University of Minnesota Press, 2016.

Nyhan, Julianne, and Andrew Flinn. *Computation and the Humanities: Towards an Oral History of Digital Humanities.* Cham: Springer, 2016.

Onwuachi-Willig, Angela. "Silence of the Lambs." In *Presumed Incompetent: The Intersections of Race and Class for Women in Academia,* edited by Gabriella Gutiérrez y Muhs, Yolanda Flores Niemann, Carmen González, and Angela P. Harris, 142–51. Denver: University Press of Colorado, 2012.

Posner, Miriam. "Some Things to Think About Before You Exhort Everyone to Code." *Miriam Posner's Blog,* February 29, 2012. https://miriamposner.com/blog/some-things-to-think-about-before-you-exhort-everyone-to-code/.

Prashad, Vijay. "Ethnic Studies Inside Out." *Journal of Asian American Studies* 9, no. 2 (2006): 156–76.

Risam, Roopika. "Diversity Work and Digital Carework in Higher Education." *First Monday* 23, no. 3 (2018). https://firstmonday.org/ojs/index.php/fm/article/view/8241/6651.

Risam, Roopika. "The Global Du Bois." 2020. https://github.com/roopikarisam/global-du-bois.

Risam, Roopika. *New Digital Worlds: Postcolonial Digital Humanities in Theory, Praxis, and Pedagogy.* Evanston, Ill.: Northwestern University Press, 2018.

Ruiz, Elsa Cantu, and Margarita Machado-Casas. "An Academic Community of 'Hermandad': Research for the Educational Advancement of Latians (REAL), a Motivating Factor for First-Tier Tenure-Track Latina Faculty." *Educational Foundations* 27, no. 1–2 (2013): 49–63.

Singh, Amardeep. "Visualizing the Uplift: Digitizing Poetry by African American Women, 1900–1922." *Feminist Modernist Studies* 1, no. 3 (2018): 269–81.

Szelényi, Katalin, and Nida Denson. "Personal and Institutional Predictors of Work-Life Balance among Women and Men Faculty of Color." *Review of Higher Education* 43, no. 2 (2019): 633–65.

Torn Apart/Separados, 2018. http://xpmethod.columbia.edu/torn-apart/volume/1/.

Wernimont, Jacqueline, and Elizabeth Losh. "Problems with White Feminism: Intersectionality and Digital Humanities." *Doing Digital Humanities: Practice, Training, Research,* edited by Constance Crompton, Richard J. Lane, and Ray Siemens, 35–46. London: Routledge, 2016.

PART II][Chapter 9

Two Volumes
The Lessons of Time on the Cross

BENJAMIN M. SCHMIDT

The Backwaters of American History

This chapter describes two parallel approaches to doing something that could be called computational history that have evolved in the last fifty years in the United States. These approaches deploy different visions of bringing computation to the human past and suggest different paths forward for computational humanities more broadly. The first, which usually calls itself "digital history" proper (a term often distinct from "digital humanities"), I argue, has developed a deeply nonscientific set of uses for computation—practices centered in public history, in exploratory analysis, and in new media. At the same time, there is a social-scientific project of history in the United States that makes use of scientific computation but happens with almost no institutional connection to the "digital humanities" or even to history departments themselves.

Many debates about digital humanities proceed from the premise that to make the humanities more *computational* means to make them more *scientific*. In Western European humanities departments, in the old tradition of "humanities computing" and in the recent push to rebrand a subset of the field as "cultural analytics," questions of scientism, calculation, and certainty play a major role.[1] In English literature, the defining feature in the contemporary digital humanities is how contemporary quantitative techniques are "blurring the traditionally sharp boundary that separated us from the quantitative social sciences" (English and Underwood, "Shifting Scales"). Advocates of "consilience" (Gottschall, "Afterword," 217) eagerly cite literary digital humanists as a step toward the (re)unification of the sciences and humanities; opponents of computational humanities criticize it for imperfectly mimicking the conventions of scientific statistical inference without generating any new meanings of its own (Da, "Computational Case").

The split in American digital history shows a way to make computation focus not on making the humanities more scientific but instead making them more creative. This is a sorely needed example.

The reasons for this lie in the particular course of interactions between history and the social sciences from about 1965 to 1985. At its heart—as with so much else distinct about the United States—is slavery. An outsize place in the whole field has been a single book, Robert Fogel and Stanley Engerman's 1974 *Time on the Cross*, which emerged as the topic of both enormous acclaim and criticism in the mid-1970s. Digital historians and historical social scientists have each evolved their own, strikingly different stories of that book's successes and failures. It is important to properly understand that controversy—and the closely related, if broader, question of how American history would grapple with its country's central trauma—to think about what it means to apply computational methods to the most central areas of social life.

Some readers may be inclined to take this story simply as a curio; an apologia for how the energy of American historians was diverted into an odd channel. I hope they won't. Although I intend to tell a myopically American story here (up to and including consistently using "American" as an adjective to describe only the United States of America), the work done by Americans in digital history gives a different charge to the question of computational humanities as a whole. While I give a descriptive account of how American digital history came, for the most part, not to be social scientific, I think that the channels into which it was re-rerouted are well worth our time. It is, in short, that computational humanities need not be quantitative humanities and *certainly* need not be scientific humanities.

Accounting for Slavery in History

Digital history of some form has been practiced for nearly a hundred years. While digital humanists still often treat Roberto Busa's work on Thomas Aquinas as the earliest digital research in the humanities, the use of digital storage and calculating machines for historical work goes back even further—at least to 1933, when William Murray published a comparative study of farm mortgages in Story County, Iowa, from 1854 to 1931 using 25,993 punched cards (Figure 9.1) (Murray, "Economic Analysis"). Writing in 1970, Robert P. Swierenga ("Clio and Computers") pointed out that leading historians including Bernard Bailyn and Merle Curti performed computational studies with punch cards in the 1950s (in both cases, under the guidance of wives who "had trained in disciplines more methodologically rigorous than history").[2]

Through the 1950s and 1960s, history was often classified as a social science in American universities. While this left scholars like Curti and Bailyn free to explore emerging technologies, the idea that history might become a science of

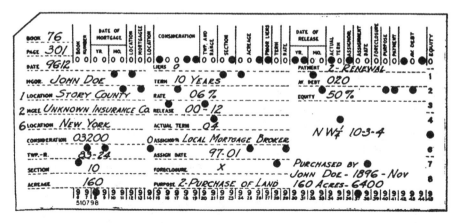

Figure 9.1. An abstracted punch card from William Murray's 1933 study of farm mortgages.

measurement drummed up organized opposition as well. In 1962, Carl Bridenbaugh, the president of the American Historical Association, notoriously described quantification as a "bitch-goddess," heretical to historical practice. The slur—adapted from a reference of William James's to the "the bitch-goddess 'success'"—is so breathtaking in how concisely it deploys tropes of sexism and orientalism together that it has somewhat overshadowed the core of Bridenbaugh's message; that the social sciences are dehumanizing because they lose sight of individual experience.

> The finest historians will not be those who succumb to the dehumanizing methods of social sciences, whatever their uses and values, which I hasten to acknowledge. Nor will the historian worship at the shrine of that Bitch-goddess, QUANTIFICATION. History offers radically different values and methods. It concerns itself with the "mutable, rank-scented many," but it fails if it does not show them as individuals whenever it can. (Bridenbaugh, "Presidential Address")

These struggles came to a head in the 1970s, and the central area of contestation was around the field of *cliometrics*. While cliometrics was never really part of the American historical profession proper, it precipitated conflicts that had riled the profession. The term—apparently first used in economics seminars at Purdue in late 1960 (Goldin, "Cliometrics and the Nobel")—initially indicated a project of bringing econometric methods to questions in economic history. In his 1972 survey of the field, Joel Silbey reported that "more and more" historians were joining the ranks of the cliometricians while acknowledging that it was dominated by economists; quantitative work on political history, likewise, was led by political science departments, leaving social history the major area of research in history (Silbey, "Clio and Computers").

The outstanding figure in the field was Robert Fogel, who had been involved in the cliometric project from the beginning. The publication of *Time on the Cross* (hereafter *TotC*) marked its apotheosis, a moment when the historical discipline began to distance itself more decisively from interdisciplinary dalliances. By laying out a grand economic history of slavery that purported to measure its effects for the first time, *TotC* sought to bring one of the central areas of American history into the econometric fold. While the book was met with initial acclaim, concern about its methods and its approach quickly boiled over. Thomas Haskell's devastating 1975 *New York Review of Books* summation outlines the shortcomings in the book; the labor historian Herbert Gutman managed to turn around a book-length critique in under a year (Gutman, *Slavery and the Numbers Game*).

Insofar as digital history tells its own story, it has explicitly distanced itself from *TotC* and the cliometric project generally. One guide to computing for historians, written in the 1990s, warned that the authors were "not champions of 'cliometrics,' 'quantification,' the 'new' history, 'scientific history,' or even what is called 'social science history'" (Mawdsley, *Computing for Historians*, referenced in Thomas, "Computing and the Historical Imagination").

American historians often treat cliometrics as a failure—in Edward Ayers's words, "a brief love affair with quantification" (Parry, "Quantitative History Makes a Comeback")—that presents something of a dead end to be avoided. Historians who learned their craft in the 1970s and 1980s have raised to me again and again a single data point that emerges in almost every account of *TotC*; namely, Fogel and Engerman's calculation that most slaves were whipped 0.7 times a year, and the attendant implication that 0.7 is not especially high. Herbert Gutman cast the same numbers in a different form: the plantation was traumatized by a public display of torture more than once a week.

The reception of *TotC* has focused on its myopia. Jessica Marie Johnson published an essay in 2018, "Markup Bodies," that gives a good account of the position that I find most important for students in the humanities to completely internalize, because it articulates two of the most important ways that historians have developed a language for talking about statistics.

> Statistics on their own, enticing in their seeming neutrality, failed to address or unpack black life hidden behind the archetypes, caricatures, and nameless numbered registers of human property slave owners had left behind. And cliometricians failed to remove emotion from the discussion. Data without an accompanying humanistic analysis—an exploration of the world of the enslaved from their own perspective—served to further obscure the social and political realities of black diasporic life under slavery. (Johnson, "Markup Bodies")

The argument is not just that data fails to capture experience—as Bridenbaugh argued in 1965—but that the *existence* of data is itself part of the record of violence.

As Johnson puts it: "Data is the evidence of terror, and the idea of data as fundamental and objective information, as Fogel and Engerman found, obscures rather than reveals the scene of the crime."

The lesson that I, myself, was taught in graduate school in the late 2000s—before I had ever heard of "digital humanities"—was similar. An attention to statistical reductionism rather than human experience struck in the face of historical practice but also served to ratify past crimes. To act statistically on individual subjects violates a kind of taboo. To this day, I am reluctant to make data visualizations in which the points are individual people. In my own work—and in my advice to any other digital historians—I generally think that human beings are among the least promising topics of statistical analysis; I choose to visualize ships, books, and land but try to avoid visualizing the *person* whenever possible. After all, people are the things we need data to understand the least. In a graduate class with the political historian Sean Wilentz, I remember vividly being walked through a slate of regression analyses of ethnic voting patterns in pre–Civil War counties in the United States and feeling that I was learning something rather important about voting patterns, then being informed that none of these methods—not one!—can tell us a single thing about why a single person voted the way they did.

In this telling, cliometrics left quantification as a still-radioactive site in the discipline, smoking from the wars of the 1970s, where you tread at your peril. Digital history turned again and again to slavery in the decades since—both in work like Johnson's and the burgeoning field of Black digital humanities (Gallon, "Making a Case for the Black Digital Humanities"). But their work did not build on *TotC* in any important way. Even rare exceptions like the Trans-Atlantic Slave Trade database—led by Engerman's student David Eltis—sat at the margins of the American profession, built largely by researchers in European centers and with much of its administrative apparatus in Hull, in the United Kingdom, until the mid-2000s.

The Split between Two Volumes

But cliometrics did not either go extinct or go into hibernation; instead, under fire, it retreated back into the social sciences whence it came. To see what cliometrics is, and how it differs from digital history, we need only look at the quite different reception of Fogel and Engerman's work in the historical social sciences.

I have occasionally taught *TotC* in graduate history classes, and two things uniformly surprise. One is that the work, which most students see as catastrophically flawed, managed to earn both the Bancroft Prize—the top award in the American historical profession—and played a major part in Fogel's Nobel Prize for Economics in 1993. The other was that students would order the book from Amazon—there are still many cheap copies of *TotC* out there—and occasionally would accidentally end up with a copy not of the narrative but of the second volume that gives the methodological apparatus for the book. There are many problems with *TotC,* and many are much more important than this. But for me, the most interesting has to do with the thinking that made this a reasonable arrangement: How did the argument and the evidence come to be so heavily separated from each other?

These two problems are related. *TotC* ratified a split between the "humanities" history and social science history—especially economics—that mirrors the split of the book itself into two volumes. While historians saw the split as part of a sleight of hand—a "silk purse of scientific exactitude," Thomas Haskell put it, separated from "the sow's ear" whence it came—economists were learning an entirely *different* set of lessons.

As the history of capitalism turns to slavery in the past few years, particularly with controversies around books by Sven Beckert and Ed Baptist, we have seen economists look with bemusement at *historians* as the species that failed to learn the lessons of *TotC*. This is a set of debates largely parallel to digital history, proper, but one crucial to understanding the future of digital history, writ small.

In a fascinating review essay, the economist Eric Hilt points to the existence of an extensive literature about slavery, worrying that historians "do not seem to have taken seriously the debates among economic historians that followed the publication of that book."

> More importantly, the lack of engagement with economic historians limited the analytical perspectives of each of these books. Most of them seem aware of Fogel and Engerman's Time on the Cross (1974), and some repeat its arguments about the profitability of slavery or the efficiency of slave plantations. But they do not seem to have taken seriously the debates among economic historians that followed the publication of that book. Some . . . challenged Fogel and Engerman [but] analyzed slavery in new ways. (Hilt, "Economic History")

Hilt inclines toward what many historians may find a surprising account: that historians are even recapitulating the core *ideological* mistake of Fogel and Engerman by cloaking the work of enslaved people in a bizarrely emancipatory rhetoric, as if developing new techniques for picking cotton quickly is an accomplishment anyone should be eager to claim.

While Hilt writes respectfully about historical work, the economist Alan Olmstead has offered a more unforgiving take. The problem is not just that historians have not read the economics literature, but that they could not understand it even if they did:

> In the past, historians and economists (sometimes working as a team) collectively advanced the understanding of slavery, southern development, and capitalism. There was a stimulating dialog. That intellectual exchange deteriorated in part because some economists produced increasingly technical work that was sometimes *beyond the comprehension of many historians*. Some historians

were offended by some economists who overly flaunted their findings and methodologies. (Olmstead and Rhode, "Cotton, Slavery, and the New History of Capitalism"; italics added)

Still, in the blame that Olmstead metes out, historians' obtuseness clearly bears the brunt of it; but past the insults lies a genuine wish to be able to have a stimulating dialogue with historians in general (although not, perhaps, any actual existing historians).

Should We Just Hope for Consilience?

One obvious takeaway is that we simply need to get these fields talking to each other again and establish interdisciplinary synergy. As I will explain in a short while, I don't fully agree: but it is a claim worth considering.

The economist Trevon Logan gave a good synopsis of this account in a series of tweets in 2018 describing how he teaches *TotC* and the economics of slavery today. His story begins with the 1975 criticism of *TotC* but moves in a different direction. While historians were avoiding the radioactive spot, economists donned their hazmat suits and wandered in. While historians view *TotC* as the end of a process, economists see Fogel's later, better work, including *Without Consent or Contract,* as the real material. As Logan puts it: "F&E [Fogel and Engerman] regroup, and they cut their losses, and they go back to the beginning. They go back to the productivity calculation. . . . F&E win on prices, output, production constraints, insurance, crop mix, etc. It's a battle of the force and in the end their original calculation is established and likely accepted by the majority of the field."[3] Efficiency is vindicated—but "with a great cost," that economic historians are excessively concerned with efficiency metrics, have an unsophisticated understanding of race in America, and thus fail to reckon with slavery's actually meaning.

Logan's account of the present-day state of economics makes a strong case for the need for economists to attend to issues of race, power, and history more seriously than they have, in a way that draws on interdisciplinary connections. This situation might seem to leave major opportunities for interdisciplinary reconciliation. The case of literary studies in the Americas provides a further example of a field that *has* managed a heavily quantitative turn in the last few years. Work in digital literary studies has taken on a much more aggressive turn toward measurement; flagship journals regularly publish work using topic modeling or word embeddings, and new journals like *Cultural Analytics* lean most heavily on an English-department core rather than history.

We have seen a firmer set of turns lately toward an insistence on argumentation as the centerpiece of digital history. Cameron Blevins argued in an earlier volume of *Debates in the Digital Humanities* that digital history suffered from a "perpetual future tense" in which practitioners wrote about what they *could* do rather than advancing their scholarly fields. Since then, several initiatives out of George Mason University, which was one of the leaders of the old form of digital humanities, launched its new journal devoted to argumentation in history. It might seem reasonable to position this new manifestation of digital history as the place where cliometric flaunting could be tempered by disciplinary knowledge. Historian Lincoln Mullen at George Mason has—as in an *American Historical Review* article with Kellen Funk on legal text reuse—begun to bring some cutting-edge computational methods to mainstream historians (Funk and Mullen, "The Spine of American Law").

In some areas—like the history of capitalism—a greater degree of numerical facility is clearly necessary. But the existence of a large field pushing back against historians attempting digital work shows that the success of social science methods in English and literature is actually the exception that proves the rule. Even back in the 2000s, during the study of humanities computing, it was already the case that English had comparatively more number-crunching and that history had many more public-facing websites in its digital portfolio. That trend has continued. And the reason for that, in part, is that there is considerably less low-hanging fruit in terms of data-driven argumentation than in literary study. In literary history, there are huge arrays of digitized data and an array of fairly amateurish informaticians, physicists, and computer scientists who desperately need advice to deal responsibly with literary matters. In the United States, computational methods manipulated by historians have little promise because they are already being used at a much higher level among social scientists than any historian can possibly pick up in a graduate program.

In the history of politics and the economy, the work of creating and analyzing cultural data has been continually underway for half a century. For economic historians, in short, the legacy of cliometrics is not one of failure As Logan and Olmstead each suggest in their way, it is, rather, one of success that has not involved historians. In questions of historical interest, the post-*TotC* split has given generations of economists, sociologists, and political scientists methodologically training and substantive knowledge about the past in discourses increasingly remote from the conversations of historians. And because of the closed-off nature of the way that these fields have tended to handle their data, the resources they create exist as data crafted for purposes much closer to social science experimentation than to humanistic narration.

The best work in the cliometric tradition followed in the path of social history. For several years, I regularly paired a text alongside *TotC* on graduate syllabi: Steven Ruggles's work on the changing American family structure. Students eventually persuaded me that it was too transparently an attempt to balance the "good" cliometrics against the bad. But while Ruggles remains a tremendously important historian, the work at the Minnesota Population Center that he leads has hewed closer and closer to the sociological mainstream than the historical one. If "computational history" really existed in America, it would need a conference; and the first challenge it would face would be justifying its existence in the face of the voluminous and sophisticated work presented each year at the Social Science History Association (SSHA), which has never bothered to brand itself as "digital humanities." Before we try to reboot computational history, we should look and see what has happened in the shadow of this divide.

The Ways Disciplines Talk about Data

Take as an example two papers from opposite sides of the disciplinary divide: a work of social science history by economists and a data-driven economic history written for American historians in the field's flagship journal.

The first is a working paper by three economists—Elliott Ash, Daniel Chen, and Suresh Naidu—from 2017. While the authors are economists, the actual contribution—summed up in a title that few historians would think debatable, "Ideas Have Consequences"—is about legal or intellectual history. It presents a powerful and discrete account of the transmission of ideas across social networks through textual analysis. The substance argues that privately funded Manne seminars in law and economics—which were attended by a substantial proportion of the federal judiciary—affected the language, decisions, and sentencing of federal justices who attended them and thus, by implication, allowed large-value conservative donors to capture the federal judiciary. The effect seems robust to a variety of covariates, and even more interestingly, they claim to detect an effect where simply being randomly impaneled with a judge who attended one of these seminars makes that second judge harsher in their future sentencing decisions.

Reading this paper was exciting, but looking through the tools and tricks and sources also made me feel like someone in a science fiction movie encountering an artifact sent back from a few decades in the future. The extraordinary quality of data that economists can obtain is almost unimaginable to humanists. It is not just a million or so circuit court votes and 300,000 opinions but also the institutional capacity to file Freedom of Information Act (FOIA) requests to get the exact years of attendance for every judge who went to the Manne program and the disciplinary capacity to casually use relatively new methods like word embeddings without spending pages slowly, gently analogizing them to some "simpler" concept. Humanists wandering through algorithms seem to have to justify using an algorithm by first identifying which Borges short story—whether about the Map of the Empire, the analytical language of John Wilkins, or Pierre Menard and the Quijote—it most closely resembles.

On the other hand, consider the 2019 digital article published in the *American Historical Review,* an analysis of bank records for mid-nineteenth-century Irish immigrants in New York City by historian Taylor Anbinder and colleagues. The authorship team is interdisciplinary enough that you could reasonably claim this piece (Anbinder, Ó Gráda, and Wegge, "Networks and Opportunities") represents cliometrics returned to the highest place in the historical profession. One of the authors, Cormac Ó Gráda, was even a fellow of the Cliometrics Society in 2016.

While the piece uses data, it in no way represents the type of data science that historical computation might seem to need. Consider some of the words that never appear in it: "model," "statistic," "regress," "counterfactual," "predict," "coefficient." Even the word "network," which is in the title and conceptually at the heart of the piece, is not a formal term: the authors explicitly disavow any engagement whatsoever with technical definitions of network science or the tools of social network analysis. The only software mentioned is Microsoft Excel, not Python or R. Although the article is fundamentally about *data,* it has almost no statistics to speak of: the entire statistical apparatus is a single correlation coefficient.

But while the methodology is simple, both the analysis and the supporting apparatus branch in many more directions. The core contribution, rather, is an elaborate and impressive apparatus for browsing the deep connections between census records and bank records created (at great expense) by the project.[4] Anbinder and colleagues carefully link the individual lives of an immigrant community together across two continents and find new ways to make those stories legible that work natively on the internet without requiring archival research or statistical presentation. This foregrounding of data points and the human experience they represent is a key characteristic of modern digital history in the United States. The scholarly apparatus is, in its own way, as sophisticated as would be a more aggressive use of data and statistics; but that sophistication is directed toward readers for whom the most important validation is evidence of experience, not statistical tests.

Digital History Is Humanistic Reproducibility

These omissions are not shortcomings of a field that has not reckoned with data; they are, rather, simply the latest iteration in a long scholarly tradition that uses computers to reshape and present historical evidence while consciously avoiding anything that could be mistaken for cliometrics. The path that digital historians built in the decades of the 1990s and 2000s while *avoiding* the shadow of cliometrics was a far more interesting one; unlike English-department digital humanities of the period, it had no motive to make history more "scientific" and instead found ways to make historical practice live on computers and—increasingly—online.

The most successful of these were efforts around digital public history, where historians found ways to bring materials into an online setting that was not amenable to books. Daniel Cohen and Roy Rosenzweig's influential 2006 book *Digital History* bore the words "a guide to gathering, preserving, and presenting the past on the web" as a subtitle. The book's vision of digital history highlighted the field as involving collecting, building an audience, and designing collections for an online audience, not engaging in statistical argument. Omeka, the public history content management system developed at George Mason University Center for History and New Media, is surely the most important and irreplaceable project out of the American digital humanities. If the problem of *TotC* was the division into two books—flashy narrative in one, supporting apparatus in another—the more recent works in the disciplines have solved the problem in their own ways. Social science history has doubled down on methods, producing papers that are, to borrow a phrase from the economist Suresh Naidu, "a fortress around a fact." Historians, as much as anyone outside of digital journalists, *have* been thinking about audience, narrative, and publics. In doing this, they have found ways to foreground and expose sources alongside their work: rather than detailing a single argument, they have created richer ways of building ways to interact with the historical record (Brennan, "Public First"; Leon, "Complexity and Collaboration").

One useful way to think about this split—and the problems addressed by the Americanist digital tradition—is in terms of reproducibility. The sciences have been plagued with crises of reproducibility and deluged with schemes for solving it. Literary and library scholars in the digital humanities (overmuch, to my mind) see one of their challenges as fully fixing those problems before they even emerge through a tangle of IPython notebooks, online linked open data, and Docker configuration files. There are, of course, crises of *historical* reproducibility as well—*TotC* may have seen controversy, but it was allowed to keep its Bancroft Prize. A more traditional work of history, Michael A. Bellesiles's *Arming America*, had the 2001 Bancroft Prize revoked over concerns that many of the supporting documents cited might not actually exist.

But one reason that archival historical narratives work is that the historical narrative is *itself* an artifact of reproducible research; you read some general arguments at the front, but it is only in the process of reading a book that the reader internalizes its individual narrative flow. The thing that we need to think more about is how to shape narratives around historical data that allow reproduction by actual historians, not econometricians. How do we make that persuasive flow work for a public that can read words, visualizations, and data but does not demand all knowledge to meet social-scientific standards of causal inference.

While American digital history has not fully answered these questions, work like Anbinder's shows that it is reaching toward a constellation of solutions that are related to new forms of digital publication exploding across the internet. In digital journalism, work in the emergent genre of "scrollytelling" often tells complex stories with data by integrating argument with visualization.[5] They are also becoming increasingly common in the areas of computer science, in which publications like Google's *Distill* elevate the "interactive explorable" to the level of a scholarly product. The conventions around this work in news media and the sciences differ; "scrollership" in the humanities (Schmidt) needs space to develop its own forms of writing and reading.

And this is a contribution that digital humanities projects can continue to make—where reproduction means facilitating the arrangement and exposure of multivalent primary sources, allowing readers to engage with evidence and change the assumptions of models. This is harder than just distributing models; it is about working with sources in the indefinitely reconfigurable ways that are now possible.

We see this happening already, even in the still-vibrant digital historiography of slavery itself. Ed Baptist is one of the participants in the database of ads seeking escaped slaves, *Freedom on the Move,* that Vanessa Holden and Joshua D. Rothman explore in chapter 11 in this volume. There are multiple works on documenting lynchings (Brown, "Printing Hate"; Burnham, "Civil Rights and Restorative Justice"; Stevenson, "Lynching in America"; Franzosi, De Fazio, and Vicari, "Ways of Measuring Agency"). Flagship digital humanities projects like the Colored Conventions project at the University of Delaware (https://coloredconventions.org) focus on surfacing documents and agency, not constructing models of human action.

More broadly, a wide variety of work is not about data per se, expanding the notion of what digitally oriented scholarship can be. If I had to single out a single institution today, I would point to the University of Richmond, with work like the masterful *American Panorama,* an atlas of U.S. history edited by Robert Nelson and Edward Ayers, or Lauren Tilton and Taylor Arnold's work on the Photogrammar (https://photogrammar.org), a project about already digitized photos at the Library of Congress. And work that does use data, like Robert Lee and Tristan Atonahe's accounting of how American universities benefited from land expropriated from Native Americans in the nineteenth century (Lee et al., "Land Grab Universities"), models a practice of presenting datasets not as statistical aggregates but as individual points that would be overwhelming in their number in any medium other than the digital.

This kind of attention to audience, to reordering, and to narrative engagement evolved in part *because* of the weight of *TotC*. This—not warmed-over introductory econometrics—is the real contribution to intellectual life that digital humanities stands to make. And it is one that historians, with their multiple sources and strong subfield of public history, are better positioned to execute than any other field in the digital humanities—although not exclusively, I would add. North American literary scholars like Stephen Ramsay and the late Stefan Sinclair have also impressively modeled a form of literary engagement based on exploration, interaction, and play (Ramsay, *Reading Machines*).

The language of scientism—of which the emphasis on "intervention" and "argument" are, I would argue, part—dangles a promise that we can finally end conversations in the humanities by providing firm quantitative evidence. The rich public digital tradition in history offers, by contrast, a set of tactics and models for using the new media of communication to make the historical past more present and more reconfigurable and to help it speak to a variety of different circumstances. This work—computational but not quantitative, historical before it is historiographical—may not be the future of the past, but I hope it will be.

Notes

1. For the attitudes toward proof of the old humanistic tradition, see David Hoover, "Argument, Evidence, and the Limits of Digital Literary Studies." On the European tradition, see the "Proceedings of the Workshop on Computational Humanities Research (CHR 2020) Amsterdam, the Netherlands, November 18–20," *CEUR Workshop Proceedings* 2723 (2020), http://ceur-ws.org/Vol-2723/. When the American Historical Association convened a panel on "Computational Cultural History" in New York in 2020, only one of the four panelists was actually an American trained in history; two were European and one a scholar of literature.

2. I thank Lauren Tilton for referring me to Swierenga's work, which includes the reference to Murray.

3. Trevon Logan (@TrevonDLogan), "As promised . . . a thread on how I teach US slavery in my course on American economic history," Twitter, February 18, 2018, https://twitter.com/TrevonDLogan/status/965262267267846149.

4. This map is not even hosted by the *American Historical Review* itself; instead, it sits on a George Washington University server (https://map.beyondragstoriches.digital.library.gwu.edu/?annotation=6&nycbounds=40.728,-74.02%7C40.71,-73.99). The security certificate for the website expired on September 17, 2022; as of January 9, 2024, the site remains accessible only to users willing to ignore their web browser's warnings about attackers who might steal their personal information.

5. For an overview, see Bill Shander's "The Past, Present, and Future of Scrollytelling." See also Badger et al., "Income Mobility Charts for Girls, Asian-Americans and Other Groups. Or Make Your Own"; Wu et al., "How the Virus Got Out"; and Ford, "What Is Code?"

Bibliography

Anbinder, Taylor, Cormac Ó Gráda, and Simone A. Wegge. "Networks and Opportunities: A Digital History of Ireland's Great Famine Refugees in New York." *American Historical Review* 124, no. 5 (December 2019): 1591–1629. https://doi.org/10.1093/ahr/rhz1023.

Ash, Elliot, Daniel L. Chen, and Suresh Naidu. "Ideas Have Consequences: The Effect of Law and Economics on American Justice." SSRN Scholarly Paper. June 26, 2017. https://papers.ssrn.com/abstract=2992782.

Badger, Emily, Claire Cain Miller, Adam Pearce, and Kevin Quealy. "Income Mobility Charts for Girls, Asian-Americans and Other Groups: Or Make Your Own." *New York Times,* March 27, 2018. https://www.nytimes.com/interactive/2018/03/27/upshot/make-your-own-mobility-animation.html.

Bellesiles, Michael A. *Arming America: The Origins of a National Gun Culture.* New York: Alfred A. Knopf, 2000.

Blevins, Cameron. "Digital History's Perpetual Future Tense." In *Debates in the Digital Humanities 2016,* edited by Matthew K. Gold and Lauren F. Klein. Minneapolis: University of Minnesota Press, 2016. http://dhdebates.gc.cuny.edu/debates/text/77.

Brennan, Sheila. "Public First." In *Debates in the Digital Humanities 2016,* edited by Matthew K. Gold and Lauren F. Klein. Minneapolis: University of Minnesota Press, 2016. http://dhdebates.gc.cuny.edu/debates/text/77.

Bridenbaugh, Carl. "Presidential Address. American Historical Association Meeting, the Conrad Hilton Hotel, Chicago, Illinois, December 29, 1962." *American Historical Review* 68, no. 2 (January 1963): 315–31. https://www.historians.org/about-aha-and-membership/aha-history-and-archives/presidential-addresses/carl-bridenbaugh.

Brown, DeNeen. "Printing Hate." 2021. https://lynching.cnsmaryland.org/.

Burnham, Margaret. "Civil Rights and Restorative Justice." https://crrj.org/reading-room/.

Carroll, Joseph, Dan P. McAdams, and Edward O. Wilson. *Darwin's Bridge: Uniting the Humanities and Sciences.* Oxford: Oxford University Press, 2016. http://books.google.com?id=UxA9DAAAQBAJ.

Cohen, Daniel J., and Roy Rosenzweig. *Digital History: A Guide to Gathering, Preserving, and Presenting the Past on the Web.* Philadelphia: University of Pennsylvania Press, 2006.

Colored Conventions Project, University of Delaware. https://coloredconventions.org/.

Da, Nan Z. "The Computational Case against Computational Literary Studies." *Critical Inquiry* 45, no. 3 (March 2019): 601–39. https://doi.org/10.1086/702594.

English, James F., and Ted Underwood. "Shifting Scales: Between Literature and Social Science." *Modern Language Quarterly* 77, no. 3 (September 2016): 277–95. https://doi.org/10.1215/00267929-3570612.

Fogel, Robert, and Stanley L. Engerman. *Time on the Cross: The Economics of American Negro Slavery.* 2 vols. New York: W. W. Norton, 1974.

Ford, Paul, "What Is Code?" *Businessweek,* June 11, 2015. https://www.bloomberg.com/graphics/2015-paul-ford-what-is-code/.

Franzosi, R., G. De Fazio, and S. Vicari. "Ways of Measuring Agency: An Application of Quantitative Narrative Analysis to Lynchings in Georgia (1875–1930)." *Sociological Methodology* 42, no. 1 (2012): 1–42. https://doi.org/10.1177/0081175012462370.

Funk, Kellen, and Lincoln Mullen. "The Spine of American Law: Digital Text Analysis and U.S. Legal Practice." *American Historical Review* 123, no. 1 (2018).

Gallon, Kim. "Making a Case for the Black Digital Humanities." In *Debates in the Digital Humanities 2016,* edited by Matthew K. Gold and Lauren F. Klein. Minneapolis: University of Minnesota Press, 2016. http://dhdebates.gc.cuny.edu/debates/text/77.

Goldin, Claudia. "Cliometrics and the Nobel." *Journal of Economic Perspectives* 9, no. 2 (June 1995): 191–208. https://doi.org/10.1257/jep.9.2.191.

Gottschall, Jonathan. "Afterword." In *Darwin's Bridge: Uniting the Humanities and Sciences,* edited by Joseph Carroll, Dan P. McAdams, and Edward O. Wilson, 217. Oxford: Oxford University Press, 2016.

Gutman, Herbert George. *Slavery and the Numbers Game: A Critique of Time on the Cross.* Urbana: University of Illinois Press, 1975.

Haskell, Thomas L. "The True & Tragical History of 'Time on the Cross.'" *New York Review,* October 2, 1975. https://www.nybooks.com/articles/1975/10/02/the-true-tragical-history-of-time-on-the-cross/.

Hilt, Eric. "Economic History, Historical Analysis, and the 'New History of Capitalism.'" *Journal of Economic History* 77, no. 2 (June 2017): 511–36. https://doi.org/10.1017/S002205071700016X.

Hoover, David. "Argument, Evidence, and the Limits of Digital Literary Studies." In *Debates in the Digital Humanities 2016,* edited by Matthew K. Gold and Lauren F. Klein. Minneapolis: University of Minnesota Press, 2016. http://dhdebates.gc.cuny.edu/debates/text/77.

Johnson, Jessica Marie. "Markup Bodies: Black [Life] Studies and Slavery [Death] Studies at the Digital Crossroads." *Social Text* 36, no. 4 (137) (December 2018): 57–79. https://doi.org/10.1215/01642472-7145658.

Lee, Robert, Tristan Ahtone, Margaret Pearce, Kalen Goodluck, Geoff McGhee, Cody Leff, Katherine Lanpher, and Taryn Salinas. "Land Grab Universities." *High Country News* (2020). https://www.landgrabu.org/.

Leon, Sharon. "Complexity and Collaboration." In *The Oxford Handbook of Public History,* edited by Paula Hamilton and James B. Gardner. Oxford: Oxford University Press, 2017.

Leon, Sharon, and Tom Scheinfeldt. *Bracero History Archive.* https://braceroarchive.org/.

Mawdsley, Evan, and Thomas Munck. *Computing for Historians: An Introductory Guide.* Manchester: Manchester University Press, 1993.

Murray, William G. "An Economic Analysis of Farm Mortgages in Story County, Iowa, 1854–1931." *Iowa Agriculture and Home Economics Experiment Station Research Bulletin* 12, no. 156 (1933): art. 1.

Nelson, Robert, and Edward Ayers, eds. *American Panorama.* University of Richmond. https://dsl.richmond.edu/panorama/.

Ngu, Ash, and Sophie Cocke. "Hawaii's Beaches Are Disappearing." *ProPublica/Honolulu Star-Advertiser,* December 29, 2020. https://projects.propublica.org/hawaii-beach-loss/.

Olmstead, Alan L., and Paul W. Rhode. "Cotton, Slavery, and the New History of Capitalism." *Explorations in Economic History* 67 (January 2018): 1–17. https://doi.org/10.1016/j.eeh.2017.12.002.

Parry, Marc. "Quantitative History Makes a Comeback." *The Chronicle of Higher Education,* February 25, 2013. https://www.chronicle.com/article/Quantifying-the-Past/137419.

Ramsay, Stephen. *Reading Machines: Towards an Algorithmic Criticism.* Champaign: University of Illinois Press, 2011.

Ruggles, Steven. "The Transformation of American Family Structure." *American Historical Review* (February 1994): 103–28.

Schmidt, Benjamin. "Scrollership: A New Word for Some New Ways of Writing." In *DH2020 Book of Abstracts,* edited by Laura Estill, Jennifer Guiliano, and Constance Crompton. Alliance of Digital Humanities Organizations, 2020.

Shander, Bill. "The Past, Present, and Future of Scrollytelling." *Nightingale: Journal of the Data Visualization Society,* August 25, 2020. https://nightingaledvs.com/the-past-present-and-future-of-scrollytelling/.

Silbey, Joel H. "Clio and Computers: Moving into Phase II, 1970–1972." *Computers and the Humanities* 7 (1972): 67–79.

Stevenson, Bryan. "Lynching in America." 2015. https://lynchinginamerica.eji.org/about.

Swierenga, Robert P. "Clio and Computers: A Survey of Computerized Research in History." *Computers and the Humanities* 5, no. 1 (1970): 1–21.

Thomas, William G., III. "Computing and the Historical Imagination." In *A Companion to Digital Humanities (Blackwell Companions to Literature and Culture),* edited by Susan Schreibman, Ray Siemens, and John Unsworth. Oxford: Blackwell Publishing Professional, 2004. http://www.digitalhumanities.org/companion/.

Thomas, William G., III, and Edward L. Ayers. "The Differences Slavery Made: A Close Analysis of Two American Communities." *American Historical Review* 108, no. 5 (December 2003).

Wu, Jin, Weiyi Cai, Derek Watkins, and James Glanz. "How the Virus Got Out." *New York Times,* March 22, 2020. https://www.nytimes.com/interactive/2020/03/22/world/coronavirus-spread.html.

PART II][Chapter 10

Why Does Digital History Need Diachronic Semantic Search?

BARBARA MCGILLIVRAY, FEDERICO NANNI, AND KASPAR BEELEN

Searching for Meaning in Research

Situated at the intersection between historical research, library and information studies, information retrieval (IR), and natural language processing (NLP), searching digital heritage collections connects the humanities with computing. As large digital collections become available to scholars, the way they are searched is as important as ever and should be attuned to each discipline's research practices. In this chapter, we focus on the practices of digital history research, and therefore our examples will be drawn from this discipline. In addition to the specific research practices adopted by the discipline under investigation, search of historical digital collections should take into account the longitudinal nature of the data (the fact that the data were gathered over a period of time) and the diachronic focus of the research questions (the study of the evolution of a phenomenon over time, which is a major area of interest in historical research). The affordances of search shape the scholarly interaction with (and the interpretation of) historical collections: what cannot be searched for and be found. In this sense, it is critical to understand how the activity of search is bounded by the digital infrastructure on which it operates. In this chapter, we raise the debate on how search might be conceived and approached differently to meet the needs of digital historians. We do so by focusing on the broad and intangible but omnipresent category of diachronic semantic search—that is, search that is centered around meaning as it changes over time. In particular, we investigate how this highlights specific aspects of a corpus (compared to traditional keyword-based systems) or casts shadows on other parts of a digital collection. Semantic search lets us reach the level of meaning of a text (or at least of its words), thus allowing historians to conduct their research without reducing the concepts and ideas they intend to explore to mere combinations of keywords, which would allow you to find relevant documents even if they do not explicitly mention the terms typed. A mismatch between keywords and documents is a well-known challenge in digital history and information retrieval as a whole. It would, for instance, occur when searching for diachronically sensitive words—for example, the term *partigiani* (partisans) in the historical archive of the Italian newspaper *La Stampa*. This search would lead to very few results in the entire period of the Second World War because the newspaper was aligned with the government of the National Fascist Party, thus they were instead using words such as "bandits" or "communists" when describing specific events.[1] False positives are another problem often encountered with traditional string-based search systems. As many words are polysemous, a mismatch can appear between the meaning projected on a query and the results it returns.

While historical documents from digital collections can typically be searched at a superficial level (through character- or string-matching) or through keywords, semantically enhanced exploratory search systems are not yet available or are still highly constrained. This is critical, as many words are polysemous (i.e., have more than one meaning). For example, "depression" can refer to a mental health condition or to a lowering of the atmospheric pressure. If we search for the string "depression" in a collection with the aim to study the mental health condition, we are presented with instances of both meanings, and we need to read each context to tease them apart. For small collections, this may be time-consuming but feasible, but for larger collections, it is likely to be a completely impossible task. Moreover, current search systems do not provide chronological depth because they do not allow users to retrieve meaning information that is time-sensitive. This is an important gap when dealing with historical texts, as the meaning of words is constantly subject to change. Take, for example, the word "tablet," which has traditionally meant "a smooth stiff sheet for writing on" (Oxford English Dictionary, entry "tablet, n."), but since the beginning of the twenty-first century, the word now refers to "a small portable computer in the form of a flat tablet" (Oxford English Dictionary, entry "tablet, n."). Diachronic semantic search would allow us to identify the different meanings of a search term like "tablet" and connect them with their textual instances.

The semantic web community has provided definitions of semantic search (Guha, McCool, and Miller). In information retrieval contexts, this term broadly refers to approaches for retrieving and organizing documents in ways that go beyond the superficial level of strings and tokens. In this chapter, the term "semantic search" refers to a framework for navigating text collections that draws on information derived from (textual) data enrichment. Text enrichment adds meaning by bringing in external information from knowledge bases or surfacing and embedding information in a shared semantic space. This information can be expressed in multiple forms: from automatically generated metadata (i.e., genre classification) to entity linking (i.e., links between named entities such as names of people or places and an external knowledge base, for instance, Wikidata) or distributional semantics (i.e., the set of methods that extract meaning information from word usage statistics in texts).

While understanding the central meaning of a user query has been a long-term ambition of information retrieval systems and digital libraries (Croft et al., "Query Representation and Understanding Workshop"), addressed over the decades through various models of the latent semantics of an information need (Deerwester et al., "Indexing"; Mitra and Craswell, "Neural Models," among others), search becomes more complex in digital humanities contexts, where profound semantic changes between the context of the researchers posing a query and the period when the corpus was created play a major role. For example, the concept of nation changed from an economic category to a political and cultural category during the nineteenth century. This concept, which encompasses a sense of community but also geographical proximity and shared cultural values, is captured by many more words and expressions than just the word "nation," and this has changed over time (Hengchen, Ros, and Marjanen, "A Data-Driven Approach to the Changing Vocabulary"). It is currently impossible to find instances of a concept like nation in texts from a certain historical period without specifying all relevant words and at the same time considering that certain words have changed their meaning in time. Recent NLP research has shown the potential of computational models of semantic change that complement manual approaches (cf. Kutuzov et al., "Diachronic Word Embeddings and Semantic Shifts"; Tahmasebi et al., "Survey of Computational Approaches to Lexical Semantic Change"). However, such systems are still far from addressing the needs of humanities researchers, in spite of some attempts at addressing this (e.g., McGillivray et al., "A Computational Approach to Lexical Polysemy in Ancient Greek"). This situation is, to some extent, similar to the disconnect between NLP research and literary studies, highlighted in David Bamman's chapter, "Born Literary Natural Language Processing," in this volume. We believe that research in computational semantics will benefit from a closer interaction with digital historians with the aim of improving current search capabilities.

This chapter opens a debate on the importance of diachronic semantic search for digital history. We argue that this is a very challenging task to address for the digital history field and a problem that should not be underestimated by historians. We do not aim to offer a comprehensive overview of the field. For this reason, we offer examples for each issue we discuss, and we present them as suggestions to the reader with the aim to offer a way to dig deeper into the various aspects of our argumentation. We believe it is necessary for digital history to focus on improving computational search systems to efficiently explore large diachronic and longitudinal text collections; therefore, we present a series of recommendations for future projects. We start by offering an overview of the challenges that diachronic semantic search poses for digital humanities research, from identifying shifts in word meaning to the difficulties of deriving diachronic representations of a domain of knowledge.

We argue that search in the humanities is more than document retrieval: it is intrinsically intertwined with a process of sense-making and interpretation and therefore interfaces with hermeneutics (Putnam, "The Transnational and the Text-Searchable"; Guldi, "Critical Search"). Among other things, search assists historians with demarcating the boundaries of a concept, and there is a long tradition of defining, tracing, and analyzing concepts in history, led by many prominent scholars, including the History of Concepts Group.[2] The digital affordance (i.e., the means by which humanists can explore and navigate an archive) influences their interpretation and results. When confronted with large collections, the scholar's information need is often vaguely defined. Similarly, the target of the search emerges in conversation with historical documents. As the initial query forms a rough approximation of a more general concept, semantically enhanced search can foreground relations between documents, capture how users understand specific concepts, or extend and refine the scope of a search operation. Alex Olieman and colleagues ("Good Applications for Crummy Entity Linkers?"), for example, show how these issues play a role when searching for documents that relate to (i.e., refer to) historical periods such as the Dutch Golden Age, which is a container collating various persons and events into an overarching colligatory concept. Semantic search can assist the scholar with articulating what the concept comprises by showing potentially relevant entities (based on relations as encoded by a knowledge base), which can then guide the search and allow the user to demarcate their information needs by (de)selecting entities and documents.

In this chapter, we also focus on the importance of semantic change for retrieving historical documents, as semantics resides in the corpus as well as in the language of the query itself. All aspects of language are subject to change over time, of course, and not just semantics. Spelling, morphology, syntax, for example, are elements that tend to change at different rates, and this change needs to be accounted for in search. In this chapter, we focus on semantic change (or lexical semantic change) in words, because we believe this has particularly profound implications for the role of search in historical research. Our proposal advocates for search engines that can meet the needs of historical research. Unlike commercial search engines, which are optimized for navigation and precision of retrieval, historical practice requires more recall-oriented results, suitable for poorly defined and variable information needs, often without an initial knowledge of how the desired phenomenon is described in a historical period. The practice of search for historians, therefore, needs specific design and intentional tool building. This perspective leads us to explore issues about the overall epistemology of search and its distinction from a collection of specific technologies. While many of the other essays in this volume reflect the systems, collaborations, and institutional structures that support digital humanities (DH) work, we also reflect on what would be needed to support diachronic semantic search. We believe our suggestions are relevant especially when read in the context of other chapters in this book that touch on the usage or development of a search interface, such as "Freedom on the Move and Ethical Challenges in the Digital History of Slavery" by Vanessa Holden and Joshua D. Rothman in this volume. Their interface showcases the benefits and affordances of semantic search. By including semantic enrichments (as conscientiously recorded by volunteers), users of the database can explore the collection of runaway advertisements in nuanced and complex ways that go beyond simple keyword search. For example, they can include metadata about the ad, as well as information about the enslaved individual (or enslaver), to find content and study the language and history of slavery. In this sense, semantic search provides a technique to traverse historical data based on the rich and multifaceted biographical information embedded in runaway ads. Moreover, diachronic semantic search could also provide suggestions for query terms that are specific to the historical period and unfamiliar to us today.

Why Search?

Search is a common practice in historical scholarship, which is usually based on identifying sources in archives. The process of searching and the archives themselves have changed substantially in the last forty years, with the advent of the personal computer, then the internet and the web, Google search, digital libraries, and the Internet Archive (Graham, Milligan, and Weingart, "Exploring Big Historical Data"; Story et al., "History's Future"). Nevertheless, while the way that today's historians access sources is almost always mediated by a search tool, a digital archive, an advanced search interface, or complex queries, this topic tends to be discussed only marginally in digital history.

While historians tend to prefer "browsing" (digital) sources (Allen and Sieczkiewicz, "How Historians Use Historical Newspapers"), methodologically, the use of keyword search has become an accepted, frequent, and almost unremarkable activity (as opposed to, for example, the use of text mining methods that are currently practiced only by a very small number of historians). The debate on macro/quantitative versus micro/qualitative approaches usually receives more attention, even though few historians engage with data mining and many use search boxes to craft their argument. See, for instance, how often topics such as culturomics (Michel et al., "Quantitative Analysis of Culture") and distant reading (Moretti) are mentioned as part of the Debates in the Digital Humanities series, compared to discussions related to information retrieval.

The act of search, which is different from the act of modeling (e.g., plotting word-frequency over time), generally remains in the background.[3] A few papers have, however, explicitly questioned the impact of search on historical scholarship. Digital search opens, according to Lara Putnam ("The Transnational and the Text-Searchable"), "shortcuts that enable ignorance as well as knowledge" because the ease with which scholars can now interrogate online collections disconnects transnational history "from place-based research practices that have been central to our discipline's epistemology and ethics alike" (Putnam, 379). The speed and granularity enabled by full-text indexing facilitates discovery but risks the loss or underappreciation of contextual knowledge needed to properly interpret the found materials. Putnam is not as much concerned with technicalities of search as with how the general affordances of online access to historical sources can shape research practices for better or worse. Nonetheless, a major distinction with archival search—as is often repeated—is that historians can now "find without knowing where to look" (Putnam, 377). An interesting case, in this respect, is Osmond (2015), who, following Featherstone (2013), characterizes search as "chasing snippets and shadows." He shows how keyword queries combined with a "queer eye" allows him to trace often implicit mentions and representations of homosexuality in the sporting press before the 1950s. Also reflecting on the digitized press, Brake ("Half Full and Half Empty") emphasizes how the affordances of the interfaces mediate and structure access to databases, noticing how they mostly invite users to navigate a collection using keyword search but are less amenable to browsing series or titles. As these studies show, retrieving information is a critical part of historical analysis, and digitization is proving increasingly influential. Understanding the process by which historians collect materials from an archive is fascinating because it has at least three layers of complexity, which are the focus of the remainder of this section.

First, historians are interested in complex, abstract, and (often) latent concepts. This contrasts with fact-oriented queries that we are used to from popular web search engines like Google. For instance, historians might be interested in concepts that do not appear in the textual content because it was illegal to mention them or that are referenced differently based on the political affiliation or the cultural background of the writer. Clearly, this type of research is not adequately addressed by the string-based search functionality currently available in archives. It is therefore particularly important to allow historians to access a more advanced search that can access the level of meaning of the texts. This is what we refer to as semantic search. Second, historians work with historical collections, which typically span over a long period of time. As language changes constantly, the change in the meanings of words is a crucially important factor to be accounted for whenever texts are searched, analyzed, and interpreted. This phenomenon is called semantic change in linguistics and concept drift in other disciplines.

Finally, aware of this semantic shift, when retrieving information from an archive, historians attempt (as much as they can) to adapt their query to the period under investigation and the perceived contemporaneous meanings. Nevertheless, the meaning of words today still plays a relevant role in the way queries are formulated and documents are interpreted, especially to assess the relevance of the retrieved results. Scholars might say that an expert should simply know their subject and its contextual meanings; this, we argue here, is only partially true, and diachronic semantic search approaches could assist the expert in challenging their assumptions while exploring a collection. This approach is in line with what Hannah Ringler describes in this book in the chapter on computation and hermeneutics: Semantic search is a way of "asking questions *with*" computational methods and, by interacting with the results of the tool, a way of "asking questions *about*" computational methods. Nevertheless, it is important to keep in mind that searching is a completely different activity from reading. What search lacks in deep immersive understanding is gained in processing speed. Therefore, when discussing search, the focus should not only be on how a computational method is applied to a collection but especially how the same method helps the user define the query. Moreover, query rewrite logs are one of the best signals used by search engines for disambiguation and fine-tuning. As users, we often end up writing a query on Google repeatedly to point the tool in the direction we want to go. This is helpful because it guides us to define more explicitly what we are looking for.

Approaches toward Semantic Search

Capturing the meaning expressed in textual materials has been one of the overarching ambitions of researchers in NLP, IR, semantic web, and DH. This would allow, among many other things, retrieving information relevant to a user query beyond simple string matching: for example, as mentioned previously, Olieman and colleagues ("Good Applications for Crummy Entity Linkers?") attempt to find entities related to the concept of the Dutch Golden Age, such as painters and buildings related to this period. But there are other strategies to move from the textual to the semantic level. Here, we describe what we see as three core approaches for modeling (word) semantics that have emerged across the research community over the last decades.

The first set of approaches includes initiatives for enriching a collection of documents with layers of (semantic) meta-information. Since its origins, the DH community has deeply engaged in such approaches. This is exemplified by the body of work related to the Text Encoding Initiative (TEI), whose major accomplishment has been the creation of a framework for enriching documents with extensible markup language (XML) schemas (Cummings). These layers of semantic annotation are often modeled to encode the latent or implicit structure of a document and allow researchers to formulate more complex queries, searching only through specific parts of the document. However, manually encoding documents is labor intensive, and automatic annotation of documents requires a significant computational effort. Another form of enrichment results from the application of automatic tagging, which is often implemented by NLP tools that generate morpho-syntactic annotations (i.e., focused both on parts of speech and words, such as nouns and verbs, for example, and the structure of sentences). Linguistic annotation allows scholars to disambiguate and refine their queries—for example, by defining a combination of tokens and part-of-speech tags such as "book [VERB]." Newer interfaces such as Nederlab (Brugman et al.) allow researchers to create detailed query patterns to search diachronic heritage collections.

A core aspect of these approaches to modeling semantics is that they rely on the existence of a structured representation of a specific domain of knowledge. For this reason, such research is highly intertwined with the advent and affirmation of the semantic web and the overall goal of a computationally processable way of representing knowledge (Berners-Lee, Hendler, and Lassila). For instance, the Digging into Linked Parliamentary Data project offers a combination of a structured knowledge base and documents semantically enriched with information derived from the knowledge base itself.[4] This project tackled the double goal of semantically encoding implicitly structured documents (such as debates in parliament, which follow a distinct pattern of speech turns) and linking them to relevant knowledge bases (such as DBpedia, but also domain-specific parliamentary databases).

A related research area aims at automatically enriching documents with links to the information contained in the knowledge bases. Such efforts, embodied, for instance, in so-called entity-linker tools (Shen, Wang, and Han, "Entity Linking with a Knowledge Base") have reached the digital humanities community.[5] Such approaches allow the retrieval of occurrences of a specific entry from a knowledge base (containing, for instance, people or places) in the corpus. Moreover, these approaches make it possible to execute more complex structured queries—for instance, to find colligatory concepts such as the French Revolution that encompass a specific set of people, places, and events. WideNet (Olieman et al.) exploits the structure between entities to generate queries that aim to capture a diverse set of entities related to a concept and retrieve relevant documents. However, in addition to the focus on names of entities such as people and places rather than common nouns to denote concepts, applying knowledge bases risks introducing contemporary biases to historical data. For instance, some people were largely unknown to contemporaries and only acquired fame posthumously, which risks inducing a certain recency bias in our knowledge bases by overemphasizing information that is important from a present-day (but not necessarily from a historical) perspective. Entity linking, when not properly trained and evaluated, can amplify such biases and project them on historical data by, as an example, erroneously associating the string "Van Gogh" with the (not then famous) painter Vincent. Other projects, such as Impresso (Ehrmann et al., "Introducing the CLEF 2020 HIPE Shared Task"), have made substantial improvements regarding historical entity linking for newspaper data.[6]

The second group of approaches to modeling semantics that we consider here is from the information retrieval community (Schütze, Manning, and Raghavan). Instead of relying on a structured representation of knowledge and a collection where occurrences of entities have been linked to a knowledge base, such approaches mostly focus on better modeling the information needed by the user by expanding the query with additional semantic information. Here we highlight a few ways in which the IR community tackles this problem. One way, which bridges information retrieval and semantic web approaches, involves enriching the user query with entity links in the same way that the corpus has been previously enriched (Dalton, Dietz, and Allan, "Entity Query Feature Expansion Using Knowledge Base Links") and in line with the things-not-strings Google approach.[7] A different way of capturing/expanding the meaning of the query would be to have a so-called implicit reference feedback from the corpus: retrieving an initial set of documents that are relevant to the query, identifying a series of frequently occurring words from the set, and running a second query on the corpus (Xu and Croft, "Query Expansion Using Local and Global Document Analysis"). A final way would be to keep the user in the loop and ask for further specification on the initial query, both through a "Do you mean this?" prompt and through a filtering process of possibly related words, entities, or concepts.

A final approach of modeling semantics and allowing the user to retrieve information from a collection of documents relies on current advances in NLP, specifically concerning distributional semantics approaches. Capturing the underlying semantic similarity across documents has been a core area of research between NLP and IR. Such efforts have focused on latent semantic indexing (Hofmann, "Probabilistic Latent Semantic Indexing") and have led to the development of topic modeling algorithms, among which one of the most widely used is latent Dirichlet allocation (Blei, Ng, and Jordan). The development of compact vector representations (so-called word embeddings) that capture the meaning of words, sentences, or documents (Mikolov et al., "Distributed Representations"; Devlin et al.) has allowed for the retrieval of documents based on measuring the semantic similarity between a query and the content of documents (Mitra and Craswell, "Neural Models"; Beelen et al., "When Time Makes Sense"). The advent of such representation learning approaches has been a major breakthrough for context-sensitive and semantic search.[8] In particular, these approaches allow us to go beyond matching a user query with content, without the need for an external knowledge base or a relevance feedback involving the user. However, compared to the approaches described above, which are explicit in highlighting the similarities, the most important drawback of distributional semantics approaches is their lack of interpretability, because it is very difficult for the user to determine why their query is judged by the system to be semantically similar to the retrieved documents. As all three of these approaches demonstrate, semantic search can be achieved in different ways, each with a set of strengths and drawbacks. In the next section, we touch on the role played by time in it.

When Does Time Play a Role?

It is well known that language is a dynamic system (Traugott, "On the Persistence of Ambiguous Linguistic Contexts over Time"), and, like many other aspects of language, word meaning changes with time. Words associated with certain concepts may be different in different time periods. To take a classic example, let us consider the English adjective *gay*. It originally meant "happy" and "joyful," but in the twentieth century, it started being used to refer to people who are attracted to people who identify as their same gender identity, and this is now its predominant current meaning.[9] This change in word meaning is referred to by linguists as lexical semantic change, and it is a complex phenomenon. The original meaning of a word may coexist with a newer one, and sometimes certain meanings are limited to (or created in) particular sociopolitical and cultural contexts.[10] Nowadays, we can expect to find the original bird-related meaning of *tweet* as "chirp of small birds" in texts about birds, but in general the more recent meaning, "a post on the social media platform X (formerly known as Twitter)," is more common in other contexts. Lexical polysemy can take various shapes.[11] A word may have a concrete and an abstract meaning, related metaphorically to each other (cf. "grasp," meaning "seize" in the physical domain and "understand" in the mental domain), or a word may have opposite polarity values (e.g., "sick" as in "ill" has acquired the positive meaning of "excellent" since the early 1980s).

Word meaning change results from a series of interconnected linguistic, cognitive, social, cultural, and contextual factors, and it is often led by innovative language users and communities (Traugott, "On the Persistence of Ambiguous Linguistic Contexts"; Croft, *Explaining Language Change*; Andersen, "Markedness and the Theory of Linguistic Change"). All these complex phenomena affecting word meaning are not just relevant to (historical) linguistics research, but they have a direct effect on the effectiveness of search in historical research and on the expectations that researchers pose on it. For example, we often do not know which words were used in the past to describe feelings or phenomena, which makes it particularly hard to trace the linguistic expressions of a concept over time. Because search has always had an implicit temporal perspective, the crucial questions become how to make this perspective explicit, and how to connect the temporal anchoring of a query to the temporal aspects of the document.[12]

Two related but different semantic change scenarios can have an impact on the process of searching through a historical archive:

1. Modeling the change in meaning of words (e.g., "gay")
2. Modeling the change in linguistic expressions of the underlying concepts (e.g., "happiness-wellbeing-eudaemonia")

In the first scenario, if we take the perspective of a user performing a search for the word "happy," we can assume that their understanding of the meaning of this word corresponds to its most common contemporary definition.[13] In this case, we would like to find all contemporary documents containing the string "happy" or its morphological inflections "happier" and "happiest" and also contemporary documents containing synonyms of the term, such as "content" or "cheerful." This requires that the users specify all these synonyms in their query to retrieve the relevant texts. If the search involves historical documents (from the eighteenth century, for example), it would be desirable for the search engine to return documents containing words that meant "happy" at the time—for example, "gay." For this to happen, it is critical that the change in the meaning of search terms is accounted for in the search engine. Currently, however, the user needs to be fully informed about which synonyms were appropriate in each time period under investigation, which is only partially possible thanks to historical dictionaries, as these resources rely on often large but necessarily limited textual evidence.

In the second scenario, if we want to find documents containing instances of a semantic concept, we need to be aware of the different linguistic expressions that can be used to express that concept. To take the same example used above, the adjective "gay" can be associated to the concept of *happiness* in texts dated up to the early twentieth century. Starting from this point in time, *gay* acquired the meaning of "homosexual" alongside the original meaning of "cheerful," and therefore if our search involves texts from the twentieth or twenty-first century, this new meaning should be taken into account. In this case, what we would need is a way to associate words to concepts and to do that over the different time periods we are interested in.

Current approaches to semantic search are still limited in the two aforementioned scenarios. The semantic representation approaches that rely on manually encoding semantic information in the texts are not easily scalable. Manual semantic annotation is a very time-consuming task and cannot be done for all the texts that researchers may want to search. Some semantic resources like dictionaries and thesauri (the Oxford English Dictionary or the Historical Thesaurus of English, for example) map words' meanings to the historical periods in which they were in use, but most knowledge bases do not have this diachronic aspect. NLP research has led to various new approaches to representing words' changing semantics using word embeddings (Hamilton, Lescovec, and Jurasfky, "Cultural Shift or Linguistic Drift?"; Kutuzov et al., "Diachronic Word Embeddings and Semantic Shifts"). Another line of research has focused on identifying lexical semantic change from large historical corpora (Tahmasebi, Borin, and Jatowt, "Survey of Computational Approaches to Lexical Semantic Change"). In particular, there are rare examples of information retrieval approaches that rely on word embedding representations and have developed basic diachronic search engines such as the Diachronic Explorer for Spanish (Gamallo, Rodríguez-Torres, and Garcia, "Distributional Semantics for Diachronic Search"). However, these are still far from being accurate and detailed enough to satisfy the needs of historical research. In the next section, we present a series of recommendations that will hopefully help further this research.

Our Vision: Diachronic Semantic Search

Through the overview we presented above, our intention was to shed some light on the challenges lying ahead for digital historians who intend to develop systems for diachronic semantic search. This is especially true when searching for information on broad, complex, and abstract topics. We conclude this chapter by highlighting a few ways forward that can help researchers appreciate the extent of these challenges, while at the same time developing approaches for addressing the task.

What is needed in order to develop a diachronic semantic change system? First, a knowledge representation that captures information in the best possible way from the perspective of the period under study. Second, we need historical distributional word vectors that represent historical language use in the form of a geometrical space (a vector space). These two elements are essential because it is only through their combination that it would become possible to model both well-known sociopolitical changes (a city changing its name—for instance, Leningrad) as well as more latent long-term cultural variations (see, for instance, Light, "When Computers Were Women"). However, obtaining such resources presents multiple challenges across the spectrum of current and, as we argued, future computational humanities research.

For instance, distributional representations of the meaning of words can be derived directly from large collections. However, assessing their quality requires setting up a complex procedure to evaluate the type of semantic information captured by the model (e.g., similarity versus relatedness of meaning) and to quantify the distinction between changes in meaning and variations in language usage (Erk, McCarthy, and Gaylord, "Investigations on Word Senses and Word Usages"; Gonen et al., "Simple, Interpretable and Stable Method for Detecting Words"). Such evaluation strongly relies on the expertise of the language and the culture of the period under study. A structured knowledge representation of the period (or periods) under study will be even more difficult to obtain. In fact, while diachronic dictionaries and gazetteers exist, their coverage is necessarily just partial. For instance, gazetteers often lack relational information between entries (e.g., Florence as the capital of the Reign of Italy between 1865 and 1867). At the same time, the large majority of current knowledge graphs and entity linking tools are developed on the type of information available on Wikipedia, ranging from info-boxes to textual context around links, from redirect pages to categories as structures. This therefore limits the possibility of plugging in a pipeline that works in a contemporary setting unless the same type of knowledge information on the period under study is offered as input—for example, by having a Wikipedia of the nineteenth century. While efforts in this direction are complex and will require a long time to be implemented, we are already aware of the limitations of contemporary knowledge graph tools when applied to non-twenty-first-century mainstream sources.[14]

Further, while we need a way to assess the overall reliability of this semantic retrieval system, doing this in the context of historical research is challenging because of the complexity and abstract nature of the queries and the subjective interpretation that each historian will bring when assessing the relevance of a retrieved document based on a specific query. For this reason, we recommend that researchers move away from a pure ranking-based information retrieval paradigm (as a matter of fact, search results are much more than a ranking) and embrace different ways to establish the relevance of the obtained results. For instance, we can consider exploratory faceted search.[15] You can also consider active learning, which is a machine learning setting where the user interacts with the algorithm by iteratively labeling new data points with the desired outputs to improve the performance. These are closer to the way a historian would normally interact with a collection: first through a broad overview and then further and further into a specific topic. While the performance of an end-to-end diachronic semantic search system may be too complex to evaluate in its entirety, especially when the users are domain experts, the usefulness of each component could still be measured. For instance, we could assess how diverse the selection of an exploratory interface is or how well an active learning system picks up the signal of the user. Digital interfaces for historical research need to balance user requirements with technical constraints. Establishing the equilibrium between these aspects remains the topic of ongoing research.

The complexity of offering diachronic semantic search in a digital history context should not be underestimated and, as a community, we should not follow a data-driven paradigm that reduces context to the creation of a gold standard or a benchmark averaging the opinion of experts (McGillivray et al., "Digital Humanities and Natural Language Processing"). And, even more importantly, this does not apply only to digital history or computational humanities but all across the academic spectrum, to any discipline that relies on the use of computational methods for conducting research. As stressed by Catherine D'Ignazio and Laurent Klein (*Data Feminism,* chap. 6), "data are not neutral or objective. They are the products of unequal social relations, and this context is essential for conducting accurate ethical analysis." So, instead of ignoring, reducing, or simplifying the context, we should benefit from its complexity in order to build tools and systems that will bring us closer to the full experience of search that we envision. The analysis of meaning in digital resources is neither a purely algorithmic nor a solely manual task. Instead, we argue that it is situated at the interface of human and machine reading; it arises through a complex interaction between interpretive strategies and semantic technologies. And, as we believe, it will flourish as a result.

Notes

All authors reviewed and approved the final version of this essay. They have joint responsibility for the first and last sections. Kaspar Beelen has primary responsibility for the "Why Search?" section, Federico Nanni for "Approaches toward Semantic Search," and Barbara McGillivray for the section "When Does Time Play a Role?"

1. See the last example at "Frequently Asked Questions," *La Stampa*. Accessed January 15, 2024. http://www.archiviolastampa.it/component/option,com_lastampa/task,faq/Itemid,4/.

2. https://www.historyofconcepts.net.

3. There are some notable exceptions (e.g., Underwood, "Theorizing Research Practices," and Putnam, "Transnational and the Text-Searchable").

4. The archives for "Digging into Linked Parliamentary Data" are available at https://blog.history.ac.uk/tag/digging-into-linked-parliamentary-data/ (last accessed January 15, 2024).

5. See also Rovera et al., "Domain-Specific Named Entity Disambiguation"; Ardanuy and Sporleder, "Toponym Disambiguation"; Munnelly and Lawless, "Investigating Entity Linking"; McDonough, Moncla, and van de Camp, "Named Entity Recognition."

6. Information on the Impresso project and Impresso app are available at https://impresso-project.ch/ (last accessed January 15, 2024).

7. See Amit Singhal, "Introducing the Knowledge Graph: Things, Not Strings," *The Keyword* (blog), May 16, 2012, https://www.blog.google/products/search/introducing-knowledge-graph-things-not/ (last accessed January 15, 2024). Regarding the broader role of Google in the information retrieval community, a good starting point is Brooks's 2003 article on "Web Search: How the Web Has Changed Information Retrieval."

8. See also the advent of a new "deep learning" evaluation track in 2019 at TREC, the Text REtrieval Conference (Craswell et al.).

9. Cf., for example, "gay, adj., adv., and n." at Oxford English Dictionary (OED) Online, accessed July 14, 2020, https://oed.com/view/Entry/77207?rskey=JyQmyU&result=1&isAdvanced=false.

10. Consider, for instance, the communication on social media in order to avoid censorship; see https://www.amnesty.org/en/latest/news/2020/03/china-social-media-language-government-censorship-covid/.

11. See Bréal, "Les lois intellectuelles du langage"; Ullmann, *Semantics*; Blank, "Why Do New Meanings Occur?"; Koch, "Meaning Change and Semantic Shifts."

12. The structure and classification of archives also change over time. This point is outside the scope of the present chapter, but it is an important element to be considered.

13. See https://www.dictionary.com/browse/happy (last accessed January 15, 2024).

14. As discussed in Ardanuy and Sporleder, "Toponym Disambiguation"; Olieman et al., "Good Applications for Crummy Entity Linkers?"; Rovera et al., "Domain-Specific Named Entity Disambiguation"; Munnelly and Lawless, "Investigating Entity Linking"; McDonough, Moncla, and van de Camp, "Named Entity Recognition Goes to Old Regime France"; Ardanuy et al., "A Deep Learning Approach to Geographical Candidate Selection through Toponym Matching," among others.

15. A good example of faceted search tailored toward the research needs of historians and the content of the database is "Freedom on the Move" (https://freedomonthemove.org). This interface allows users to formulate a detailed search based on recurrent descriptions of fugitives and enslavers in American "runaway ads." See also chapter 11 in this volume.

Bibliography

Allen, R. B., and R. Sieczkiewicz. "How Historians Use Historical Newspapers." *Proceedings of the American Society for Information Science and Technology* 47, no. 1 (2010): 1–4.

Andersen, H. "Markedness and the Theory of Linguistic Change." In *Actualization: Linguistic Change in Progress*, edited by H. Andersen, 21–57. Amsterdam: John Benjamins, 2001.

Ardanuy, M. C., and C. Sporleder. "Toponym Disambiguation in Historical Documents Using Semantic and Geographic Features." In *Proceedings of the 2nd International Conference on Digital Access to Textual Cultural Heritage*, 175–80. New York: Association for Computing Machinery, 2017.

Ardanuy, M. C., K. Hosseini, K. McDonough, A. Krause, D. van Strien, and F. A. Nanni. "Deep Learning Approach to Geographical Candidate Selection through Toponym Matching." In *Proceedings of the 28th International Conference on Advances in Geographic Information Systems*, 385–88. New York: Association for Computing Machinery, 2020.

Beelen, K., F. Nanni, M. C. Ardanuy, K. Hosseini, G. Tolfo, and B. McGillivray. "When Time Makes Sense: A Historically-Aware Approach to Targeted Sense Disambiguation." In *Findings of the Association for Computational Linguistics: ACL-IJCNLP 2021*, 2751–61. Association for Computational Linguistics, 2021.

Berners-Lee, T., J. Hendler, and O. Lassila. "The Semantic Web." *Scientific American* 284, no. 5 (2001): 34–43.

Blank, A. "Why Do New Meanings Occur? A Cognitive Typology of the Motivations for Lexical Semantic Change." *Historical Semantics and Cognition* 13, no. 6 (1999).

Blei, D. M., A. Y. Ng, and M. I. Jordan. "Latent Dirichlet Allocation." *Journal of Machine Learning Research* 3 (2003): 993–1022.

Brake, L., "Half Full and Half Empty." *Journal of Victorian Culture* 17, no. 2 (2012): 222–29.

Bréal, M. "Les lois intellectuelles du langage: fragment de sémantique." *Annuaire de l'Association pour l'Encouragement des Études Grecques en France* 17 (1883): 132–42.

Brooks, T. A. "Web Search: How the Web Has Changed Information Retrieval." *Information Research* 8, no. 3 (2003).

Brugman, H., M. Reynaert, N. van der Sijs, R. van Stipriaan, E. T. K. Sang, and A. van den Bosch. "Nederlab: Towards a Single Portal and Research Environment for Diachronic Dutch Text Corpora." In *Proceedings of the Tenth International Conference on Language Resources and Evaluation (LREC'16)*, 1277–81. Göttingen: 2016.

Craswell, N., B. Mitra, E. Yilmaz, D. Campos, and E. M. Voorhees. "Overview of the TREC 2019 Deep Learning Track." *ArXiv:2003.07820* (2020).

Croft, W. *Explaining Language Change: An Evolutionary Approach*. Harlow, Essex: Longman, 2000.

Croft, W. B., M. Bendersky, H. Li, and G. Xu. "Query Representation and Understanding Workshop." *SIGIR Forum* 44, no. 2 (December 2010): 48–53.

Cummings, J. "The Text Encoding Initiative and the Study of Literature." In *A Companion to Digital Literary Studies,* edited by Ray Siemens and Susan Schriebman. Blackwell, 2013.

Dalton, J., L. Dietz, and J. Allan. "Entity Query Feature Expansion Using Knowledge Base Links." In *Proceedings of the 37th International ACM SIGIR Conference on Research and Development in Information Retrieval,* 365–74. 2014.

Deerwester, S., S. T. Dumais, G. W. Furnas, T. K. Landauer, and R. Harshman. "Indexing by Latent Semantic Analysis." *Journal of the American Society for Information Science* 41, no. 6 (1990): 391–407.

Devlin, J., M. W. Chang, K. Lee, and K. Toutanova. BERT: Pre-training of Deep Bidirectional Transformers for Language Understanding. In *NAACL-HLT* 1 (January 2019).

D'Ignazio, C., and L. F. Klein. *Data Feminism.* Cambridge, Mass.: MIT Press. 2020.

Ehrmann, M., M. Romanello, S. Bircher, and S. Clematide. "Introducing the CLEF 2020 HIPE Shared Task: Named Entity Recognition and Linking on Historical Newspapers." In *European Conference on Information Retrieval,* 524–32. Cham: Springer, 2020.

Erk, K., D. McCarthy, and N. Gaylord. "Investigations on Word Senses and Word Usages." In *Proceedings of ACL-IJCNLP 2009—Joint Conference of the 47th Annual Meeting of the Association for Computational Linguistics and 4th International Joint Conference on Natural Language Processing of the AFNLP,* 10–18. Stroudsburg, Pa.: Association for Computational Linguistics, 2009.

Featherstone, L. "Snippets and Shadows of Stories: Thoughts on Sources and Methods When Writing an Australian History of Sexuality." In *Intimacy, Violence and Activism: Gay and Lesbian Perspectives on Australasian History and Society,* edited by G. Willett and Y. Smaal, 74–89. Melbourne: Monash University Publishing, 2013.

Gamallo, P., I. Rodríguez-Torres, and M. Garcia. "Distributional Semantics for Diachronic Search." *Computers and Electrical Engineering* 65 (October 2018): 438–48. https://doi.org/10.1016/j.compeleceng.2017.07.017.

Gonen, H., G. Jawahar, D. Seddah, and Y. Goldberg. "Simple, Interpretable and Stable Method for Detecting Words with Usage Change across Corpora." In *Proceedings of the 58th Annual Meeting of the Association for Computational Linguistics,* 538–55. Stroudsburg, Pa.: Association for Computational Linguistics, 2020. https://doi.org/10.18653/v1/2020.acl-main.51.

Graham, S., I. Milligan, and S. Weingart. *Exploring Big Historical Data: The Historian's Macroscope.* Singapore: World Scientific Publishing, 2015.

Guha, R., R. McCool, and E. Miller. "Semantic Search." In *Proceedings of the 12th International Conference on World Wide Web,* 700–709. New York: Association for Computing Machinery, 2003.

Guldi, J. "Critical Search: A Procedure for Guided Reading in Large-Scale Textual Corpora." *Journal of Cultural Analytics* 3, no 1 (2018). https://doi.org/10.22148/16.030.

Hamilton, W. L., J. Leskovec, and D. Jurasfky. "Cultural Shift or Linguistic Drift? Comparing Two Computational Measures of Semantic Change." In *Proceedings of the 2016*

Conference on Empirical Methods in Natural Language Processing, 2116–21. Association for Computational Linguistics, 2016.

Hengchen, S., R. Ros, and J. Marjanen. "A Data-Driven Approach to the Changing Vocabulary of the Nation in English, Dutch, Swedish and Finnish Newspapers, 1750–1950." In *Proceedings of the Digital Humanities (DH) Conference.* 2019.

Hofmann, T. "Probabilistic Latent Semantic Indexing." In *Proceedings of the 22nd Annual International ACM SIGIR Conference on Research and Development in Information Retrieval,* 50–57. 1999.

Koch, P. "Meaning Change and Semantic Shifts." In *The Lexical Typology of Semantic Shifts,* edited by P. Juvonen and M. Koptjevskaja-Tamm, 21–66. Berlin: De Gruyter, 2016.

Kutuzov, A., L. Øvrelid, T. Szymanski, and E. Velldal. "Diachronic Word Embeddings and Semantic Shifts: A Survey." In *Proceedings of the 27th International Conference on Computational Linguistics,* 1384–97. Association for Computational Linguistics, 2018.

Light, J. S. "When Computers Were Women." *Technology and Culture* 40, no. 3 (1999): 455–83.

McDonough, K., L. Moncla, and M. van de Camp. "Named Entity Recognition Goes to Old Regime France: Geographic Text Analysis for Early Modern French Corpora." *International Journal of Geographical Information Science* 33, no. 12 (2019): 2498–522.

McGillivray, B. "Computational Methods for Semantic Analysis of Historical Texts." In *Research Methods in the Digital Humanities,* edited by K. Schuster and S. Dunn, 261–74. London: Routledge, 2020.

McGillivray, B., S. Hengchen, V. Lähteenoja, M. Palma, and A. Vatri. "A Computational Approach to Lexical Polysemy in Ancient Greek." *Digital Scholarship in the Humanities,* 34, no. 4 (2019): 893–907. https://doi.org/10.1093/llc/fqz036.

McGillivray, B., T. Poibeau, and P. Ruiz Fabo. "Digital Humanities and Natural Language Processing: 'Je t'aime . . . Moi non plus.'" *DHQ: Digital Humanities Quarterly* 14, no. 2 (2020).

Michel, J. B., Y. K. Shen, A. P. Aiden, A. Veres, M. K. Gray, J. P. Pickett, D. Hoiberg, et al. "Quantitative Analysis of Culture Using Millions of Digitized Books." *Science* 331, no. 6014 (2011): 176–82.

Mikolov, T., I. Sutskever, K. Chen, G. S. Corrado, and J. Dean. "Distributed Representations of Words and Phrases and Their Compositionality." In *Advances in Neural Information Processing Systems,* 3111–19. Curran Associates, 2013.

Mitra, B., and N. Craswell. "Neural Models for Information Retrieval." *ArXiv:1705.01509* (2017).

Moretti, F. *Distant Reading.* London: Verso Books, 2013.

Munnelly, G., and S. Lawless. "Investigating Entity Linking in Early English Legal Documents." In *Proceedings of the 18th ACM/IEEE on Joint Conference on Digital Libraries,* 59–68. New York: Association for Computing Machinery, 2018.

Olieman, A., K. Beelen, M. van Lange, J. Kamps, and M. Marx "Good Applications for Crummy Entity Linkers? The Case of Corpus Selection in Digital Humanities." In *Proceedings of the 13th International Conference on Semantic Systems,* 81–88. New York: Association for Computing Machinery, 2017.

Osmond, G. "'Pink Tea and Sissy Boys': Digitized Fragments of Male Homosexuality, Non-Heteronormativity and Homophobia in the Australian Sporting Press, 1845–1954." *International Journal of the History of Sport* 32, no. 13 (2015): 1578–92.

Putnam, L. "The Transnational and the Text-Searchable: Digitized Sources and the Shadows They Cast." *American Historical Review* 121, no. 2 (2016): 377–402. https://doi.org/10.1093/ahr/121.2.377.

Rovera, M., F. Nanni, S. P. Ponzetto, and A. Goy. "Domain-Specific Named Entity Disambiguation in Historical Memoirs." In *Proceedings of the Fourth Italian Conference on Computational Linguistics CLiC-IT 2017*, 287–91. Aachen, Germany: CEUR, 2017.

Schütze, H., C. D. Manning, and P. Raghavan. *Introduction to Information Retrieval*. Cambridge: Cambridge University Press, 2008.

Shen, W., J. Wang, and J. Han. "Entity Linking with a Knowledge Base: Issues, Techniques, and Solutions." *IEEE Transactions on Knowledge and Data Engineering* 27, no. 2 (2014): 443–60.

Story, D. J., J. Guldi, T. Hitchcock, and M. Moravec. "History's Future in the Age of the Internet." *American Historical Review* 125, no. 4 (2020): 1337–46.

Tahmasebi, N., L. Borin, and A. Jatowt. "Survey of Computational Approaches to Lexical Semantic Change." *ArXiv:1811.06278* (2018). https://arxiv.org/abs/1811.06278.

Traugott, E. C. "On the Persistence of Ambiguous Linguistic Contexts over Time: Implications for Corpus Research on Micro-Changes." *Corpus Linguistics and Variation in English*, 231. 2012.

Ullmann, S. *Semantics: An Introduction to the Study of Meaning*. Basil: Blackwell, 1962.

Underwood, T. "Theorizing Research Practices We Forgot to Theorize Twenty Years Ago." *Representations* 127, no. 1 (2014): 64–72. https://doi.org/10.1525/rep.2014.127.1.64.

Xu, J., and W. B. Croft. "Query Expansion Using Local and Global Document Analysis." Proceedings of the 19th Annual International ACM SIGIR Conference on Research and Development in Information Retrieval. January 1996.

PART II][Chapter 11

Freedom on the Move and Ethical Challenges in the Digital History of Slavery

VANESSA M. HOLDEN AND JOSHUA D. ROTHMAN

Nancy fled in January 1844. According to an advertisement placed for her capture in the New Orleans *Daily Picayune* by her enslaver, Willis Holmes, she was forty years old and about five feet tall. Holmes described Nancy as "stout" and "thick set" with a "black complexion and good countenance," and he claimed she wore a dress of blue homespun when she left his residence on St. Charles Street, in the American section of the city just outside the French Quarter. Nancy had not been in New Orleans for long. Holmes reported that she had been shipped there from Charleston on the brig *Powhatan* only weeks before she absconded, and he suspected she would try to return to South Carolina, warning the "public generally," but "masters of vessels and steamboats" especially, from "harboring her, under the penalty of the law." Holmes offered a $10 reward for anyone who delivered Nancy to him or had her placed in a New Orleans jail (New Orleans *Daily Picayune*).

The notice Holmes took out as he pursued Nancy in the hopes of re-enslaving her was one of hundreds of thousands of similar advertisements that appeared in American newspapers over the course of more than 150 years before slavery's abolition in 1865. Colloquially known as "runaway ads," these are documents with seemingly boundless genealogical, educational, and research potential. They are pocket biographies of individual enslaved people, with details about their physical appearances, skills, relationships, and histories that often appear nowhere else in the archive of slavery. They reveal the priorities and calculations of slaveholders, they demonstrate the constant resistance of the enslaved, and they reveal American slavery as cruel and intractable yet also unstable, rife with friction, and in constant motion. They are relatively simple and straightforward documents that are nevertheless rich with information about the material culture of slavery, the domestic slave trade, the geographies of enslavement, the demographics of flight, and the systematic surveillance and captivity of enslaved people in which an entire nation participated. Yet, even writing this summary mirrors some of the challenges researchers face when confronting the documents and the archive comprising the data extracted from them.

In 2013, a small group of historians began collaboration on a project titled Freedom on the Move (FOTM), whose aim is to collect, digitize, and make available online every one of these advertisements. Since the founding of the project, the number of collaborators has grown and expanded to include additional historians from a range of public and private universities, as well as software engineers, data librarians, education researchers, and grant specialists. FOTM has garnered over $1 million in grants, hired dozens of undergraduate and graduate student researchers, built a preliminary database and a website with a robust user interface, and collected more than 30,000 advertisements.

Over the course of the last eight-plus years, we have learned some important lessons that are applicable to a wide range of digital humanities projects and perhaps especially applicable to projects grappling with Black history and the history of American slavery.

Though imagined and driven in important ways by scholars with expertise in their fields, any public-facing project must bring audiences and builders of various kinds—scholars, programmers, funders, educators, students, and multiple publics—into partnership and collaboration from the outset, and that partnership and collaboration must be made integral to the project's development and evolution. Simultaneously, the various stakeholders must be aware that new interventions and ideas will come into play as the project unfolds. There will be new partners and communities to engage, and there will be unforeseen moral dilemmas and interpretive questions that need to be negotiated among stakeholders who bring different priorities and understandings of the project's goals and significance to the table. Ultimately, gathering the historical materials that compose the foundation of a digital humanities project centering on the history of slavery and enslaved people is no mean feat, yet FOTM demonstrates that it may be the simplest and most straightforward element of the project. Making those materials into an ethically sound archive, accessible and responsive to a wide range of contributors, builders, and users, is a more profound challenge.

In the digital humanities, we would suggest that the challenge is best considered as an ongoing process rather than a matter with a clearly definable end (see Lothian). Documenting and drawing attention to the ethical choices that go into the creation of archives and datasets is imperative, and those choices ought to be continuously documented as they unfold over time. Creating this kind of archive and dataset within the archive maintains the spirit of openness, accessibility, and care critical to computational humanities as a discipline. It also reminds scholars that attending to Black life in database projects requires us to work at the intersection of the digital humanities and computational humanities. Because enslaved people were valued in numerical forms as much and as often as their social, legal, or even spiritual personhood (or lack thereof), projects that appear to be focused on the digital humanities

(DH) but engage histories of slavery are also and always computational humanities projects as well—projects dealing in large datasets where mathematical formulas, programming, and numerical calculations on a large scale overlap with qualitative research on the everyday lives of, in this instance, enslaved people.

Building the Team: Centering Collaboration

Historians have used runaway advertisements before to demonstrate enslaved people's persistent resistance, enslavers' commitment to slavery, and the construction of race as a social category over time. Mostly, these historians built their own databases and research files by scouring newspaper collections from various archives and publishing collections of advertisements. Some of these collections have been digitized and some have not, and when we began FOTM, we had a vision for a comprehensive open-source archive that would be available and legible to researchers, genealogists, educators, students, and multiple publics alike. As Crystal Eddins notes, DH projects have the potential to engage with the long Black Radical Traditions of marronnage. Among the potential maroon characteristics that Eddins posits are the "creation of solidarity networks of people who share social position and liberatory goals."[1] From the start, we prioritized collaboration with programmers and the many constituencies we imagined would find the project useful. We designed the project to incorporate a crowdsourcing model to code and organize data points, asking users to help build the archive and find new ways to use it. As Mia Ridge has observed, at its best, crowdsourcing can connect "people, culture, history, and collections while providing the public with platforms for enjoyable, meaningful activity" (Ridge, 435).

But through team meetings, alpha and beta testing groups, and workshops with K–12 educators, we came to understand that the diverse publics we imagined using FOTM would not merely contribute time and labor to the project. We were not adding their response to our work in our revisions of the site. They would work alongside us as collaborators in building the archive *and* designing it, a welcome realization that nonetheless brought to the fore a set of knotty concerns (see Bailey; Thomas). Perhaps the most generative quandary has been the ethical issue of reifying the violence of reducing self-emancipated people to data to be "extracted" and "analyzed" from sources whose creators were intent on making them slaves when they so clearly stated with their feet that they were indeed free people. This is where computational humanities and analytics play an important role, but only alongside the digital humanities more broadly. Interrogating where, for example, linked open data might be useful, as in a project like Enslaved.org, alongside where and whether that approach does or does not repeat the commodification of enslaved lives is a key discussion point at FOTM. For scholars like Daryle Williams, defining core sets of metadata allows scholars to combine large datasets (of enslaved people's biographical information) that may otherwise vary widely by empire, archive collection practices, and research preferences. For FOTM, the issues of collaboration and public engagement play as much a role as the metadata and formulas for searching the ads and has shaped our project's inquiries.

The process of engaging and collaborating with scholars, students, and the general public in viewing, building, and designing the archive implicates them and compounds that ethical conundrum. The priorities and interests of the historians, programmers, and university grant and contract agents are not always in alignment, and efforts to foreground the experiences of the enslaved are inevitably compromised by orientations toward outcomes and resources. At FOTM, we are conscious of these and other dilemmas, many of which are endemic to the digital history of slavery and to Black digital humanities projects more broadly. We have attempted to build into the project itself ways to address these concerns. Even as we recognize that they are often ultimately irresolvable, we would argue that their potential damage and harm can be acknowledged, reduced, and made into productive, important, and integral components of FOTM and its possibilities. We believe our experience points toward an instructive model for computational humanities projects grappling with similarly challenging materials and variegated stakeholders.

Archives of Fugitivity: Fragments of Self-Emancipated Lives

For contemporary users, what is it like to transcribe data categories easily gleaned from each ad? How should the programmer deal with each data point? A dropdown menu? A blank to fill in? What do those choices mean at a computational level? What about at the interpretive level for users? What about users who encounter the long list of racial categories across multiple languages that appear in the advertisements available for transcription? What if they are deeply offended by the racist terms used for enslaved people in the past? The challenge most intrinsic to FOTM is also perhaps the most inextricable from it, which is that by amassing evidence of fugitivity, breaking down that evidence into discrete and detailed categories, and enabling it to be collated for examination, study, and research, we risk replicating some of the imperatives and hierarchies of slavery itself.

One cogent answer comes in the form of a found poem: *"I/loved/her/but/that/ white man/took/her/from/me."* From a photocopy of an advertisement found in the FOTM database, these words peek out from between redactions made with black permanent marker to conceal most of the words on the page. Concealed sections, chosen by an eighth-grade student, serve as a mimetic for archival silence. Those left visible attest to the way that even fraught sources, produced by enslavers, often reveal the pervasive resistance of the Black people they were so intent on enslaving. There, among words meant to transform a person back into chattel, to deny the self-emancipation evident in one person's flight from bondage, a contemporary middle-school student left legible only the part that reveals one definition of freedom: love and intimacy. The collaborative mission of the project is explicitly to

Freedom on the Move and Ethical Challenges in the Digital History of Slavery [199

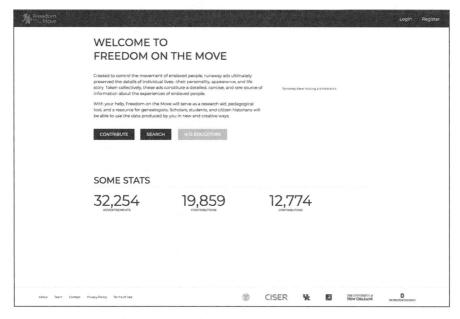

Figure 11.1. Freedom on the Move welcome page. Visitors to the website make a choice here to contribute to or search the database of advertisements for fugitives from slavery.

build with students like the poem's author, not to anticipate their needs and teach them what they need to know. Time and again, the range of collaborative voices on the project have revealed things that did not catch the attention of professional historians.

When most users begin working with FOTM, they select whether they prefer to "contribute" to or "search" the database (Figure 11.1). Selecting "contribute" gives users the options to "extract data," to "group advertisements," or to "moderate" (Figure 11.2). The first option is the most involved. Choosing it takes users to a page of advertisements and asks them to pick one, transcribe it from a pdf image into text, answer a lengthy series of questions that disaggregate the text into several dozen metadata categories, submit their work into the system, and then, if they wish, begin anew on another advertisement. Users who select "group advertisements" are asked to examine a series of advertisements, determine whether any of them were placed repeatedly over time, and link them together as a group of duplicates. Users who select "moderate" are asked to proofread and check the accuracy of contributions already made by other users and thus to provide an element of editing and quality control for the database. Users who select at the outset to "search" the database, meanwhile, can look for keywords or pull together one or more categories of metadata from every advertisement entered by previous users.

Not every "runaway advertisement" ever placed is still extant, as not every American newspaper from before the Civil War is still extant, and so even at its most complete, the project will only ever be able to claim comprehensiveness of

Figure 11.2. Freedom on the Move page where visitors choose to contribute to the site by extracting data (filling out information about an advertisement, fugitives from slavery, and enslavers), grouping multiple instances of an advertisement, or moderating content provided by others.

the surviving evidence base. Nevertheless, the number of advertisements that has survived is so tremendously large that we do not yet have a reliable way to make a precise estimate of it. Indeed, these advertisements are, by far, the most voluminous and systematic evidence base ever created for the phenomenon of fugitivity from slavery in the United States. Moreover, they are usually the only surviving written evidence documenting the lives and efforts of tens of thousands of individual enslaved people to achieve their own liberation.

Retrieving, documenting, and sharing that evidence can advance a deep and authoritative understanding of the phenomenon. It offers the opportunity to dignify those lives and efforts, and the harnessing of computational power to a digital archive of the evidence lets us see things at both fine-grained and holistic levels that might otherwise be impossible. Organizing and investigating the metadata extracted from the FOTM database can tell us, for example, about the ebbs and flows of flight from slavery by geographic location and time of year, about the linguistic skills and the presumed literacy of fugitives, and about the items they chose to bring with them when they attempted their escapes. We can see in the particular and the aggregate alike the ages of those who fled from slavery and how often they fled alone, with family members, or with one or more other enslaved people. We can even map the likely paths and directions they took while trying to elude their enslavers. Information about these and dozens of other aspects of fugitivity, ranging across thousands and thousands of instances of flight, would traditionally require immensely time-consuming and painstaking work, but they can be revealed in seconds by the FOTM engine. Moreover, and importantly, being able to parse the material from so many different angles and with the input of so many voices and collaborators helps counter, at least in some measure, the problematic gaze of the enslavers who created it.

An Ethic of Care: Participant Users and the Fraught Nature of Slavery's Archive

Yet there is no denying that runaway advertisements still reflect the voices, priorities, and concerns of the enslavers and jailers who placed them, and that users inevitably "speak" in those voices when they transcribe them. There is no denying that asking users to enter information about the ages, physical characteristics, racial categories, skills, possessions, and rewards offered for fugitives can be a discomfiting request. Seeking out and entering such information so that it might be sorted and arranged, after all, arguably asks users to recreate the inspections and quantifications of Black people and their worth, which, as scholars such as Walter Johnson and Daina Ramey Berry have demonstrated, made their capital, reproductive, and labor values assessable under slavery.

The inescapable moral dualism of creating and analyzing the data in FOTM extends to users who perform searches as well. Currently, for example, a researcher who performs a keyword search of "lame" will retrieve 899 advertisements. Among them are accounts of Sampson, "an African" and "a Shoemaker by trade" who "walks lame in consequence of the loss of his toes by frost"; Albert, who was "lame from a defect in his hip"; and George Guy, who was "lame of one leg, and had on when he left an iron collar around his neck" (Charleston *Courier*). Such information can tell us about the conditions under which enslaved people worked, the punishments inflicted on them, the lengths to which they would go to escape their bondage, and the intersecting histories of slavery and disability. Retrieving the information also conjures up the violence of slavery and forced labor as a matter of course. As Jessica Marie Johnson has argued, the "devastations" of the archive of Atlantic world slavery easily "reproduce themselves in digital architecture" (58).

The problems here are unsettling, and they can seem especially so given that many if not most users of the project are likely uninitiated to the problems when they begin working on FOTM. Some users of FOTM are researchers affiliated with the project, the directors themselves, or other scholars. But the project website currently indicates that more than 11,000 contributors have transcribed advertisements, extracted data from them, or moderated content. The vast majority are high school and college students using it as part of a classroom assignment, members of the general public who have read or heard about the project and want to help, or genealogists who come to the site curious about what they might find and decide to do some transcription or metadata work during their visit. Some among these various kinds of users may understand that their activities on the FOTM site evoke some of what sustained the enslavement of the very people described on their screens. But it seems probable that the numbers who do or who have thought about the issue are relatively few.

Regardless of whether or not users are struck by the implications of their engagement with FOTM, the dilemmas of those implications are, in some ways, insoluble, and we do not attempt the fruitless task of resolving them. Rather, we confront them. We try to use them as an opportunity to encourage users and researchers alike to recognize how power is perpetuated through the historical archive, to see how engaging the archive through FOTM can be a small but not insignificant way to oppose that power, and to be purposeful and careful about how they use the data derived from it. As both Benjamin Schmidt and Crystal Nicole Eddins note in this volume, DH projects allow for a unique opportunity to engage sources and participants in this way.[2] As Schmidt writes, one of the things made possible is having participants "change the assumptions of models" and work "with sources in the indefinitely reconfigurable ways that are now possible." While FOTM, for example, presents itself as a database of fugitives from American slavery, visitors to the splash page of the project see it foregrounded as an endeavor in rediscovering the stories of self-liberating people. They can watch a short promo video that juxtaposes a voice-over reading of a runaway advertisement taken out by Thomas Jefferson with visuals centered particularly on the struggles and the flights of enslaved people from bondage. The FOTM website reminds users that even as the advertisements in the database were "created to control the movements of enslaved people," they "ultimately preserved the details of individual lives" that enslavers could never completely control and that the voices of those who lived them are discoverable when advertisements are read critically and against the grain. And we remind users that working with the project is a responsibility. They drive the research and its outcomes.

Yet the act of transcription can result in users reinscribing the power relations that the documents evidence. Nearly any digital project that asks users to transcribe materials whose very existence reflects the selective and heavily mediated nature of the historical archive deals with this predicament. In the particular case of FOTM, the predicament means reinscribing the power relations and hierarchies of slavery. Users do not annotate each document. Instead, they extract metadata and make each document searchable by a list of terms set by the project directors. Users do not edit racist descriptors that advertisers used to describe the self-emancipated people who enslavers hoped to thwart and recapture. Users do not challenge each enslaver's claim to the power to re-enslave the self-emancipated. FOTM thus simultaneously risks the realities of transcription never resonating with users and also alienating users who either come to consciousness about this duality while participating or who encounter the project and question how participation incriminates them in the discursive violence of the documents and physical violence they record.

Akin to the printers who featured these advertisements in their periodicals, users of the project complete the labor of making an enslaver's or a jailer's desires legible to a wider public. Trained scholars, researchers, and archivists are often aware of this reality: each ad represents an individual who fled enslavement, but the representation captured by each ad is the product of an enslaver's views, desires, and hopes to make each self-emancipated person into a slave. Just because an ad includes a person's height, an age, or a name does not mean that the information is accurate. Nor does an ad's description represent how a self-emancipated person would have described themselves, the name their kin called them, or their true final destination. As Sharon Block and Daina Ramey Berry have shown, in both the eighteenth and nineteenth centuries, whites often estimated or approximated the physical characteristics of African descended people. Social markers like skin color, manner of dress, and even age were mediated categories that shifted by region, time period, and imperial jurisdiction. Using the ads as historical sources requires a sophisticated understanding of what, exactly, they do and do not leave a record of for those interested in consulting them.

But educators, students, genealogists, and laypeople unfamiliar with the extant archival materials of the eighteenth and nineteenth centuries may not be aware that each ad does not contain an objective description of its African American subject. Enslavers did, after all, construct each ad as an authoritative statement of their own power to make slaves of full human beings, to define the character and desires of Black people, and to entice readers to join them in enslaving people who had absconded. In fact, the privileged access enslavers had to the very medium of newspapers, and the right to dictate the information circulating within them, was a mechanism for monitoring and controlling the enslaved. The question for our team as designers of the crowdsourcing platform became how to impart this kind of knowledge and these sorts of understandings and lessons to users from diverse backgrounds with varying levels of experience with the archive of Atlantic slavery. We had to determine how to teach users to read, transcribe, code, and learn from each ad without falling into the trap that enslavers from hundreds of years ago so carefully laid for readers. The issue at hand here is not unlike the broader challenges faced by researchers who want to encourage the work and enthusiasm of "citizen scientists" with widely disparate backgrounds, knowledge, and training. We wanted to do what we could to have "users" of FOTM actually be "participants" or "builders" of FOTM. We wanted them not to be passive absorbers of the material they engaged with or simply processors of information; rather, we wanted them to be "citizen scholars" who would bring a critical eye to bear on their work and who would have a deeper appreciation for its ramifications. When building a dataset through crowdsourcing, those involved in the computational humanities must be attuned to how the process of data creation can end up relaying troublesome elements of the data to users. FOTM presents one possible model for addressing the issue.

Collaboration in Community: Participant Users and the Labor of Archive Building

We built the crowdsourcing platform of FOTM to foreground the collaborative nature of the project, and we ask users solely to transcribe ads as they appear. We chose to carefully embed moments of reflection right into the process of contributing to it. We remind users in each part of the transcription process that they are working with a form that we, the FOTM team, built. Furthermore, we explain that we built the platform to carefully code a set of historical documents that are themselves constructions of enslavers' making. We worked with programmers to construct both the transcription platform and the forms for coding information that users harvest from the ads so that they serve multiple purposes: to capture information, to communicate the fraught nature of each ad as a historical source, and to train users to think like historians.

To meet these goals, the team considered not only what we would ask users to do but how we would ask them to complete each task. Importantly, while these deliberations were driven initially by the FOTM team, they evolved such that the deliberations themselves became a collaboration between the team and project users. As users began engaging with the project, for example, we solicited feedback and listened to questions about the information that appears in advertisements, about why the project aimed to collect certain kinds of data, and about the uses to which such data might be put. We realized that we had failed to explain sufficiently both the problematic nature of the advertisements and the research and other purposes for which the data in them might be significant.

In response, we made a series of adjustments. We developed, for instance, a glossary of terms to guide participants unfamiliar with eighteenth- and nineteenth-century terms, particularly for race and appearance. The glossary allows us to reiterate that terms used in the documents are archaic, racist, and carry historically contingent meanings, and that cataloging them can further efforts to undermine their power even as it risks reifying their meanings. We built a tutorial to guide participants through the transcription process and to signal more clearly, as users learned the form and the process, what working with the ads truly means—namely, they would be handling a weapon that enslavers employed to hunt down and enslave Black people. The tutorial teaches users what the documents are as it teaches them how to transcribe and code them in the archive.

We designed a series of forms that lead users through the process of coding information in each document. We start with transcription as a way to reiterate that users are working with sources and not reading accurate life histories. We then ask for information on the advertiser(s), for details that the advertiser gives about the runaway event, information the ad contains about individual runaways, and finally, information about their enslaver. We begin with the source and then guide users through how each advertiser constructed the source. This signals, at each click to a new form, that the ad is a carefully constructed document and one specific action used by enslavers to enslave.

Careful choices of phrasing foreground the unstable nature of each document. We ask users, "What is the primary name given for this runaway?" rather than simply labeling the response box with the words "full name" or "runaway's name." This question reminds users that they are reading an ad placed by an enslaver or jailer, that the ad's author and not the self-emancipated person supplied the name listed, and leaves open the question of what each runaway may have called themselves. We provide a question mark icon that, when hovered over or clicked, indicates that enslavers sometimes gave enslaved people names that they themselves did not use or prefer. We open the possibility that the ad offers one story, not *the* story of each runaway event. We ask users over and over again, in each form, what the advertisement constructed by enslavers and jailers says and not "what happened."[3]

The form we collaborated on has a pedagogy that also ultimately involves the users in building a database with searchable categories. We do not just invite users to supply data or to transcribe uncritically. We challenge them, through the form we constructed, to consider what each ad can and cannot tell us. We also ask them, both informally and through periodic focus groups, to tell us how we can make the aims of the project clearer and more conscientious about its procedures and aims.

We hope and believe this mutually collaborative process has improved the project itself and made FOTM more responsive to and inclusive of its multiple audiences. We know it has made the directors of the project more acutely aware of the impact of every one of our choices. We understand and try to consider how each of our decisions has implications for FOTM, its meaning, and the arguments it makes and will potentially make. That the interface (Figure 11.3) presents an image of the original advertisement at all times for the user, for example, rather than disappearing once a transcription is made, serves as a subtle but important reminder of the historical tangibility of an enslaved person's experience and of an enslaver's aim to thwart their escape. Along the same lines, the logo we selected for FOTM includes both the male and female printer's icons of fugitives, reveals the text of runaway advertisements through those icons as if they were transparencies, and arranges the title of the project so the words "freedom" and "move" stand out prominently. All were conscious choices that set fugitives themselves at the forefront and highlight their decisions and goals rather than those of their enslavers, while simultaneously alluding to the source material at the heart of the project and gesturing toward how that source material haunted the enslaved at every turn.

Considerations of how we ask users to engage with challenging content in the FOTM database, and what those engagements mean for thinking about the history of slavery and for the subjective experiences of the users themselves, are issues whose relevance is linked mostly to the front end of the project. User feedback and input are important for refining the project infrastructure, but users are not privy to most of the process of actually creating it. Nor are they exposed to plans and

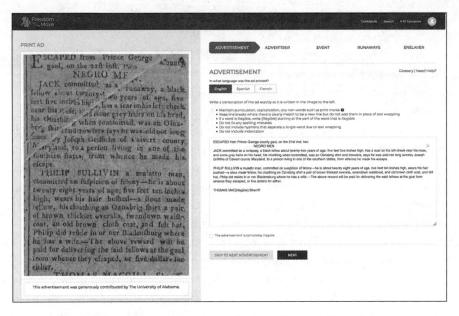

Figure 11.3. Example from the Freedom on the Move website of an entry for an advertisement, including a transcription of the text.

conversations that have been ongoing for years and continue to play out among project personnel about everything from grant proposals to building pathways through the user interface to which fonts to use in the website design. Yet those plans and conversations, those decisions and choices made behind the scenes, are the bedrock on which we ask users to construct a landscape. And fault lines lie in that bedrock because it rests on the expertise of individuals with wide-ranging skills and training and varying senses of the goals and significance of FOTM. Computational humanities projects of almost any significant size and scale will rely on extensive and cross-disciplinary personnel, which in turn demands an understanding of what every member of a team brings to a project and a purposeful consideration of how the various strengths of those members can work in tandem instead of at cross-purposes.

Toward Equitable Access and Collaboration

FOTM grew out of the research questions of historians, and the project was in many ways not especially original or novel in its conception. Historians have been gathering "runaway advertisements" for decades. Some compiled them simply as text that constituted "databases" before the internet existed, and they published them in book form that was then the most effective way to make the advertisements available to an audience mostly of scholars and genealogists. Technological advances led some in ensuing generations of historians to put sets of advertisements from particular eras, states, or regions online and to make them accessible and searchable in a fashion that presages FOTM. Many of those projects still exist and are ongoing, and they serve in some ways as valuable models for what we imagined FOTM could be. If what sets FOTM apart is its effort at comprehensiveness and its invitation for input from all sorts and any number of users, it most certainly draws on precursors with similar if usually more limited goals. It incorporates in some cases the data of those precursors, and it is part of a family of digital humanities projects focused on fugitivity (Windley).[4] FOTM is also part of a movement of projects within the broad heading of slavery and data that are deeply invested in doing more than calculating figures from slavery's archive and in fact demonstrate that the binaries and boundaries between digital humanities and computational humanities dissolve in the face of marginalized historical subjects.

Accomplishing comprehensiveness, allowing broad public access, and encouraging multiple audiences to contribute to the project, however, has also entailed and required participation from people with skill sets historians typically lack. Mostly working together with the Cornell Institute for Social and Economic Research (CISER), we have and continue to rely on the expertise of programmers and data specialists who understand how to translate information from the printed page into digital spaces, construct functional and logical data models and workflows, build an elegant programming interface, and manage and administer a database whose crowdsourced content changes and expands all the time. We draw on staff efforts in offices of sponsored programs at multiple universities to identify and pursue grant opportunities to fund the research and development that make FOTM possible. And we work closely with data services and grant managers who are vital bridges between historians and programmers. Crucial personnel who think about the long term and the big picture, they make sure that everyone involved in the project understands their roles at given points in time, that projected benchmarks are met, that plans for maintenance and sustainability often unnecessary in the traditional humanities but essential to the digital humanities are in place and carried out, and that progress is being made on grant applications and grants-in-effect alike. We consider every person in these capacities to be members of the FOTM "team" no less than the project directors, and we indicate as such on the project website to ensure that labor is equitably credited and acknowledged.

Somewhat remarkably, we have been fortunate that the relationship between the historians directing FOTM and the funders of the project has not been nearly as knotty as it sometimes can be. The grant agencies we have worked with appear to share our goals and understand why FOTM matters. They have asked only that the project carry out the plans detailed in grant proposals in a timely fashion, and to date, they have put almost no restrictions on our ability to reallocate portions of the project's budgets as priorities and needs shift. Still, the varied personnel indispensable to FOTM bring varied ambitions and objectives to bear. Programmers and data specialists come at the project and the advertisements it comprises as an interesting "problem" to be solved and as a set of technological hurdles to clear. Staff in grant offices engage the project in terms of bringing funds to their respective universities, conducting those funds through appropriate channels, and ensuring that the bureaucratic particulars of applications and budgets are carried out effectively. Data services and grant managers, meanwhile, must superintend everything all at once and keep everyone on task. It is no criticism of any of them to observe that their respective responsibilities and talents mean that enslaved people at the heart of the project can fall out of focus. It is understandable that histories of slavery and fugitivity can drift from the center amid the very practical considerations of continuing to pay for FOTM and make it function well for users. Such practical considerations inevitably pull us as historians into such results-oriented calculations, and there is no avoiding those calculations altogether.

Take, for example, the lengthy discussion we had with all the FOTM personnel about how to gather metadata on the "race" of fugitives and how to ask users to help us do it. At the outset, most of the project programmers and other nonhistorians considered the matter an obvious one. Enslavers might describe fugitives in advertisements as, for example, "black," "negro," "mulatto," or "yellow," and collecting data was as simple as having users click a category or fill a text box with whatever description was provided. The historians on the project, however, observed that the physical descriptions of fugitives captured "color" as often as they did "race." They noted that categories appearing in advertisements included terms such as "griffe," "mustee," or "octoroon" that are not only racist but are also sometimes archaic and almost certainly unfamiliar to users. They pointed out that descriptors did not necessarily capture anything objective or correlative to the appearance of fugitives other than what their enslavers saw and that asking users to pull the thread of racial descriptors from advertisements unproblematically was to reify the artificiality of race in any number of ways. In short, programmers saw the question of race mostly as a matter of ensuring that users could capture and indicate every category and descriptor, while historians saw the categories and descriptors themselves as impossibly unsteady and fictive.

Ultimately, we settled on something like a compromise in which users do indicate racial descriptors that appear in the advertisements while also having their attention drawn to the constructed and evolving natures of race and racism. Users have access to a pulldown menu of descriptors and can include new ones in a text box, but above that box they are asked to tell us "what racial category is assigned" to a fugitive in an advertisement rather than "what race is" the person. Hovering over an informational link next to the question, meanwhile, informs users that categories of "color" and "race" were inventions enslavers deployed to keep the enslaved in bondage, and that although many of the categories are offensive, collecting them allows us to "map changes in how racism shifted its terms across space and time."[5]

Ours is not a perfect solution. But it satisfied, at least provisionally, the aims of the programmers and the historians alike, both of whom learned from the discussion a great deal about the mindsets, needs, and concerns of the other. Moreover, this quandary, and others like it, has led all of us to grapple more deeply with the significance and import of FOTM. Eddins notes that one characteristic of marronnage that can be present in DH projects is the "disruption of capital accumulation processes that extract resources from Black spaces."[6] The historians have come to think harder about the compromises required when turning the experiences of enslaved people into data for the sake of better understanding those experiences. The nonhistorians have developed new sensitivities and appreciation for a painful yet liberatory past and the complexities of translating that past into the present. Many of them have said that being asked to think in these new ways invigorates a sense of mission unlike projects they have worked on before, even as most of our programmers have worked with or for universities and university faculty for years. While the capital here is in the form of the power to shape the archive, this social capital typically is not distributed to participants. FOTM is stronger for users at the front end thanks to the dialogue they may never see at the back end. Many projects in the computational humanities could surely benefit from having the kinds of dialogues described here, which both produce greater clarity about a project's stakes and a more effective presentation for users and audiences.[7]

Publics and Partnerships

As we now aim to provide greater access to a greater range of publics through a museum kiosk that can be duplicated in multiple institutions, K–12 lesson plans and resources for educators, and expanded access for laypeople, we continue to grapple with the totality of what we are asking of users. Engaging users as collaborators and partners in the project of archiving this collection of sources means recognizing that they provide more to the project than volunteer labor. Especially as the project becomes a part of how classroom teachers deliver content about the period of Atlantic slavery, we are asking users to take on an interpretive mindset even as they transcribe advertisements. We are asking them to learn to think like historians, particularly about what those advertisements can and cannot tell us about the enslaved people and acts of resistance about which the ads purport to present accurate information.

We view this as an opportunity for a frank reckoning with the many realities of preserving, studying, and teaching America's past and the important dilemmas of which educators, students, and laypeople should be more, not less, aware. The history of slavery, enslavers, and the enslaved is not a history that wraps neatly into enjoyable activities and lessons. The "history is fun" or "people in the past, they're just like us" framing, which accompanies some attempts to engage people in learning about the past, does not fit. Typical "living history" models for other topics are very fraught with multiple histories coming to bear for public historians engaged in interpreting sites of Black history. From the National Museum of African American History and Culture in Washington, D.C., to sites such as the Whitney Plantation in southern Louisiana, there are certainly many examples of public history locations that grapple with slavery and its legacies seriously. Too often, however, we still see mock slave auctions, auction posters as creative projects, and "history roleplay" lessons that are perhaps the best of the worst of trying to "funnify" or "gamify" a history that should be engaged with care. Field trips to the farms and plantations where enslavers treated people of African descent as property should have a decidedly different tone for students than a field trip to an amusement park. Instead of providing the many publics we are trying to reach with the tools to study and learn the history of American slavery by couching the history as "fun," we ask participants to view FOTM as their own but also as everyone's collective effort to amplify enslaved people's resistance and the violent reality of American slavery.

Emphasizing partnership and collectivity is particularly important because it is easy to slip into the language of commerce when speaking about crowdsourced DH projects. Proposals for funding are rife with language like "stakeholders," "sense of ownership," "investment," and "returns." In our own conception of the project, we moved away from asking users to "take ownership," a particularly unsuitable term given that each advertisement in the collection is a part of enslavers' attempts to turn a person into property. Instead, we want users to join us in collaboration, to share the archive they helped to build, and to walk away with a new language for why the project is important. The ads, after all, draw each user's attention to both the active project of enslavement and Black people's pervasive culture of resistance.

Our system is evolving and imperfect. Our translation of historians' understanding of historical categories sometimes falls short. For example, the historians, programmers, and other team members engaged in a lengthy conversation about how FOTM would code for the sex and gender of historical actors. But the result still does not quite capture the nuance of gender and gender expression for which we had hoped. Now, our form asks, "Based on the ad, do you think the enslaver was male or female?" and then the form provides the categories "male," "female," "other," and "not provided." We signal that we are asking the user to read the ad and supply information from the ad, rather than provide accurate information about the biological sex of a particular person. Again, we encourage users to question the way that enslavers read Black people's bodies.

We acknowledge that the ads are not always complete or clear pictures of the individuals they concern and that, in fact, biological sex is not binary. But the way that we have worded our questions and presented users with possibilities still reinscribes binary understandings of sex as either "male" or "female." "Other" and "unknown" are exceptions and implicitly less valid than the first two choices. We do not account for the many gender identities possible for self-emancipated people and instead ground our question in biological sex. While perhaps asking about biological sex is a less anachronistic way to discuss how the historical people in question may or may not have thought of themselves, our question closes rather than opens possibilities for users.

If an advertiser misgenders a self-emancipated person after capturing them and insists that they are male, for example, or if that advertiser uses only male pronouns and insists on a name typically given to men in the period, a user may just go with the advertiser's word. After all, we ask, "Based on the ad . . ." We also close off the diverse gender expression possible for fugitives from slavery that printers might have signaled with their use of printing plates known as stereotypes. Stereotypes came in sets and provided printers with stock images that they could use to draw readers' eyes and to signal what content each section of a periodical contained. More than once in the archive, a newspaper uses a female stereotype absconding with a bindle to accompany an ad that describes a male enslaved person. Was it a printer's mistake? A missing stereotype from a set? Or did this combination signal something else to eighteenth- and nineteenth-century readers? We may not know exactly, but FOTM is currently not asking for this metadata from users. This issue requires revision and careful consideration. Our team is committed to both.

Crowdsourcing an archive of ads that were originally placed by enslavers for the purpose of re-enslaving those who took to their feet and defied enslavement remains a challenge and a messy process. One way that our team has committed to an ethic of care in this work that combines pedagogy, service to various communities, and knowledge production is to start with the assumption that revision to both our plans and our project can and should be ongoing. While we can embed efforts at harm reduction and acknowledgment, we cannot as a team of historians, programmers, and project managers completely avoid implicating ourselves and project users in the violence that our sources evidence. This is part of the work: fully acknowledging the harrowing reality and legacies of American slavery involves, on some level, the acknowledgment that no one can escape its echoes. But as Catherine D'Ignazio and Lauren Klein observe in *Data Feminism*, "counting and measuring do not always have to be tools of oppression. We can also use them to hold power accountable, to reclaim overlooked histories, and to build collectivity and solidarity" (123). While the shadows of the historical subjects who appear in these extant advertisements may have been cast by slavery, those subjects, numbering in the hundreds of thousands, have also left us evidence of their persistent quest to define themselves through resistance and defiance.

Willis Holmes advertised in the New Orleans *Daily Picayune* at least thirty-one times over the course of more than two months in 1844 in his efforts to recapture Nancy. His advertisement remained the same but for the fact that near the end of March, he increased the reward he offered from $10 to $25. He seems to have finally stopped advertising about two weeks later. Whether or not that meant his elevated reward led to the results he wanted or that he abandoned any hope of taking Nancy back into slavery is unknown, and we do not ultimately know Nancy's fate. Like the broader archive of slavery itself, the archive we have created in FOTM leaves as many questions as it provides answers. As we continue to build it, alongside our team of partners and our growing set of users, we hope it shows an ethical and responsible model for other computational humanities projects that deal with difficult materials and that it remains part of larger conversations about them. If we have learned a great deal so far, we know we still have a great deal to learn.

Notes

1. See chapter 7 in this volume.
2. For Schmidt and Eddins, respectively, see chapters 7 and 9 in this volume.
3. To date, we have not gathered data on how often users turn to the glossary, the question marks embedded in the interface, or other explanatory materials as they work on the project. Such data would be potentially illuminating in any number of ways and could help further improve and refine FOTM as a resource. But when users come to the project, they are asked only to provide an email address to create an account, and they provide no other identifying information. This is in part because we know that many users of the project are middle and high school students, and ethical (and sometimes legal) issues might arise were we proactively to collect data about how particular users engage with FOTM.
4. Lathan A. Windley published what are probably the best-known series of printed volumes of runaway advertisements, a four-volume set of eighteenth-century ads entitled *Runaway Slave Advertisements*. Other print volumes include Graham Hodges and Alan Brown's *"Pretends to Be Free,"* and Billy Smith and Richard Wojtowicz's *Blacks Who Stole Themselves*. Windley's collections, supplemented with other digitized materials, appear online at "The Geography of Slavery in Virginia," based at the University of Virginia (http://www2.vcdh.virginia.edu/gos/). Other online advertisement collections include "North Carolina Runaway Slave Advertisements, 1750–1865," based at the University of North Carolina-Greensboro (http://libcdm1.uncg.edu/cdm/landingpage/collection/RAS), and the "Texas Runaway Slave Project" at Stephen F. Austin State University (https://digital.sfasu.edu/digital/collection/RSP). Though not focused on fugitivity per se, other important digital projects focusing on the liberation of the enslaved and its aftermath include "Visualizing Emancipation," based at the University of Richmond (https://dsl.richmond.edu/emancipation/), and "Last Seen: Finding Family after Slavery," at Villanova University (https://informationwanted.org/).
5. FOTM does not currently link to data and materials on the historical construct of race and racial categories outside the project itself, but as the database becomes larger, more extensive ancillary and related materials and data on this and other questions may get added to the project website, freedomonthemove.org.
6. See chapter 7 in this volume.
7. See chapter 7 in this volume.

Bibliography

Bailey, Moya Z. "All the Digital Humanists Are White, All the Nerds Are Men, but Some of Us Are Brave Journal of Digital Humanities." *Journal of Digital Humanities* 1, no. 1 (Winter 2011). http://journalofdigitalhumanities.org/1-1/all-the-digital-humanists-are-white-all-the-nerds-are-men-but-some-of-us-are-brave-by-moya-z-bailey/.

Berry, Daina Ramey. *The Price for Their Pound of Flesh: The Value of the Enslaved, from Womb to Grave, in the Building of a Nation.* Boston: Beacon Press, 2017.

Block, Sharon. *Colonial Complexions: Race and Bodies in Eighteenth-Century America.* Philadelphia: University of Pennsylvania Press, 2018.

Charleston *Courier.* May 20, 1822. Available at *Freedom on the Move,* freedomonthemove.org. Accessed July 27, 2020.

D'Ignazio, Catherine, and Lauren F. Klein. *Data Feminism.* Durham, N.C.: Duke University Press, 2020.

Earhart, Amy E. "'Can Information Be Unfettered? Race and the New Digital Humanities Canon." In *Debates in the Digital Humanities,* edited by Matthew K. Gold, chap. 18. Minneapolis: University of Minnesota Press, 2012. https://dhdebates.gc.cuny.edu/read/untitled-88c11800-9446-469b-a3be-3fdb36bfbd1e/section/cf0af04d-73e3-4738-98d9-74c1ae3534e5.

Earhart, Amy E., and Toniesha L. Taylor. "Pedagogies of Race: Digital Humanities in the Age of Ferguson." *Debates in the Digital Humanities 2016,* edited by Matthew K. Gold and Lauren F. Klein, 251–64. Minneapolis: University of Minnesota Press, 2016. https://doi.org/10.5749/j.ctt1cn6thb.24.

Hodges, Graham R., and Alan E. Brown. *"Pretends to Be Free": Runaway Slave Advertisements from Colonial and Revolutionary New York and New Jersey.* New York: Garland, 1994.

Johnson, Jessica Marie. "Markup Bodies: Black [Life] Studies and Slavery [Death] Studies at the Digital Crossroads." *Social Text* 36, no. 4 (137) (December 2018): 57–79.

Johnson, Walter. *Soul by Soul: Life Inside the Antebellum Slave Market.* Cambridge, Mass.: Harvard University Press, 1999.

Lothian, Alexis, and Amanda Phillips. "Can Digital Humanities Mean Transformative Critique?" *Journal of E-Media Studies* 3, no. 1 (2013). https://doi.org/10.1349/PS1.1938-6060.A.425.

McPherson, Tara. "Why Are the Digital Humanities So White? Or Thinking the Histories of Race and Computation." In *Debates in the Digital Humanities,* edited by Matthew K. Gold, chap. 9. Minneapolis: University of Minnesota Press, 2012. https://dhdebates.gc.cuny.edu/read/untitled-88c11800-9446-469b-a3be-3fdb36bfbd1e/section/20df8acd-9ab9-4f35-8a5d-e91aa5f4a0ea.

New Orleans *Daily Picayune.* June 13, 1845, and September 15, 1846. Available at *Freedom on the Move,* freedomonthemove.org. Accessed July 27, 2020.

Noble, Safiya Umoja. "Toward a Critical Black Digital Humanities." In *Debates in the Digital Humanities 2019,* edited by Matthew K. Gold and Lauren F. Klein,

27–35. Minneapolis: University of Minnesota Press, 2019. https://doi.org/10.5749/j.ctvg251hk.5.

Ridge, Mia. "From Tagging to Theorizing: Deepening Engagement with Cultural Heritage through Crowdsourcing." *Curator: The Museum Journal* 56, no. 4 (2013): 435–50.

Risam, Roopika. "Beyond the Margins: Intersectionality and the Digital Humanities." *Digital Humanities Quarterly* 009, no. 2 (September 2015).

Smith, Billy G., and Richard Wojtowicz. *Blacks Who Stole Themselves: Advertisements for Runaways in the Pennsylvania Gazette, 1728–1790.* Philadelphia: University of Pennsylvania Press, 1989.

Thomas, William. "What We Think We Will Build and What We Build in Digital Humanities." *Journal of Digital Humanities* 1, no. 1 (Winter 2011).

Williams, Daryle. "Digital Approaches to the History of the Atlantic Slave Trade." *Oxford Research Encyclopedia of African History,* November 20, 2018. https://doi.org/10.1093/acrefore/9780190277734.013.121.

Windley, Lathan A. *Runaway Slave Advertisements: A Documentary History from the 1730s to 1790 Virginia.* Westport, Ct.: Greenwood, 1983.

PART II][Chapter 12

Of Coding and Quality
A Tale about Computational Humanities

JULIA DAMEROW, ABRAHAM GIBSON,
AND MANFRED D. LAUBICHLER

Most if not all fields of research rely on computers. Some fields like physics rely so heavily on computers that many curricula include basic computer science classes. Other fields, among them most of the humanities, are only starting to explore the full potential of computing. Even though more and more digital humanities programs offer computer science and programming courses, many practitioners of computational humanities are still self-taught. This raises two questions. First, what are the consequences of this situation regarding the quality of code of computational humanities projects? And second, does the quality of source code matter to the research results? In this chapter, we argue for better quality control of source code produced for research because we are convinced that poor code quality not only negatively affects research outcomes but also slows down the progression of the field as a whole. We advocate for improving the computer science training of humanities researchers as well as working with research software engineers. The latter point reflects the necessity for computational humanities to work in collaborative teams (rather than the traditional single scholar approach). Such teams, however, need the right kind of support and expertise. Research software engineers can facilitate here and also provide the tacit knowledge and continuous support that complements formal education in computer science and coding.

We will start by talking about the differences between coding, programming, and software engineering. We then discuss a concept from software engineering called "leaky abstractions" to demonstrate why some fundamental computer science knowledge is important not just for professional software engineers but also for computational humanists. Next, we turn our attention to programming bugs and code quality and why this is important to computational research. After that, we discuss possible approaches to improve code quality and minimize bugs. As (missing) recognition of programming work in the digital and computational humanities is part of the problem of low code quality, we will turn to this topic before we summarize our main discussion points in the conclusion.

Let's Code!

The question whether humanists should learn how to code has been debated for several decades (Ladurie; Hockey). Blog posts by humanities scholars describing their experiences teaching themselves programming, or web pages with helpful resources for the aspiring digital humanities (DH) programmer are plentiful (McDaniel; Sadler; Weingart; Afanador-Llach et al.). For the computational humanities, the question is more or less settled. If you are a computational humanist, you have to know how to code; you have to know how to "hack" and not just how to "yack" (Nowviskie). But what exactly does this mean? To answer that question, we will first define how we understand the different terms often used to describe the activity of writing code: coding, programming, and software engineering.

Generally, when speaking of coding, it refers to writing code—for example, writing a Python script that sorts and renames files. Often coding is associated with writing scripts or simple programs that have one specific goal (e.g., download a dataset from an API or running a specific analysis on a dataset). Programming goes beyond the simple activity of writing code; it encompasses planning, documentation, and an understanding of the bigger picture of the resulting program. Examples would be the generalization of a piece of code to be used by others or to be published as a package as well as the initial development of a web application. Software engineering, in contrast, has an even more holistic view of the process of creating software. It does not only focus on the implementation of a program but also on its design by taking into account issues such as hardware, user, and infrastructure requirements. For instance, getting a web application to run locally on a laptop requires in many cases "just" programming. Adding test cases, setting up a continuous integration and delivery pipeline, making sure it can be deployed to different servers by externalizing configuration, and preparing it to be translated into other languages would require software engineering. We believe that code quality is an important factor to consider no matter if a scholar is "just" coding or if a software engineer is developing an application to serve several research groups at a time. The methods and strategies might just have to be adjusted to fit a particular use case.

Lauren Klein raises this issue: "the real question, however, isn't whether or not students should learn how to code; it's what they should learn by doing so." Learning to code can be a valuable experience for any digital humanist, even if they do not end up using it for their research. However, if the goal is to use coding for computational research, we believe one should aim to learn how to program. Knowing how to write a for-loop in Python is in most cases not enough to develop programs that can be trusted to produce accurate research results. Miriam Posner remarks that bootcamps are a good form of training in the digital humanities. However, she states that "a two-day long bootcamp, and even a week-long training opportunity, is not the ideal. The ideal is long-term collaboration with people you come to know and trust over the years." While we agree with this statement, Posner might have a different group of people in mind. She suggests that bootcamps should be followed by regular meetings to create a community of like-minded people. While such a community can be very beneficial, it might not include the people who are on the more technical end of the spectrum of computational humanists; the ones that might not even call themselves computational humanists but software engineers who work on computational or digital humanities projects. Such people will likely not attend a bootcamp that teaches humanists how to code or how to develop a web application, but they are the ones who will be able to support scholars in becoming programmers rather than coders or to take the coding work of a scholar and turn it into a reusable and sustainable program.

Here we do not want to further engage in the discussion whether humanities scholars should learn how to code or what specifically they should learn, but we want to briefly introduce an idea from software engineering that adds another dimension to that debate. It is the concept of "leaky abstractions" that was popularized by Joel Spolsky in 2002. To understand what leaky abstractions are, however, we first need to understand what abstractions in programming are. At the core, any program consists of just ones and zeros. You don't have to write these ones and zeros because there are several layers that abstract from it. Before a Java program can be run, there is another program (the compiler) that translates the Java code into another form of code, called Java bytecode (much less human friendly). That code will then be executed by yet another program that turns it into machine code, which is even less understandable by a human. This process continues until the code is made up of ones and zeros that can be executed on computer hardware. Each step in this process represents an abstraction. Java bytecode abstracts from machine code. Java abstracts from bytecode. Abstractions make programming easier. A Java programmer usually does not have to worry about registers or even memory allocation. However, sometimes the lower levels bleed through, and a programmer has to understand the underlying mechanisms to avoid pitfalls or to fix a bug. This is what Spolsky calls a leaky abstraction.[1] A Java programmer, for example, might encounter an "OutOfMemoryError" message. Unless they understand what memory management is and how Java handles it, it is difficult to fix or avoid such a scenario. Other prominent examples involve encoding issues. While most programming languages make it fairly easy to deal with file encodings when processing text files, many programmers do not quite understand what a file encoding actually is. This often leads to copy-pasted solutions from the internet or comments such as "then I had to remove all the question marks that appeared in my text." The details of how characters are represented in a computer by bits and bytes leak through to the programming layer that abstracts from them and can only be correctly handled if fully understood.

The problem with leaky abstractions is that it is often not obvious how they manifest or that they are even there. Additionally, many programming courses and tutorials promise that a language is easy to learn and emphasize how much can be accomplished in a short time frame. While this is often true, those resources forget to mention that there is a lot more under the hood that might affect the outcomes. Similarly, coding "recipes" that provide solutions to common scenarios, including copy and paste solutions for often-encountered issues, are very popular. While it is very helpful to have these resources available, they often result in people copying code without actually understanding what it is doing. This not only introduces unintended side effects but also has a big potential to introduce leaky abstractions. Spolsky so pointedly observes that "even as we have higher and higher level programming tools with better and better abstractions, becoming a proficient programmer is getting harder and harder." In 2019, Jayanti Bhandari Neupane and colleagues found that a Python script that was used for certain chemistry calculations returned different results depending on the operating system that was used. The authors point out that this could invalidate the research findings of multiple papers. Although Python abstracts from the underlying operating system, the fact that different file systems handle file sorting differently leaked through and influenced the calculations of the script (Neupane et al.). Leaky abstractions inevitably affect projects in computational humanities. The question is, what can we do about it?

My Code Has Bugs

Every programmer makes mistakes, which means that basically every program contains bugs (Soergel). If anything, self-taught programmers are likely to make more mistakes than fully trained software engineers because they are, among other things, often less prepared to handle leaky abstractions. Depending on the maturity of the code, the general estimation is that 1,000 lines of code contain from 1 to 50 bugs (Harrison). Now consider that 1,000 lines of code is not that much. Depending on the programming language used, this number is reached relatively quickly with just mildly complex code. The Python script linked in the footnote to index documents downloaded from HathiTrust in Elasticsearch is about 200 lines of code.[2] The Pymarc Python library to work with Marc21 records consists of about 1,500 lines of code.[3] Neither of these examples are very complex, but code grows fast.

In addition to a possibly higher rate of programming bugs compared to industry software, there is the potential issue of a lack of fundamental computer science knowledge among DH programmers. Others have observed "a worrying trend, in that the minimum requirement for scholars working in this field should be that they at least have an understanding of the difference between a markup language like XML, and a more sophisticated programming language such as Python" (O'Sullivan, Jakacki, and Galvin, i145–46). While more research is needed on that topic, personal experiences suggest that there does indeed exist a lack of understanding regarding fundamental computer science concepts, technologies, and skills. Examples include ignorance of the existence of and need for virtual environments in Python, unawareness of programming best practices such as version control and unit testing, and a lack of knowledge about multithreading and parallel processing. By no means does a computer science background guarantee knowledge or experience in these topics, but it is more likely that there exists at least some basic understanding of the form "I know what I don't know" and that there is more foundational knowledge to understand those leaky abstractions.

There is a debate whether the same quality standards that are used in professional software engineering projects should be applied to computational research. Some argue that scientific code does not have to follow software engineering best practices because the users of the code are programmers with in-depth knowledge of the internal workings of the code and hence don't require it to be well documented or maintainable (Bull; Anonymous). We disagree. While it is probably true that a lot of code developed for research is only used within the same lab by a small group of people, this does not mean that they would not benefit from good documentation and coding best practices. Things like spaghetti code (long code blocks with no structure or recognizable organization), bad variable naming, or missing tests count as bad practice in software engineering for good reasons. They make it hard to understand, check, and trust code. At the very least, understanding and modifying badly written code takes a lot longer than understanding and modifying well-documented code that follows best coding practices. Worst case, it makes it a lot more likely that the code contains bugs that are hard if not impossible to find. The argument that scientists write code that is free of any bugs that would affect research outcomes because they check carefully that any change they make does not lead to wrong or inaccurate research results is simply not true (see, for example, a case described by Miller). Furthermore, leaky abstractions are a good example why this view is problematic. The Wikipedia community even makes it a point to emphasize that "a particularly problematic cause of software defects" is "the reliance of the software developer on an abstraction's infallibility" (Wikipedia Contributors). But abstractions are created by developers, who make mistakes, which means abstractions are never flawless. It is hard to believe that researchers would not rely on the trustworthiness of, for example, a programming language or popular library.

In fact, there are many examples of papers that have been retracted because of programming bugs. For example, in 2020, a paper in *Current Biology* (Letzner, Güntürkün, and Beste) was retracted by the authors because of an error in their MATLAB script. If specific results are used to inform policy decisions, things get especially complicated. A piece of code called covid-sim, developed by Professor Neil Ferguson and his team at Imperial College, London, was used to inform the United Kingdom's policy on Covid-19, and it got a lot of public attention after it was released on GitHub.[4] Reviewers criticized its overall quality and its inability to reproduce the same results given the same starting conditions (Boland and Zolfagharifard). There are quite a few different issues that can and should be discussed regarding this situation, and we do not intend to engage in the United Kingdom's Covid-19 lockdown discussion, but it is a prime example of how research in general needs to change in order to deal with the complexity of computational approaches. The computational humanities are no exception. So, let us briefly look at some of the main issues of covid-sim and relate them to the computational humanities.

The first issue to note is that the code was not published until April 2020. Reportedly, the code had been worked on for multiple years and was used in other scenarios before it was uploaded to GitHub (see Boland and Zolfagharifard). Unfortunately, it is a quite common scenario that code is not or only later published in a version control system and made public. A survey conducted by the library of the University of St. Andrews found that out of 124 participants who developed programs only thirty-five (28 percent) used a form of version control (McCann). A survey by Yurdagül Ünal and colleagues came to a similar conclusion, stating that "gaps are evidenced" by, for example, "file naming systems and version control" (Ünal et al.). While neither of these two surveys were targeting digital or computational humanities scholars in particular, it is reasonable to assume a similar situation in this field. If code is not published, research relying on that code cannot be reproduced, improved, or applied to other datasets and projects, which means not only can research results not be validated but every project has to start at zero instead of building on previous programming work, slowing down research as a whole.

Another issue of the covid-sim code is that it contains multiple bugs (Boland and Zolfagharifard). It does not adhere to software engineering standards like modular design to make it easier to read and maintain. More important is the possibility that the code does not produce the same results when run under the same conditions as reported in a GitHub issue (U.K. RAMP "RED TEAM"). While this is, according to the discussion thread of the issue, acceptable in some scenarios, it is also suggested that it could be the result of a bug. The issue here is not that the program might produce different results for different executions, since this is the nature of some algorithms, but that it is not clear if this is the case or if the code is flawed.

While programming bugs in general are to an extent unavoidable even under perfect circumstances, it would be a manageable issue if proper review and publication practices for code existed. However, while the awareness grows for code quality, such practices are still not the standard. Additionally, in the computational humanities, most projects will not get the public attention that, for instance, the covid-sim model received. In many cases, even if the code is published, nobody will ever actually look at it, let alone take the time to review and test it. This also means that code developed for one project is unlikely to be reused for another project as it is too hard or too time-consuming to understand and modify. Instead of building off each other's work, improving it, and eradicating bugs, developers repeat what others have already done, slowing down research.

So, What Can Be Done about It?

Tara McPherson states that "we must have at least a passing familiarity with code languages, operating systems, algorithmic thinking, and systems design. We need database literacies, algorithmic literacies, computational literacies, interface literacies" (McPherson, "Moving beyond Our Boxes").[5] While we absolutely agree with this statement, a "passing familiarity" might in many cases not be enough to achieve high-quality code. If a scholar develops some code to analyze an image or text dataset in C or C++, then they need to understand how memory allocation and management works. Similarly, if a researcher (or research team) creates a web application to allow users to run certain analyses on the web, there needs to be an awareness of the complications of multithreading environments. Depending on the goals of a project, there will be a point when a humanist scholar with some (potentially formal) computer science training simply won't be enough. While some people are able to master both fields—for instance, a humanities discipline and software engineering—most of us will tend to be an expert in one but not both. As we look toward ways that we can develop, integrate, and support the programming expertise that we are calling for in DH, we offer several models and ideas.

One potential model DH can draw on is the concept of the "research software engineer" (RSE). In the past couple of years, the term RSE has become increasingly popular to describe those who apply their software engineering and other related skills to research problems in a number of disciplines (Vanessasaurus). In 2014, the Research Software Engineer Association was created to provide a "community and raise awareness of the UK's Research Software Engineers" (UKRSE Association, "Welcome"). The association has now been succeeded by the Society of Research Software Engineering.[6] Similar efforts are underway in several other countries, among them the United States, Germany, and the Netherlands.[7] The Research Software Engineers Association described RSEs as "people in a variety of roles who understand and care about both good software and good research" (UKRSE Association, "What Is an RSE?"). By now, many institutions employ RSEs that can help scholars with their coding. There are even a few RSE units specializing in DH, such as King's Digital Lab at King's College, the Center for Digital Humanities at Princeton University, and the Digital Innovation Group at Arizona State University.[8]

In the digital humanities, however, a more common model than RSE units is the one in which a single person embedded in a DH project, lab, or department does all the programming work or in which a humanities scholar works with developers from a library. Often these people do not have a formal computer science background but are self-taught and might have a higher degree in a humanities discipline (see the survey results in DHTech). Additionally, they would often not describe themselves as RSEs, although they are doing at least some work typical for an RSE role. This hesitancy toward adopting the term "research software engineer" might partially stem from not having formal training in software engineering and not doing (and not wanting to do) software engineering 100 percent of the time. Another reason could be that titles can convey different meanings and areas of expertise depending on their contexts (the term "lecturer" has very different connotations in U.S. and U.K. systems, for example). Choosing a position as a research software engineer might raise concerns about future competitiveness when applying for more traditional academic jobs.

Scholarship best advances within professional groups. To meet the challenges related to computing in the humanities, professional communities geared toward people doing RSE work in the digital humanities can provide an important platform for networking and exchange.[9] Certain types of software bugs, such as the ones originating from leaky abstractions, can best be avoided through continuous learning and support from other like-minded people. A community can provide and advertise training and career development opportunities and connect its members to benefit from each other's expertise. This does not only mean that more skilled developers offer advice or training for less experienced ones but also that developers with, for example, formal computer science background and no humanities training can learn the intricacies and pitfalls they might encounter in a digital humanities project. For instance, issues like incorporating uncertainty in date representation or text extraction of 200-year-old manuscripts are not typically part of a computer science curriculum. In the interest of brevity, we will hereafter use the term "RSE" to encompass all people doing RSE work that identify with the description of the RSE role even if not with the term itself.

Quinn Dombrowski and colleagues ("Voices from the Server Room," in this volume) describe their experiences about providing high-performance computing (HPC) support to humanists. They describe challenges when working with users in regard to missing background knowledge. This is another area in which RSEs or people with an RSE-like skill set could be helpful for any computational humanities scholar who does not (yet) possess the skills to work with HPC resources. RSEs could provide support to aid in the communication between HPC support staff and humanities scholars or to support execution of locally developed code on HPC resources.

However, simply adding an RSE to a research group is not the solution to all problems. There might be multiple desired outputs of a research project, such as a script to analyze a specific dataset and a web application to visualize and analyze results. Often all these tasks are simply lumped together as programming work. However, very different skill sets are needed for the different types of work. Many scholars doing computational work may have learned a programming language such as Python or R at some point to be able to automate calculations they know how to do on paper. This often works well, and all that might be needed is some guidance on, for example, proper version control. Good coding practices become important, however, when a scholar aims to allow others to use their code by developing libraries. A 200-line spaghetti code script is not easy to read or maintain, but it is usually doable by the author of the script. If that is turned into a library, however, meant to be used by others and possibly extended, that is a different story. Adding code to messy code keeps increasing its complexity and messiness and eventually makes it almost impossible to understand. It is at that point that we believe that scholars competent in programming but whose passion and interest do not lie with software development should start considering adding RSEs to a project. They can ensure that coding best practices are considered in the development process and make informed decisions about what infrastructure to best use for distribution and what quality assurance measures can be taken. Software development projects that go beyond scripts and libraries, such as projects that plan to develop web or desktop applications, should especially consider adding RSEs because this is what many software engineering programs focus on and it requires a very different skill set than writing short analysis scripts. While it is, of course, possible to acquire expertise and experiences in several different areas and for a scholar to also be a skilled software developer, most people do not start out with these skills. The practical experiences of a software developer have a big influence on the quality of their software. The more experienced a software developer is, the more knowledgeable they usually are with coding best practices, making them better equipped to deal with leaky abstractions. But experiences have to be acquired, which can be a long process full of mistakes and bugs.

Which brings us to our next point. Providing humanists with formal computer science training and adding RSEs to projects to increase code quality is just one piece of the puzzle. There will always be bugs in code, no matter how skilled and knowledgeable the programmer. Finding and eradicating those bugs is aided by measures an individual programmer can take such as writing tests. There are also procedures that can be put in place by teams of developers and the community at large. In particular, we are referring to code reviews (see, for example, Sadowski et al.). During a code review, a programmer other than the author inspects a piece of code with the goal of finding defects and suggesting improvements. Code reviews are generally valued as a measure to improve code quality (Sadowski et al.); however, a 2018 RSE survey suggests that many projects have only one developer (Philippe et al.), which can make team-internal code reviews difficult if not impossible. As Rebecca Sutton Koeser so pointedly observes: "no one will ever read my code.... In fact, in practical terms, the better I do my job, the less likely it is that someone will read my code, since the most likely reason for someone to trawl through code is because they have to do so in order to find and fix a bug" (Koeser, "[Re]viewing the Code," 386).[10] And even this is only likely to happen if someone reuses or extends someone else's code.

A solution to this problem could be to establish a community code review and publication process that allows developers to submit their code to be reviewed by other programmers. There are journals that publish articles about software, but the code review part is limited, for good reasons.[11] If done right, a community code review process could not just improve code quality overall but also give scholars more confidence when reusing the programs of other projects. An example of such an effort is the Network for Computational Modeling in the Social and Ecological Sciences (CoMSES Net), which aims to improve computational modeling in the social and ecological sciences (CoMSES; Rollins et al.). The digital and computational humanities community would greatly benefit from such a system, and there are in fact plans for a CoMSES sister project that focuses on digital humanities code as well as a newly created working group that was started at the Association for Computers and the Humanities (ACH) conference in 2021.[12]

However, implementing a generally accepted code review process faces multiple obstacles. Most importantly, cleaning up code enough to submit it, finding reviewers to review it, and then improving code according to reviewer comments is a time-consuming task. While probably most researchers can see the benefits of it, actually engaging in that process could be hampered by time and money constraints. Funding agencies and publishers are in the position to support and facilitate this process. They could put requirements in place for projects to publish their code in a way that ensures at least a minimum of code quality. Funding agencies could require implementation details, infrastructure, and personnel considerations that take into account required skills and technologies for projects that plan a computational component. It is also not unreasonable to require that an RSE or someone with similar experiences be on any grant that plans to develop software.

That is only part of the problem, though. As mentioned previously, many people doing RSE-related work in the computational humanities do not have a formal computer science education; in fact, many are self-taught. They might hesitate to submit code for review worrying that it is not good enough and that they might be shamed for it. A prominent example of how difficult it can be to ask coding-related questions and expose one's own work is Stack Overflow.[13] As of this writing, this question-and-answer site for programmers has 12 million users with 8,700 questions asked per day (Stack Exchange). While the Stack Overflow site is widely used by programmers, it has often been criticized for its unwelcomeness; coding beginners especially are afraid of judgmental and unfriendly comments on the site (Chipps). Similar observations can be made for the covid-sim project. There are several issues and discussions that lack productive criticism and are simply not helpful to the authors (see, for example, MrHash; pdehaye). Jeff Leek ("Simply Statistics") describes an experience in which someone reviewing their code commented in a way that was "clearly designed for the sole purpose of embarrassing us (the authors) and discrediting our work." It is therefore crucial that any code review process for computational humanities provides a safe space that allows for productive feedback, with the goal to improve code quality and coding skills, and it is not meant to be used as a tool to discredit another researcher's work. Leek calls for a process that encourages researchers to share their code for review, recognizes that code inevitably contains mistakes, and suggests strategies to achieve positive outcomes for the author and the community when bugs are discovered.

This is especially important in the context of the discussion around computational humanities and gender bias (Latex Ninja, "The Computational Humanities and Toxic Masculinity?"). At the time of this writing, the original list that collected names of people interested in a computational humanities community included 24 percent women and 74 percent men.[14] The Computational Humanities Research forum that was based on that list has 450 members (at the time of this writing), of which 36 percent identify as women and 55 percent as men.[15] DHTech, a community of "technical people" in DH, has 19 percent female members and 80 percent male members.[16] These numbers show that the computational humanities have a similar gender imbalance as computer science, which makes it likely that the situation for other minorities is not much different, either. A badly designed code review process could have the potential to make these numbers even worse if, for example, the process would be perceived as intimidating and requiring too much expertise of the reviewee. Guidelines on how to provide feedback must therefore be carefully crafted. A code review platform has to encourage and accept anyone writing code for a humanities project to submit to it, no matter how confident the author is. The community has to embrace the diverse backgrounds of its members. Only then can the overall quality of code in the computational (and digital) humanities increase.

It might also be useful to add other initiatives that go beyond just reviewing code to encourage more people interested in computational humanities. The idea of mentorship programs has entered discussions in the research software engineering community. Such programs could provide more hands-on support for coding beginners, and they could also specifically target certain minorities to make them feel more welcome in the community. Roopika Risam's chapter in this volume, "Double and Triple Binds," is a great presentation of the different factors that might keep researchers from learning to code and engage with computational humanities. Her experiences with having a team of people offering support when learning to program is especially relevant here. We need a community to provide this kind of support to any researcher who wants to learn how to code and program.

Whose Work Needs to Be Recognized?

Besides improving code quality, a generally accepted code review process would also have another benefit, which concerns the recognition of coding work. Depending on the project, there are various degrees of programming work involved in the implementation of a project. Oftentimes, however, this work is not being fully credited. In some cases, the computational part of a project might consist of the development of a script to clean and analyze a dataset. Usually, one of the authors is the author of that script and receives credit for their work through the publication of articles. While this does not address the issue of code quality, the author of the programming work is given credit for career advancement. In many cases, however, there are multiple applications or people involved in collecting, cleaning, and managing data, and often the work that is being done is only mentioned as a side note rather than being cited (e.g., in case of software applications or datasets; see Smith, Katz, and Niemeyer; Mooney and Newton) or being attributed academic recognition. Writing a script for data collection and cleaning is in many cases not recognized as an academic endeavor and therefore does not count toward career progression (Sula, Hackney, and Cunningham; D'Ignazio and Klein).

There are multiple issues associated with this situation. First of all, if cleaning up and publishing code does not provide any advantage for the author of the code in terms of career advancement, it is usually not very high on the list of things to do. In better cases, code is at least pushed to a repository. In worst cases, code is kept on the programmer's hard drive to be lost potentially forever.[17] If the goal is to develop a program, get results, and then publish these results, it might not matter to the author that much if the code follows standard best practices, is well tested, documented, readable, and maintainable. A clean, well-documented, and versioned code base optimizes flexibility (especially regarding the cyclical nature of computational research with lots of pivoting and refocusing), but it is difficult for early career scholars to justify spending time on improving something that will not count toward a tenure-track evaluation. Although this is slowly changing, it still presents an issue for many young scholars.[18] But even in cases in which code counts for a scholar's career progression, the question then becomes what does count. It might be easier to decide this question in cases of a web application that gets traffic that can be measured, but what about a Python library for analyzing citations? Does it count how often it has been forked on GitHub? How many projects use it? Or how well has the programmer documented it? Again, a code review and publishing platform might be a solution to at least some of these questions. This is where professional organizations such as the Open Modeling Foundation enter the picture. These are large enough organizations establishing broad standards that can be understood by tenure and promotion and other advancement committees. Similar to a traditional article, publication would allow scholars to show that they produced quality work.

However, this practice might not be appropriate in all cases. While code reviews are realistic for shorter scripts and possibly smaller libraries, it becomes less manageable for bigger web applications, desktop applications, or comprehensive libraries. Nonetheless, there should be a discussion about how such projects can leverage community support through, for example, partial or ongoing code reviews or third-party testing strategies to ensure the quality of the developed software. A code review process also does not account for reuse and application of a program. This problem exists across disciplines, and there is an active working group (see Katz and Chue Hong) that has produced principles and guidelines for citing software and giving credit (see, for example, Katz, Chue Hong, and Fenner; Smith, Katz, and Niemeyer).

Computational humanities, possibly to an even greater extent than digital humanities, requires a shift from the traditional one-person research project that is common in the humanities toward a more team-oriented approach that is typical of science. Even small projects can require several different skill sets and might only be realizable through collaboration. RSE units that exist in some universities can be well-suited collaborators for some projects (see, for example, University of Sheffield, "Research Software Engineering"). They can provide guidance in project planning and development support for projects and can be a way to ensure long-term maintenance of projects. Often these groups also provide training for scholars to, for instance, facilitate good coding practices and make sure researchers who do computational work possess basic computer science knowledge. This, however, is not necessarily a good fit for every project or not even a possibility in places where such a group simply does not exist. In such cases especially, we need more community support and infrastructure to ensure research results that can be trusted. A community code review process could be one important cornerstone of such infrastructure. Furthermore, providing opportunities for RSE-focused roles embedded in computational humanities projects (as opposed to service units) and a clearer career path for such roles could contribute to the development of the necessary expertise to successfully move the field of computational humanities forward.

While in this chapter we focused on programming work, there are many more areas of expertise that may be needed, such as that of a statistician, data analyst, or designer. Hence, for the computational (as well as the digital) humanities, we need to engage in conversations about new career paths and recognition, about training and publication, about community and collaboration. Only if we have these conversations can we achieve the code quality needed to establish trust in the results of our research. To paraphrase Douglas Adams, by doing so, we may not be going where we intended to go, but we believe we will end up where we need to be.

Notes

This chapter was written during the 2020 Covid-19 pandemic with two of the authors having small children and no day care. Some of these sentences were literally written with a two-year-old clinging on the writer's back. Funding by NSF SBE 1656284 RCN: Mapping Authorities and Ontologies in Computational and Digital HPS and from the Smart Family Foundation is gratefully acknowledged.

1. Spolsky was not the first to put this concept into words, but he popularized the term by defining the law of leaky abstractions that says that "all non-trivial abstractions, to some degree, are leaky."
2. https://github.com/diging/utilities/blob/master/ht-elastic/ht_index.py.
3. https://github.com/JaimieMurdock/pymarc.
4. https://github.com/mrc-ide/covid-sim.

5. From the section "Moving Beyond Our Boxes" in McPherson, "Why Are the Digital Humanities So White?," 152.

6. https://society-rse.org/.

7. For the association in the United States, see https://us-rse.org/. The German association for people behind research software is at https://de-rse.org/. The Netherlands group is at https://nl-rse.org/.

8. For the website of King's Digital Lab at King's College, see https://kdl.kcl.ac.uk/. The Center for Digital Humanities at Princeton University website can be found at https://cdh.princeton.edu/ and the website of the Digital Innovation Group at Arizona State University is https://diging.asu.edu/.

9. See DHTech, a special interest group of the Alliance of Digital Humanities Organizations (ADHO), https://dh-tech.github.io/; see also Research Software Engineering in den Digital Humanities, https://dh-rse.github.io/.

10. From the section "Reviewing the Code" in Koeser, "Trusting Others to 'Do the Math.'"

11. See the *Journal of Open Research Software* (https://openresearchsoftware.metajnl.com/), and the *Journal of Open Source Software* (https://joss.theoj.org/).

12. See the DHTech Community Code Review Working Group (https://dhcodereview.github.io/). The CoMSES community has, in the meantime, established the Open Modeling Foundation to provide a broader platform for computing and modeling across a number of disciplines (see https://openmodelingfoundation.github.io).

13. https://stackoverflow.com/.

14. The percentages are from https://github.com/cohure/CoHuRe/issues/1. In this case, gendered names and pictures were used to decide gender. Some users could not be identified by using just these two criteria, hence the percentages do not add up to 100 percent.

15. See Computational Humanities Research at https://discourse.computational-humanities-research.org/. Again, the percentages do not add up to 100 because the same counting method as before (gendered names and pictures) was used.

16. https://dh-tech.github.io/.

17. We acknowledge that this practice has become less common with GitHub being increasingly accepted by the DH community, but we believe it is still a not negligible issue. Data collected by Lisa Spiro and Sean Morey Smith ("Evaluating GitHub") also still show that there is a gap between working on a DH project and having a GitHub account.

18. See, for example, CDRH, "Promotion and Tenure Criteria."

Bibliography

Afanador-Llach, Maria José, James Baker, Adam Crymble, Victor Gayol, Martin Grandjean, Jennifer Isasi, et al. "2019 Programming Historian Deposit Release." *Programming Historian*. 2019. November 1, 2019. https://doi.org/10.5281/zenodo.3525082.

Anonymous. "Discussion of 'Why We Can Ignore Reviews of Scientific Code by Commercial Software Developers.'" *Hacker News*, May 18, 2020. https://news.ycombinator.com/item?id=23221697.

Boland, Hannah, and Ellie Zolfagharifard. "Coding That Led to Lockdown Was 'Totally Unreliable' and a 'Buggy Mess,' Say Experts." *The Telegraph,* May 16, 2020. https://www.telegraph.co.uk/technology/2020/05/16/coding-led-lockdown-totally-unreliable-buggy-mess-say-experts/.

Bull, Phil. "Why You Can Ignore Reviews of Scientific Code by Commercial Software Developers." *Lumps "n" Bumps,* May 10, 2020. https://philbull.wordpress.com/2020/05/10/why-you-can-ignore-reviews-of-scientific-code-by-commercial-software-developers/.

CDRH. "Promotion and Tenure Criteria for Assessing Digital Research in the Humanities Evaluating Digital Scholarship." Center for Digital Research in the Humanities University, University of Nebraska–Lincoln. Accessed June 8, 2020. https://cdrh.unl.edu/articles/promotion.

Chipps, Sara. "What a Very Bad Day at Work Taught Me about Building Stack Overflow's Community." *Stack Overflow Blog,* July 18, 2019. https://stackoverflow.blog/2019/07/18/building-community-inclusivity-stack-overflow/.

CoMSES. "A Growing Collection of Resources for Computational Model-Based Science." CoMSES Network. Accessed May 21, 2020. https://www.comses.net/.

DHTech. "DH RSE Survey Results." DHTech. Accessed August 9, 2021. https://dh-tech.github.io/survey-results-2020.

D'Ignazio, Catherine, and Lauren F. Klein. "Show Your Work." In *Data Feminism,* 173–201. Cambridge, Mass.: MIT Press, 2020.

Harrison, W. "The Dangers of End-User Programming." *IEEE Software* 21, no. 4 (2004): 5–7.

Hockey, Susan. "Workshop on Teaching Computers and the Humanities Courses." *Literary and Linguistic Computing* 1 (1986): 228–29.

Katz, Daniel S., and Neil P. Chue Hong. "Software Citation in Theory and Practice." In *Mathematical Software—ICMS 2018.* Lecture Notes in Computer Science, edited by James H. Davenport, Manuel Kauers, George Labahn, and Joseph Urban, 289–96. Cham: Springer, 2018.

Katz, Daniel S., Neil Chue Hong, and Martin Fenner. "FORCE11 Software Citation Implementation Working Group." *GitHub Force11/Force11-Sciwg.* Accessed May 27, 2020. https://github.com/force11/force11-sciwg.

Klein, Lauren F. "Code." In *Digital Pedagogy in the Humanities,* edited by Rebecca Frost Davis. Accessed May 27, 2020. https://digitalpedagogy.hcommons.org/keyword/Code.

Koeser, Rebecca Sutton. "Trusting Others to 'Do the Math.'" *Interdisciplinary Science Reviews* 40, no. 4 (2015): 376–92. https://doi.org/10.1080/03080188.2016.1165454.

Ladurie, Emmanuel Le Roy. "La fin des érudits." *Nouvel Observateur,* May 8, 1968.

Latex Ninja. "The Computational Humanities and Toxic Masculinity? A (Long) Reflection." *Latex Ninja* (blog). April 19, 2020. https://latex-ninja.com/2020/04/19/the-computational-humanities-and-toxic-masculinity-a-long-reflection/.

Latex Ninja. "News on the DH and Gender Equality." *Latex Ninja* (blog). May 24, 2020. https://latex-ninja.com/2020/05/24/news-on-the-dh-and-gender-equality/.

Leek, Jeff. "Simply Statistics: How Could Code Review Discourage Code Disclosure? Reviewers with Motivation." *Simply Statistics,* September 26, 2013. https://simplystatistics.org/posts/2013-09-26-how-could-code-review-discourage-code-disclosure-reviewers-with-motivation/.

Letzner, Sara, Onur Güntürkün, and Christian Beste. "Retraction Notice to: How Birds Outperform Humans in Multi-Component Behavior." *Current Biology* 30 (2020): 754.

McCann, Patrick. "Research Software Engineering Inside and Outside the Library." Presentation at RLUK Conference 2017. Accessed May 19, 2020. https://research-repository.st-andrews.ac.uk/bitstream/handle/10023/10488/rse_in_out_lib.pdf?sequence=1&isAllowed=y.

McDaniel, Caleb. "Interview with Jason Heppler." *Digital History @ Rice,* March 27, 2013. http://digitalhistory.blogs.rice.edu/2013/03/27/interview-with-jason-heppler/.

McPherson, Tara. "Why Are the Digital Humanities So White? Or Thinking the Histories of Race and Computation." In *Debates in the Digital Humanities,* edited by Matthew K. Gold, 139–60. Minneapolis: University of Minnesota Press, 2012.

Miller, Greg. "A Scientist's Nightmare: Software Problem Leads to Five Retractions." *Science* 314, no. 5807 (2006): 1856–57.

Mooney, Hailey, and Mark P. Newton. "The Anatomy of a Data Citation: Discovery, Reuse, and Credit." *Journal of Librarianship and Scholarly Communication* 1, no. 1 (2012). https://doi.org/http://dx.doi.org/10.7710/2162-3309.1035.

MrHash. "Archive This Project and Start Again." GitHub Issues for Covid-Sim. May 7, 2020. https://github.com/mrc-ide/covid-sim/issues/174.

Mullen, Lincoln A. *Computational Historical Thinking: With Applications in R.* 2018. Accessed June 19, 2020. http://dh-r.lincolnmullen.com/.

Neupane, Jayanti Bhandari, Ram P. Neupane, Yuheng Luo, Wesley Y. Yoshida, Rui Sun, and Philip G. Williams. "Characterization of Leptazolines A–D, Polar Oxazolines from the Cyanobacterium Leptolyngbya Sp., Reveals a Glitch with the 'Willoughby–Hoye' Scripts for Calculating NMR Chemical Shifts." *Organic Letters* 21 (2019): 8449–53. https://doi.org/10.1021/acs.orglett.9b03216.

Nowviskie, Bethany. "On the Origin of 'Hack' and 'Yack.'" In *Debates in the Digital Humanities 2016,* edited by Matthew K. Gold and Lauren F. Klein. Minneapolis: University of Minnesota Press, 2016. https://dhdebates.gc.cuny.edu/read/untitled/section/a5a2c3f4-65ca-4257-a8bb-6618d635c49f#ch07.

O'Sullivan, James, Diane Jakacki, and Mary Galvin. "Programming in the Digital Humanities." *Digital Scholarship in the Humanities* 30, supp. 1 (2015): i142–47. https://doi.org/10.1093/llc/fqv042.

pdehaye. "Work with the *Actual* Professionals at Opening Up Code." GitHub Issues for Covid-Sim. May 11, 2020. https://github.com/mrc-ide/covid-sim/issues/209.

Philippe, Olivier, Martin Hammitzsch, Stephan Janosch, Anelda van der Walt, Ben van Werkhoven, Simon Hettrick, Daniel S. Katz, et al. "softwaresaved/international-survey: Public Release for 2018 Results (Version 2018-v.1.0.2)." *Zenodo.* Accessed June 8, 2020. http://doi.org/10.5281/zenodo.2585783.

Posner, Miriam. "Here and There: Creating DH Community." In *Debates in the Digital Humanities 2016*, edited by Matthew K. Gold and Lauren F. Klein. Minneapolis: University of Minnesota Press, 2016. https://dhdebates.gc.cuny.edu/read/untitled/section/c6b8f952-acfd-48b6-82bb-71580c54cad2.

Rollins, Nathan D., C. Michael Barton, Sean Bergin, Marco A. Janssen, and Allen Lee. "A Computational Model Library for Publishing Model Documentation and Code." *Environmental Modelling and Software* 61 (2014): 59–64. https://doi.org/10.1016/j.envsoft.2014.06.022.

Sadler, Jesse. "New Kinds of Projects: DH 2.0 and Coding." *Jesse Sadler—A Blog about Early Modern History and Digital Humanities*, August 16, 2017. https://www.jessesadler.com/post/new-kinds-of-projects/.

Sadowski, Caitlin, Emma Söderberg, Luke Church, Michal Sipko, and Alberto Bacchelli. "Modern Code Review: A Case Study at Google." In *ICSE-SEIP '18: Proceedings of the 40th International Conference on Software Engineering: Software Engineering in Practice*, 181–90. New York: Association for Computing Machinery, 2018. https://doi.org/10.1145/3183519.3183525.

Smith, Afron M., Daniel S. Katz, and Kyle E. Niemeyer. "Software Citation Principles." *PeerJ Computer Science* 2:e86 (2016): 1–31. https://doi.org/10.7717/peerj-cs.86.

Soergel, David A. W. "Rampant Software Errors May Undermine Scientific Results." *F1000Research* 3, no. 303 (2015). https://doi.org/10.12688/f1000research.5930.1

Spiro, Lisa, and Sean Morey Smith. "Evaluating GitHub as a Platform of Knowledge for the Humanities." Presentation at Digital Humanities 2016. Accessed June 8, 2020. https://digitalscholarship.files.wordpress.com/2016/07/spirosmithdh2016githubpresentationfinal.pdf.

Spolsky, Joel. "The Law of Leaky Abstractions." *Joel on Software*, November 11, 2002. https://www.joelonsoftware.com/2002/11/11/the-law-of-leaky-abstractions/.

Stack Exchange. "Stack Exchange." Accessed May 26, 2020. https://stackexchange.com/sites?view=list#users.

Sula, Chris A., S. E. Hackney, and Phillip Cunningham. "A Survey of Digital Humanities Programs." *Journal of Interactive Technology and Pedagogy* 11 (2017). https://jitp.commons.gc.cuny.edu/a-survey-of-digital-humanities-programs/.

UK RAMP "RED TEAM" at Edinburgh University. "Apparent Unexpected Difference in Results When Re-Using a Binary Network File." GitHub Issues for Covid-Sim. April 21, 2020. https://github.com/mrc-ide/covid-sim/issues/116.

UKRSE Association. "Welcome to the UK Research Software Engineer Association." Accessed May 25, 2020. https://rse.ac.uk/.

UKRSE Association. "What Is an RSE?" Research Software Engineer Association. Accessed May 25, 2020. https://rse.ac.uk/what-is-an-rse/.

Ünal, Yurdagül, Gobinda Chowdhury, Serap Kurbanoğlu, Joumana Boustany, and Geoff Walton. "Research Data Management and Data Sharing Behaviour of University Researchers." *Proceedings of ISIC: The Information Behaviour Conference* 24, no. 1 (2019). http://informationr.net/ir/24-1/isic2018/isic1818.html.

University of Sheffield. "Research Software Engineering Sheffield." Accessed May 27, 2020. https://rse.shef.ac.uk/.

Vanessasaurus. "The Story of the Research Software Engineer." *Vanessasaurus Fun*, July 9, 2019. https://vsoch.github.io//2019/the-research-software-engineer/.

Van Zundert, Joris J., and Ronald Haentjens Dekker. "Code, Scholarship, and Criticism: When Is Code Scholarship and When Is It Not?" *Digital Scholarship in the Humanities* 32, supp. 1 (2017): i121–33. https://doi.org/10.1093/llc/fqx006.

Weingart, S. "Teaching Yourself to Code in DH." *The Scottbot Irregular*. Accessed January 3, 2020. https://scottbot.net/teaching-yourself-to-code-in-dh/.

Wikipedia Contributors. "Leaky Abstraction." *Wikipedia*. Last modified September 29, 2023. https://en.wikipedia.org/wiki/Leaky_abstraction.

PART II][Chapter 13

The Future of Digital Humanities Research
Alone You May Go Faster, but Together You'll Get Further

MARIEKE VAN ERP, BARBARA MCGILLIVRAY,
AND TOBIAS BLANKE

Breakthroughs in artificial intelligence and the collection of large cultural datasets have led to renewed excitement about computational literary studies, digital history, and other advanced computational analysis in the humanities. Applied work with artificial intelligence and machine learning has mainly become relevant in the context of a new discipline called "data science" that is broadly concerned with extracting meaning from digital data. Because digital humanities shares this interest, we are beginning to see more and more joint work between the two areas. The emergence of data science has fundamentally changed the relationship between computer science and humanities. This chapter provides insights on this model of collaboration based on our experiences in European projects around machine learning and data engineering that we have conducted over the past fifteen years. These projects have strengthened our conviction that the best approach to take on digital humanities research is to collaborate across disciplines. Through transnational frameworks of the European Union and also national funding collaborations, these projects should not be read as the initiative of one (usually Western) European country; rather, they incorporate different perspectives from Eastern or Southern Europe. They are generally multilingual in nature and focused on different (cultural) histories. While we cannot cover all relevant projects and perspectives, we aim to present a diverse set of examples that generalize to other initiatives.

The new breakthroughs in scientific data analysis, which we label as machine learning, data science, and large-scale language models, also came with a broadening of the availability of advanced computational analysis tools that can now be easily used by new groups of users that do not necessarily have PhDs in statistical modeling. New toolkits, often built around open-source languages such as R and Python, have allowed users to focus on their data work rather than having to implement machine learning algorithms from scratch. Python's *sklearn* or R's *caret* do not just embed computational analysis into well-defined processing pipelines; they also provide a range of advanced data processing tools. They have largely contributed to the wider adoption of digital methodologies as a whole—also in the humanities. This has radically shifted the relationship between computer science and humanities and allowed for a new dialogue to emerge with much more computational input from the humanities. Ted Underwood has summarized that digital humanities is unified "by reflection on digital technology." In his 2012 contribution to *Debates in Digital Humanities,* Dave Parry wrote: "Digital humanities did not invent collaborative scholarship, but it does make such work more acceptable and transparent." So, what has changed?

Not too long ago, the collaboration between humanities and computer science in projects often entailed a division of work where computer science had to create the "services" that humanities defined in requirement studies. Not only has this reduced the computer science work to software engineering work, but the humanities, too, were often not an integral part of the digital production process. Project applications generally contained standard lines that the humanities lagged behind other disciplines in their computational knowledge and therefore appreciated the role of consumers of technologies. Advances in computational modeling have meant that the traditional division of labor with requirements from humanities and engineering from computing science is still there, but we also see new projects with a more direct interaction. These are often smaller projects that work directly with a given dataset.

Humanities and computer science have both changed very fast, have become more complex along the way, and have driven new critical research. This chapter begins with the history and current account of the sometimes difficult collaboration of computer science and (digital) humanities and then offers insights into our current work bringing the two together. We demonstrate in particular how humanities can contribute to advanced computational research based on new collaborations in data science and data publication.

Doing a Better Job: Balancing the Computational and the Humanities

Computer science and humanities have found further connections due to the growing prominence of data science as well as machine learning techniques becoming more easily available. Nevertheless, they still divide work in very large projects in Europe, such as the CLARIAH collaborations or efforts to create Europeana. These large-scale projects often entail the complicated cocreation of data between content experts and digital professionals. While both academic disciplines share similarities—namely, in academic career ladders, their need to operate in a global network, and their hunt for external funding—there are marked differences. These differences are most apparent in the publication cultures. For computer science, the focus is on competitive eight-page conference publications, whereas humanities scholars are generally evaluated on books and journal articles. These different publication cultures affect the research pace and the unit of publication, which tends to be smaller for the computational sciences. In this section, we showcase several projects in which we were and are involved in order to detail how disciplinary differences influenced the work in the projects and how the teams balanced these issues. These projects were selected because they show how the collaboration between computing sciences and humanities can lead to a successful cross-fertilization of perspectives. Both initiatives are large enough for all involved disciplines to have their own specific work areas, but they would have not been successful had the disciplines not successfully cooperated on data integration and analysis. We need to spend that time to develop a common understanding of the issues to be addressed. Both projects managed to argue for this successfully with their funders.

The European Holocaust Research Infrastructure (EHRI) has worked on the integration of Holocaust materials in Europe, the United States, and Israel for over ten years (Blanke and Kristel, "Integrating Holocaust Research"). EHRI employs in almost equal measures historians, archivists, and computer experts and has developed a sophisticated data integration framework where content experts concentrate on data that is not yet well described or needs to be newly created (Blanke et al., "The European Holocaust Research Infrastructure Portal"). The computer experts, on the one hand, have set up a semiautomated data integration system covering the many already existing large-scale archives in the field. Archivists and computer scientists, on the other hand, have worked together on translating archival principles of information access such as provenance and fonds into a novel digital framework using graph databases. Given the size of the challenges with over 2,000 collection-holding institutions and datasets at the terabyte scale, a clear division of labor has emerged and remains necessary.

The story of EHRI's disciplinary collaboration is repeated across several other initiatives in Europe that focus on a diverse set of skills in order to develop and integrate humanities resources. EHRI's focus is on difficult to reach resources from Eastern and Southeastern Europe and to integrate them. It is very much transnational, but similar large-scale collaborations are also repeated in individual member states of the European Union. Between 2004 and 2014, eighteen projects were funded by the Dutch Research Council called CATCH: Continuous Access to Cultural Heritage. The goal was for each project team to consist of a PhD student (four years), a postdoctoral researcher, and a scientific programmer (each three years).[1] This team would spend a considerable amount of time at a cultural heritage institution.[2] CATCH had a coining influence on the digital humanities ecosystem in the Netherlands, leading to one of the most advanced research communities in the world that is unique in advocating for the involvement of computer science research in the humanities.

In the first round of CATCH projects, starting in 2005, partners from both computer science and cultural heritage were involved, followed by a strong focus on a humanities component. As such, the team needed to include researchers from both computer science and humanities.[3] Besides embedding the teams in cultural heritage institutions and often having them share an office, the program coordinators regularly organized events for all ongoing projects to establish the division of work between computer science and humanities and keep it close to the institutional interests. These events would typically take place at one of the participating cultural heritage institutions, and the project team based at that institute would be responsible for the scientific program of the meeting. The results of putting together researchers from different disciplines in direct contact with heritage professionals resulted in a close-knit community of over 100 people (including project leaders and coordinators) who still work together in various follow-up projects such as CLARIAH[4] and networks such as the Dutch Digital Heritage Network[5] can call on each other for guest lectures or student excursions.

The Netherlands easily lends itself to such a network because it takes about four hours to drive from the country's northernmost tip to the farthest corner in the south. The Netherlands is also rich enough for its research councils to spend ten million euros on a ten-year research program. Therefore, replicating this setup is not easy. However, the pandemic years taught us that digital collaborations can facilitate such partnerships, too, albeit at a somewhat slower pace and lower resolution. The most important thing to make research truly interdisciplinary in such larger projects is to spend time on the equality in research questions and mutual understanding. This means that the research is driven by interests from both sides. Neither humanities nor computer science should define the project alone with the other in a supporting role. Formulating research projects with central research questions from the different parties is an excellent starting point.

Furthermore, mutual understanding is key. Naturally, most humanities scholars will not immediately grasp the finer details of computer science methods within a three-year project or even in a long-standing collaboration, while computer scientists struggle with the focus on details in the humanities and its research interests. However, to a certain extent, one does need to understand the other's research field as long as the division of labor is well defined and collaboration is built into the work. This includes research questions, methodologies, workflows, and research culture. It is incredibly difficult to achieve such an in-depth understanding without working together often and closely. Discussing a shared project in a meeting room for an hour a week and then spending the rest of the week in one's own office is not enough. From our experience, it is necessary to talk often and then also about nitty-gritty details, to recommend core publications from your field and read your colleague's core publications from her field. It is unrealistic to expect the first six months of the project to yield scientific breakthroughs, but getting to the bottom of the research problem and building an understanding of each other's disciplines will be beneficial in the long run.

CATCH entailed several detailed collaborations between computer science and humanities. Its Agora project, for example, attempted to connect different cultural heritage collections through a historical dimension—that is, through the events depicted or related to collection objects instead of standard metadata regarding the object's type, dimensions, and maker. Furthermore, the project's research questions were formulated from both humanities and computer science perspectives. Fairly early on in the project, the project team started investigating the use of events as a link between different heritage collections, such that you could relate a weapon from the Rijksmuseum collection used in a conflict to a documentary from the Netherlands Institute for Sound and Vision on that conflict, thus providing additional context to those collection objects. One of the main difficulties, which is as yet unresolved, was to define what an event is and how it can be modeled. Indeed, there are several event models (cf. Scherp et al.; Shaw, Troncy, and Hardman and Van Hage et al.) and datasets that describe events in a structured format, but these are fairly simple and lack the complexity that events denote to historians. The project team thus took a step back and started spending afternoons talking and whiteboarding to try to define and model workable prototypical object-event and event-event relationships to support the interpretation of objects in cultural heritage collections. This led to a paper that was copresented by one of the historians and one of the computer scientists on the team and that also received a nomination for the best paper award at that conference (Van den Akker et al., "Digital Hermeneutics"). More importantly, the process required bridging a huge gap between the two different project angles, both on the content and on how the work is approached and the expected results of a "unit of research." The team realized that they could only come to a successful collaboration if they understood each other's process and learned to ask what the other meant when they talked about "modeling," "vocabulary," or "event."

In EHRI and CATCH, humanities scholars and computer scientists have found innovative ways to work together over long sustained periods of time. In this process, they developed their own joint vocabulary along a distinct division of work. As the computational humanities grows, so will our work with colleagues from fields such as computer and data science. Our doing a better job in clarifying and establishing a shared language will be even more important. EHRI and CATCH are in many ways typical for a large number of digital humanities projects in Europe in the last decade where vocabularies are integrated but the work remains divided. Next, we present new styles of collaborations that we are seeing where both work and vocabularies are brought together. They are made possible by a broadening of the availability of data science tools as well as new data environments that allow for a joint publication of data. One of these new data environments is the work on humanities-specific data publication journals.

Sharing Is Caring

The widespread availability of large digital datasets for humanities research and the growing interest in computational and data-intensive methods in digital humanities go hand in hand with questions about how to ensure that the work of creating and sharing the datasets is correctly credited in the humanities as well. In this section, we argue that publishing papers in data journals should be encouraged among humanities scholars and that this becomes part of the standard publication strategy for humanities research projects. This way, data journals become symbols of new data-driven research work specific to the humanities.

In the humanities, digital datasets are now more available and do not always have to be created from scratch, which often required large-scale collaborations across disciplines in Europe. In a context where novel research within particular fields of humanities is encouraged and called for and where traditional schemes in research funding acquisition, higher-education program structures, and academic career paths are challenged (McGillivray, "Computational Methods for Semantic Analysis of Historical Texts"), the topic of data publication venues and data sharing is of particular relevance. It has been shown that humanities research based on freely available and openly licensed datasets is more likely to be cited (e.g., Colavizza et al., "The Citation Advantage"), leading to increased reproducibility rates and greater public confidence in the research. Next to ensuring the long-term preservation of and access to the datasets and resources, it is important to enhance the discoverability and intellectual context of datasets by positioning them within a broader area of research. Like many other disciplines, humanities scholars across the language and historical disciplines have started to investigate how to ensure that the work of creating and sharing of datasets is correctly credited and recognized as a valuable contribution to the scholarly community.

Important initiatives such as DataCite have contributed to setting standards in the area of data sharing, recognizing the importance of all types of research outputs, and providing a persistent digital object identifier (DOI) for all research outputs.[6] However, given the dominant role played by journal publications in academic careers in the humanities, it is important that incentives are in place for the scholars themselves to create and share datasets. Data journals provide scholars with this incentive and are, in Europe at least, a sign that humanities scholars themselves have become more data-active. Data journals are academic journals that publish articles describing and analyzing datasets rather than presenting new findings, theories, or interpretations. They are a relatively new concept in academic publishing, first appearing only a decade ago. The first data journals originated in scientific publishing to ensure that the creators and curators of datasets are rewarded for their work and that data sharing is facilitated and encouraged. Examples of such journals dedicated broadly to a range of scientific disciplines include *Scientific Data*,[7] *GigaScience*,[8] and *F1000Research*.[9]

Following the example of scientific disciplines, two data journals specifically dedicated to the humanities have appeared in the past few years in Europe: the *Journal of Open Humanities Data*[10] and *Research Data for the Humanities and Social Sciences*.[11] Although they are a growing niche within the academic publishing market,[12] data journals constitute a great opportunity to support and enhance research in the data-driven humanities (Marongiu et al., "Le Journal of Open Humanities Data"). Thanks to their nontraditional format and scope, they have the ability to adapt to the evolving needs of this research. For example, the *Journal of Open Humanities Data* publishes both short data papers dedicated to the description of specific research objects, full-length research papers, and longer narratives devoted to the discussion of "methods, challenges, and limitations in the creation, collection, management, access, processing, or analysis of data in humanities research, including standards and formats."[13] The flexibility of the latter format allows authors to report on the challenges and methodological aspects and techniques, which is particularly important for computational research in the humanities. To further stress the tight connection between data objects and computational research, the *Journal of Open Humanities Data,* moreover, has published so far nine articles in the special collection dedicated to Computational Humanities Research Data.[14] We believe that a focus on data sharing and data publication can help develop more data-driven humanities work across the disciplines. Joint efforts aimed at enabling reproducible research, crediting resource-creation, ensuring digital preservation, and crucially being part of the same data-centric innovative process in academic publishing can contribute to bridging gaps and empowering more data-driven research in the humanities.

In EHRI and CATCH, data issues required an organized division of labor between computer science and humanities. To facilitate reuse of datasets and future integration of computing and humanities interests, humanities-specific data journals offer an opportunity to publish and receive recognition for research data outputs. Data journals, just like their traditional counterparts, provide researchers with the means to gain recognition for their research outputs and should thus encourage the publications of datasets in all disciplines that will, in turn, allow for more directly humanities-driven research. They have significantly contributed to the wider availability of data in the humanities that has, in our experience, brought about a new collaboration toward data-driven humanities. Consider, for example, a dataset of the annual ethnic fractionalization index for 162 countries across the world from 1945 to 2013 (Drazanova, "Introducing the Historical Index of Ethnic Fractionalization [HIEF] Dataset"). This dataset was reused in a number of further quantitative and computational studies on rebel rivalry (Tokdemir et al., "Rebel Rivalry and the Strategic Nature of Rebel Group Ideology and Demands"), political polarization of nations (Davis and Vila-Henninger, "Charismatic Authority and Fractured Polities"), and racism and economic inequality of countries (Caller and Gorodzeisky, "Racist Views in Contemporary European Societies").

Advancing Data-Driven Humanities

The growing level of interaction and exchange between computational sciences and humanistic disciplines has had a strong effect on data-sharing practices, as we described in the previous section. It has also changed the relationship between computer science and humanities. Research work is not simply divided anymore but shared. On the one hand, this has led to a general recognition that new and better methodological frameworks for quantitative research in the humanities are needed (e.g., Clifford et al.; Jenset and McGillivray; Bode; McGillivray, Colavizza, and Blanke, to name a few) and that this has implications for the relationship between the tools being developed and the research questions that can be answered with them (as argued in Scheinfeldt, "Where's the Beef?"). This has been taken critically by some, who have supported the view that computational and digital methods in the humanities, and particularly history, have led the field away from argument-driven scholarship toward tool building and resource accessibility (Blevins, "Digital History's Perpetual Future Tense"). On the other hand, scholars have expressed views on which infrastructural considerations best enable high-quality research at scale (cf., e.g., Smithies, "Software Intensive Humanities") and have voiced a call for more reproducible and open research practices (Liu, "Assessing Data Workflows for Common Data 'Moves' across Disciplines"), which are particularly topical in the case of research at the interface between computer science and humanities. This section reports on some of the projects that we have been involved with where this new type of quantitative open research has succeeded in enhancing humanities understandings.

The HiTime project (Van de Camp, "A Link to the Past") took a data-centric approach to create social networks between people, professions, locations, events, and schools of thought in the labor movement from 1850 to 1940. By analyzing a database containing information about strikes and newspaper articles, the project team uncovered links between the strikes mentioned in the database and those mentioned in the newspapers, as well as a host of "almost" strikes mentioned in newspapers but that were canceled and thus never appeared in the database (Van den Hoven, Van den Bosch, and Zervanou, "Beyond Reported History"). The potential of this dataset became apparent only by discussing the text analytics results early and often with the historians and repeating the experiments frequently, otherwise they could have easily been dismissed as not relevant because the strikes did not take place. Small changes make a big difference in data-driven humanities.

In another example, our interdisciplinary team developed a "materialist sociology of political texts" of post-1945 U.K. government white papers (Blanke and Wilson, "Identifying Epochs in Text Archives"). We focused on U.K. government white papers to map connections and similarities in political communications from 1945 to 2010. These are 888 documents and 19.3 million words in total. Rather than discovering large-scale trends since 1945 in the political documents, we were interested in how we could deconstruct standard perceptions of political epochs that are related to, for instance, government changes or major historical events such as wars. The team relied on machine learning to classify historical time periods by means of the ambiguity, fairness, morality, and political sentiments in the documents. Three longer-term epochs of political communications emerged from correlating these sentiments: from 1945 to 1965, from 1965 to 1990, and from 1990 onward. This way the team was able to then trace changes of meaning in key political concepts across these three epochs using topic models and word2vec word embeddings. Each approach reinforced the strong differences in political communication in the three epochs, underlining that such projects can use computational methods to alter typical perceptions of historical epochs.

A "computational genealogy" was developed (Blanke and Aradau, "Computational Genealogy") using the inaugural addresses of U.S. presidents over time. The goal of the project was to find out together with researchers from critical studies how computational methods can help to articulate discontinuity and moments of dissent that have been central to critical historical work. In our experience, this runs counter to the computational science tendency to look for patterns and trends. The team had to learn how to integrate new vocabularies of discontinuity as they appear in computational analysis: anomalies, spikes, outliers, influence, detrending, and so on. Even in a fairly small and closed corpus such as the inaugural addresses, there are no clear trends and differences that seem to dominate. The analysis focused on machine learning techniques that surface differences, such as anomaly detection and detrending. For example, Donald Trump's inaugural rhetoric was found to be distinct not so much from his direct Democrat predecessors but from other Republicans. Trump's speech highlights a struggle within the Republican party and the disappearance of Dwight Eisenhower's internationalist ideas. The trend toward Trump is most influenced by Ronald Reagan's conservatism and Republican ultra-nationalism. It is interrupted, however, also by Abraham Lincoln's national consolidation and Eisenhower's internationalism. This example shows that contributions to data-driven humanities can be made with relatively small existing datasets and readily available tools.

Another project further illustrates a fruitful interdisciplinary collaboration where the humanistic perspective of classics scholars met the interests of statisticians and machine learning scientists, with an ambitious aim to lead to original research in both fields. This project's goal was to develop new computational models for semantic change in Ancient Greek.[15] The task was identifying the change in meaning of words over time (McGillivray, "Computational Methods for Semantic Analysis of Historical Texts"). The starting point of this research was work done in computational linguistics, which relies on distributional representations of word meaning based on word co-occurrence statistics in large corpora (cf. Tahmasebi, Borin, and Jatowt, "Survey of Computational Approaches," for an overview). These models use time as the only metadata field, thus risk missing subtle nuances in word meaning, which are particularly important in the case of ancient languages.

Computational linguists tend to be interested in developing state-of-the-art models that can automatically identify words as they change meaning in a certain time span. This has a range of applications, including lexicography, information retrieval, opinion, and sentiment mining. From the point of view of classicists, semantic shifts can help explore questions about the semantics of Ancient Greek words in relation to historical, stylistic, cultural, and geographical factors. Bridging the gap between the two sets of interests required careful consideration. One very positive aspect of this interdisciplinary exchange was that it led to an innovative contribution to the design of the computational model itself. The insight that polysemy and semantic change are particularly closely related in ancient languages, and that genre plays a very important role in the semantics of Ancient Greek words, led to the development of a new computational model that incorporates genre as a key factor in the distributional contexts of words (Perrone et al., "GASC").

These examples show that new methods allow scholars to answer different (types) of research questions and gain new insights—in our cases, finding unexpected patterns indicating events that did not happen or rhetorical differences not between politicians of opposite parties but of different politicians within a party over time. Big data and computational methods allow us to effectively present a different lens on a domain as a complement to traditional close-reading methods.

Going Forward

Combining the digital with the humanities does not only pose research challenges, but it also challenges our research cultures. In our experience, bridging these cultures is where many of the current challenges for collaboration lie. This focus on collaboration is by no means new to the discourse on digital humanities; Spiro ("'This Is Why We Fight'"), for example, highlights collaboration among the core values for the digital humanities community, and Davidson ("Humanities 2.0") discusses collaboration and customization in the context of the cocreation of collective projects (particularly archives) involving the public. In this chapter, we stress the importance of collaboration specifically with the community of researchers in computer science and discuss what shape this collaboration can take. We also point to new developments, which come with the development of data science as a separate discipline and the larger availability of advanced computational methods.

Where the computer science publication culture puts a lot of emphasis on conferences with low acceptance rates, the humanities publication culture is focused on books and journal articles.[16] These different publications (and, by extension, the field's research evaluation measures) demand different research cycles that currently bar optimal cross-pollination between the fields. It is unlikely that any of the different disciplines will radically change their research and publication culture. However, interdisciplinary projects can try to use this as a feature rather than a bug and present their projects to the different communities represented in their project. With multiple project members, each can take the lead in tailoring the project's results to their research community's preferred format.

We also need to rethink our research evaluation strategies that currently behave as silos between the different research fields. More and more early-career researchers are becoming digital humanities scholars and may not fit one or the other publication culture paradigm, so they are at risk of falling behind when it comes to having their CVs evaluated for project proposals and next career steps. The trend to share datasets and code also calls for expanding research evaluation metrics to also include types of work that are extremely valuable to the community but are often not included in standard evaluations.[17]

We observe progress in the growing acceptance of computational cultures from within the appointment panels that we have participated in. There is also clearly a fairly well-funded attempt by research councils in Europe to bring together computer science and humanities. However, we expect the most sustained impact to come from changes within the disciplines themselves. The emergence of data science has widened the scope of computing research to work with more diverse data. In the humanities as well, we see concerted efforts to bridge the gaps presented in this chapter. Through data publications, humanities scholars can participate in the creation of datasets that can be shared and reused and still achieve recognition comparable to other research outputs like journal articles. Inspired by similar efforts in other disciplines and in active collaboration with them, numerous data-driven humanities projects are now underway that are based on small teams working around specific research questions and interests in the humanities.

Notes

1. In rare cases, the Dutch Research Council allowed two postdoctoral researchers or another configuration of the team.
2. https://www.nwo.nl/catch.
3. Disclaimer: one of the authors was involved in two CATCH projects, one as a PhD student and one as a postdoctoral researcher.
4. https://clariah.nl/en/.
5. https://www.netwerkdigitaalerfgoed.nl/en/.
6. https://www.datacite.org.
7. https://www.nature.com/sdata/.
8. https://academic.oup.com/gigascience.
9. https://f1000research.com/.
10. https://openhumanitiesdata.metajnl.com/.
11. https://brill.com/view/journals/rdj/rdj-overview.xml?lang=en.

12. Although it is not a dedicated data journal, the *Journal of Cultural Analytics* also has a section on datasets (https://culturalanalytics.org/section/1579-data-sets). Datasets are defined as offering "lengthy discussions of curatorial choices associated with new data sets relevant to cultural study" (https://culturalanalytics.org/about).

13. https://openhumanitiesdata.metajnl.com/about/.

14. https://openhumanitiesdata.metajnl.com/collections/computational-humanities-research.

15. See "Computational Models of Meaning Change in Ancient Greek," a project from the Alan Turing Institute, at https://www.turing.ac.uk/research/research-projects/computational-models-meaning-change-ancient-greek.

16. Cf. "ACL 2019 Acceptance Rates," June 18, 2019, http://acl2019pcblog.fileli.unipi.it/?p=161, and "NeurIPS 2019 Stats," September 9, 2019, *Medium*, https://medium.com/@dcharrezt/neurips-2019-stats-c91346d31c8f.

17. In 2010, the Altmetrics manifesto was published (https://altmetrics.org/manifesto/), calling for a broader approach to measuring research impact. Since 2019, all the universities of the Netherlands, the Royal Netherlands Academy of Arts and Sciences (KNAW), the Dutch Research Council (NWO), the Netherlands Organisation for Health Research and Development (ZonMw), and the university hospitals have been working on Recognition & Rewards, a national program to shape a different and broader approach to recognizing academic staff for the work they do. For more information, see https://www.knaw.nl/en/publications/recognition-and-rewards-agenda-2022-2025.

Bibliography

Blanke, T., and C. Aradau. "Computational Genealogy: Continuities and Discontinuities in the Political Rhetoric of US Presidents." *Historical Methods: A Journal of Quantitative and Interdisciplinary History* (2019): 1–15.

Blanke, T., and C. Kristel. "Integrating Holocaust Research." *International Journal of Humanities and Arts Computing* 7, no. 1–2 (2013): 41–57.

Blanke, T., M. Bryant, M. Frankl, C. Kristel, R. Speck, V. V. Daelen, and R. V. Horik. "The European Holocaust Research Infrastructure Portal." *Journal on Computing and Cultural Heritage (JOCCH)* 10, no. 1 (2017): 1–18.

Blanke, T., and J. Wilson. "Identifying Epochs in Text Archives." In *IEEE International Conference on Big Data (Big Data), Boston, MA,* 2219–24. 2017. https://ieeexplore.ieee.org/document/8258172.

Blevins, C. "Digital History's Perpetual Future Tense." In *Debates in the Digital Humanities 2016,* edited by Matthew K. Gold and Lauren F. Klein. Minneapolis: University of Minnesota Press. 2016. https://dhdebates.gc.cuny.edu/read/untitled/section/4555da10-0561-42c1-9e34-112f0695f523.

Bode, K. *A World of Fiction: Digital Collections and the Future of Literary History.* Ann Arbor: University of Michigan Press, 2018. https://doi.org/10.3998/mpub.8784777.

Caller, S., and A. Gorodzeisky. "Racist Views in Contemporary European Societies." *Ethnic and Racial Studies* (2021). https://doi.org/10.1080/01419870.2021.1952289.

Clifford, J., B. Alex, C. Coates, A. Watson, and E. Klein. "Geoparsing History: Locating Commodities in Ten Million Pages of Nineteenth-Century Sources." *Historical Methods* 49, no. 3 (2010): 115–31. https://doi.org/10.1080/01615440.2015.1116419.

Colavizza, G., I. Hrynaszkiewicz, I. Staden, K. Whitaker, and B. McGillivray. "The Citation Advantage of Linking Publications to Research Data." *PLoS ONE* 15, no. 4 (2020): e0230416. https://doi.org/10.1371/journal.pone.0230416.

Davidson, C. N. "Humanities 2.0: Promise, Perils, Predictions." In *Debates in the Digital Humanities*, edited by Matthew K. Gold, 476–89. Minneapolis: University of Minnesota Press, 2012.

Davis, A. P., and L. Vila-Henninger. "Charismatic Authority and Fractured Polities: A Cross-National Analysis." *British Journal of Sociology* 72 (2021): 594–608. https://doi.org/10.1111/1468-4446.12841.

Drazanova L. "Introducing the Historical Index of Ethnic Fractionalization (HIEF) Dataset: Accounting for Longitudinal Changes in Ethnic Diversity." *Journal of Open Humanities Data* 6, no. 1 (2020): 1–8. https://doi.org/10.5334/johd.16.

Jenset, G. B., and B. McGillivray. *Quantitative Historical Linguistics. A Corpus Framework.* Oxford: Oxford University Press, 2017.

Liu, A. "Assessing Data Workflows for Common Data 'Moves' across Disciplines." *Alan Liu*, May 6, 2017. https://doi.org/10.21972/G21593.

Marongiu, P., N. Pedrazzini, M. Ribary, and B. McGillivray. "Le Journal of Open Humanities Data: enjeux et défis dans la publication de data papers pour les sciences humaines." In *Humanités numériques et science ouverte*. Lille, France: Presses Universitaires du Septentrion, 2022.

McGillivray, B. "Computational Methods for Semantic Analysis of Historical Texts." In *Routledge International Handbook of Research Methods in Digital Humanities*, edited by Kristen Schuster and Stuart Dunn, 261–74. Abingdon-on-Thames: Routledge, 2020.

McGillivray, B., G. Colavizza, and T. Blanke. "Towards a Quantitative Research Framework for Historical Disciplines." In *COMHUM 2018: Book of Abstracts for the Workshop on Computational Methods in the Humanities 2018*, edited by M. Piotrowski, 53–58. Lausanne: Université de Lausanne, 2018. https://zenodo.org/record/1312779#.W2B4I62ZNTY.

McGillivray, B., T. Poibeau, and P. Ruiz Fabo. "Digital Humanities and Natural Language Processing: 'Je t'aime . . . Moi non plus.'" *DHQ: Digital Humanities Quarterly* 14, no. 2 (2020).

Parry, D. "The Digital Humanities or a Digital Humanism." In *Debates in the Digital Humanities*, edited by Matthew K. Gold. Minneapolis: University of Minnesota Press, 2012.

Perrone, V., M. Palma, S. Hengchen, A. Vatri, J. Smith, and B. McGillivray. "GASC: Genre-Aware Semantic Change for Ancient Greek." In *Proceedings of the 1st International Workshop on Computational Approaches to Historical Language Change 2019*, edited by Nina Tahmasebi, Lars Borin, Adam Jatowt, and Yang Xu, 56–66. Florence, Italy: Association for Computational Linguistics, 2019.

Scheinfeldt, T. "Where's the Beef? Does Digital Humanities Have to Answer Questions?" In *Debates in the Digital Humanities*, edited by Matthew K. Gold. Minneapolis: University of Minnesota Press, 2012.

Scherp, A., T. Franz, C. Saathoff, and S. Staab. "F—A Model of Events Based on the Foundational Ontology Dolce+ DnS Ultralight." In *K-CAP'09: Proceedings of the Fifth International Conference on Knowledge Capture*, 137–44. New York: Association for Computing Machinery, 2009.

Shaw, R., R. Troncy, and L. Hardman. "Lode: Linking Open Descriptions of Events." In *Asian Semantic Web Conference*, 153–67. Berlin: Springer, 2009.

Smithies, J. "Software Intensive Humanities." In *The Digital Humanities and the Digital Modern*, 153–202. Basingstoke: Palgrave Macmillan, 2017.

Smithies, J. "Towards a Systems Analysis of the Humanities." In *The Digital Humanities and the Digital Modern*, 113–51. Basingstoke: Palgrave Macmillan, 2017.

Spiro, L. "'This Is Why We Fight': Defining the Values of the Digital Humanities." In *Debates in the Digital Humanities*, edited by Matthew K. Gold. Minneapolis: University of Minnesota Press, 2012.

Tahmasebi, N., L. Borin, and A. Jatowt. "Survey of Computational Approaches to Diachronic Conceptual Change." *ArXiv:1811.06278 [cs.CL]* (2018).

Tokdemir, E., E. Sedashov, S. H. Ogutcu-Fu, C. E. M. Leon, J. Berkowitz, and S. Akcinaroglu. "Rebel Rivalry and the Strategic Nature of Rebel Group Ideology and Demands." *Journal of Conflict Resolution* 65, no. 4 (2021): 729–58. https://doi.org/10.1177/0022002720967411.

Underwood, T. "A Genealogy of Distant Reading." *Digital Humanities Quarterly* 11, no. 2 (2017).

Van de Camp, M. "A Link to the Past: Constructing Historical Social Networks from Unstructured Data." PhD thesis, Tilburg University, 2016.

Van den Akker, C., S. Legêne, M. van Erp, L. Aroyo, R. Segers, L. van der Meij, J. van Ossenbruggen, et al. "Digital Hermeneutics: Agora and the Online Understanding of Cultural Heritage." In *WebSci'11: Proceedings of the 3rd International Web Science Conference*, 1–7. New York: Association for Computing Machinery, 2011.

Van Hage, W. R., V. Malaisé, R. Segers, L. Hollink, and G. Schreiber. "Design and Use of the Simple Event Model (SEM)." *Journal of Web Semantics* 9, no. 2 (2011): 128–36.

Van den Hoven, M., A. van den Bosch, and K. Zervanou. "Beyond Reported History: Strikes That Never Happened." In *Proceedings of the First International AMICUS Workshop on Automated Motif Discovery in Cultural Heritage and Scientific Communication Texts, Vienna, Austria*, 20–28. 2010.

PART II][Chapter 14

Voices from the Server Room
Humanists in High-Performance Computing

QUINN DOMBROWSKI, TASSIE GNIADY, DAVID KLOSTER,
MEGAN MEREDITH-LOBAY, JEFFREY THARSEN, AND LEE ZICKEL

High-performance computing (HPC) is a technical resource that can vastly reduce the processing time necessary for computationally intensive digital humanities work. HPC is generally considered to involve aggregating or parallelizing computational resources. This includes tasks such as very large-scale optical character recognition (hundreds of thousands of pages or more), photogrammetry for generating 3D models, or dependency parsing corpora of thousands of documents for text analysis. While centrally run HPC clusters with free or low-cost access for faculty are common service offerings at research universities, national HPC resources in the United States and Canada are available to anyone affiliated with a university or college. In the annual usage reports prepared by HPC service providers, disciplinary diversity is valued as a way to show that the considerable funds directed toward HPC are serving the entire research community and not just the "usual suspects" in astrophysics or computational chemistry. In this context, humanities examples of HPC use are particularly valued. And yet, despite the utility of HPC for certain kinds of digital humanities (DH) work and the desire of HPC staff for humanists to use their services, HPC use by humanists remains rare and is often marked by frustration on both sides.

This chapter, focusing on HPC labor and the North American institutions in which the resources are located, draws on the experiences of five humanists who work (or have worked) in HPC support roles at institutions or national organizations in order to identify some of the barriers to HPC use by humanists and to assess the ways in which humanists can better engage with and in institutional HPC infrastructure, locally or nationally. Awareness of potential pitfalls and ways to mitigate them is important for managing the expectations of both the new HPC user and the HPC providers. In this chapter, we describe the value of having humanities disciplinary experts as part of HPC support staff, with the goal of offering readers arguments to advocate for these roles at their institutions or as part of national HPC centers open to all institutionally affiliated scholars. Particularly for scholars who do not have access to local HPC staff, we describe the peer support resources available through three national centers and how scholars can get involved with those groups. Finally, given the expanding number of HPC support roles open to humanists, we describe the skills necessary to succeed in such a role and the diverse ways of pursuing such a professional pathway.

In addition, we argue for the ongoing need for humanists on the service provider side of HPC and advocate for greater consideration of HPC support as a meaningful alt-ac career path.

Humanities Use Cases for HPC

The growing availability of large datasets, such as those created and maintained by cultural heritage institutions, has increased the likelihood that scholars in the humanities may be confronted with more data than they can realistically process on their own computers. At the same time, there have been advances in useful but computationally expensive methods, such as the creation and application of machine learning models for everything from optical character recognition (OCR) to text analysis and image classification. They have increased the need for humanists to have access to more powerful hardware than has traditionally been common outside of fields that process multimedia.

Despite the demand for better computational resources stemming from more data and more complex methods, the number of projects that have been able to take advantage of the HPC resources offered locally at R1 institutions and nationally for any institutionally affiliated scholar in the United States and Canada has been limited.[1] Typically, projects that have successfully used HPC have involved collaboration with DH-aware staff on HPC support teams or staff with a mix of technical and disciplinary expertise in the library, DH centers, or similar groups. Melissa Terras and colleagues describe a series of case studies where a team collaborated with humanities scholars to help them use large datasets from the British Library—one involving tracking the term "cholera" over time and another tracking changes in the size and technique of images as they corresponded to book genre. A number of projects have used HPC to perform OCR at scale (e.g., Köntges et al.) or develop systems to improve OCR quality for particular kinds of text (e.g., Christy et al.). Others describe the use of HPC for photogrammetry to generate high-quality 3D models for researchers in fields including cultural heritage and architecture (Gniady et al.; Ruan et al.). HPC also has a role in managing large textual corpora at the Stanford Literary Lab (McClure et al.). And work such as the large-scale investigations of maps without first rendering them as vectors, as described by Katherine McDonough in "Maps as Data" in this volume, is likewise well-suited to HPC.

But just because there is a match between the technical needs of humanists doing the kinds of work described here and the computational resources provided by HPC centers locally or nationally, it does not mean that there is always an easy path for humanists to use HPC. In the next section, we describe the translation work that needs to take place to go from a humanist's needs (e.g., around large-scale text or image analysis or computationally intensive processing tasks like OCR or dependency parsing a corpus) to a successful engagement with HPC service providers.

Domain Translation

When we talk about support for HPC in the humanities, it helps to broaden the view to think less about large servers and compute nodes and more about a digital research infrastructure. What is digital research infrastructure? The PARTHENOS training project, part of the European Commission DARIAH network, defines research infrastructures for humanities as "shared, unbounded, heterogeneous, open, and evolving socio-technical systems comprising an installed base of diverse information technology capabilities and their user, operations, and design communities."[2] This definition works for digital research using HPC as well as for any other research computing context. But how do the needs of DH scholars differ from those of other disciplines, and how can institutions (including national HPC centers) address those needs through the development of digital research infrastructures that better support humanities scholars?

The area in which DH scholars benefit the most from domain-specific HPC support is in translating humanistic inquiries into questions that a computer can answer. The questions posed by humanists are often fundamentally different from the mathematical or scientific questions historically solved by computing clusters. John Unsworth, in a 2006 report on cyberinfrastructure for the humanities and social sciences from the American Council of Learned Societies, wrote:

> Humanities scholars and social scientists will require similar facilities but, obviously, not exactly the same ones: grids of computational centers are needed in the humanities and social sciences, but they will have to be staffed with different kinds of subject-area experts; comprehensive and well-curated libraries of digital objects will certainly be needed, but the objects themselves will be different from those used in the sciences; software toolkits for projects involving data-mining and data-visualization could be shared across the sciences, humanities, and social sciences, but only up to the point where the nature of the data begins to shape the nature of the tools.[3]

Importance of Local Support

Supporting this domain-to-domain translation for DH scholars wishing to use HPC can best be realized with local, institutionally situated support from members of the HPC support staff.[4] Having a staff member on the HPC team who understands who is doing DH and how they are doing DH at the institution can increase the success of researchers wanting to access the infrastructure. This diversity of DH needs can also be addressed where the HPC staff also understands the backgrounds of other members of the HPC support team and their ability and willingness to work with humanists and act as a go-between where necessary.

It is well known that DH is a field often defined more for its broad scope than for specific tools or methods common across the field. Entire institutions themselves often specialize in only a few genres of DH. One institution may have a number of people working on large-scale text analysis of thousands of written documents and centered in an English department, while another may have archaeologists whose datasets are a heterogeneous mix of text, images, and physical objects, such as soil samples and artifacts, and the digital analogues of the same. Lack of support at the local level can mean that researchers are unable to bridge the gaps between their disciplinary needs and the infrastructure available at the institution.

In addition to helping individual researchers, advocating upward for digital research infrastructure that supports DH is an important part of a humanities liaison role. When money is available for system improvements, it is more likely to go toward the kinds of features that make HPC more accessible for humanists (e.g., user-friendly portals of various kinds) if someone on the HPC support staff is advocating for them and soliciting use cases from local humanities faculty. For an institution to achieve something close to Unsworth's vision of "grids of computational centers," there needs to be support from staff who understand humanities research, are well versed in how humanities research translates into digital research, and can articulate the infrastructure needs of the humanities community to those who build and support that infrastructure.

This brings us to the challenges facing DH scholars who do not have access to someone with experience in both humanities research and HPC systems. Though this researcher may be able to access HPC infrastructure through their institution or nationally, receiving help on specific problems may require going through a service process or ticketing support service that may not address the full context of the challenges the researcher is facing. Researchers in this position can look toward national HPC platforms, such as the Digital Research Alliance of Canada or ACCESS for help.[5] Looking toward a group like this, even if it is not in your home country, is one way of finding others with similar challenges and receiving help with best practice.

Navigating Culture Clashes in HPC Support

The translation needed by most humanists to successfully engage with HPC is not limited to bridging the gap between humanities research questions and the specific technical affordances of HPC resources. The presentation of HPC service offerings and the customer service style typically employed in addressing requests and questions from users is steeped in scientific culture and expectations. Long-standing HPC support staff are accustomed to a particular kind of collegially terse exchange with their expected users: scholars for whom programming is an integral, basic part of their academic training and for whom navigating command-line interfaces is as intuitive and familiar as humanists find navigating bibliographies. The move toward opening HPC to all scholars as a core resource has had some welcome effects from the perspective of HPC support teams (i.e., additional funding), but many of the new users, including scholars from the humanities, do not have the background knowledge that HPC staff are used to.

Humanists are not alone here—computational biologists, psychologists, and many others do not share the expectations and practices of the HPC mainstream core user block from fields like astrophysics, nuclear engineering, and chemistry. A question about how to run code on the cluster may be "answered" with a one-line response containing a link to highly technical documentation that covers specific parameters and variables used by that individual cluster but none of the scaffolding needed to get to the point where one could make use of that information. Important information that can often be overlooked includes how to log in, how and where to transfer files, how compute-time allocations work or how long one might wait in a queue, the importance of parallelization and how to do it, and how to install software or run containers. A synchronous conversation can surface these gaps quickly, but a user facing documentation in isolation may not even realize what prerequisites have been omitted until they can't make the instructions "work." These kinds of exchanges are highly frustrating for both parties: HPC staff grow annoyed that their usual responses are met with bafflement instead of gratitude, and scholars outside traditional HPC disciplines conclude that HPC is too complicated and the staff can't be counted on to make it any easier.

One way to improve this relationship could be to implement technical scaffolding documents as well as documentation with some basic explanation of why a process works and what it is doing. A humanities domain expert on the HPC support team is well positioned to develop these kinds of documents and help both nontraditional HPC users and HPC support staff navigate moments of culture clash.

While the addition of humanists to HPC staff groups is a significant step toward better support for nontraditional HPC users, the overall impact is limited when the HPC team takes the approach of directing all "unusual" requests to the staff member with the unusual background rather than adopting a more integrated cross-training model. Humanists working with HPC groups (at their institution or at national organizations) that lack a "translator" can benefit from reaching out to colleagues in similar disciplines who use HPC to see if they can help navigate the process or serve as a kind of advocate for humanists with the HPC group.

Online workshop materials are another resource to support those unfamiliar with HPC, especially complete beginners. An example is HPC Carpentry.[6] These self-directed courses may be daunting for scholars who have never worked with the command line or code or those who prefer some hands-on training. However, working through some preliminary Programming Historian tutorials that explain the command line may be enough of an on-ramp to then work through HPC Carpentry successfully.[7] An introductory overview like HPC Carpentry can, at a minimum, provide scholars with enough of a vocabulary to ask the kinds of specific questions that are more likely to get a useful answer from HPC staff if there is no humanities domain expert who can serve as a translator.

Peer Support Groups for HPC

National HPC organizations, such as Compute Canada, XSEDE, or the HathiTrust Research Center (HTRC), can play a significant role in ensuring that the entire DH community, regardless of individual institutional resources, is not left out of the HPC ecosystem and its opportunities. The national reach of these organizations allows them to interact with the DH community across broad geographic areas and collaborate more easily across institutional boundaries. Each of these organizations has its own emphasis and strategies for user engagement, as described below.

THE DIGITAL RESEARCH ALLIANCE OF CANADA (THE ALLIANCE)

The Digital Research Alliance of Canada (formerly Compute Canada) uses the model of a national disciplinary support team. One opportunity for DH scholars to build on this model would be through discipline-specific support teams within a broader DH team. This could take the shape of discipline-specific mini teams within national HPC organizations, headed by a member of the national team with members drawn from the research communities. A national disciplinary support team could also encourage more collaboration among the researchers using national HPC systems. This is a strategy that would not only work in the humanities but would help support all researchers using national digital research infrastructure to share best practices and stories of things that went well and things that could have gone better and to give coordinated feedback to national coordination teams on user needs, challenges, and opportunities. An example might be a group made up of all DH projects hosting a project on the Alliance infrastructure using the Islandora platform or a group of researchers whose projects are all hosted on Alliance cloud infrastructure. There is also room for HPC practitioners at the national level to engage in prototyping for the community on national infrastructure in order to allow DH scholars to more easily use the infrastructure and integrate datasets from outside sources such as the cultural heritage datasets (described in Terras et al., "Enabling Complex Analysis of Large-Scale Digital Collections"). Finally, DH researchers, with some coordination at the national level, should take a more active role in helping to shape future funding calls that take into account the needs of DH scholars in terms of sustainability of web-based research projects and the need for expertise in development and tool-building.

ACCESS

Even though ACCESS (previously XSEDE) and its service providers are based in the United States, ACCESS has community groups to help promote global outreach around HPC resources. The ACCESS acronym stands for Advanced Cyberinfrastructure Coordination Ecosystem: Services & Support and is funded by the National Science Foundation, yet it offers help for DH practitioners in the form of MATCH Services. With MATCH Services the researcher submits an engagement request and a mentor and student are assigned based on the project needs, including DH projects. Additionally, Campus Champions are still offered as an assistance option with ACCESS as they were with XSEDE. While some champions are domain specific, other champions are specific to an institution (campus champions) or a region (regional champions), the latter of which could be a resource for scholars whose institution does not have its own HPC services. In addition, ACCESS offers online training and YouTube video tutorials to help new users. However, concerns about gaps in The Alliance's support are also applicable to ACCESS. Even with DH assistance, there is a need for training and workshops developed with humanists in mind. These humanist-specific trainings and workshops could be more easily created within a DH support team made up of humanists from different disciplines, as suggested above.

HTRC

Another global resource that offers HPC services is the HathiTrust Research Center. While the HTRC is not a traditional HPC resource in the same vein as ACCESS and The Alliance, it is an asset for humanists looking to leverage not only additional computing power but datasets, tools, and resources not available with other national or global HPC organizations. The HTRC allows users access to over 16 million digitized volumes in the HathiTrust Digital Library and provides built-in analytics tools as well as Linux data capsules where users can pull both volumes that are in and out of copyright and perform various text analysis algorithms using tools like Voyant or their own scripts.[8] In addition, the HTRC provides access to volume metadata and lets users create worksets of volumes and then share those worksets with other users, who can then pull them into their data capsules and run their own analyses. Finally, HTRC users are not limited to what is in the HathiTrust; they can transfer their own datasets via secure file transfer protocol (SFTP) or download them from their preferred cloud storage option while the capsule is in maintenance mode. This allows users to combine their texts or other data with other texts or data in the HathiTrust. While these tools and resources are invaluable, the HTRC data capsules only allow a default maximum of twenty gigabytes of RAM and ten CPUs. This makes a data capsule about as powerful as a decent laptop. However, if more computing power is needed for special projects, it is possible to request additional resources, apply for special project grant money outside of HTRC, or apply to be one of the Advanced Collaborative Support (ACS) projects offered yearly by the HTRC. The ACS projects come with specialized expertise, developer time, and compute resources. Outside the ACS projects, the HTRC has a combination of programmers and computer scientists as well as DH specialists on hand to provide support to users and help bridge the gap between humanists and developers.

Pursuing Professional Paths in HPC Support

HPC support groups have been expanding to better serve disciplinarily diverse audiences by hiring specialists from a wider variety of fields who have deep expertise in HPC. As a result, the kinds of humanities liaison roles we have described here have become a viable alt-ac career path for many humanities scholars. Unlike the digital scholarship librarian position, which is becoming an increasingly well-defined (and credentialed) career path, humanists come to HPC support roles through many different routes. Humanists working in HPC groups tasked with helping other humanists use available HPC resources need to be able to communicate effectively in both worlds, which means having training and experience in both domains. The academic paths taken by humanists in HPC support roles are as varied as the field of DH itself.

A quick look at the backgrounds of the authors for this publication attests to this diversity. Many have advanced humanities degrees, and they acquired their computational expertise through vocational roles before earning their degrees, while earning their degrees, or after the fact. Others have multiple degrees, often combining a humanities degree as well as a degree in informatics, computer science, or library science with some emphasis in digital libraries or, in more increasing instances, digital humanities. For example, Indiana University's Department of Information and Library Sciences offers a specialization in digital humanities for their Master in Library Science and Master in Information Science degrees, the University of Central Florida offers a DH minor, and Loyola University–Chicago offers an MA in DH.[9] The common thread is that humanists in HPC (or even DH in general) have a degree in a humanities discipline, be it undergraduate or graduate, and a degree or vocational experience in a computational or informatics discipline.

Another popular degree trend is the aforementioned library science and/or information science degree or an MA in digital humanities. The appeal of earning these degrees is that it can be a one-stop-shop for those seeking to gain the knowledge and skills necessary to acquire employment in a DH position, such as providing HPC support to humanists. For those with a library science (as opposed to information science) degree, a focus in digital libraries or digital humanities is helpful if a job working with humanists and HPCs is desired. However, even with the digital library or digital humanities focus, much on-the-job learning is necessary in order to help humanists with their HPC needs as these specializations, at best, provide only introductory training. Many universities house their DH centers in the library, and they are often funded, at least partly if not entirely, by the library. In the absence of a DH center, many academic libraries employ librarians whose job descriptions require skills that are well suited to help with potential DH projects. This close association between DH and libraries and library degrees has led to many taking this road to obtain the degree, knowledge, and skills necessary to gain employment in a DH position.

For individuals not currently holding a PhD, having an MLS/MIS degree is a qualifying alternative when applying for library-associated DH positions. The proliferation of these types of jobs has led to the notion that a library degree is an advantage in the field. This route has become so popular that the other degree paths mentioned above are often viewed as less conventional, even when bridging the HPC and humanities gap. However, many library-based DH specialists do not have the experience or training needed to help with HPC needs that may arise. This is why even with a library-based DH center or DH librarian, a person who understands HPCs in addition to humanities scholarship is necessary. While the MLS/MIS degrees can provide a good base to prepare for a DH position involving HPCs, it should be expected that the lion's share of the learning will be done as part of the vocation until MLS/MIS degree programs begin to offer more courses on HPC systems. This would allow those interested in a DH career to qualify for DH positions in both the library-centric DH world as well as the emerging world of DH in the information technology (IT) centers supporting HPC systems. Until this happens, university IT centers looking to hire people who can bridge the gap between humanists and HPCs will need to understand that unless they happen to find one of the handful of people who are not already employed and already have experience or training with HPC systems, they will need to be patient and provide the necessary training.

TRADITIONAL AND NONTRADITIONAL PATHS TO EXPERTISE IN TECH/COMPUTER SCIENCE AND DH

The traditional path to advanced computer science skill-building comes through a degree or concentration in computer science, often during undergrad, when basic and advanced algorithm design in languages like C++ or Java, training in a variety of data structures, and working daily within a command-line environment on an HPC cluster are all part of the standard curriculum. Few digital humanists take this route, however, as students wishing to pursue both humanistic and computer science training must balance their workload and fulfill degree requirements across divisions that often do not coordinate well. The far more common path is for a student pursuing a humanities degree to become aware of and interested in applications of technology (including computer science) to further their research and then to begin learning those technologies on an ad hoc basis with a research goal in mind. Other humanities-focused students have found a general knowledge of technology (including computer science) can be beneficial as they work to diversify their skill sets and serves to open professional career options that would otherwise not be available with solely a humanities degree.

In DH, even for those working in high-performance computing, all of these tracks can be viable options, depending on one's area of specialization, overall skill set, and the primary needs of the research community. While formal training in computer science affords a deeper understanding of some forms of technology—algorithm design in particular—advanced competency and even expertise can be achieved by the dedicated student. This skill set includes, but is not limited to, a scripting language such as Python or R, methods such as text analysis or network analysis, and technologies such as geographic information systems (GIS) and natural language processing (NLP).

Indeed, a broader skill set is likely more useful in the long run for translator positions and for supporting the needs of humanistic and social scientific research across the academic spectrum, especially when combined with an MLS or MIS degree and deep knowledge in a specific discipline such as art history, digital media, linguistics, or philology. Skills acquired within a computer science (CS) curriculum are generally easier for potential employers to measure than skills gained without certification. Researchers without a CS degree (or analogous certificate) wishing to demonstrate their competency will likely want to spend some time either working professionally in information technologies (for example, as a developer or software engineer, either in the private sector or at a public institution) or by taking certification exams offered by leading information technology corporations like Microsoft, Google, or Amazon/AWS.

As with most disciplines, there are no real shortcuts to mastery of any part of DH. However, an achievable short-term goal is focusing on one area or specialization that will allow the digital humanist interested in working in HPC to become competent, proficient, and ultimately an expert in one part of the spectrum that makes up the current range of digital and computational approaches to humanistic inquiry. Many of these core skills can also be learned in concert; for example, most modern programming languages tend to use similar logical structures, and gaining an understanding of the command line and *NIX operating systems is excellent preparation for working within an HPC environment. Many skill sets within the geographical sciences tend to build on each other (from basic GIS to spatial data science to complex computational approaches to urban design). Similarly, a focus on textual data and corpus creation can lead to expertise in corpus linguistics, digital philology, or library collection and federation practices.

Another skill component to DH HPC is project management. Strong project management skills allow for the articulation of research goals into achievable and usually quantifiable outcomes.[10] Experience working on and ultimately managing projects is an excellent way to learn how to identify potential pitfalls and roadblocks and how to avoid them, how to plan for the entire lifetime of a project, and how to help make the process as efficient and as appropriate for the needs of the project researchers and stakeholders as possible. We would again like to emphasize that the DH practitioner need not enter HPC as an expert programmer. The fact that humanities disciplinary liaisons are required to navigate different communication styles, levels of technical fluency, and types of documentation, as well as to advocate for humanities-oriented priorities in infrastructure development, means that high levels of coding proficiency are less crucial than in roles such as research software engineers (described by Damerow et al., "Of Coding and Quality," in this volume). Skill-building and gaining expertise in DH methods using HPC resources is a process, and no single practitioner can reliably claim expertise in the entirety of the field. As is the case with most disciplines, a broad base of general knowledge supplemented by knowledge acquisition in particular areas can most reliably predict individual success.

National computing resources in the United States and Canada have made strides in opening up their infrastructures to humanities practitioners, not only by making available computing resources but by creating staff positions for disciplinary experts who can translate humanists' questions and needs to HPC support staff, and vice versa. Many R1 institutions have likewise moved in this direction. In both local and national contexts, there continues to be a need for humanities scholars to advocate for better support for the kinds of work they are interested in doing with HPC, be it through the hiring of additional staff fluent in DH methods or by fostering communities of practice oriented toward humanities tools and methods.

The urgency around this kind of support has increased significantly in the wake of the Librarian of Congress granting a 2020 request for a new exemption to section 1201 of the Digital Millennium Copyright Act (DMCA) that supports the computational analysis of multimedia, including texts (in the form of encrypted ebooks) and video (in the form of encrypted DVDs). While this exemption paves the way for more U.S.-based humanities scholars to legally use cultural materials that have until recently been rendered inaccessible by digital rights management and other technological protection measures, the onerous security and access conditions on the exemption will inevitably lead humanities scholars to the doorstep of HPC support groups, with requests akin to those from the medical school.

The likely expansion of HPC support with an eye toward a growing humanities user base will foster new humanities career tracks. For students in the humanities who are considering different career options, the path toward becoming a humanities domain specialist in an HPC group shares some overlap with paths for digital scholarship librarians, developers, or research software engineers. However, the lack of HPC-specific courses in programs such as LIS degrees means some degree of personal motivation and self-study is likely part of the journey. Having more humanities students develop some exposure to the research methods that HPC enables, and then take up HPC staff roles themselves, will lead to increasing support for humanists using computational methods. In the meantime, scholars—particularly faculty with the power to influence their institutions or advocate nationally—can make strides toward this vision by developing some technical know-how, through the formal and informal paths to mastery we have laid out, and engaging with HPC support staff, if only to speak up for their needs. This combination of advocacy from senior scholars and skill-building among students who are then positioned to pursue careers in HPC support will establish a path for the successful and sustainable use of HPC in the humanities.

Notes

1. According to the Carnegie Classification of Institutions of Higher Education 2021 update, R1 institutions are those that give research a "very high" institutional priority. The classification includes "institutions that awarded at least 20 research/scholarship doctoral degrees during the update year and also institutions with below 20 research/scholarship doctoral degrees that awarded at least 30 professional practice doctoral degrees in at least 2 programs." In addition, these institutions had "at least $5 million in total research expenditures" (https://carnegieclassifications.acenet.edu/carnegie-classification/classification-methodology/basic-classification/).

2. "Welcome to the PARTHENOS Project," https://www.parthenos-project.eu/.

3. J. B. Unsworth, "Our Cultural Commonwealth: The Report of the American Council of Learned Societies Commission on Cyberinfrastructure for the Humanities and Social Sciences" (New York: ACLS, 2006), 8.

4. We recognize that every institution will be able to provide local support and address other means of HPC support elsewhere. However, there are advantages to having someone on the ground who is able to facilitate HPC interaction and effectively advocate for changes, where necessary, to support practices in order to better meet humanists' needs. Scholars using national-level cluster resources (e.g., when local resources do not exist at their institution) can also benefit from establishing a working relationship with a staff person at the national cluster who is familiar with humanities questions (e.g., the digital humanities specialist role at Compute Canada), though that person may not be able to provide the same level of attention and one-on-one support as a local, institutional person.

5. The Digital Research Alliance of Canada (https://alliancecan.ca/en/services/advanced-research-computing/national-services/humanities-and-social-sciences), for instance, has a national humanities and social sciences group that consults regularly with researchers and conducts outreach and training for the DH community. ACCESS

(previously XSEDE; https://support.access-ci.org/match/overview) matches you with a mentor and student based on your research project and computing needs.

6. https://hpc-carpentry.github.io/.

7. As an example of a tutorial, see the "set up" category of lessons at Programming Historian here: https://programminghistorian.org/en/lessons/?topic=get-ready.

8. The main page for the built-in tools can be found at https://analytics.hathitrust.org/explore. Some examples include the HTRC Feature Reader (https://github.com/htrc/htrc-feature-reader), the workset builder (https://solr2.htrc.illinois.edu/solr-ef/), and use of data capsules (https://analytics.hathitrust.org/staticcapsules).

9. To learn more about the degrees at IU, UCF, and Loyola-Chicago, see, respectively, https://ils.indiana.edu/programs/specializations/digital-humanities.html, https://www.ucf.edu/degree/digital-humanities-minor/, and https://www.luc.edu/digitalhumanities/.

10. Currently, end goals/outcomes often come in the form of statistics to support a research conclusion, data visualizations, or interactive environments, but these are just a few of many viable (project) outcomes.

Bibliography

Christy, Matthew, Anshul Gupta, Elizabeth Grumbach, Laura Mandell, Richard Furuta, and Ricardo Gutierrez-Osuna. "Mass Digitization of Early Modern Texts with Optical Character Recognition." *Journal on Computing and Cultural Heritage* 11, no 1 (December 2017): 1–25. https://doi.org/10.1145/3075645.

Gniady, Tassie, Guangchen Ruan, William Sherman, Esen Tuna, and Eric Wernert. "Scalable Photogrammetry with High Performance Computing." In *PEARC'17: Proceedings of the Practice and Experience in Advanced Research Computing 2017 on Sustainability, Success and Impact,* art. 72, 1–3. New York: Association for Computing Machinery, 2017. https://doi.org/10.1145/3093338.3104174.

Köntges, Thomas, Rhea Lesage, Bruce Robertson, Jennie Sellick, and Lucie Wall Stylianopoulos. "Open Greek and Latin: Digital Humanities in an Open Collaboration with Pedagogy." *IFLA World Library and Information Congress* (2019). http://library.ifla.org/2551/1/178-kontges-en.pdf.

McClure, David, Mark Algee-Hewitt, Steele Douris, Erik Fredner, and Hannah Walser. "Organizing Corpora at the Stanford Literary Lab. Balancing Simplicity and Flexibility in Metadata Management." In *Proceedings of the Workshop on Challenges in the Management of Large Corpora and Big Data and Natural Language Processing (CMLC-5+BigNLP) 2017, Including the Papers from the Web-as-Corpus (WAC-XI) Guest Section.* Mannheim: Institut für Deutsche Sprache, 2017. https://ids-pub.bsz-bw.de/frontdoor/index/index/docId/6261.

Ruan, Guangchen, Eric Wernert, Tassie Gniady, and Esen Tuna. "High Performance Photogrammetry for Academic Research." In *PEARC'18: Proceedings of the Practice and Experience on Advanced Research Computing,* art. 45, 1–8. New York: Association for Computing Machinery, 2018. https://doi.org/10.1145/3219104.3219148.

Terras, Melissa, James Baker, James Hetherington, David Beavan, Martin Zaltz Austwick, Anne Welsh, Helen O'Neill, et al. "Enabling Complex Analysis of Large-Scale Digital Collections: Humanities Research, High-Performance Computing, and Transforming Access to British Library Digital Collections." *Digital Scholarship in the Humanities* 33, no. 2 (2018): 456–66. https://doi.org/10.1093/llc/fqx020.

PART II][Chapter 15

A Technology of the Vernacular
Re-centering Innovation within the Humanities

LISA TAGLIAFERRI

The technology of language and writing, as an endeavor, has been held firmly by humanists. During the early codification of the vernacular language in the fourteenth century, Boccaccio asks why the *Decameron* should be denied to half of the potential reading population: "E chi negherà questo, quantunque egli si sia, non molto piú alle vaghe donne che agli uomini convenirsi donare?" ("Who will deny, that it should be given, for all that it may be worth, to gentle ladies much rather than to men?"[1]) (Proemio, 008–009). Though this positionality is not entirely without a tongue in the author's cheek, Boccaccio could have readily written this work—like others of his—in Latin instead, but doing so would exclude almost all women as readers, not to mention men who were not educated in Latin. The effort to use and further develop the vernacular in its written form was a calculated choice that opened up literacy and knowledge production to more practitioners.

In the early thirteenth century, one of the first known Italian poems was composed in the Umbrian dialect by Francesco d'Assisi. The *Laudes creaturarum* was a religious song written to enable the general public to pray in their own language, and is an example of a true accessibility innovation in our collective understanding of European history. Vernacular practitioners alongside Francesco included other community leaders and literary innovators, like Dante. Italian poets—who were notaries and other professionals by day—treated a wide range of subjects, from metaphysics to astronomy to optics, as in Guido Cavalcanti's *Donna me prega*. A foundation of intellectual poetry and community work would set the stage for continued investment in the technology of the vernacular not just in Italy but across Europe, allowing for texts to circulate and be translated from one vernacular to another.

The shift away from writing exclusively in Latin—the language of the wealthy, powerful, and elite—to a growing number of texts in the vernacular—the regional spoken languages of roughly everyone—came just ahead of a number of other important accessibility innovations that notably include the European printing

[261

press. An everyday language that, at this historical juncture, gets codified into writing corresponded with an increase in literacy due, in part, to the more accessible nature of the written expression of language people were already using (Latin was not generally spoken in the piazza). Indeed, Francesco and Dante may be interested to know that the question of the vernacular is still relevant to today's Catholic Church, as Pope Francis reimposed restrictions on the Latin Mass in favor of the vernacular.[2] In our current disciplinary understanding, language, the material book, and literature are all within the purview of the humanities, and the innovations of the late medieval and early Renaissance periods laid foundations for growing literacy and increased knowledge production among an expanding number of participants.

Through the historical example of the vernacular, my aim here is to demonstrate the role of the humanities in enabling cross-disciplinary innovation by providing foundations that include the technology of language. What was at stake at this time period—who had access to learning, who was able to produce knowledge—echoes in today's technological landscape of who has access to peer-reviewed research, who has access to inspect the software that runs on their devices, and who has access to build that software. The digital humanities—and the computational humanities in particular—sit at the confluence of the humanities and technology and could play a more critical role in driving access and innovation. The computational humanities offer a site for vernacular innovation built around open-source inclusive code, literate technologists, and collaborative interdisciplinary innovation. While our communities become more enmeshed and reliant on the digital, the use and development of technology must become more accessible and relatable to the public writ large. As computational and digital humanists, standing at the intersection of fields of study, we must work to move technology into a shared and accessible vernacular.

Inclusion, Community, Literacy: Vernacular Innovation

One beneficiary of the rise in vernacular was Caterina da Siena, who would live as a community builder, ambassador, and mystic writer, despite having been born both female and non-noble in 1347. As an uncloistered nun, Caterina was credited with returning the pope to Rome from Avignon, became canonized in the century after her death, and was made a doctor of the church in 1970. Probably, Caterina's impressive CV would not have been possible without her ability to read and write. A member of the artisanal class, Caterina gained literacy through her relationships with other women: her fellow *Mantellate* of the third order who included noble widows. Her choice of the Dominican order provided her with a rich intellectual environment, and Caterina learned across fields from religious studies to biology. She became a prolific writer in the last few years of her short life.

Despite her achievements and ability to teach others, reading and writing in the vernacular was not considered to be true literacy in a Latinate world. Though Caterina was born half a century after Dante's death, little had changed regarding the status of the Italian and Latin languages and what participating in those language communities meant. Latin—the language of upper-class men, intellectual humanists, and the church—presented a clear barrier that prevented the general public and women in particular from accessing information. Though Caterina did learn Latin (the extent to which we cannot be sure), she consciously and strategically chose Sienese Italian as her language of writing and speech. She so believed in the power of the vernacular that she wrote to the popes of her time in Sienese, such that it was required for her letters to be read aloud to them in Latin, *viva voce*. This approach was not for the faint of heart, considering the power of the papal seat at the time. As a spiritual figure serving her community, offering comfort, advice, and care to the prisoners, penitent women, and ill of Siena, how could Caterina choose to communicate in a language that the majority of those around her would not be able to understand?

About 30 percent of Caterina da Siena's nearly 400 extant letters were written to women, indicating a thriving vernacular female readership in Italy as early as the fourteenth century. More than those addressed to women, many of her letters contain the echoes of full literate communities as they capture the voices of all those physically in the room when a letter was penned. Among Caterina's scribes were her own female followers, revealing literary production—and the technical ability to write with fourteenth-century tools—outside masculine spaces. Letters, sometimes, are considered alongside ephemera and are not afforded the full weight of other texts. Caterina, who wrote a book, some prayers, and these letters, employed unique and consistent metaphors and imagery across her corpus and also persuasively enacted diplomacy through her writing, indicating a poetic and rhetorical prowess. A somewhat earlier medieval figure, Brunetto Latini—a philosopher, notary, and Dante's famous damned teacher—argues that Cicero's teachings on speeches also apply to letters in his French work *Tresor*.[3] Caterina writes her letters with the decorum one may expect of the period, especially when addressing the pope, and we do know that the technical act of writing was more laborious than it is today, suggesting that these texts of spiritual teachings for her followers were not intended to be thrown away.

Indeed, Caterina thought very much of her legacy and, on her deathbed, she asked the most trusted men of her *famiglia* followers to gather her writings together and watch over them. They would eventually collect these works for her canonization proceedings and to further distribute them across Europe in manuscripts and translations. The first printed edition of her letters was an early vernacular book run by Aldus Manutius in 1500, prior to his printings of Dante and Petrarca.[4] Her book, *Il dialogo*, is a multi-century bestseller: the first printed edition was done in 1472 by Azzoguidi in Bologna, and a print run has taken place every seven to eight years since then (Cavallini, xiii). Her books would prove to have a lasting impact on her reception and also would be among those texts working to solidify Italian as a language on the global stage.

Caterina represents innovation in the emerging vernacular language and in a community approach that was fueled through her interest in the technology of writing. She used new language that signaled a new spiritual approach and leveraged the language of the general public for effective political discourse. While she often positioned herself outside privileged and exclusive spaces, Caterina was able to negotiate these sites and work within and against them to push forward the community-based project of developing a recognized and elegant vernacular. The record of her work reveals a wide literary exchange with people who could read and write Italian from all walks of life in the fourteenth century, inviting them into the commons of knowledge rather than casting them out.

Although history often preserves a single hero and single date for many inventions and innovations, this work is actually slow, iterative, often intergenerational, and generally the result of many building on the efforts of others. At its best, innovation can drive access, but often access will drive innovation by including more people who can anticipate more angles and approaches to solving a given problem. Dante is often credited with being the father of the Italian language, but the project of Italian began before him and persisted after. Like Caterina da Siena, there were many other spiritual community builders working in the Italian peninsula in the thirteenth through fifteenth centuries, including Franciscan friar and poet Iacopone da Todi, Franciscan mystic and writer Angela da Foligno, and Augustinian tertiary and healer Elena da Udine. These figures innovated on the language spoken by the people in their urban areas and developed a public repertoire outside institutions of power and privilege, seeking to drive inclusion and access through public speech and written texts. Through distancing themselves from a separate and self-monitoring elite group, those who emphatically wrote texts or gave speeches in Italian included communities historically excluded. This work helped to bring women, prisoners, the poor, the disabled, and other marginalized people into broader public discourse. Though inequity was not eradicated, there were increased avenues for literacy and communication across class lines.

While many other factors contributed to the growing rise in global literacy, the impact of the shift from Latin to the vernacular in the late Middle Ages and into the early modern period cannot be overstated. With data from several data stores, including the World Bank, Max Roser and Esteban Ortiz-Ospina have created a number of compelling graphs on the rise of global literacy, which as of 2019 rests just above 86 percent (World Bank).

With the concession that older data come with many caveats, Eltjo Buringh and Luiten van Zanden have estimated that 15 percent of the population in Italy were literate within the timeframe of 1451 to 1500. They have come to this conclusion in part based on their data for per capita consumption of printed books annually across countries, which can certainly erase many readers, as we know one book can be read by many, which was notably the case in monasteries.[5] In the figures available on Manifold, Roser and Ortiz-Ospina collapse that period to 1475; I have added the percentages onto the countries within the map. Of the European countries with data available, with the exception of the Netherlands, Italy has the highest literacy rate, which arguably correlates with the earlier adoption of the vernacular language as well as Italy's high production of manuscripts (see Buringh and Van Zanden, "Charting the 'Rise of the West,'" for data on book production across Europe). Italy would continue to accelerate on literacy through 1800, where it caps at 23 percent. By then, the Netherlands achieved 85 percent literacy and Great Britain 54 percent, based on Buringh and Van Zanden's estimates.

Literacy would not have risen without certain innovations. Of those innovations, some may belong more firmly to the purview of what we today consider to be the sciences and technology (we may include better access to resources and healthcare, and more intuitive writing technology as belonging to these disciplines), but in working together with the innovation of the vernacular language—led by humanists who wrote literature and built communities—we have all benefited from more reading, more writing, and more knowledge sharing. Had historical innovators not been able to drive these outcomes, inviting more interlocutors into an expanding discourse, we would not be so well positioned today with a wealth of recorded knowledge that we can continue to build on.

The work to expand access and invite more interlocutors is an ongoing effort. As the inheritors of both humanistic and technological traditions, the computational humanities are in a position to meet people where they are, to speak in languages more people understand (here, let us include digital and other literacies besides human language), and to drive greater inclusion. There is so much that is at stake, and those who are at the crossroads of where computation meets the humanities have a unique opportunity to increase the number of potential stakeholders we need today through expanding literacy and what literacy may mean.

Open Source and Vernacular Code

Today, there is another kind of literacy where many are excluded and where much is at stake. As of 2021, roughly 0.379 percent of the global population can code (Mleczko).[6] This is compared to the nearly 59.5 percent of the global population (4.66 billion) who are active internet users worldwide in 2021 (Statista). Of course, this does not mean that under 1 percent of the population produce content on the internet, but it does reveal a stark disparity between how many people can create software versus how many people can consume only the user-interface element of software.

More than a decade ago in 2011, venture capitalist Marc Andreessen published his famous op-ed "Why Software Is Eating the World" in the *Wall Street Journal*, signaling the growing rise of software and how it is increasingly important to how we live today. Significantly, software is not only entrenched within our digital and virtual realities, but it also tangibly impacts our physical world, as software is part of what runs cars (not just self-driving ones), space vehicles, and elevators, and is used to create other smart appliances and material objects.[7] While some of this software is proprietary, a lot of it is community-built open-source software, and more often than not, for-profit proprietary software is built on open source.

Open-source software refers to software in which source code is made available to others so that they may inspect, reuse, and modify it, and oftentimes open-source software is developed collaboratively in public. Closely related in ethos to open access, the open-source and free software movements represent a site of community-based technology building. The hundreds of millions of lines of code that underlie processes in modern vehicles are largely coming from open-source libraries, and NASA's small helicopter Ingenuity flew on Mars thanks to many open-source contributors building software to automate and innovate over years and decades (Holmes; Vaughan-Nichols). These examples are just a small fraction of what runs on open source today. Crucially, open source can be read by anyone who is literate in code, and inspecting open-source libraries can give insight into what is happening under the hood of not just cars but computers, apps, and websites, too. Open source could therefore be thought of as a kind of vernacular in that it lays bare its algorithms and developers can build on top of it and innovate on it. But it is not vernacular in the sense that people on the streets are speaking that language—what would a native, vernacular Java programming language look like? On the other hand, proprietary software represents code that cannot be read or modified, which is why it is hard to determine if there is algorithmic bias on social media platforms that rely on closed instructions and opaque data stores.[8]

Though it is not the only platform where people can host and collaborate on software projects, GitHub is one of the most popular examples. Founded in 2008, the platform had 10 million repositories by 2013, and today it has more than 190 million repositories (at least 28 million of those being open source). The rapid growth of open-source software generally is hard to track in totality, but the data provided by GitHub ("2020 State of the Octoverse") can provide a sense of the acceleration and scale of software projects—both open source and proprietary. GitHub was acquired in 2018 by Microsoft; it is hugely problematic that much of the open-source software ecosystem is hosted on the closed-source platform of a giant tech company.

One of the problems with the tech industry broadly, and open source in particular, is diversity. I am referring here to the broadest possible intersectional diversity, but we need to rely on common metrics to start to understand the degree of monoculture that exists in tech. In industry, underrepresented women of color do not make up even 10 percent of major tech companies in the United States. The data in the chart available on Manifold demonstrate that there is a large gender disparity, and an even larger disparity when one considers race and gender together (Fussell). How can the software and products built at these companies equitably serve all communities when their workforce does not even approximate the demographics of the United States?

Open-source software is even less representative. In 2017, the Open Source Survey was conducted by GitHub with partners in academia and industry, and researchers found that open source was orders of magnitude away from a diverse space. A full 95 percent of respondents to the survey identified as male, only 3 percent identified as female, and just 1 percent as nonbinary. In terms of race, 16 percent of respondents to this survey said they belonged to ethnic or national groups that are in the minority in the country in which they live. My pessimistic suspicion is that there have not been any more recent surveys because the data have not indicated that tech and open source have become more inclusive, but I would be happy to be proved wrong. The more generous read is that this small group of people, homogeneous though they may be, have created some substantial innovations that have permanently changed the way we work, play, and live. What would our world look like if there were a vernacular programming language that enabled more people to participate? How could those precluded from technocratic power get involved in open source as literate technologists and stakeholders?

Technology will only truly serve all communities if more individuals from more contexts are building technology and leading innovation. By "literate technologist" I mean someone who understands how software works, not necessarily a programmer. By "vernacular" I would like to invite expansive readings—what would it look like for technology to be truly vernacular, to be something that people "speak" in everyday life, where there is not a barrier for them to enter into discourse like a computational language that they must learn and gain fluency in? Historically, we know that when one closed, self-monitoring group is in charge of language, information, and knowledge, then many people are kept out. Once more people are invited in, there are increased opportunities for knowledge sharing and knowledge production, and more individuals can work to innovate in ways that benefit the communities they represent. Some answers to vernacular code are already being developed. There have been interesting programming language innovations that represent natural languages other than just English in their keywords (the heritage of imperialism is long), and there has been a proliferation of "no code" and "low code" platforms as well. The right kind of solution here demands an interdisciplinary approach that can likely benefit from an undergirding grounded in the humanities.

I feel so strongly that we must work to lower barriers of entry to building software that I have dedicated my post-academic career to making progress in driving technical literacy and advocating for open source. I am currently the senior director of developer enablement at Chainguard, a software supply chain security startup with a long-term mission of making secure software development the default. I work closely with several open-source projects, and the Sigstore project in particular, which provides tools to make the open-source ecosystem more secure. This work supports broader efforts in software ethics, allowing technologists to understand the code they are implementing, preventing cyberattacks, and supporting a trust root in software. I have previously built open-source learning platforms and maintain open-source repositories for teaching purposes. Among my colleagues at Chainguard with interdisciplinary academic backgrounds are Kathleen Juell, a software engineer who holds a PhD in early American literature, and John Speed Meyers, a security data scientist who holds a PhD in policy analysis. While I discuss my work with a long view to the Italian vernacular, Juell discusses her web development work in the context of world-making from the literature she researched.

My previous roles were at Sourcegraph, a code search company; and DigitalOcean, a cloud computing company. In my industry roles, I have built teams that develop software, open-access technical tutorials and documentation, free ebooks, and interactive web-based terminals for learning (innovative as an educational sandbox that hooks into cloud infrastructure).[9] With the weight of a company behind you, there are resources to scale work like this; my ebook *How to Code in Python* was downloaded over 150,000 times, and my single-authored tutorials have been accessed over 45 million times to date. Monthly, about 5 million unique users visit the DigitalOcean web properties; to me, this represents a lot of opportunities to drive more technical literacy in incremental ways (DigitalOcean Holdings, "Form S-1/A"). The tech industry has afforded me with a wider reach than I had access to in the academy, and I am able to build things with and for a wider community, with the intention of making that community larger through education.

I met (hired, promoted) other humanities PhDs throughout my tech career to date. Erin Glass currently leads my former team at DigitalOcean. Her PhD was in English and her dissertation was titled "Software of the Oppressed: Reprogramming the Invisible Discipline"—if you think that the tech industry has no room to employ those who wield critical discourse, think again. DigitalOcean more recently hired Jeanelle Horcasitas as a developer educator; she completed a PhD in literature and cultural studies and was a HASTAC Scholar like myself. On the technical editorial team, which works alongside Developer Education, recent hires include Rachel Lee, whose English PhD focused on Romantic literature, and Caitlin Postal, who was a fellow panelist of mine on a digital humanities session at the International Congress on Medieval Studies in Kalamazoo (she completed her English PhD in 2022). A previous technical editor was Matt Abrams—PhD in art history—who is now a community support engineer at Grafana Labs, a monitoring startup. A former user research colleague of mine at DigitalOcean was Michele Tepper, who is currently director of user experience on the Platform Developer Experience team at Salesforce. Scott Bailey, who was technical content marketing manager when we worked together at Sourcegraph, completed graduate work in philosophical theology and had a career working as a digital humanities developer and librarian at university libraries before making this transition into tech.

I do not share these names to say that tech startups have been particularly interested in humanities PhDs; rather, I would like to draw attention to the fact that we humanists are already in tech. We perform many different roles; we are collaborating with many others across our organizations; we are bringing our training to us. And I am glad that we are here because we need to be among those leading technical innovations and outcomes alongside our colleagues with training in the physical and social sciences.

The question of the vernacular language of tech and how to drive inclusion are among the most compelling problems that humanists can begin to address, and there are many additional areas where the humanistically minded can innovate within tech. PhDs and other post-academics interested in joining the tech industry are particularly well suited to startups where their skill combination of high agency, fast learning, strong communication (teaching and writing), skillful research, and strong analysis proves to be very valuable. I do not think there are prescriptive pathways to follow; we are software developers, marketers, product managers, solutions architects, relationship partners, customer engineers, executive-level leaders, and more. I would love to have you as colleagues. But humanists need not be in industry to make an impact within the technology sector and to drive innovation generally; there is much that can be done from the academy and other alt-ac spaces to influence tech, create a vernacular for technologists of the future, and build something new.

Computational Humanities as a Site of Interdisciplinary Innovation

The digital humanities and computational humanities have many opportunities to shift the way research is done and counted to enable humanists to participate in interdisciplinary innovation. Research that brings together a group of experts across fields to create new methodologies and new knowledge is one avenue to explore. Unlocking History is a group of "conservators, paleographers, literary scholars, historians, publishers, book-artists, imaging experts, engineers, and scientists" who research letterlocking, an early form of material information security. They have been able to virtually unfold and read documents that remained sealed for hundreds of years, and their approach and findings were published in *Nature Communications* in 2021 (Dambrogio et al.). The researchers were able to apply X-ray microtomography scans and computational flattening algorithms to reconstruct and virtually unfold letters that were complexly locked to be read again. More than this, the group has been very engaged in the public humanities space through letterlocking workshops and a YouTube channel with over 17,000 subscribers.[10] The team is co-led by Jana Dambrogio, a conservator at MIT Libraries, and Daniel Starza Smith, a lecturer in early modern English literature at King's College, London, and they are joined by contributors in fields ranging from algorithm engineering and computer science to dentistry and material science.[11] Given the wide scope of security and letters, along with sizable archives of unopened locked letters (the Brienne Collection has 577 unopened letters), this project is compelling and incredibly innovative. No team had ever been able to read a letter locked in this manner without damaging it before.

There are other recent examples of interdisciplinary projects that bring together humanists with those in the sciences or other disciplines. *Viral Visualizations: How Coronavirus Skeptics Use Orthodox Data Practices to Promote Unorthodox Science Online* is one example. Led by Crystal Lee, an incoming assistant professor of Computational Media and Design at MIT, along with a team of computer scientists and an anthropologist, this timely research brings scientific approaches in content and method (the spreading of falsified science alongside data visualizations) together with humanistic inquiry.[12] Another example is the 2019 book *Language and Chronology: Text Dating by Machine Learning* by Gregory Toner, professor of Irish at Queen's University, Belfast, and Xiwu Han, a computer scientist and research fellow also at Queen's University. The book is part of the LexiChron project that uses machine learning to determine the chronology of ancient and medieval texts with unclear or no dates. The book seeks to more precisely date Irish sagas (ca. 700–ca.1700) through several approaches. The text's conclusion underscores that humanists with domain knowledge must interpret machine learning results. If only we could encourage more stakeholders in industry to think about their own machine learning algorithms with a similarly interdisciplinary eye.

Consider how much we as a society could innovate and drive equity if humanists trained in gender theory, queer theory, and critical race studies would be in a position to directly collaborate with others in technology and science.[13] We are at a pivotal moment where humanists have the opportunity to recognize and act on the ways in which we can disrupt some increasingly dystopian trends before we get further locked into a technological society without coleadership from philosophers, historians, and ethicists. In their chapter "Manufacturing Visual Continuity" in this volume, Fabien Offert and Peter Bell discuss the implications of what could be achieved if digital humanists did not limit themselves to established techniques of computer science, but explored new innovations from the field. I would like to take this further and involve humanists not only in the application of evolving technology but in the production of new and more equitable technologies. This call to action is with the caveat that Roopika Risam rightly points out in her chapter, "Double and Triple Binds," in this volume: we as humanists must hold ourselves accountable, "redistribute resources to assist scholars who do not have access to them," and fight against systemic racism within digital and computational humanities practices. We are in a position to fight against structural inequity within technology; let us not propagate it.

Outside of science, technology, engineering, and mathematics (STEM) fields, academics may believe we cannot participate in the software ecosystems that increasingly provide the infrastructure for our research and teaching. With increasing budget cuts, less access to institutional relationships and resources, and an increased likelihood of trained humanists having a precarious academic job—or a job outside the academy altogether—it is hard to think about the positions of power that humanities scholars do have. When evaluating what the digital humanities as a field has to offer, we must reframe how we recognize work and support the growth of our practitioners. We may consider how to encourage and fund contributions to open source, how to assess software as scholarship, how to equally recognize collaborative research in addition to single-author research, and how we may effectively participate in research projects across disciplines, like the team digital humanities projects I mentioned above. Damerow, Gibson, and Laubichler make a strong case for new approaches in their chapter ("Of Coding and Quality") in this volume, "Computational humanities... require a shift from the traditional one-person research project that is common in the humanities toward a more team-oriented approach that is typical of science." Alongside this, we can be champions of open access, ensuring that everyone has access to (often government-funded) research—rather than have it be locked behind expensive paywalls—so that we can all read the code that informs the ever-expanding repository of human knowledge.

Perhaps most importantly, we need to critically consider how we can engage with and properly compensate and recognize humanists who are in precarious positions or who are no longer institutionally or departmentally affiliated, because humanities work is not limited to the work of the traditional tenured faculty member in a disciplinary department. If we can begin to make other kinds of scholarship more legible, we can begin to participate more fully in the production of humanistic technology—it would no longer be something that is carved out alongside single-authored traditional research but can instead become the primary location of research output. It is of increasing importance that we pursue opportunities to not only participate in the governance of the software that we are using to do research and to teach, but also to be among those who are building this software. And we are well positioned to do so. To serve these ends, we need to stop creating ever more impossible barriers to entry in our disciplines and start recognizing digital, public, and technology-focused humanities work for the vital work that it is.

If we can imagine how to reward projects outside the single-authored, peer-reviewed paper and single-authored monograph, we can recognize collaborative work in the field, as the examples mentioned above suggest. We will open up more possibilities for practice of the computational humanities. How many humanists are there in open source? Can we onboard more humanists onto these platforms as part of our teaching and research? How can the academy commit to open scholarship and incentivize scholars to open source their research data or software? What models can we borrow from other fields, and what new methodologies can we create to help teams of researchers who build on each other's humanities open-source projects? How can we recognize non-code contributions in software development and open source? As trained humanists with deep knowledge of computation, we can strengthen our public practice as technical communicators to support more technology consumers from understanding what is at stake with proprietary software and the collection of user data. Many of our colleagues in the sciences collaborate on teams and with industry, and they do this work in a cross-disciplinary manner. David Gray Widder, a PhD student in computer science at Carnegie Mellon University, was the lead author on a paper entitled "Limits and Possibilities for 'Ethical AI' in Open Source: A Study of Deepfakes," which provides analysis and possibilities for open-source communities to practice an ethics of artificial intelligence (AI). He collaborated with not only academic computer scientists but also Dawn Nafus, an anthropologist who is in industry at Intel Labs. How may humanities scholars develop relationships to create working groups, benefit from funding, drive research, and provide humanistic perspectives in potential cross-disciplinary and cross-sector partnerships?

I would like to invite more relationships and inroads between the humanities and the tech industry (I include here both for-profit companies and nonprofits). There are many sites for collaboration, from user research and product research to education and community to software development and DevOps. We have already witnessed what happens when the tech industry builds software for use in higher education without true collaboration with the end users they will serve. Turnitin and Course Hero have each had their fair share of criticism from plagiarism and privacy concerns to the ethical use of data. As educators, we are all too familiar with subpar learning management systems that are adopted across a given institution that never seem developed with our use cases in mind. However, even platforms that have been started by higher education institutions like edX have been handed over to for-profit organizations. What does true vernacular humanities software look like? The best examples may be truly distributed software projects that bring together universities, academic professional groups, and the tech industry. Commons In A Box (CBOX) is the open-source software behind projects like the Humanities Commons and CUNY Academic Commons, and it is built by a number of groups including the Modern Language Association of America (MLA), City University of New York (CUNY), and those in industry.[14] Danica Savonick and I have argued that the use of CBOX as part of the Futures Initiative courses offered across the CUNY Graduate Center and the CUNY undergraduate campuses enabled students to be more participatory with their studies. The digital host of the Debates in Digital Humanities series, Manifold, is also a cross-industry and open-source endeavor with the CUNY Graduate Center, the University of Minnesota Press, and Cast Iron Coding among the collaborators and funding from the Andrew W. Mellon Foundation. This project can very well be the future of open-access publishing.

Part of the work of creating more vernacular software is to create space and structure for collaboration across sectors, including with humanists who have left the academy and today may be precluded from academic collaborations. Those trained in the humanities who are working in different industries often lose institutional access to resources, have limited time to do labor that is not compensated through a research line, and are not always considered to be part of the larger academic community. Some initial steps that universities and academic departments can take to support those who leave academia include providing continued library access to alumni,[15] keeping track of the career outcomes of all alumni, and creating visiting affiliations for those outside institutions to be part of a research community.[16] Those alumni in turn may be able to work with their employers to support internships for current students, provide free versions of their software (or other product) to researchers, or teach technical workshops. In the beginning of this chapter, I gestured toward the professional lives of vernacular innovators whose work outside the "life of the mind" has long been central to the humanist endeavor. Now, with ever-ubiquitous technology, there is much at stake, and there are many sites where humanists (whether inside or outside academia) can begin to become engaged, from open source to industry to centers of ethics and technology.

We need everyone involved in the critique and production of computational technology if we are going to build technology that serves everyone. In these endeavors, humanists bring nuance, ask relevant questions that may diverge from their STEM peers, draw from other fields of knowledge, and advocate for the end user. Humanists can interrogate how ethical machine learning algorithms can be, consider what is at stake when corporate entities collect data, and imagine different use cases for the same technologies. It is important that the humanities are among those driving the development of technology.

Returning briefly to Caterina da Siena, I would like to share an abridged quote from a letter she wrote to her confessor, Raimondo da Capua. Though we do not have any of her (or her scribes') original manuscript letters today, she tells him that this letter and another she sent him were written by her own hand rather than by the hands of scribes. She relates to him the pure joy of being able to complete the technical act of writing by hand alongside the technical act of communicating her thoughts onto physical material.

> This letter and another I already sent you I wrote in my own hand . . . I was full of self-admiration . . . and of his abundant providence toward me that provided me relief in the aptitude for writing, a consolation I did not have knowledge of due to my ignorance—so that when I descended from the high I had a little something with which I could vent my heart, so that it would not burst. . . . Forgive me for too much writing, it is because my hands and my tongue are in harmony with my heart.[17]

Caterina uses the quite humanistic symbolism of the hands, tongue, and heart working together to convey her message and to describe how this effort both brings her out of her ignorance and makes her proud of the accomplishment. Moreover, being able to communicate in this way relieves her, for she has had so much she wanted to share and was not able to without being able to use the tools of broader discourse. Imagine what it is like to be completely precluded from intellectual discourse because you were not taught Latin; to be something of a foreigner in your own land. I, too, have felt what she expresses: proud when an essay I have written resonates with others, relief when writing software that compiles (eureka!), and joy when software I launched is adopted or built upon by others. Being able to communicate, learn, and collaborate with others is vital across all fields of human pursuit, and always has been across contexts, regions, and time, which is why being able to do these acts effectively—with a shared vernacular—is so crucial.

The poets and community builders who innovated the vernacular language and invited more people into knowledge production come from a common foundation with us today. If we do not continue this work and bring everyone into the production of technology, then we risk losing ground on combating discriminatory search results and ungoverned data collection, and we may be unable to drive inclusion and the creation of equitable algorithms. We, as humanists, must take stock of our rich history and its intersections with other fields of learning. We must work to subvert current power hierarchies in the eternal projects of meaning-making and knowledge production in order to empower all who engage with technology, whether they are the builders, the readers, or both.

Notes

This chapter is dedicated in memory of Hollie Haggans, builder and innovator of inclusive tech communities.

1. Trans. J. M. Rigg.
2. See Pullella, "Pope Francis Renews Curbs on Latin Mass in Rebuff to Conservatives."
3. "Or dit li mastres que la escience de retorique est en .ii. mainieres, une qui est en dissant de boche & une autre que l'en mande par letres; mais li ensegnement sont comun, car il ne puet chaloir que l'en die ou en conte ou que l'en mande par letres. . . ." (Latini, *Li livres dou tresor*, 296). For a full discussion of the Ars dictaminis and Brunetto Latini, see Ronald Witt's "Brunetto Latini and the Italian Tradition of Ars Dictaminis."
4. Aldus Manutius printed Petrarca in 1501 and Dante in 1502.
5. One example relevant to Catherinian studies is the case of Syon Abbey in England, which would circulate books not only among nuns but among laywomen in the nuns' networks; many women readers can be left uncounted in this way (for more on this see Tagliaferri, *Lyrical Mysticism*, ch. 5).
6. Admittedly, every counting body likely approaches the questions of what coding is and who a coder is differently, but other estimates I have found go no higher than 0.5 percent. However, a more generous calculation may be to use GitHub's registered user base, which is 56 million as of September 2020. There may be duplicate users, but this would certainly include nonprofessional developers, bringing the percentage total to 0.72 percent of the world population (GitHub, "2020 State of the Octoverse"). See also discussion and some sources on Quora (https://www.quora.com/How-many-people-on-earth-know-computer-programming) and 2014 data from IDC (https://www.infoq.com/news/2014/01/IDC-software-developers/).

7. If you want to know why McDonald's ice cream machines are often broken, it seems to have something to do with proprietary software and willful obfuscation of knowledge working together to drive unchecked profit (see Greenberg, "They Hacked McDonald's Ice Cream Machines—and Started a Cold War").

8. See, for example, Safiya Noble's *Algorithms of Oppression: How Search Engines Reinforce Racism* and popular articles such as Rebecca Heilweil's "Why Algorithms Can Be Racist and Sexist."

9. Credit for this software goes largely to Jamon Camisso, DevOps engineer, developer educator, who studied information studies and teaches system administration at York University.

10. "Letterlocking Videos," @Letterlocking, YouTube channel at https://www.youtube.com/channel/UCNPZ-f_IWDLz2S1hO027hRQ.

11. For information on the Unlocking History research team, see https://letterlocking.org/team.

12. The MIT Visualization Group page is http://vis.csail.mit.edu/pubs/viral-visualizations.

13. In her essay "Humanities 2.0: Promise, Perils, Predictions," Cathy N. Davidson makes a compelling argument not only about the role of the humanities in scientific discovery but also what is at stake in the early twenty-first century.

14. I am on the technical advisory board of Humanities Commons. I share this to both disclose my interest in the platform and also to note that those working on the Humanities Commons are interested in perspectives from a wide audience (including mine as an academic in industry). My personal view is that this is a forward-looking move that will support innovative development of the platform, and I would like to thank the Humanities Commons for including me on the board.

15. Here, I would like to recognize the librarians, faculty, and staff of the CUNY Graduate Center and the Mina Rees Library who provide me with considerable access to resources and databases as an alum. I would also like to thank the librarians and staff of the New York Public Library and its MaRLI (Manhattan Research Library Initiative) program, which provides me with world-class access to books and other resources. I encourage other libraries and universities to learn from these programs.

16. In the spring 2022 semester, I was a visiting scholar in the Italian department at Rutgers University, where I taught a graduate-level course on the digital humanities and gave invited talks and workshops as part of Digital Humanities and Public History programming. I believe my experience in the tech industry, combined with my academic background, was valuable to my students, and I would like to thank the program for my personal opportunity and their leadership in this area.

17. Letter T272, following Noffke. "Questa lettera, e un'altra ch'io vi mandai, ho scritte di mia mano . . . ma piena d'ammirazione ero di me medesima . . . e la sua Providenzia; la quale abondava verso di me, che per refrigerio, essendo privata della consolazione, la quale per mia ignoranzia io non cognobbi, m'aveva dato, e proveduto con darmi l'attitudine dello scrivere; acciocchè discendendo dall'altezza, avessi un poco con chi sfogare 'l cuore, perchè

non scoppiasse.... Perdonatemi del troppo scrivere, perocchè le mani e la lingua s'accordano col cuore."

Translation mine. Note that this is a mystical text, and the "high" is generally understood to be a mystical elevation and the "providence" is divine.

Bibliography

Alighieri, Dante. *The Divine Comedy of Dante Alighieri*. Translated by Allen Mandelbaum. New York: Bantam Books, 2004.

Andreessen, Marc. "Why Software Is Eating the World." *Wall Street Journal*, August 20, 2011. https://www.wsj.com/articles/SB10001424053111903480904576512250915629460.

Boccaccio, Giovanni. *The Decameron*. Translated by J. M. Rigg. Private Print for the Navarre Society, 1921.

Boccaccio, Giovanni. *Decameron*. Milan: Mondadori, 2015.

Buringh, Eltjo, and J. L. Luiten van Zanden. "Charting the 'Rise of the West': Manuscripts and Printed Books in Europe: A Long-Term Perspective from the Sixth through Eighteenth Centuries." *Journal of Economic History* (2009).

Caterina da Siena. *Dialogo della serafica vergine, et sposa di Christo S. Catherina da Siena*. Venetia: appresso Giacomo Cornetti, 1589.

Caterina da Siena. "Le Lettere Di Santa Caterina Da Siena." In *Santa Caterina Da Siena: Opera Omnia*, edited by Antonio Volpato and Fausto Sbaffoni. Pistoia: Provincia Romana dei Frati Predicatori, 2002. CD-ROM.

Caterina da Siena. *The Dialogue*. Translated by Suzanne Noffke. New York: Paulist Press, 1980.

Caterina da Siena. *The Letters of Catherine of Siena*. Vol. 1–4. Translated by Suzanne Noffke. Tempe, Ariz.: Center for Medieval and Renaissance Studies.

Cavalcanti, Guido. *Rime*. A cura di Marcello Ciccuto. BUR Poesia, 2010.

Cavallini, Guiliana. *Catherine of Siena*. London: Bloomsbury Academic, 2005.

Center for Medieval and Renaissance Studies. *The Prayers of Catherine of Siena*. Translated by Suzanne Noffke. New York: Paulist Press, 1983.

Dambrogio, Jana, Daniel Starza Smith, and the Unlocking History Research Team. *Dictionary of Letterlocking* (DoLL). February 23, 2021. https://letterlocking.org/dictionary.

Dambrogio, Jana, Amanda Ghassaei, Daniel Starza Smith, Holly Jackson, Martin L. Demaine, Graham Davis, David Mills, et al. "Unlocking History through Automated Virtual Unfolding of Sealed Documents Imaged by X-Ray Microtomography." *Nature Communications* 12 (2011): 1184. https://doi.org/10.1038/s41467-021-21326-w.

Davidson, Cathy N. "Humanities 2.0: Promise, Perils, Predictions." In *Debates in the Digital Humanities*, edited by Matthew K. Gold. Minneapolis: University of Minnesota Press, 2012. https://dhdebates.gc.cuny.edu/read/untitled-88c11800-9446-469b-a3be-3fdb36bfbd1e/section/c6fc3cc1-5751-4c6b-aac5-b9890206930f#ch28.

DigitalOcean Holdings, Inc. "Form S-1/A DigitalOcean Holdings, Inc." *EDGAR.* U.S. Securities and Exchange Commission, March 15, 2021. https://sec.report/Document/0001193125-21-090653/.

Foligno, Angela da. *Angela de Fulginio, in quo ostenditur nobis vera via qua possumus sequi vestigia nostri Redemptoris.* apud Guillelmum Chaudiere, via Iacobaea sub signo Temporis, & Hominis Syluestris, 1598.

Francesco d'Assisi. "Laudes creaturarum." *Produzione e fruizione: antologia della letteratura italiana.* Edited by Giuseppe Petronio and Vitilio Masiello. Palermo: G. B. Palumbo & C. Editore S.P.A., 1988.

Fussell, Sidney. "The Alarming Downsides to Tech Industry Diversity Reports." Gizmodo, December 13, 2016. https://gizmodo.com/the-alarming-downsides-to-tech-industry-diversity-repor-1789797486.

GitHub. *The 2020 State of the Octoverse.* Accessed September 2020. https://octoverse.github.com.

GitHub. *Open Source Survey.* 2017. https://opensourcesurvey.org/2017/.

Greenberg, Andy. "They Hacked McDonald's Ice Cream Machines—and Started a Cold War." *Wired,* April 20, 2021. https://www.wired.com/story/they-hacked-mcdonalds-ice-cream-makers-started-cold-war/.

Heilweil, Rebecca. "Why Algorithms Can Be Racist and Sexist." *Vox,* February 18, 2020. https://www.vox.com/recode/2020/2/18/21121286/algorithms-bias-discrimination-facial-recognition-transparency.

Holmes, Freddie. "Auto Industry's Thirst for Software Is Quenched by Open Source." *Automotive World,* October 8, 2018. https://www.automotiveworld.com/articles/auto-industrys-thirst-for-software-is-quenched-by-open-source/.

Latini, Brunetto. *Li livres dou tresor.* Edited by Spurgeon W. Baldwin and Paul Barrette. Tempe, Ariz.: Arizona Center for Medieval and Renaissance Studies, 2003.

Lee, Crystal, Tanya Yang, Gabrielle D. Inchoco, Graham M. Jones, and Arvind Satyanarayan. "Viral Visualizations: How Coronavirus Skeptics Use Orthodox Data Practices to Promote Unorthodox Science Online." In *Proceedings of the 2021 CHI Conference on Human Factors in Computing Systems,* 1–18. New York: Association for Computing Machinery, 2021. https://doi.org/10.1145/3411764.3445211.

Mleczko, Anna. "How Many Developers Are There in the World in 2021?" *Business Blog, Future Processing.* Accessed May 20, 2020. https://www.future-processing.com/blog/how-many-developers-are-there-in-the-world-in-2019/.

Noble, Safiya. *Algorithms of Oppression: How Search Engines Reinforce Racism.* New York: NYU Press, 2018.

Petrarca, Francesco. *Petrarch's Lyric Poems: The Rime Sparse and Other Lyrics.* Cambridge, Mass.: Harvard University Press, 1976.

Pullella, Philip. "Pope Francis Renews Curbs on Latin Mass in Rebuff to Conservatives." *Reuters,* July 16, 2021. https://www.reuters.com/world/europe/pope-francis-renews-curbs-latin-mass-rebuff-conservatives-2021-07-16/.

Roser, Max, and Esteban Ortiz-Ospina. "Literacy." *Our World in Data*. Accessed 2016. https://ourworldindata.org/literacy.

Savonick, Danica, and Lisa Tagliaferri. "Building a Student-Centered (Digital) Learning Community with Undergraduates." *DHQ: Digital Humanities Quarterly* 11, no. 3 (2017). https://www.digitalhumanities.org/dhq/vol/11/3/000306/000306.html.

Statista. "Global Digital Population as of January 2021 (in Billions)." Accessed January 2021. https://www.statista.com/statistics/617136/digital-population-worldwide/.

Tagliaferri, Lisa. "Lyrical Mysticism: The Writing and Reception of Catherine of Siena." PhD diss., City University of New York, 2017. https://academicworks.cuny.edu/cgi/viewcontent.cgi?article=3117&context=gc_etds.

Todi, Jacopone da. *Jacopone Da Todi: Lauds*. Translated by Serge Hughes and Elizabeth Hughes. New York: Paulist Press, 1981.

Todi, Jacopone da. *Laude: a cura di Franco Mancini*. Laterza, Italy: GLF editori, 2006.

Toner, Gregory, and Xiwu Han. *Language and Chronology: Text Dating by Machine Learning*. Leiden: Brill, 2019.

Vaughan-Nichols, Steven J. "Flying on Mars Fueled with Open-Source Software." *ZDNet*, April 19, 2021. https://www.zdnet.com/article/flying-on-mars-fueled-with-open-source-software/.

Widder, David Gray, Dawn Nafus, Laura Dabbish, and James Herbsleb. "Limits and Possibilities for 'Ethical AI' in Open Source: A Study of Deepfakes." In *FAccT '22: Proceedings of the 2022 ACM Conference on Fairness, Accountability, and Transparency, June 21–24, 2022, Seoul, Republic of Korea*, 2035–46. New York: Association for Computing Machinery, 2022.

Witt, Ronald G. "Brunetto Latini and the Italian Tradition of Ars Dictaminis." *Stanford Italian Review* 3, no. 3 (1983): 5–24.

World Bank. "Literacy Rate, Adult Total (% of People Ages 15 and Above)," September 2020. https://data.worldbank.org/indicator/SE.ADT.LITR.ZS.

Acknowledgments

The editors are greatly appreciative of the work and generosity of the contributors. The initial call for contributions began with an ambitious timeline in 2019. No one anticipated the emergence of a global pandemic or the short- and long-term impact of the fear, loss, and hope that ensued. We are grateful to the contributors for continuing with this project, providing feedback through a peer-to-peer review process, revising, and then incorporating feedback from external peer reviewers over the past four years. Along with working to make sure the chapters resonate with each other and the debate, we heeded the advice of Sarah Ahmed, who encouraged the use of citations as a means of acknowledgment and as a navigation aid. Thank you to the authors for doing the extra work of engaging with a range of scholarship that traversed disciplinary, geographical, and methodological boundaries to enrich and expand the debates. The volume is richer and more intellectually vibrant because of your engagement.

Our personal lives and embodied experiences also shape our scholarship. Along the way, collaborators experienced pain from the loss of a loved one, along with incredible joy with the birth of children. Timelines and deadlines came and went. This was our decision as editors. No chapter is more important than the health and wellness of each other. Thank you to everyone for your patience and understanding. We thank series editors Matt Gold and Lauren Klein, whose constant support and enthusiasm for the volume helped us navigate these past four years when the uncertainty of 2020 and 2021 seemed indefinite. Thank you as well to Anne Carter, Leah Pennywark, and the University of Minnesota Press for their support, particularly working to get the book to press under a tight timeline.

Our work as editors was possible because of the support of our institutions, families, and friends. Jessica Marie Johnson is grateful to the community of researchers, artists, and community members who make up LifexCode: DH against Enclosure, including cofounder Dr. Christina Thomas. Thank you to the Johns Hopkins University Krieger School of Arts and Sciences, the Mellon Foundation, and the National Historic Publications and Records Commissions for supporting the kind of work that makes it possible to envision and revise computational humanities and debate the digital humanities, including projects like the Diaspora Solidarities Lab, Black beyond Data, and Keywords for Black Louisiana. Jessica's work on this volume is dedicated to Mary Nuñez née Matos, who found her way home over the course of the making of this volume, and the teachers and youth scholars of the

Acknowledgments

New Generations Scholars and African Diaspora Alliance of Baltimore, who teach us all what it means to break and abolish all enclosures. David Mimno is grateful to Cornell Information Science for proving that computational science and humanities scholarship are not only compatible but exciting. Jennifer Mimno has been the best partner for this journey. The broader digital humanities community has provided endless opportunities to learn, to be challenged, and to make a difference. The University of Richmond School of Arts and Sciences and Lauren Tilton's department, Rhetoric and Communication Studies, have from day one been supportive of digital humanities and open to a range of scholarly forms that animates computational humanities. There is no way to fully describe what it means to work among an interdisciplinary, liberal arts community that seeks to support and amplify new forms and avenues of scholarship; it lends a kind of experimental and creative freedom that models the radical futures that are possible within higher education. Lauren Tilton is deeply appreciative of her family, including her intellectual and life partner Taylor Arnold, whose support was critical during several health struggles, and the sweetness and silliness of our four-legged furballs, Roux and Sarge.

Contributors

MARK ALGEE-HEWITT is associate professor of digital humanities and English at Stanford University, where he directs the Stanford Literary Lab. He is the author of *The Afterlife of Aesthetics: Literature, the Sublime, and the Art of Criticism in the Long Eighteenth Century*.

DAVID BAMMAN is associate professor in the School of Information at the University of California, Berkeley.

KASPAR BEELEN is technical lead, digital humanities, at the School of Advanced Study, University of London.

PETER BELL is professor of art history and digital humanities at Philipps-University Marburg and coeditor of the *Computing Art Reader*.

TOBIAS BLANKE is university professor in AI and humanities at the University of Amsterdam and coauthor of *Algorithmic Reason: The New Government of Self and Other*.

JULIA DAMEROW is lead scientific software engineer in the School of Complex Adaptive Systems at Arizona State University.

QUINN DOMBROWSKI is a member of the digital humanities staff in the Division of Literatures, Cultures, and Languages and the library at Stanford University and has served as the copresident of the Association for Computers and the Humanities.

CRYSTAL NICOLE EDDINS is associate professor of sociology at the University of Pittsburgh and the author of *Rituals, Runaways, and the Haitian Revolution: Collective Action in the African Diaspora*.

ABRAHAM GIBSON is assistant professor of history at the University of Texas at San Antonio and the author of *Feral Animals in the American South: An Evolutionary History*.

TASSIE GNIADY is systems application manager for the Monroe County Community Public School System.

Contributors

CRYSTAL HALL is associate professor of digital humanities and affiliated faculty in Italian studies at Bowdoin College. She is the author of *Galileo's Reading* and codirector of GaLiLeO: Galileo's Library and Letters Online.

VANESSA M. HOLDEN is associate professor of history and African American and Africana studies at the University of Kentucky, where she directs the Central Kentucky Slavery Initiative. She is the author of *Surviving Southampton: African American Women and Resistance in Nat Turner's Community*.

JESSICA MARIE JOHNSON is associate professor of history at Johns Hopkins University and director of LifexCode: Digital Humanities Against Enclosure. She is author of *Wicked Flesh: Black Women, Intimacy, and Freedom in the Atlantic World*.

DAVID KLOSTER is systems programmer/analyst for UITS research technologies visualization and data lab's IU3D lab at Indiana University, where he implements lidar scanners, drones, and high-performance computers to create digital twins of spaces and structures.

MANFRED D. LAUBICHLER is Global Futures Professor and President's Professor of Theoretical Biology and History of Biology at Arizona State University, where he is also the director of the School of Complex Adaptive Systems and the Decision Theater.

KATHERINE MCDONOUGH is lecturer in digital humanities at Lancaster University and senior research fellow at the Alan Turing Institute.

BARBARA MCGILLIVRAY is lecturer in digital humanities and cultural computing at King's College London. She is author of *Methods in Latin Computational Linguistics* and coauthor of *Quantitative Historical Linguistics: A Corpus Framework* and *Applying Language Technology in Humanities Research: Design, Application, and the Underlying Logic*.

MEGAN MEREDITH-LOBAY is associate director of the research computing group at Simon Fraser University.

DAVID MIMNO is associate professor of information science at Cornell University.

FEDERICO NANNI is senior research data scientist at the Alan Turing Institute, working as part of the research engineering group.

FABIAN OFFERT is assistant professor of the history and theory of the digital humanities at the University of California, Santa Barbara. He serves as principal investigator for the international research project AI Forensics, funded by the Volkswagen Foundation.

HANNAH RINGLER is assistant teaching professor of rhetoric and director of the Communication across the Curriculum program in the humanities department at Illinois Institute of Technology.

ROOPIKA RISAM is associate professor of film and media studies and of comparative literature in the digital humanities and social engagement cluster at Dartmouth College. She is author of *New Digital Worlds: Postcolonial Digital Humanities in Theory, Praxis, and Pedagogy* and coeditor of *The Digital Black Atlantic* (Minnesota, 2021), among other volumes.

JOSHUA D. ROTHMAN is professor of history at the University of Alabama. He is a codirector of Freedom on the Move: A Database of Fugitives from American Slavery and the author of *The Ledger and the Chain: How Domestic Slave Traders Shaped America*.

BENJAMIN M. SCHMIDT is vice president of information at Nomic, an information cartography company in New York.

LISA TAGLIAFERRI is senior director of developer education at the software supply-chain startup Chainguard. An interdisciplinary researcher in tech and the humanities, Tagliaferri teaches digital humanities at Rutgers University and is the author of popular books and tutorials on Python, machine learning, cloud infrastructure, and software security.

JEFFREY THARSEN is associate technology director for digital studies at the University of Chicago, where he serves as technical domain expert for digital and computational approaches to humanistic inquiry. He is author of *Chinese Euphonics: Phonetic Patterns, Phonorhetoric and Literary Artistry in Early Chinese Narrative Texts*.

LAUREN TILTON is E. Claiborne Robins Professor of Liberal Arts and Digital Humanities at the University of Richmond. She is coauthor of *Distant Viewing: Computational Exploration of Digital Images*.

MARIEKE VAN ERP is department head of the digital humanities research lab at the Royal Netherlands Academy of Arts and Sciences' humanities cluster.

LEE ZICKEL is applications manager for [U]Tech's enterprise applications at Case Western Reserve University and has been in IT and the humanities for more than twenty years.